LITERATURE AND THE SIXTH SENSE

BY PHILIP RAHV

FABER AND FABER
London

First published in England in 1970
by Faber and Faber Limited
24 Russell Square London WC1
Printed in Great Britain by
John Dickens & Co Ltd Northampton
All rights reserved

ISBN 0 571 09497 X

cc

To Lily and Theo

The author wishes to thank the following editors and publishers for permission to reprint some of the essays which appear in this volume:

Commentary; Farrar, Straus & Giroux; Folio; Holt, Rinehart and Winston; The Kenyon Review; Meridian Books; New Directions; The New Leader; The New Republic; The New Statesman; The New York Herald Tribune, Inc. (Book Week); The New York Review of Books; Partisan Review.

Farrar, Straus & Giroux: "A Note on Bernard Malamud" is reprinted with the permission of Farrar, Straus & Giroux, Inc. from The Malamud Reader by Bernard Malamud, copyright © 1967 by Farrar, Straus & Giroux, Inc.; Holt, Rinehart and Winston: Philip Rahv's Introduction to The Friend of the Family and The Eternal Husband by Fyodor Dostoevsky, Rinehart Edition. Introduction copyright © 1963 by Holt, Rinehart and Winston, Inc., reprinted by permission of Holt, Rinehart and Winston, Inc.; Partisan Review: "Twilight of the Thirties: Passage from an Editorial," "The Unfuture of Utopia," and "A Season in Heaven" appeared first in Partisan Review (Summer 1939, Vol. 6, no. 4, July 1949, Vol. 16, no. 7, and June 1936, Vol. 3, no. 5, respectively); The Southern Review: "Proletarian Literature: A Political Autopsy" is reprinted with permission of The Southern Review, copyright © 1939 by The Southern Review; The Washington Post Company: "Two Subversive Russians" first appeared in the May 1, 1966, edition of Book Week as a review of The Trial Begins and On Socialist Realism by Andrei D. Sinyavsky, copyright © 1966 by The Washington Post Company.

FOREWORD

NIETZSCHE was surely right in his observation that the development of historical insight in the modern epoch represents what is virtually a new faculty of the mind, a sixth sense. But how does this sense function? As I see it, it functions both as an analytic instrument largely unapprehended by the past cultures and as a new, bracing resource of the modern sensibility. And in selecting the essays comprised in this collection from a body of critical work going as far back as 1936, I was struck by the extent to which I have myself drawn upon this resource, by the way in which my own strong interest in historical reality as well as historical reason has in the long run affected my literary attitudes and judgments. To my mind, this sufficiently justifies the title of the book, reflecting as it does one of the more salient characteristics of my ventures in criticism. However, this should not be taken to mean that I subscribe to some formal theory of "historicism," nor that historical consciousness is the sole attribute that the reader can legitimately expect to encounter in these pages.

I think that the origins of my predilection for a heightened form of historical awareness can be traced primarily though not exclusively to my early training in Marxism. Even if through the years I have pulled back from a good deal that was implicit in that training at its very inception (such as, for instance, the metaphysics of dialectical materialism and the messianic role assigned to the working class) I have nonetheless retained from it a certain approach, a measure of social and ideological commitment and, I make bold to say, a certain kind of realism, not untouched with hope and expectancy, in my outlook on society and the human potential as articulated in the constructs of the imagination. The polemical tone of some of my pieces is also in part derived from the Marxist tradition. In saying this I have in mind, of course, the assault, in earlier years, on the blatant deceptions practiced by the party-liners in the Communist literary movement as well as, in later years, my protests against nihilism on the one hand — including the latter-day nihilism, commercialized to the core, which finds it opportune to masquerade in the vestments of the classic avant-garde — and, on the other hand, against a variety of empty spiritualizations of the world that finally and inexorably change nothing at all, leaving the world exactly as it is.

But that is far from being all so far as influences are concerned. Also discernible is the force and pressure of other modes of historical thought, embodied in the work of a number of thinkers and writers, ranging from that of Hegel and Nietzsche to the sociology of Karl Mannheim and the criticism of T. S. Eliot (insofar, that is, that it remains germane to the present cultural situation without surrendering, as at times it certainly does, to archaistic nostalgia). It goes without saying, too, that the influence of the Freudian theory which, even if centered on the problems of the individual, has its own peculiar historical dimension, is not to be overlooked. The purely literary influences are much too diverse to be subject to enumeration.

It is hardly necessary to note that the workings of the historical sense, in criticism as in other fields, depends as much on intuition as on knowledge, though what may be involved is a special kind of intuition that one would find it very difficult to define with any precision. Yet it is precisely that kind of intuition, easily recognizable even if hard to pin down in a formula, which one ordinarily misses in academic historical studies purporting to deal with literary art. Such studies are sometimes given over to the methodological fashions of the moment (the "new criticism," for example, was one such fashion), but for the most part they are devoted to the sheer accumulation of historical facts for their own sake, as it were, without regard to their relevance, to their weight and importance in the shaping of creative trends and ideas. For the academic mind at work on literary materials tends to assume, altogether gratuitously I think, that such matters will somehow take care of themselves in good time so long as the facts, however trivial, are more or less stated correctly. Thus most literary scholars, confined by narrow horizons, evade the hazard no less than the power of the historical imagination by immersing themselves in sheer facticity; and though this facticity, for all its amorphousness and automatism, may have its professional rationale in the English departments of our universities, it very seldom appertains in any meaningful way to the critical act.

To be sure, if he is to do his job properly the literary critic must cultivate an acute sense of fact. Without it he is lost, and to acquire it he must have recourse to the literary scholars among others. Yet mere presumptions of expertise fail to impress him. Facts are of value to him if their historical significance is elucidated and clearly related to the imaginative transaction; but random facts left hanging in the air, so to speak, facts explicated just because they happen to be available for scholarly citation, are of no use to him.

This volume contains a good many of the essays and reviews that were included in two previous critical collections, *Image and Idea* and *The Myth and the Powerhouse*. It also contains more than a dozen pieces that have not heretofore appeared in book form. Excluded from this book are the essays I have written on some of Dostoevsky's major novels, as I mean to place them as individual chapters within a longer study of the Russian novelist which I plan to publish in the near future. The piece on Dotoevsky's shorter novels, originally written as an introduction to the Rinehart paperback edition of *The Friend of the Family* and *The Eternal Husband*, is reprinted here for the reason that it does not suit the design of the longer study.

In the interest of maintaining unity of tone I have excluded from this collection all articles dealing directly with political issues. In my view, mixing literary-critical discourse with comment of an immediately political nature cannot make for coherence of presenta-

tion. Part II of the book consists of shorter pieces, many of them
written as reviews. The criterion of selecting reviews for reprint
has been quite simply that of leaving out those that deal with books
or authors that are of little or no relevance in the contemporary
situation.

The earliest piece in this volume was written in 1936 as a review
of T. S. Eliot's play *Murder in the Cathedral.* It was published in
Partisan Review, at that time still connected, though somewhat am-
biguously to be sure, with the official Communist movement in this
country. Needless to say, my defense of Eliot against the then
prevalent charge of fascist allegiance struck the orthodox party-
liners as verging on heresy. I was implicitly deprecating official
cultural policy and preparing to quit; and it was only a year later
that I broke completely with that movement; in 1939 I was so far
gone in opposition that I was able, in the pages of *The Southern
Review,* to subject "proletarian literature" to the political autopsy it
deserved. At that point *Partisan Review,* of which I was still actively
an editor, had become openly hostile to Stalinism and all its manifestations in politics and in culture.

My personal experience with Stalinism had been short-lived but
extremely educative — for me at least. The leaders of that movement appeared to me to be out-and-out opportunists and the rank
and file members at bottom religious-minded people, true believers
who had converted the Soviet Union and the Bolshevik party, under
whatever leadership, into objects of sectarian worship. The Marxism
they professed, leaders and followers alike, was a scandalous and
vicious caricature not only of the classic doctrine but of Lenin and
Trotsky as well. Piety, of whatever sort, being alien to my temperament, I had very little difficulty breaking away from the conventicle
of orthodoxy. I might add that this distaste for the stances of piety
has stayed with me through the years. It accounts to some degree
for the thrust of the last essay in this collection — the criticism of
F. R. Leavis and D. H. Lawrence written in 1968 — which is in
effect a reaction to the excesses of the Lawrence cult and its assidu-
ous promotion by Leavis' all too reverent but quite unilluminating
exhortations.

I have made very few changes in the work collected in this volume, for certainly one way to look at it is as a document of critical

response to three quite distinct periods in American literary life. The first is that of the socially oriented thirties and the entanglement of many radical writers of that time with the Soviet version of Communism. The second, which lasted nearly till the end of the fifties, was fundamentally conservative in nature, taking form among the then dominant group of "new critics" in a perfervid adherence to "tradition" as well as the onset of a peculiarly belated and shallow kind of religiosity among literary intellectuals. The prevailing mood was one of total revulsion from all political activity and ideas that smacked in any way of the old Leftism. The third and present period, that of the "swinging" sixties, is still with us. It is a period exhibiting very little cohesion — a mere jumble of mutually contradictory trends. For on the one hand we have witnessed a renewal of political consciousness and a penchant for political action among younger people, and on the other hand our attention is continually solicited by the self-elected spokesmen of a new aestheticism, or "new sensibility" as it is called at times. These spokesmen retain nothing more than the cultist mannerisms of the classic avant-garde; they ape its dissidence and revolt while actually constituting themselves as a veritable academy, and a ruling academy at that, fawned upon in the most respectable quarters even as it turns out art objects as consumer goods.

In America, whose second name, I sometimes think, should be "amnesia," the historical sense in this century chronically suffers one lesion after another as literary periods crowd each other out with extreme celerity, each presenting itself as the culmination of the imaginative process of all times. In consequence our literary world is afflicted with an acute loss of memory, so much so that one meets nowadays graduate students in English who have only the vaguest notion of what the "new criticism" was all about and scarcely any notion at all of what the radical literary movement of the thirties really came to. The value of these collected essays, if any, might well lie in the implicit summons they contain to recognize and in that sense restore a proper perspective on what has transpired in American literary culture during the past thirty years.

PHILIP RAHV
April 1969

CONTENTS

Part II: Sketches in Criticism

PART I

PALEFACE AND REDSKIN

VIEWED HISTORICALLY, American writers appear to group themselves around two polar types. Paleface and redskin I should
like to call the two, and despite occasional efforts at reconciliation
no love is lost between them.

Consider the immense contrast between the drawing-room fictions
of Henry James and the open-air poems of Walt Whitman. Compare Melville's decades of loneliness, his tragic failure, with Mark
Twain's boisterous career and dubious success. At one pole there
is the literature of the lowlife world of the frontier and of the big
cities; at the other the thin, solemn, semiclerical culture of Boston
and Concord. The fact is that the creative mind in America is frag-
mented and one-sided. For the process of polarization has produced
a dichotomy between experience and consciousness — a dissociation
between energy and sensibility, between conduct and theories of
conduct, between life conceived as an opportunity and life conceived as a discipline.

The differences between the two types define themselves in every
sphere. Thus while the redskin glories in his Americanism, to the
paleface it is a source of endless ambiguities. Sociologically they

1

2/*Literature and the Sixth Sense*

can be distinguished as patrician vs. plebeian, and in their aesthetic
ideals one is drawn to allegory and the distillations of symbolism,
whereas the other inclines to a gross, riotous naturalism. The paleface is a "high-brow," though his mentality — as in the case of
Hawthorne and James — is often of the kind that excludes and repels
general ideas; he is at the same time both something more and
something less than an intellectual in the European sense. And the
redskin deserves the epithet "low-brow," not because he is badly
educated — which he might or might not be — but because his reactions are primarily emotional, spontaneous, and lacking in personal
culture. The paleface continually hankers after religious norms,
tending toward a refined estrangement from reality. The redskin,
on the other hand, accepts his environment, at times to the degree
of fusion with it, even when rebelling against one or another of its
manifestations. At his highest level the paleface moves in an exquisite moral atmosphere; at his lowest he is genteel, snobbish, and
pedantic. In giving expression to the vitality and to the aspirations
of the people, the redskin is at his best; but at his worst he is a
vulgar anti-intellectual, combining aggression with conformity and
reverting to the crudest forms of frontier psychology.

James and Whitman, who as contemporaries felt little more than
contempt for each other, are the purest examples of this dissociation.* In reviewing *Drum Taps* in 1865 the young James told off the
grand plebeian innovator, advising him to stop declaiming and go
sit in the corner of a rhyme and meter school, while the innovator, snorting at the novelist of scruples and moral delicacy, said
"Feathers!" Now this mutual repulsion between the two major figures in American literature would be less important if it were mainly
personal or aesthetic in reference. But the point is that it has a profoundly national and social-historical character.

James and Whitman form a kind of fatal antipodes. To this, in
part, can be traced the curious fact about them that, though each
has become the object of a special cult, neither is quite secure in his
reputation. For most of the critics and historians who make much
of Whitman disparage James or ignore him altogether, and vice

* According to Edith Wharton, James changed his mind about Whitman late
in life. But this can be regarded as a private fact of the Jamesian sensibility,
for in public he said not a word in favor of Whitman.

versa. Evidently the high valuation of the one is so incongruous with the high valuation of the other that criticism is chronically forced to choose between them — which makes for a breach in the literary tradition without parallel in any European country. The aristocrat Tolstoy and the tramp Gorky found that they held certain values and ideas in common, whereas James and Whitman, who between them dominate American writing of the nineteenth century, cannot abide with one another. And theirs is no unique or isolated instance.

The national literature suffers from the ills of a split personality. The typical American writer has so far shown himself incapable of escaping the blight of one-sidedness: of achieving that mature control which permits the balance of impulse with sensitiveness, of natural power with philosophical depth. For the dissociation of mind from experience has resulted in truncated works of art, works that tend to be either naive and ungraded, often flat reproductions of life, or else products of cultivation that remain abstract because they fall short on evidence drawn from the sensuous and material world. Hence it is only through intensively exploiting their very limitations, through submitting themselves to a process of creative yet cruel self-exaggeration, that a few artists have succeeded in warding off the failure that threatened them. And the later novels of Henry James are a case in point.

The palefaces dominated literature throughout the nineteenth century, but in the twentieth they were overthrown by the redskins. Once the continent had been mastered, with the plebeian bourgeoisie coming into complete possession of the national wealth, and puritanism had worn itself out, degenerating into mere respectability, it became objectively possible and socially permissible to satisfy that desire for experience and personal emancipation which heretofore had been systematically frustrated. The era of economic accumulation had ended and the era of consummation had arrived. To enjoy life now became one of the functions of progress — a function for which the palefaces were temperamentally disqualified. This gave Mencken his opportunity to emerge as the ideologue of enjoyment. Novelists like Dreiser, Anderson, and Lewis — and, in fact, most of the writers of the period of "experiment and liberation" — rose against conventions that society itself was beginning to abandon. They helped to "liquidate" the lag between the enormous riches of the nation and its morality of abstention. The neo-humanists were among the last of the breed of palefaces, and they perished in the quixotic attempt to reestablish the old values. Eliot forsook his native land, while the few palefaces who managed to survive at home took to the academic or else to the "higher" and relatively unpopular forms of writing. But the novelists, who control the main highway of literature, were, and still are, nearly all redskins to the wigwam born.

At present the redskins are in command of the situation, and the literary life in America has seldom been so deficient in intellectual power. The political interests introduced in the 1930s have not only strengthened their hold but have also brought out their worst tendencies; for the effect of the popular political creeds of our time has been to increase their habitual hostility to ideas, sanctioning the relaxation of standards and justifying the urge to come to terms with semiliterate audiences.

The redskin writer in America is a purely indigenous phenomenon, the true-blue offspring of the Western hemisphere, the juvenile in principle and for the good of the soul. He is a self-made writer in the same way that Henry Ford was a self-made millionaire. On the one hand he is a crass materialist, a greedy consumer of experience, and on the other a sentimentalist, a half-baked mystic listening to inward voices and watching for signs and portents. Think of Dreiser, Lewis, Anderson, Wolfe, Sandburg, Caldwell, Steinbeck, Farrell, Saroyan: all writers of genuine and some even of admirable accomplishments, whose faults, however, are not so much literary as faults of raw life itself. Unable to relate himself in any significant manner to the cultural heritage, the redskin writer is always on his own; and since his personality resists growth and change, he must continually repeat himself. His work is ridden by compulsions that depress the literary tradition, because they are compulsions of a kind that put a strain on literature, that literature more often than not can neither assimilate nor sublimate. He is the passive instead of the active agent of the *Zeitgeist*, he lives off it rather than through it, so that when his particular gifts happen to coincide with the mood of the times he seems modern and contemporary, but once the mood has passed he is in danger of being quickly discarded. Lacking the qualities of surprise and renewal, already Dreiser and Anderson, for example, have a "period" air about them that makes a rereading of their work something of a critical chore; and one suspects that Hemingway, that perennial boy-man, is more accurately understood as a descendant of Natty Bumppo, the hero of Fenimore Cooper's "Leatherstocking Tales," than as the portentously disillusioned character his legend makes him out to be.

As for the paleface, in compensation for backward cultural conditions and a lost religious ethic, he has developed a supreme talent for refinement, just as the Jew, in compensation for adverse social conditions and a lost national independence, has developed a supreme talent for cleverness. (In this connection it is pertinent to recall T. S. Eliot's remark about Boston society, which he described as "quite refined, but refined beyond the point of civilization.") Now this peculiar excess of refinement is to be deplored in an imaginative writer, for it weakens his capacity to cope with experience and induces in him a fetishistic attitude toward tradition; nor is this species of refinement to be equated with the refinement of artists like Proust or Mann, as in them it is not an element contradicting an open and bold confrontation of reality. Yet the paleface, being above all a conscious individual, was frequently able to transcend or to deviate sharply from the norms of his group, and he is to be credited with most of the rigors and charms of the classic American books. While it is true, as John Jay Chapman put it, that his culture is "secondary and tertiary" and that between him and the sky "float the Constitution of the United States and the traditions and forms of English literature" — nevertheless, there exists the poetry of Emily Dickinson, there is *The Scarlet Letter*, there is *Moby Dick*, and there are not a few incomparable narratives by Henry James.

At this point there is no necessity to enter into a discussion of the historical and social causes that account for the disunity of the American creative mind. In various contexts a number of critics have disclosed and evaluated the forces that have worked on this mind and shaped it to their uses. The sole question that seems relevant is whether history will make whole again what it has rent asunder. Will James and Whitman ever be reconciled, will they finally discover and act upon each other? Only history can give a definite reply to this question. In the meantime, however, there are available the resources of effort and understanding, resources which even those who believe in the strict determination of the cultural object need not spurn.

1939

PROLETARIAN LITERATURE:
A POLITICAL AUTOPSY

THERE IS HARDLY a literary critic in America who has not at one time or another taken a hand in the controversy concerning proletarian literature. Few of the contributors to this historic controversy, however, were aware of its concrete political background and perspectives. What was new about the proletarian literary movement was its emphasis on political and social relations; and in approaching this movement the critics, it is true, discussed the connection between art and politics and between art and society. But they failed to notice that it is not these general and abstract connections but primarily its specific political history which explained proletarian literature.

Like other types of literary creation, this literature undoubtedly reflected class interests, needs, and attitudes; yet unlike other types, it reflected such interests, needs, and attitudes through the coordinated medium of a political party. That party is the Communist Party, which alone of all parties in the labor movement displayed any solicitude for proletarian literature — a solicitude, needless to say, in full measure returned by its recipient.

It is impossible, in my opinion, to understand the development of this literature, its rise and fall, without understanding its relation to the Communist Party. There are other factors, of course, but all of them have been modified by this one fundamental relation. Thus the Marxist doctrine, for example, whose existence antedates that of the Communist International but in whose name the Communist literary critics habitually speak, has been generally taken as the theoretical basis of proletarian literature and its source of values. In identifying their own views — that is, the views of their party — with those of Marxism, these critics constructed a strategic mystification which had important consequences. One can place most of the books and essays dealing with Marxism and literature under the heading of this mystification, for what they actually deal with is literature and the particular interpretation of Marxism held by the official party. As such it is a perfectly legitimate subject, but the writers who use it should be aware of its real nature and hence of its limitations. Another result has been that it is the Marxist philosophy and not specifically the Communist Party which has been held responsible for the excesses and crudities of proletarian literature and which has drawn the fire of its opponents; and yet there are Marxist thinkers of reputation who believe that the theory behind this literature has nothing in common with revolutionary thought. Manifestly, a subject as intricate and contradictory as proletarian literature needs more than a purely theoretical analysis. Let us look first to its political history.

To revolutionary optimists the triumph of the left-wing in American literature seemed inevitable in the early 1930s. And, on the whole, in looking back at those years, the expectation of this triumph appears to have been based on plausible enough grounds. At face value most of the factors entering into the situation were indeed favorable to a realignment of letters along radical lines.

The suffering imposed on the bulk of the population by the economic crisis elevated the "common man" to a martyrdom that almost overnight integrated him into the sympathies of the literary artist. Humanized by the calamities that befell him, the "common man" now began figuring in the imaginative scheme with positive force. Notwithstanding the contempt heaped upon him for many years as a mobster and a boob, he now emerged as the ideal-carrier of fictions, invocations in verse, and critical manifestoes. In the part of petty beneficiary of a prosperous and soulless materialism he had long typified the negation of values; cast in the role of at once a piteous victim and militant rebel he typified their revival. And his apotheosis was consummated when writers made a practice of detaching him from his ordinary human environment in order to place him within "the glorious collectivity of the embattled proletariat."

A further causative factor was provided, of course, by the exhaustion of the literary modes current in the twenties. Being for the most part expressions of disillusionment with society, these modes could not cope with the demands for its reconstruction. The various regional programs, designed as they were for local uses, appeared inconsequential in the face of a national crisis involving profound spiritual and material transformations. The proletarian program, on the other hand, invoking history in all its tenses to confirm its ambitions, laid claim to a universality and radicalism of outlook poles asunder from the restricted and polite values of the past.

Furthermore, a political party existed in America, the Communist Party, which made haste to identify this literary program as a part of its own larger perspective and which welcomed into its political home all writers wishing to realize in practice their conversion to the revolutionary cause. This party, at that time virtually in sole occupation of the Marxist arena, thus became the organizer of proletarian literature and its ultimate court of appeal. The Left literary magazines were published under its auspices or edited by its members. It appointed political commissars to supervise the public relations of the new literary movement and to minister to its doctrinal health. It furnished it with an initial audience and with an organizational base; and, finally, it conditioned the writers that had come under its control to conceive of the Soviet Union, its own source of strength and seat of highest authority, as the living embodiment of their hopes for socialism.

Nominally, despite the elaborate and often weirdly sectarian theories proclaimed by individual members, the program of this literary movement was quite simple and so broad in its appeal as to attract hundreds of writers in all countries. It can be reduced to the following formula: *the writer should ally himself with the working class and recognize the class struggle as the central fact of modern life.* Beyond that he was promised the freedom to choose his own subjects, deal with any characters, and work in any style he pleased. The Communist Party was seldom mentioned directly in connection with this formula of conversion. Granville Hicks's book, *The Great Tradition,* was in effect nothing more than a historical argument for the realization of this formula by American literature, whose liberation from "confusion, superficiality, and despair" was predicted as the reward of compliance.

This formula, however, despite its deceptive simplicity, is actually a complicated political mechanism. Its abstract political meaning conceals multiple confusions that proved to be as beneficial to the fortunes of the Communist Party as they were pernicious in their consequences for literature. In the first place, it should be noted that this formula is empty of aesthetic principle and advocates no particular aesthetic direction; second, it establishes no defensible frontiers, so to speak, between art and politics — it merges them; third, it draws no distinctions between the politics of writing in a *generic and normative sense* and the politics of an individual writer in a particular historical period; and lastly, it fails to define in what way a writer's alliance with the working class is or is not an alliance with any particular political party of that class. Through this formula the writer was actually offered a contract of an unprecedented character, but all the specific stipulations were left to be written in after he had attached his signature to it. The principal mystification involved in this transaction consisted of the fact that while the writer thought he was allying himself with the working class, in reality he was surrendering his independence to the Communist Party, which for its own convenience had fused the concepts of party and class.

The Communist critics, sometimes deliberately and sometimes through ignorance, cultivated these mystifications, for it is with their aid that they succeeded in stuffing the creativity of the Left into the sack of political orthodoxy. In their criticism, opinions as to the literary merit of a work of art were by no means ruled out, but the fundamental criteria concerned themselves with the author's loyalty to the working class and his interpretation of the class struggle. And it is exactly at that point, of course, that the literary critic resigned in favor of his party. Loyalty to the working class? Interpretation of the class struggle? What are these if not political matters, and who is better versed in political matters than the party under whose patronage proletarian literature was developing? No critic, regardless how learned in Marxism, could possibly presume to pit his own judgment against the party's political sway and reputed infallibility in the reading of the law and the prophets. To impugn the party's political authority meant to court excommunication. Thus it turned out that a novel or a play was certificated "revolutionary" only when its political ideas — existing or latent — corresponded to those of the party. And since the party had long ago awarded itself a monopoly of *correct* politics, the seemingly liberal formula that had enticed so many recruits was soon filled with a content altogether at variance with its manifest meaning. If not in origin then in function it became no more than an administrative tool, a political contrivance for imposing party views on critical and creative writing. What we were witnessing was a miniature version of the process which in Russia had resulted in the replacement of the dictatorship of the proletariat by the dictatorship of the Communist Party. Within the brief space of a few years the term "proletarian literature" was transformed into a euphemism for a Communist Party literature which tenaciously upheld a fanatical faith identifying the party with the working class, Stalinism with Marxism, and the Soviet Union with socialism. The "literary movement" droned these beliefs into its members with the result that instead of revolutionary writing — which may mean a thousand and one things depending upon time, place, and individual bias — an internationally uniform literature was created whose main service was the carrying out of party assignments. For strategic purposes, of course, the official spokesmen found it advisable to conceal their essentially factional inspiration and narrow standards under a variety of pseudonyms designed to give the appearance of flexibility, objectivity, freedom from control, etc. However (and I think I can allow myself the dogmatism of saying this), unless we understand the relation of these pseudonyms to their referents we can learn very little about Left writing in America, or, for that matter, in any other country.

It is essential to understand the difference between the literature of a class and the literature of a party. Whereas the literature of a class represents an enormous diversity of levels, groupings, and interests, the literature of a party is in its very nature limited by utilitarian objectives. It cannot properly be called literature, for it tends to become a vehicle for the dissemination of special policies and views; a party is too small a unit of social life to serve as the base for the formation of a spiritual and artistic superstructure. Expressing the historic being and consciousness of an entire sector of society, the literature of a class accumulates organic traditions and norms. Confident of its past and frequently of its future as well, it permits a free exchange and conflict of feelings and ideas. A true class literature constantly strives and partially succeeds in overcoming and transcending its given social limitations; its aim is the all-human pattern and image, though this aim may be frustrated by historical needs of the opposite character. A party, however, being merely the political instrument of a class and usually of only one of several groupings in that class, must necessarily reproduce itself in literature in all its narrowness and rigidity.

But there are classes and classes, as there are parties and parties. Not all classes are capable of producing an art and literature of their own. The conception of a proletarian literature relies for its defense on abstract and formal analogies between the proletariat and the bourgeoisie. Literature is the outgrowth of a whole culture, one of its inseparable parts and manifestations. A class which has no culture of its own can have no literature either. Now in all class societies it is the ruling class alone which possesses both the material means and the self-consciousness — independent, firmly rooted, and elaborated — that are the prerequisites of cultural creation. As an oppressed class, the proletariat, insofar as it is a cultural consumer, lives on the leavings of the bourgeoisie. It has neither the means nor the consciousness necessary for cultural self-differentiation. Its conditions of existence allow it to produce certain limited and minor cultural forms, such as urban folklore, language variations, etc.; but it is powerless to intervene in science, philosophy, art, and literature. Neither is it admissible, for the purpose of proving the possibility of a proletarian culture, to compare the proletariat of today to the bourgeoisie of yesterday, when the latter was itself oppressed. While the oppression of the bourgeoisie by the feudal regime was chiefly political, the modern property relations dominate the proletariat in a *total* fashion. Because it was already an owning class, disposing of considerable wealth and leisure, the third estate could begin creating cultural values even before its political emancipation. The proletariat, on the other hand, before it can achieve the freedom that participation in culture requires, must first institute changes in society which include its own abolition. And if that historic task is ever accomplished, it will not be the proletariat — which will then no longer exist — but a classless and stateless humanity that will shape the new culture in its own image.

Virtually all the theorists of proletarian culture are fetishists of ideology, which they naively equate with and substitute for culture. And since they believe that in Marxism the proletariat possesses a distinct and separate ideology of its own, they conclude that all that is lacking for the creation of an art and literature of the working class is a plan and the will to carry it into effect. But the truth is that Marxism is not an ideology *of* the working class — it is an ideology *for* the working class brought to it from without. "The history of all countries," Lenin wrote in *What Is To Be Done?*, "bears witness that the working class is capable of developing only a trade-unionist consciousness . . . that is, the conviction of the necessity of joining together in unions, of conducting a struggle against the employer, of demanding from the government this or that legislative measure in the interests of the workers, etc. The socialist doctrine (Marxism), however, has proceeded from the philosophical, historical, and economic theories which originated with educated representatives of the owning classes, the intellectuals." Now inasmuch as proletarian literature, by the innumerable definitions* of it given by its own theorists, is nothing more than the socialist doctrine transferred to the creative sphere, it follows that it is a literature produced outside

---

* In his *The Novel and the People*, the British Communist critic, Ralph Fox, states that "Marxism gives to the creative artist the key to reality . . ." "He [the proletarian writer] will be unable to make his picture a true one unless he is truly a Marxist, a dialectician with a finished philosophical outlook." The Soviet Russian, Sergey Dinamov, speaks of the writer's "Party and class evaluation of life." The German, Otto Biha, contends that the "proletarian writer can view the world only from a consistent Marxian standpoint . . ." The American, Edwin Seaver, defines the proletarian novel by its "acceptance and use of the Marxian interpretation"; another American, Edwin Berry Burgum, defines it similarly, as "a novel written under the influence of dialectic materialism from the point of view of the class-conscious proletariat."

the proletariat and brought to it from without. But it is impossible to conceive of a literature issuing full-blown from a doctrine — it must also have some kind of concrete political basis. That political basis is none other than the Communist Party, which conceives of itself as the guardian of the socialist doctrine and its organizational embodiment.

This analysis is confirmed by an examination of the works which the official critics have accepted as proletarian. Whether we choose Soviet novels by orthodox authors like Gladkov, Fadeyev, and Sholokhov; or recent "militant" works by the Frenchmen Aragon and Malraux; or the revolutionary* prose and verse of American writers like Robert Cantwell, Fielding Burke, Michael Gold, Clifford Odets, John Howard Lawson, Albert Maltz, Jack Conroy, Ben Field, Isidor Schneider, Josephine Herbst, Kenneth Fearing, Muriel Rukeyser, Edwin Rolfe, etc. — in none of them shall we find an imagination or sensibility which is not of a piece with some variety — either plebeian or aristocratic but mostly the former — of the bourgeois creative mode. It is purely in a doctrinal-political fashion that these works differ from "the literature of another class." But even the doctrine, the one distinctive element in it, is not proletarian in any real sense; into literature as into the proletariat it is imported via a political party by "educated representatives of the owning classes" (Lenin) — the Marxist intellectuals.

It is clear that proletarian literature is the literature of a party disguised as the literature of a class. This fact explains both the speed of its development and the speed of its disintegration. Its peculiar artificiality, the devious and volatile nature of its critical principles, its artistic chaos plus its political homogeneity and discipline, its uses

* Throughout this article, in conformity with the practice of the international Communist press, the terms "proletarian literature" and "revolutionary literature" are used as synonyms. That this usage is still current is shown by Joshua Kunitz's article, *In Defence of a Term*, in the *New Masses* (July 12, 1938). There have been attempts to define "proletarian literature" as writing by people of proletarian origin about the life of their class. This definition, however, is purely formal and politically neutral. Obviously, a writer, though of proletarian origin and proletarian in his subject matter, might at the same time be fascist in his political allegiance. As a matter of fact, there are such literary types in Nazi Germany. Hence Communist critics have always insisted that the "proletarianism" of a work should be defined in relation to its political outlook rather than by its author's choice of themes or class origin.

as a cover for organizational activities — all these are explained by the periodic shifts and changes of the "party line." The growth of proletarian literature in this country between 1930 and 1935 is precisely coincident with the growth of the party during that period, when its policy was ultra-Left and opposed to any united or people's fronts. At that time the party saw the revolution as an immediate possibility, and its literature was extreme in its Leftism, aggressive, declamatory, prophetic. It was intolerant of all other schools of writing and proclaimed itself to be the sole heir of the literary creations of the ages. Its practitioners were persuaded by the party critics to turn out sentimental idealizations of the worker-types they were describing in their stories and plays. These works, most of which were quite crude as literary art, presented a silly and distorted picture of America. Despite good revolutionary intentions, their political content was schematic. Instead of giving a realistic and individualized portrayal of social experience, their authors *inferred* its characteristics by speculative methods from the theses of the Comintern about the "world-situation"; and since the Comintern had declared at that time that the workers of all countries were ready to seize power and establish socialism, they endeavored to demonstrate that the Comintern was right by showing "reality" behaving according to its directives. The better writers, of course, such as Josephine Herbst, Grace Lumpkin, Robert Cantwell, and Kenneth Fearing, avoided these fantasies by sticking to what they knew. But proletarian literature as a whole, here and abroad, followed the party in predicting and celebrating the victory of the revolution in a period when it was actually losing every battle.

At present this literature is withering away because the party no longer needs it. Since 1935 the party has acquired respectability by reconstructing itself on a reformist and patriotic basis. Having abandoned its revolutionary position and allied itself with liberal capitalism, its cultural requirements are altogether different from what they were in the past. Everything within its orbit, including the proletarian literary movement, which separates it from other reformist and Left-bourgeois tendencies is being done away with in order to expedite the "building of a democratic front." That the political party which fathered proletarian literature should now be devouring it is no cause for astonishment. A certain type of internal cannibalism — witness the Moscow trials — is intrinsic to its history and necessary for the fulfillment of its peculiar tasks.

The period of the proletarian mystification of American letters is now definitely over. To say this, however, is by no means equivalent to saying that in recent years the official Left has declined in size and in influence. On the contrary, there are more writers today extending active political support to the Communist Party than ever in the past. To read the long and diversified lists of names signed to some of the appeals or petitions issued by the League of American Writers, an organization controlled by members and sympathizers of that party, is to realize that in such centers as New York, Chicago, and Hollywood a large sector of literary opinion is in substantial agreement with the policies of the American section of the Comintern. Nothing could be more naive, however, than to equate the popularity of these policies among writers with the triumph of the proletarian literary program. The actual process is in the opposite direction.

The official Left is now engaged in reestablishing that dichotomy between the writer as citizen and the writer as artist which it once decried as a source of bourgeois infection. It has discovered how to take advantage of a dualism between art and life that in the past it pretended to find intolerable. Why examine what a writer puts into his books when the real profit is derived from regulating his political conduct as an individual to conform with that of the Communist Party. The official Left is today primarily interested not in literature but in *authors;* from them it seeks to obtain public statements approving its political program on current issues — a favor which it is only too glad to reciprocate by guaranteeing to the works of the obliging literary men immunity from its "Marxist" criticism. (In the case of the more prominent literary personalities the rate of reciprocation is, of course, much higher. Eulogies, such as have been provided for a recent novel by Ernest Hemingway, are expected and delivered.) Thus the narrow, one-sided truism of Granville Hicks and his colleagues defining *art* as a weapon becomes in practice the many-sided opportunism of converting the *artist* into one. This takes the form of extracting from him surplus publicity value by putting his public reputation to work in political testimonials which directly or indirectly refer back to the Communist Party or any of its agencies. Such political habits are in themselves sufficient to render insincere the attempt to introduce a radical content into literature, but in the present surreptitious abandonment of this attempt these habits are only of minor importance. If at present proletarian writing in this country is in the last stages of dissolution, it is largely because it is under political orders to commit suicide.

The experienced literary politicians who once acted as the apostles of proletarian literature would doubtless vehemently deny that they are in the midst of abolishing it. But that is exactly how their party code requires them to behave. It is now no longer news, except to fanatical Stalinists and reactionaries bent on maintaining a Red scare, that the Comintern has put away its revolutionary aims and embarked on national-reformist policies; and it is no friendlier to revolutionary ideas in the cultural than in the political sphere. Its literary adherents are, of course, lagging behind the "party line." A cultural lag is to be expected. All sorts of amusing inconsistencies and atavisms are to be observed in the pages of the Stalinist literary periodicals. In a purely academic way the small fry are still permitted to play with Marxist notions. The literary movement as a whole however, is being quickly dissolved in the body of American writing. It is a long time since we have read a programmatic article on proletarian "aesthetics" in the *New Masses,* which has replaced its former standards of evaluation with the abstract categories of "progress" and "reaction." This year only one novel and two volumes of verse were published in America that follow in any appreciable degree the accepted patterns of the proletarian literary mode.

In fiction the themes of unemployment and union organization have persisted. Being objectively present in the material of the social-minded writer, they cannot be arbitrarily cast aside; and neither does the politics of reformism make such a casting aside necessary. The question relates entirely to the political treatment such themes receive. If once, in following the official perspective, the proletarian writer transformed his positive characters — who invariably were either unemployed or on strike — into revolutionaries performing some act that symbolized the overthrow of the system of private property, today he would have to resolve their problems by attaching them to some activity of the New Deal. The new Communist

2

orthodoxy having decreed that peace, progress, and prosperity are possible under capitalism, the writer is unable to revolutionize his characters in any concrete sense without violating the precepts of the political faith of which, presumably, he is a loyal adherent. To be really logical, the unfortunate practitioner of the "party line" in fiction would have to substitute one of the President's fireside chats or a resolution for an immediate declaration of war on Japan for those visions of proletarian upheaval and the ultra-future of the classless society which nourished his inspiration in the past.

There are certain forms of demagogy, however, which a medium as palpable as fiction — unless it degenerates to the level of pulp propaganda — excludes by its very nature. Thus the media of art, if only by that fact alone, prove their superior humanity to the media of politics. The kind of casuistry which may easily pass for truth within the pseudo-context of a political speech or editorial, will be exposed in all its emptiness once it is injected into the real context of a living experience, such as the art of fiction strives to represent. The novel is the preeminent example of an experiential art; and to falsify the experiential terms in which it realizes itself is infinitely more difficult than to falsify abstract reasoning. Whereas politics summarizes social experience, the novel subjects it to an empiric analysis. Hence the test of the novel is more rigorous, less at the mercy of manipulation and rhetorical depravity. Proletarian fiction cannot *maintain its identity* while following its political leadership into an alliance with capitalist democracy. The only alternative for a school of writing that finds itself in such extraordinary straits is to abdicate. As citizens the members of that school are still moving within the orbit of their party, but what they write is increasingly becoming a matter that concerns no one but themselves — and the individual reader and critic, of course. The orientation toward capitalist democracy has deprived the proletarian writers of those political values which alone distinguished them from the nonproletarians. If historically American literature can be said to possess an ideology that generalizes it socially, it is none other than the ideology of capitalist democracy; and it is hardly necessary to develop a proletarian literature so that it may practice ideologically what American literature has been practicing virtually since its inception.

The other wings of cultural expression dominated by the Stalinist party are in a similar state of disintegration. That the revolutionary theater is dead no one doubts. As for Marxist criticism, it finds itself with less and less work on its hands. All that the Marxist critics can do is write conventional pieces with a slight social edge or else compose political polemics against the "counter-revolutionary fascist-aiding Trotskyites." These trenchant compositions, however, have as little in common with an analysis of art or letters as Trotskyism has with fascism. It is the absence of enemies, of course, which determines this Marxist idleness. If your critical sphere is American writing — in which there are as yet very few traces of fascism — and you have accepted the notion that your only real enemies are the fascists and that with everyone else it is necessary to cooperate, then to all intents and purposes your function as a Marxist critic has been abolished. What is left, of course, is the party-task of misrepresenting and assaulting the work of those Left writers who have repudiated Russian "socialism" and the Comintern. Michael Gold, for instance, has recently arraigned John Dos Passos before the bar of "progress" and convicted him of writing nothing but *merde.** But such critical activities are exercises in the art of abuse rather than in the art of criticism.

In the last chapter of *The Great Tradition,* revised in 1935, Granville Hicks wrote that "if revolutionary writers should become convinced, on adequate or inadequate grounds, that capitalism could survive, that revolution is unnecessary or impossible, they would cease to be revolutionary writers." Given the political milieu in which Mr. Hicks works, it was rash of him to commit himself to so definite a formula, which has the virtue of proving the statement that revolutionary literature, at least as Mr. Hicks conceived it in 1935, is no longer in existence. But it passed away without the benefit of any kind of convictions, either "on adequate or inadequate grounds," on

* In the *Daily Worker,* Feb. 28, 1938, Gold wrote: "On rereading his trilogy, one cannot help seeing how important the merde is in his psychology, and how, after a brief, futile effort, he has sunk back into it, as into a native element," etc. etc. Hailed as late as 1936 as the foremost representative of the revolutionary novel in America, he is now condemned as a hater of humanity and a decadent. This "critical" revaluation is based, to be sure, not on a "rereading" of the trilogy as Gold pretends, but on the fact that since 1936 Dos Passos has emphatically expressed his disagreement with Stalinist policies in Spain and elsewhere.

the part of Mr. Hicks's "revolutionary writers." An episode in the history of totalitarian communism, it will be remembered as a comedy of mistaken identities and the tragedy of a frustrated social impulse in contemporary letters.

1939

THE CULT OF EXPERIENCE IN
AMERICAN WRITING

EVERY ATTENTIVE READER of Henry James remembers that highly dramatic scene in *The Ambassadors* — a scene singled out by its author as giving away the "whole case" of his novel — in which Lambert Strether, the elderly New England gentleman who had come to Paris on a mission of business and duty, proclaims his conversion to the doctrine of experience. Caught in the spell of Paris, the discovery of whose grace and form is marked for him by a kind of meaning and intensity that can be likened only to the raptures of a mystic vision, Strether feels moved to renounce publicly the morality of abstention he had brought with him from Woollett, Mass. And that mellow Sunday afternoon, as he mingles with the charming guests assembled in the garden of the sculptor Gloriani, the spell of the world capital of civilization is so strong upon the sensitive old man that he trembles with happiness and zeal. It is then that he communicates to little Bilham his newly acquired piety toward life and the fruits thereof. The worst mistake one can make, he admonishes his youthful interlocutor, is not to live all one can. — "Do what you like so long as you don't make my mistake . . . Live! . . . It doesn't so much matter what you do in particular, so long as you have your life. If you haven't had that, what *have* you had? . . . This place and these impressions . . . have had their abundant message for me, I have just dropped *that* into my mind. I see it now . . . and more than you'd believe or I can express . . . The right time is now yours. The right time is any *time* that one is still so lucky as to have . . . Live, Live!"

To an imaginative European, unfamiliar with the prohibitive American past and the long-standing national habit of playing hide-and-seek with experience, Strether's pronouncements in favor of sheer life may well seem so commonplace as scarcely to be worth the loving concentration of a major novelist. While the idea that one should "live" one's life came to James as a revelation, to the contemporary European writers this idea had long been a thoroughly assimilated and natural assumption. Experience served them as the concrete medium for the testing and creation of values, whereas in James's work it stands for something distilled or selected from the total process of living; it stands for romance, reality, civilization — a self-propelling, autonomous "presence" inexhaustibly alluring in its own right. That is the "presence" which in the imagination of Hyacinth Robinson, the hero of *The Princess Casamassima*, takes on a form at once "vast, vague, and dazzling — an irradiation of light from objects undefined, mixed with the atmosphere of Paris and Venice."

The significance of this positive approach to experience and identification of it with life's "treasures, felicities, splendors and successes" is that it represents a momentous break with the then dominant American morality of abstention. The roots of this morality are to be traced on the one hand to the religion of the Puritans and, on the other, to the inescapable need of a frontier society to master its world in sober practice before appropriating it as an object of enjoyment. Such is the historical content of that native "innocence" which in James's fiction is continually being ensnared in the web of European "experience." And James's tendency is to resolve this drama of entanglement by finally accepting what Europe offers on condition that it cleanse itself of its taint of evil through an alliance with New World virtue.

James's attitude toward experience is sometimes overlooked by readers excessively impressed (or depressed) by his oblique methods and effects of remoteness and ambiguity. Actually, from the standpoint of the history of the national letters, the lesson he taught in *The Ambassadors,* as in many of his other works, must be understood as no less than a revolutionary appeal. It is a veritable declaration of the rights of man — not, to be sure, of the rights of the public, of the social man, but of the rights of the private man, of the rights of personality, whose openness to experience provides the sole effective guaranty of its development. Already in one of his earliest stories we find the observation that "in this country the people have rights but the person has none." And insofar as any artist can be said to have had a mission, his manifestly was to brace the American individual in his moral struggle to gain for his personal and subjective life that measure of freedom which, as a citizen of a prosperous and democratic community, he had long been enjoying in the sphere of material and political relations.

Strether's appeal, in curiously elaborated, varied, as well as ambivalent forms, pervades all of James's work; and for purposes of critical symbolization it might well be regarded as the compositional key to the whole modern movement in American writing. No literature, it might be said, takes on the qualities of a truly national body of expression unless it is possessed by a basic theme and unifying principle of its own. Thus the German creative mind has in the main been actuated by philosophical interests, the French by the highest ambitions of the intelligence unrestrained by system or dogma, the Russian by the passionately candid questioning and shaping of values. And since Whitman and James the American creative mind, seizing at last upon what had long been denied to it, has found the terms and objects of its activity in the urge toward and immersion in experience. It is this search for experience, conducted on diverse and often conflicting levels of consciousness, which has been the dominant, quintessential theme of the characteristic American literary productions — from *Leaves of Grass* to *Winesburg, Ohio* and beyond; and the more typically American the writer — a figure like Thomas Wolfe is a patent example — the more deeply does it engulf him.

It is through this preoccupation, it seems to me, that one can account, perhaps more adequately than through any other factor, for some of the peculiarities of American writing since the close of its classic period. A basis is thus provided for explaining the unique indifference of this literature to certain cultural aims implicit in the aesthetic rendering of experience — to ideas generally, to theories of value, to the wit of the speculative and problematical, and to that new-fashioned sense of irony which at once expresses and modulates the conflicts in modern belief. In his own way even a writer as intensely aware as James shares this indifference. He is the analyst of fine consciences, and fine minds too, but scarcely of minds capable of grasping and acting upon those ineluctable problems that enter so prominently and with such significant results into the literary art developed in Europe during the past hundred years. And the question is not whether James belonged among the "great thinkers" — very few novelists do — but whether he is "obsessed" by those universal problems, whether, in other words, his work is vitally associated with that prolonged crisis of the human spirit to which the concept of modernity is ultimately reducible. What James asks for, primarily, is the expansion of life beyond its primitive needs and elementary standards of moral and material utility; and of culture he conceives as the reward of this expansion and as its unfailing means of discrimination. Hence he searches for the whereabouts of "Life" and for the exact conditions of its enrichment. This is what makes for a fundamental difference between the inner movement of the American and that of the European novel, the novel of Tolstoy and Dostoevsky, Flaubert and Proust, Joyce, Mann, Lawrence, and Kafka, whose problem is invariably posed in terms of life's intrinsic worth and destiny.

The intellectual is the only character missing in the American novel. He may appear in it in his professional capacity — as artist, teacher, or scientist — but very rarely as a person who thinks with his entire being, that is to say, as a person who transforms ideas into actual dramatic motives instead of merely using them as ideological conventions or as theories so externally applied that they can be dispensed with at will. Everything is contained in the American novel except ideas. But what are ideas? At best judgments of reality and at worst substitutes for it. The American novelist's conversion to reality, however, has been so belated that he cannot but be baffled by judgments and vexed by substitutes. Thus his work exhibits a singular pattern consisting, on the one hand, of a disinclination to thought and, on the other, of an intense predilection for the real: and the real appears in it as a vast phenomenology swept by waves of sensation and feeling. In this welter there is little room for the intellect, which in the unconscious belief of many imaginative Americans is naturally impervious, if not wholly inimical, to reality.

Consider the literary qualities of Ernest Hemingway, for example. There is nothing Hemingway dislikes more than experience of a make-believe, vague, or frigid nature, but in order to safeguard himself against the counterfeit he consistently avoids drawing upon the more abstract resources of the mind, he snubs the thinking man and mostly confines himself to the depiction of life on its physical levels. Of course, his rare mastery of the sensuous element largely compensates for whatever losses he may sustain in other spheres. Yet the fact remains that a good part of his writing leaves us with a sense of situations unresolved and with a picture of human beings tested by values much too simplified to do them justice. Cleanth Brooks and Robert Penn Warren have recently remarked on the interrelation between qualities of Hemingway's style and his bedazzlement by sheer experience. The following observation in particular tends to bear out the point of view expressed in this essay: "The short simple rhythms, the succession of coordinate clauses, the general lack of subordination — all suggest a dislocated and ununified world. The figures which live in this world live a sort of hand-to-mouth existence perceptually, and conceptually, they hardly live at all. Subordination implies some exercise of discrimination — the sifting of reality through the intellect. But Hemingway has a romantic anti-intellectualism which is to be associated with the premium which he places upon experience as such."[*]

But Hemingway is only a specific instance. Other writers, less gifted and not so self-sufficiently and incisively one-sided, have come to grief through this same creative psychology. Under its conditioning some of them have produced work so limited to the recording of the unmistakably and recurrently real that it can truly be said of them that their art ends exactly where it should properly begin.

"How can one make the best of one's life?" André Malraux asks in

[*] Cf. "The Killers," by Cleanth Brooks and Robert Penn Warren, in *American Prefaces*, spring 1942.

one of his novels. "By converting as wide a range of experience as possible into conscious thought." It is precisely this reply which is alien to the typical American artist, who all too often is so absorbed in experience that he is satisfied to let it "write its own ticket" — to carry him, that is, to its own chance or casual destination.

In the first part of *Faust* Goethe removes his hero, a Gothic dreamer, from the cell of scholastic devotion in order to embroil him in the passions and high-flavored joys of "real life." But in the second part of the play this hero attains a broader stage of consciousness, reconciling the perilous freedom of his newly released personality with the enduring interests of the race, with high art, politics, and the constructive labor of curbing the chaotic forces in man and nature alike. This progress of Faust is foreshadowed in an early scene, when Mephisto promises to reveal to him "the little and then the great world." — *Wir sehen die kleine, dann die grosse Welt.* — The little world is the world of the individual bemused by his personal experience, and his sufferings, guilt feelings, and isolation are to be understood as the penalty he pays for throwing off the traditional bonds that once linked him to God and his fellowmen. Beyond the little world, however, lies the broader world of man the inhabitant of his own history, who in truth is always losing his soul in order to gain it. Now the American drama of experience constitutes a kind of half-*Faust*, a play with the first part intact and the second part missing. And the Mephisto of this shortened version is the familiar demon of the Puritan morality play, not at all the Goethian philosopher-sceptic driven by the nihilistic spirit of the modern epoch. Nor is the plot of this half-*Faust* consistent within itself. For its protagonist, playing Gretchen as often as he plays Faust, is evidently unclear in his own mind as to the role he is cast in — that of the seducer or the seduced?

It may be that this confusion of roles is the inner source of the famous Jamesian ambiguity and ever-recurring theme of betrayal. James's heroines — his Isabel Archers and Milly Theales and Maggie Ververs — are they not somehow always being victimized by the "great world" even as they succeed in mastering it? Gretchen-like in their innocence, they nonetheless enact the Faustian role in their uninterrupted pursuit of experience and in the use of the truly Mephistophelean gold of their millionaire-fathers to buy up the brains and beauty and nobility of the civilization that enchants them. And the later heroes of American fiction — Hemingway's young man, for instance, who invariably appears in each of his novels, a young man posing his virility against the background of continents and nations so old that, like Tiresias, they have seen all and suffered all — in his own way he, too, responds to experience in the schizoid fashion of the Gretchen-Faust character. For what is his virility if not at once the measure of his innocence and the measure of his aggression? And what shall we make of Steinbeck's fable of Lennie, that mindless giant who literally kills and gets killed from sheer desire for those soft and lovely things of which fate has singularly deprived him? He combines an unspeakable innocence with an unspeakable aggression. Perhaps it is not too farfetched to say that in this grotesque creature Steinbeck has unconsciously created a symbolic parody of a figure such as Thomas Wolfe, who likewise crushed in his huge caresses the delicate objects of the art of life.

The disunity of American literature, its polar division into above and below or paleface and redskin writing, I have noted elsewhere. Whitman and James, who form a kind of fatal antipodes, have served as the standard examples of this dissociation. There is one sense, however, in which the contrast between these two archetypal Americans may be said to have been overdrawn. There is, after all, a common ground on which they finally, though perhaps briefly, meet — an essential Americanism subsuming them both that is best defined by their mutual affirmation of experience. True, what one affirmed the other was apt to negate; still it is not in their attitudes toward experience as such that the difference between them becomes crucial but rather in their contradictory conceptions of what constitutes experience. One sought its ideal manifestations in America, the other in Europe. Whitman, plunging with characteristic impetuosity into the turbulent, formless life of the frontier and the big cities, accepted experience in its total ungraded state, whereas James, insisting on a precise scrutiny of its origins and conditions, was endlessly discriminatory, thus carrying forward his ascetic inheritance into the very act of reaching out for the charms and felicities of the great European world. But the important thing to keep in mind here is that this plebeian and patrician are historically associated, each in his own incomparable way, in the radical enterprise of subverting the puritan code of stark utility in the conduct of life and in releasing the long compressed springs of experience in the national letters. In this sense, Whitman and James are the true initiators of the American line of modernity.

If a positive approach to experience is the touchstone of the modern, a negative approach is the touchstone of the classic in American writing. The literature of early America is a sacred rather than a profane literature. Immaculately spiritual at the top and local and anecdotal at the bottom, it is essentially, as the genteel literary historian Barrett Wendell accurately noted, a "record of the national inexperience" marked by "instinctive disregard of actual fact." For this reason it largely left untouched the two chief experiential media — the novel and the drama. Brockden Brown, Cooper, Hawthorne, and Melville were "romancers" and poets rather than novelists. They were incapable of apprehending the vitally new principle of realism by virtue of which the art of fiction in Europe was in their time rapidly evolving toward a hitherto inconceivable condition of objectivity and familiarity with existence. Not until James did a fiction writer appear in America who was able to sympathize with and hence to take advantage of the methods of George Eliot, Balzac, and Turgenev. Since the principle of realism presupposes a thoroughly secularized relationship between the ego and experience, Hawthorne and Melville could not possibly have apprehended it. Though not religious men themselves, they were nevertheless held in bondage by ancestral conscience and dogma, they were still living in the afterglow of a religious faith that drove the ego, on its external side, to aggrandize itself by accumulating practical sanctions while scourging and inhibiting its intimate side. In Hawthorne the absent or suppressed experience reappears in the shape of spectral beings whose function is to warn, repel, and fascinate. And the unutterable confusion that reigns in some of Melville's narratives (*Pierre, Mardi*) is primarily due to his inability either to come to terms with experience or else wholly and finally to reject it.

Despite the featureless innocence and moral enthusiastic air of the old American books, there is in some of them a peculiar virulence, a feeling of discord that does not easily fit in with the general tone of the classic age. In such worthies as Irving, Cooper, Bryant,

Longfellow, Whittier, and Lowell there is scarcely anything more than meets the eye, but in Poe, Hawthorne, and Melville there is an incandescent symbolism, a meaning within meaning, the vitality of which is perhaps only now rightly appreciated. D. H. Lawrence was close to the truth when he spoke of what serpents they were, of the "inner diabolism of their underconsciousness." Hawthorne, "that blue-eyed darling," as well as Poe and Melville, insisted on a subversive vision of human nature at the same time as cultivated Americans were everywhere relishing the orations of Emerson who, as James put it, was helping them "to take a picturesque view of one's internal possibilities and to find in the landscape of the soul all sorts of fine sunrise and moonlight effects." Each of these three creative men displays a healthy resistance to the sentimentality and vague idealism of his contemporaries; and along with this resistance they display morbid qualities that, aside from any specific biographical factors, might perhaps be accounted for by the contradiction between the poverty of the experience provided by the society they lived in and the high development of their moral, intellectual, and affective natures — though in Poe's case there is no need to put any stress on his moral character. And the curious thing is that whatever faults their work shows are reversed in later American literature, the weaknesses of which are not to be traced to poverty of experience but to an inability to encompass it on a significant level.

The dilemma that confronted these early writers chiefly manifests itself in their frequent failure to integrate the inner and outer elements of their world so that they might stand witness for each other by way of the organic linkage of object and symbol, act and meaning. For that is the linkage of art without which its structure cannot stand. Lawrence thought that *Moby Dick* is profound *beyond* human feeling — which in a sense says as much against the book as for it. Its further defects are dispersion, a divided mind: its real and transcendental elements do not fully interpenetrate, the creative tension between them is more fortuitous than organic. In *The Scarlet Letter* as in a few of his shorter fictions, and to a lesser degree in *The Blithedale Romance*, Hawthorne was able to achieve an imaginative order that otherwise eluded him. A good deal of his writing, despite his gift for precise observation, consists of fantasy unsupported by the conviction of reality.

Many changes had to take place in America before its spiritual and material levels could fuse in a work of art in a more or less satisfactory manner. Whitman was already in the position to vivify his democratic ethos by an appeal to the physical features of the country, such as the grandeur and variety of its geography, and to the infinite detail of common lives and occupations. And James too, though sometimes forced to resort to makeshift situations, was on the whole successful in setting up a lively and significant exchange between the moral and empiric elements of his subject matter. Though he was, in a sense, implicitly bound all his life by the morality of Hawthorne, James nonetheless perceived what the guilt-tossed psyche of the author of *The Marble Faun* prevented him from seeing — that it is not the man trusting himself to experience but the one fleeing from it who suffers the "beast in the jungle" to rend him.

The Transcendentalist movement is peculiar in that it expresses the native tradition of inexperience in its particulars and the revolutionary urge to experience in its generalities. (Perhaps that is what Van Wyck Brooks meant when, long before prostrating himself at his shrine, he wrote that Emerson was habitually abstract where he should be concrete, and vice versa.) On a purely theoretical plane, in ways curiously inverted and idealistic, the cult of experience is patently prefigured in Emerson's doctrine of the uniqueness and infinitude, as well as in Thoreau's equally steep estimate, of the private man. American culture was then unprepared for anything more drastic than an affirmation of experience in theory alone, and even the theory was modulated in a semiclerical fashion so as not to set it in too open an opposition to the dogmatic faith that, despite the decay of its theology, still prevailed in the ethical sphere. "The love which is preached nowadays," wrote Thoreau, "is an ocean of new milk for a man to swim in. I hear no surf nor surge, but the winds coo over it." No wonder, then, that Transcendentalism declared itself most clearly and dramatically in the form of the essay — a form in which one can preach without practicing.

Personal liberation from social taboos and conventions was the war cry of the group of writers that came to the fore in the second decade of the century. They employed a variety of means to formulate and press home this program. Dreiser's tough-minded though somewhat arid naturalism, Anderson's softer and spottier method articulating the protest of shut-in people, Lewis' satires of Main Street, Cabell's florid celebrations of pleasure, Edna Millay's emotional expansiveness, Mencken's worldly wisdom and assaults on the provincial pieties, the early Van Wyck Brooks's high-minded though bitter evocations of the inhibited past, his ideal of creative self-fulfillment — all these were weapons brought to bear by the party of rebellion in the struggle to gain free access to experience. And the secret of energy in that struggle seems to have been the longing for what was then called "sexual freedom"; for at the time Americans seeking emancipation were engaged in a truly elemental discovery of sex whose literary expression on some levels, as Randolph Bourne remarked, easily turned into "caricatures of desire." The novel, the poem, the play — all contributed to the development of a complete symptomatology of sexual frustration and release. In his *Memoirs*, written toward the end of his life, Sherwood Anderson recalled the writers of that period as "a little band of soldiers who were going to free life . . . from certain bonds." Not that they wanted to overplay sex, but they did want "to bring it back into real relation to the life we lived and saw others living. We wanted the flesh back in our literature, wanted directly in our literature the fact of men and women in bed together, babies being born. We wanted the terrible importance of the flesh in human relations also revealed again." In retrospect much of this writing seems but a naive inversion of the dear old American innocence, a turning inside out of inbred fear and reticence, but the qualities one likes in it are its positiveness of statement, its zeal and pathos of the limited view.

The concept of experience was then still an undifferentiated whole. But as the desire for personal liberation, even if only from the less compulsive social pressures, was partly gratified and the tone of the literary revival changed from eagerness to disdain, the sense of totality gradually wore itself out. Since the 1920s a process of atomization of experience has forced each of its spokesmen into a separate groove from which he can step out only at the risk of utterly disorienting himself. Thus, to cite some random examples, poetic technique became the special experience of Ezra Pound, language that of Gertrude Stein, the concrete object was appropriated by W. C. Williams, super-American phenomena by Sandburg and related nationalists, Kenneth Burke experienced ideas (which is by no means the same as thinking them), Archibald MacLeish experienced public attitudes, F. Scott Fitzgerald the glamor and sadness of the very rich, Hemingway death and virile sports, and so on and so forth. Finally Thomas Wolfe plunged into a chaotic recapitulation of the cult of experience as a whole, traversing it in all directions and ending nowhere.

Though the crisis of the 1930s arrested somewhat the progress of the experiential mode, it nevertheless managed to put its stamp on the entire social-revolutionary literature of the decade. A comparison of European and American left-wing writing of the same period will at once show that whereas Europeans like Malraux and Silone enter deeply into the meaning of political ideas and beliefs, Americans touch only superficially on such matters, as actually their interest is fixed almost exclusively on the class war as an experience which, to them at least, is new and exciting. They succeed in representing incidents of oppression and revolt, as well as sentimental conversions, but conversions of the heart and mind they merely sketch in on the surface or imply in a gratuitous fashion. (What does a radical novel like *The Grapes of Wrath* contain, from an ideological point of view, that agitational journalism cannot communicate with equal heat and facility? Surely its vogue cannot be explained by its radicalism. Its real attraction for the millions who read it lies elsewhere — perhaps in its vivid recreation of "a slice of life" so horridly unfamiliar that it can be made to yield an exotic interest.) The sympathy of these ostensibly political writers with the revolutionary cause is often genuine, yet their understanding of its inner movement, intricate problems, and doctrinal and strategic motives is so deficient as to call into question their competence to deal with political material. In the complete works of the so-called "proletarian school" you will not find a single viable portrait of a Marxist intellectual or of any character in the revolutionary drama who, conscious of his historical role, is not a mere automaton of spontaneous class force or impulse.

What really happened in the 1930s is that due to certain events the public aspects of experience appeared more meaningful than its private aspects, and literature responded accordingly. But the subject of political art is *history,* which stands in the same relation

to experience as fiction to biography; and just as surely as failure
to generalize the biographical element thwarts the aspirant to fiction, so the ambition of the literary Left to create a political art
was thwarted by its failure to lift experience to the level of history.
(For the benefit of those people who habitually pause to insist on
what they call "strictly literary values," I might add that by "history"
in this connection I do not mean "history books" or anything re-
sembling what is known as the "historical novel" or drama. A political art would succeed in lifting experience to the level of history if
its perception of life — any life — were organized around a perspective relating the artist's sense of the *society* of the dead to his sense
of the *society* of the living and the as yet unborn.)

Experience, in the sense of "felt life" rather than as life's total
practice, is the main but by no means the total substance of literature. The part experience plays in the aesthetic sphere might well
be compared to the part that the materialist conception of history
assigns to economy. Experience, in the sense of this analogy, is the
substructure of literature above which there rises a superstructure
of values, ideas, and judgments — in a word, of the multiple forms
of consciousness. But this base and summit are not stationary: they
continually act and react upon each other.

It is precisely this superstructural level which is seldom reached
by the typical American writer of the modern era. Most of the well-
known reputations will bear out my point. Whether you approach
a poet like Ezra Pound or novelists like Steinbeck and Faulkner,
what is at once noticeable is the uneven, and at times quite distorted, development of the various elements that constitute literary
talent. What is so exasperating about Pound's poetry, for example,
is its peculiar combination of a finished technique (his special share
in the distribution of experience) with amateurish and irresponsible
ideas. It could be maintained that for sheer creative power Faulkner
is hardly excelled by any living novelist, yet the diversity and wonderful intensity of the experience represented in his narratives cannot entirely make up for their lack of order, of a self-illuminating
structure, and obscurity of value and meaning. One might naturally
counter this criticism by stating that though Faulkner rarely or never
sets forth values directly, they nonetheless exist in his work by implication. Yes, but implications incoherently expressed are no better

than mystifications, and nowadays it is values that we can least afford to take on faith. Moreover, in a more striking manner perhaps than any of his contemporaries, Faulkner illustrates the tendency of the experiential mode, if pursued to its utmost extreme, to turn into its opposite through unconscious self-parody. In Faulkner the excess, the systematic inflation of the horrible is such a parody of experience. In Thomas Wolfe the same effect is produced by his swollen rhetoric and compulsion to repeat himself — and repetition is an obvious form of parody. This repetition-compulsion has plagued a good many American writers. Its first and most conspicuous victim, of course, was Whitman, who occasionally slipped into unintentional parodies of himself.

Yet there is a positive side to the primacy of experience in late American literature. For this primacy has conferred certain benefits upon it, of which none is more bracing than its relative immunity from abstraction and otherworldliness. The stream of life, unimpeded by the rocks and sands of ideology, flows through it freely. If inept in coping with the general, it particularizes not at all badly; and the assumptions of sanctity that so many European artists seem to require as a kind of guaranty of their professional standing are not readily conceded in the lighter and clearer American atmosphere. "Whatever may have been the case in years gone by," Whitman wrote in 1888, "the true use for the imaginative faculty of modern times is to give ultimate vivification to facts, to science, and to common lives, endowing them with glows and glories and final illustriousness which belong to every real thing, and to real things only." As this statement was intended as a prophecy, it is worth noting that while the radiant endowments that Whitman speaks of — the "glows and glories and final illustriousness" — have not been granted, the desired and predicted vivification of facts, science, and common lives has in a measure been realized, though in the process Whitman's democratic faith has as often been belied as confirmed.

It is not the mere recoil from the inhibitions of puritan and neopuritan times that instigated the American search for experience. Behind it is the extreme individualism of a country without a long past to brood on, whose bourgeois spirit had not worn itself out and been debased in a severe struggle against an old culture so tenacious as to retain the power on occasion to fascinate and render impotent even its predestined enemies. Moreover, in contrast to the derangements that have continually shaken Europe, life in the United States has been relatively fortunate and prosperous. It is possible to speak of American history as "successful" history. Within the limits of the capitalist order — until the present period the objective basis for a different social order simply did not exist here — the American people have been able to find definitive solutions for the great historical problems that faced them. Thus both the Revolutionary and the Civil War were complete actions that virtually abolished the antagonisms which had initially caused the breakdown of national equilibrium. In Europe similar actions have usually led to festering compromises that in the end reproduced the same conflicts in other forms.

It is plain that until very recently there has really been no urgent need in America for high intellectual productivity. Indeed, the American intelligentsia developed very slowly as a semi-independent grouping; and what is equally important, for more than a century now and especially since 1865, it has been kept at a distance from the machinery of social and political power. What this means is that insofar as it has been deprived of certain opportunities, it has also been sheltered and pampered. There was no occasion or necessity for the intervention of the intellectuals — it was not mentality that society needed most in order to keep its affairs in order. On the whole the intellectuals were left free to cultivate private interests, and, once the moral and aesthetic ban on certain types of exertion had been removed, uninterruptedly to solicit individual experience. It is this lack of a sense of extremity and many-sided involvement which explains the peculiar shallowness of a good deal of American literary expression. If some conditions of insecurity have been known to retard and disarm the mind, so have some conditions of security. The question is not whether Americans have suffered less than Europeans, but of the quality of whatever suffering and happiness have fallen to their lot.

The consequence of all this has been that American literature has tended to make too much of private life, to impose on it, to scour it for meanings that it cannot always legitimately yield. Henry James was the first to make a cause, if not a fetish, of personal relations; and the justice of his case, despite his vaunted divergence from the pioneer type, is that of a pioneer too, for while Americans generally were still engaged in "gathering in the preparations and necessities" he resolved to seek out "the amenities and consummations." Furthermore, by exploiting in a fashion altogether his own the contingencies of private life that fell within his scope, he was able to dramatize the relation of the new world to the old, thus driving the wedge of historical consciousness into the very heart of the theme of experience. Later not a few attempts were made to combine experience with consciousness, to achieve the balance of thought and being characteristic of the great traditions of European art. But except for certain narratives of James and Melville, I know of very little American fiction which can unqualifiedly be said to have attained this end.

Since the decline of the regime of gentility many admirable works have been produced, but in the main it is the quantity of felt life comprised in them that satisfies, not their quality of belief or interpretive range. In poetry there is evidence of more distinct gains, perhaps because the medium has reached that late stage in its evolution when its chance of survival depends on its capacity to absorb ideas. The modern poetic styles — metaphysical and symbolist — depend on a conjunction of feeling and idea. But, generally speaking, bare experience is still the *leitmotif* of the American writer, though the literary depression of recent years tends to show that this theme is virtually exhausted. At bottom it was the theme of the individual transplanted from an old culture taking inventory of himself and of his new surroundings. This inventory, this initial recognition and experiencing of oneself and one's surroundings, is all but complete now, and those who persist in going on with it are doing so out of mere routine and inertia.

The creative power of the cult of experience is almost spent, but what lies beyond it is still unclear. One thing, however, is certain: whereas in the past, throughout the nineteenth and well into the twentieth century, the nature of American literary life was largely determined by national forces, now it is international forces that have begun to exert a dominant influence. And in the long run it is in the terms of this historic change that the future course of American writing will define itself.

1940

THE DEATH OF IVAN ILYICH
AND JOSEPH K.

F RANZ KAFKA is best known for his innovations. His originality
has so dazzled his readers that they tend to think of him almost
solely in terms detached from any of the historic tendencies of modern literature. In recent years, however, we have learned to suspect
excessive originality. The intensive study by modern critics of the
relation between tradition and original talent has convinced most
of us that originality at the point where it becomes the equivalent
of eccentricity is more often a sign of weakness than of strength.
In this sense, the isolation of Kafka not only delays a just estimate
of his achievement but also exposes him to the danger that we shall
merely gape at his fantastic performance and pass on.

The real question is whether Kafka's isolation is justified. Now
while it is true that in certain respects Kafka is an idiosyncratic
writer and that it would not do to underrate the extent to which he
departed from the norms of the literary imagination, still it can be
argued that the characteristic vision of his work is associated — at a
level beyond surface "strangeness" or purely private inspiration —
with other modern creations not generally regarded as unique or

abnormal. This may be demonstrated by comparing Kafka's novel *The Trial* with Tolstoy's *The Death of Ivan Ilyich*, a shorter narrative more widely known perhaps than any of Kafka's writings. The two narratives, though quite dissimilar in their formal subject matter and literary methods, seem to me essentially similar in theme and conception. Above all they share a common ideological tendency, which is objective in the sense that it exists on a social and historical rather than personal plane. This tendency can be defined as a tendency against scientific rationalism, against civilization, against the heresies of the man of the city whose penalty is spiritual death.

It is two works I am comparing, of course, not two writers. In the hierarchy of modern literary art Tolstoy obviously ranks higher than Kafka. Indeed, considered as creative personalities the two men are poles apart. One was an aristocratic yet elemental genius, whose initial identification with the natural world was more profound than his subsequent recoil from it; the other was an invalid and a neurotic, a prey to all the fears that beset the small, lost people of the city, who was driven by an obsessive feeling of guilt to burrow into the very foundations of reality. All the more startling, then, to hear the Tolstoyan cry from above, from the heights, also issuing from below, from the Kafkan underground.

It is not, of course, as an existential study of death that *Ivan Ilyich* falls into the same framework as *The Trial*. The Tolstoyan concern with mortality is not shared by Kafka, who found life so nearly impossible that he could hardly muster the strength to look beyond it. In associating the two narratives the first thing that comes to mind, rather, is their common religious basis, for both echo with the Augustinian imprecation, "Woe unto thee, thou stream of human custom!" But the religious basis, though important, is much too general and variable to serve directly as a unifying principle. Patently Tolstoy's system of Christian anarchism excludes Kafka's dominant hypothesis of the incommensurability of the human and divine orders. It is above all within the range of depicted experience, of the applied attitudes toward the real and the unreal, that the correspondence between the two works reveals itself most clearly.

In the midst of their ordinary, and, to them, wholly satisfactory lives, Ivan Ilyich and Joseph K. are stricken down by mysterious catastrophes. Just as K., failing to win his case in the unknown and unknowable Court which tries him on an unspecified charge, is finally executed, so Ilyich, failing to recover from an "unheard of" illness, which no doctor is able to diagnose, finally dies in agony after screaming incessantly for three days and three nights. The "case" and the "illness" are variations of the same device, which permits the author to play God so as to confront an ordinary, self-satisfied mortal with an extraordinary situation, to put to rout his confidence in reason and in the habitual limits of his consciousness, and in the end to destroy him utterly.

Incapable of distinguishing themselves either for good or evil, neither Ilyich nor K. are sinners in the accepted sense. Nevertheless the inquisitorial art of their authors burns them at the stake as heretics. And their heresy consists simply of their typicality.

Standardized urban men, K. and Ilyich are typical products of a quantitative civilization. Neither rich nor poor and at all times removed from any material or spiritual extremity, they conform to the conventions with the regularity of a law of nature. Both are professional men: K. a bank official and Ilyich, a state functionary, member of the "Judicial Council." They aspire to and ordinarily succeed in leading a life of lighthearted agreeableness and decorum. The history of Ilyich, says Tolstoy, "was the simplest, the most ordinary, and the most awful." He marries and children are born to him; but inevitably husband and wife get to despise each other, she becoming steadily more ill-tempered, and he striving to make the relationship void by hiding behind his social and official duties.

K., on the other hand, like Kafka, is a bachelor. Necessarily so, for that is a telling item in Kafka's indictment of him — an indictment which on the human plane is in fact no indictment at all — thus causing unwary readers to consider him innocent — but which on another plane contributes to his guilt. Kafka's letters and diaries show him to have been continually haunted by the image of family life. Because of his personal deracination, he tended to idealize any human bond which rooted an individual in the community and supported him in his efforts to attain a status sanctified by the earthly as well as celestial powers. A projection of that side of his personality which Kafka wished to punish, K. concentrates within himself some of the faults of his author's condition and character, including the absence of family ties.

But from the chrysalis of the Kafkan self there also emerges another figure who, by means of a psychic transformation, assumes the role of judge and avenger. This dread antagonist summarily lifts K. out of his rationalist sloth and plunges the metaphysical knife into his breast. However, this antagonist is not a character whom we can recognize, he is not a living actor in the drama of K.'s fate. He is, rather, a transcendental emanation taking shape in the actual plot of the novel, which is really a plot against K.'s life — and, in the last analysis, against the human faith in visible reality.

The catastrophe which overtakes K. is immaculately conceived, and thus much more mysterious in its nature than the one which Tolstoy inflicts upon Ilyich. Kafka clears in one bound the naturalist barrier to his symbolist art; and insofar as he describes everyday scenes and objects, he does so on his own terms, with the aim of producing effects of irony, contrast, and suspense. *The Trial* opens with the sentence: "Someone must have been telling lies about Joseph K., for without having done anything wrong he was arrested one fine morning." This beguilement of the reader continues throughout the story, and though before long he begins doubting the "realism" of what he is told, he is not resentful of having been taken in by a false show, but, on the contrary, finds himself yielding entirely to this mockery of the real.

Kafka unites within one framework the realistic and symbolic, the recognizable and mysterious, in a way that severs the continuity of assumption between author and reader which has in a short time made the most difficult modern works universally accessible. To read him rightly one has, as it were, to learn to read anew; and to feel at home in his world it is first necessary to grasp his fundamental attitude toward life. At bottom the reason his meaning is so illegible is that he viewed life as essentially illegible, incomprehensible; which does not mean, however, that he thought it meaningless. Having made his main premise the unknowability of the relations within which man lives, Kafka could permit himself a free range of hypotheses concerning their true character. His narratives are speculations translated into the language of the imagination; they

are myths whose judicious, mock-scientific tonality at once dissociates them from the myth as an historical product. Experimental in
tendency, they are not so much findings about reality as methods of
exploring it. One might call them experimental myths. As meanings
they move strictly in a circle, for they always return to their point
of departure, namely, the uncertain, the unknown, the unfathomable. Hence their beginnings and ends are really identical: the
origin and culmination of a Kafkan story tend to fuse in our minds
into a single mystery. Obviously the myth as *procedure,* the myth
as a technique of investigation, is the myth inverted, the myth standing on its head; and in demonstrating its uses Kafka achieved a new
mutation in the art of prose fiction.

But Kafka's myths are not experimental in the sense of an inner
lack of commitment; nor are they experimental in the sense of a
playful tentativeness of design. In one of his notebooks he gives
us a clue to his intention. What he wished most, he writes, was to
recreate life in such a way that "while still retaining its natural full-
bodied rise and fall, it would simultaneously be recognized no less
clearly as a nothing, a dream, a dim hovering . . . Considered as a
wish, somewhat as if one were to hammer together a table with
a painful and methodical and technical efficiency, and simultaneously do nothing at all, and not in such a way that people would
say: 'Hammering a table together is nothing to him,' but rather
'Hammering a table together is really hammering a table together
to him, but at the same time it is nothing,' whereby certainly the
hammering would become still bolder, still surer, still more real
and, if you will, still more senseless."

Kafka realizes his wish. His forms dissolve the recognizable world
even as they hold us to it by their matter-of-fact precision of detail.
K. is persecuted by chimerical powers while he works at his desk
in a bank, lives in an ordinary boardinghouse on an ordinary street,
and is subject to normal impressions and distractions. Kafka succeeds in joining the two planes, in "hammering" them together until
both are equally real and yet equally unreal. His intrinsic ambivalence found here its ideal expression. His myths, though experimental, unfold like dreams, and like dreams they banish the sense
of "perhaps" and are predominantly made up of visual images.
Their terror is like nothing so much as the sensation of drowning;

it is the terror of sinking so deeply into workaday reality that, magically transformed, it turns into a dream, an illusion.

However, this illusion, this "nothing, dream, dim hovering," has a content. It is the cruel and unfathomable poetry of relations, the alchemy of fate. Phenomena are known, explicable — hence the naturalistic description of backgrounds — but relations are inexplicable and fantastic. These relations Kafka personifies with bold literalness in the form of a summary Court in perpetual session, a divine hierarchy, an irrational aggregate of rules and regulations known as the Law. Utterly alienated from nature, he sees everything in terms of society, which he conceives as the totality of being within which dwell both the known and unknown, the earthly and heavenly, the divine Law and the human litigant. Kafka's fear and its objects are in the main social; his divinities are fantastic personifications of irrational relationships chiefly rendered in the fear-and-dependence imagery of the Father.

In his stories the immemorial symbolism of the divine is inverted. Brightness, purity, immateriality — what reason is there to believe that these are really the attributes of Heaven? Instead Kafka houses his Court in a slum and fills the dilapidated rooms with bad air. Even the Castle, which is seen through a medieval haze, is in reality a squat office building where the functionaries — the angels and demons — are preoccupied with writing letters and filing documents. It is both easy and difficult to handle these functionaries; there are no fixed principles for dealing with them. Beyond their zeal in behalf of the Law, they share all the vices of humanity; and like the sons of God mentioned in the Book of Genesis, they pursue the daughters of man.

The officials of the Law never go hunting for crime among the populace: they are simply drawn toward the guilty. No errors are possible, and if such errors do occur, who is finally to say that they are errors? And man is not tried by means of his high ambitions, by the foiling of his heroic designs, but on the level of a realistic humanism, by the failure of his effort to define his status in the community and win a measure of control over his social and personal destiny. What is particularly original here, as well as baffling of course, is the combination of the archaic and modern. Reviving the furies of antiquity, the fatality lurking at the roots of existence,

Kafka at the same time contrives to enclose them within the prosaic framework of litigations, petty documented worries, and bureaucratic tedium.

The metaphysical end sought by Kafka is accomplished by Tolstoy in a different way, for his realistic method is sober and "heavier." Whereas Kafka plays, as it were, both ends against the middle, Tolstoy always proceeds from the external to the internal. In his apartment, one day, Ilyich goes up a ladder to have some hangings draped, misses a step and slips; "but, like a strong and nimble person, he clung on, and only knocked his side against the corner of a frame. The bruised place ached, but it soon passed off." In time, however, he begins complaining of an uncomfortable feeling on the "left side" of his stomach, and soon we see him hovering over the edge of an abyss. While his world is falling apart, his physicians are engaged in balancing the probabilities "between a loose kidney, chronic catarrh, and appendicitis." They never manage to come to a decision; nor are they able to mitigate the patient's suffering, let alone save him from his fate. And as the story goes on, the disease which lays Ilyich low gradually loses its verisimilitude, until finally it takes on the form of an occult visitation. Manifestly in order to get the better of the accepted normality of the world, the naturalism of Tolstoy's narrative must come to an end at the precise point where the symbolism of Kafka's begins: at a crisis not only of conscience but of objective reality. The devised catastrophe must reach a dimension where normal explanations cease to operate. Only within that dimension can it function properly. At the close of his life Ilyich realizes that the horrible thing that goes on within him — the irresistible "It" — is at once a disease and yet not a disease. Is it not, after all, the voice of his soul, just as K.'s Court is perhaps nothing more than a machine of persecution invented by his alter ego to penalize K.'s death in life? (In one of his parables Kafka envisions a prisoner who, seeing a gallows being erected in the courtyard of his prison, "mistakenly" believes it is meant for him, and that night he slips out of his cell and hangs himself.) But this simple explanation holds only on the level of ordinary religious psychology, in the light of which the ordeals of Ilyich and K. merely illustrate once again the eternal struggle between man's brute nature and his soul. The real problem, however, is to discover the particular meanings, social and historical, of Ilyich's contrite soul and K.'s machine of persecution.

In the loneliness of his pain Ilyich understands at last that his life had been trivial and disgusting. In this accounting which he gives to himself he thinks of what he now desires. To live and not to suffer, yes, but how? And his reply: "Why, live as I used to live before, happily and pleasantly," shows that as yet no real change has occurred in him. But during the last three days and nights he feels himself being thrust by an invisible force into a black sack; and his agony is due to his being in the black sack of course, and — "still more to not being able to get right into it." What hinders him from fully getting into the black sack? The pretense that his life had been good. — "That justification of his life held him fast and would not let him go forward, and it caused him more agony than all." Only on freeing himself of this pretense, of this illusion, does the terror of death leave him and he expires.

Morally, the death of K. duplicates the death of Ilyich. He, too, at first mistakes his apocalyptic fate, not perceiving the shape of a hidden god outlined in the petty event of his arrest. He expects to return to his normal state of well-being as soon as the matter of the absurd and obscure charge against him is cleared up. But after a few scuffles with the agents of the Court, he realizes the gravity of his situation and engages lawyers to defend him. These lawyers might as well be Ilyich's doctors. Both Ilyich and K. feel that their ostensible protectors are wasting time in irrelevant and supposedly scientific generalities, while they — patient and defendant — want to know only one thing: Is their condition serious?

Much like Ilyich, K. is impelled to give an accounting of his life, his case requiring, he decides, that he put it in the form of a written plea for justice containing a complete review of his career down "to the smallest actions and accidents formulated and examined from every angle." And just as Ilyich can no longer keep his mind on his legal documents, but must ask everybody questions concerning sick people, recoveries and deaths, so K. is continually distracted from his duties at the bank by his need to hunt out other defendants and compare experiences with them. Tolstoy's description of Ilyich's mounting incapacity to cope with his daily routine in view of that "matter of importance" which he must constantly keep before him, forms an almost exact parallel to those scenes in *The Trial* when K. stands looking out of his office window, so overwhelmed by his "case" that he can no longer face his business callers. And toward the end — on the evening of his execution — as two men in frock coats and top hats who look like old-time tenors arrive to take him away, K. likewise contents himself with half-truths. Though he allows his warders to lead him off, still he is not entirely resigned but must make a last-minute attempt to shake them loose. He is half in and half out of the black sack. But finally he understands that there is nothing "heroic" in resistance: "I have always wanted to snatch at the world with twenty hands, and not for a very laudable motive either. That was wrong, and am I to show now that not even a whole year's struggle with my case has taught me anything? Am I to leave this world as a man who shies away from all conclusions?" And thinking of that High Court to which he had in vain striven to penetrate, he suffers the knife to be turned in him twice.

II

The use to which Kafka puts the categories of law in *The Trial* is to some extent analogous to Tolstoy's use of medicine in *Ivan Ilyich*. Representative disciplines, institutions, conspicuous structures erected by man's progress and science, law and medicine are fortresses against which those who spurn the authority of progress and science must take up arms. But the assault takes different forms. Whereas Tolstoy makes a frontal attack, openly jeering at the doctors for their silly airs and pose of omniscience, and even accusing them of lying, Kafka enters the fortress disguised as a friend. Emotionally ambivalent, he sympathizes at once with the divine judge and with the human defendant; hence even as he demonstrates the meaninglessness of the notion of justice he wears the mask of legality. His unusual irony converts juridical relations, which we are accustomed to think of as supremely rational, into the very medium of irrationality. K. discovers that the enactments and ordinances of the Court are not motivated by a love of order but by caprice and every kind of disorderly impulse. Bent on proving the disjunction between justice and necessity, human intention and destiny, Kafka created in his myth of the Law a wonderfully imaginative, albeit emotionally cruel, equivalent of a philosophical idea.

Against this Law, which abhors reason, it is impossible to revolt; nor are reforms to be thought of. Combined action of the defendants (the socialist recommendation) is out of the question, for "each case is judged on its own merits, the Court is very conscientious about that . . ." The arbitrariness of the system of justice impels the accused men to suggest improvements, and that is one of the sources of their pathos. The only sensible thing to do is to adapt oneself to existing conditions. "This great organization remains . . . in a state of delicate equilibrium, and if someone took it upon himself to alter the disposition of things around him, he ran the risk of losing his footing and falling to destruction while the organization would simply right itself by some compensating reaction in another part of its machinery . . ."

Manifestly in this scheme of things the outlook for social progress is entirely blank, and Kafka's acceptance of its perils is unconditional. True, it is an irrational world, but its irrationality, he suggests, is perhaps no more than the specific illusion, the particular distortion, inherent in the human perspective. "In the fight between you and the world back the world!" he wrote. Such "backing" must be understood as a derangement of the attitudes native to Western literary art. This art has always pitted itself against the world, the heroes it created struck out and often conquered it, at the very least they protested against its injustices and insufficiencies. Kafka, on the other hand, refuses to cheat the world of its triumph, and the peculiarly austere tone of his prose evolves out of the tension between his sympathy for his heroes and the doom to which he consigns them.

This doom, articulated in narrative terms through the device of the mysterious catastrophe, requires that before the final blow is struck the victim be subjected to a process of dehumanization. If to be human is to be what K. and Ilyich are, then to dehumanize is to spiritualize them — such is the logic of this process. Kafka ensnares K. in the web of an inhuman law; Tolstoy, ever steadfast in his naturalism, crushes his victim physically. The latter method is simpler and entirely orthodox as religious procedure. Invoking as it does the old dualism of body and spirit, it suggests modern ideas as well, such as the idea of kinship between disease and spirit stressed by Nietzsche and in his wake by Thomas Mann. "Disease," writes Mann in his essay *Goethe and Tolstoy*, "has two faces and a double relation to man and his human dignity. On the one hand it is hostile; by overstressing the physical, by throwing man back upon his own body, it has a dehumanizing effect. On the other hand, it is possible to feel about illness as a highly dignified human phenomenon." And while it may be going too far, he adds, to claim that disease and spirit are identical, still the two conceptions have much in common. "For the spirit is pride; it is a willful denial and contradition of nature; it is detachment, withdrawal, estrangement from her." Mann's observations are supported by Tolstoy's practice in *Ivan Ilyich*. The story, which has the qualities of a rite of purification, was published in 1886, several years after the author's "conversion"; and the disease which ravages Ilyich evidently represents Tolstoy's reaction against the natural world with which he formerly identified himself and his advance toward a rational religiosity and an ethical conception of social existence.

But *The Trial* is a purer, a more ideal instance of a magical rite. In the psychology of its author it is not difficult to recognize the symptoms of a compulsion-neurosis. The conscience-phobia, the morbid scruples and self-depreciation, the ceremonial "correctness" of behavior conceived as a supple bargaining, as a counterbalance to the threatening maneuvers of fate, the compensatory altruism and humility — all are obvious symptoms. Freud remarks that the primary obsessive actions of compulsion neurotics are "really altogether of a magical nature"; and in another context he notes that insofar as the neuroses are caricatures of social and cultural creations, the compulsion-neurosis is like a caricature of a religion. More: aside from sexual features the Freudian theory detects in this and similar neuroses a regression in time to the world-pictures of primitive men. The collective representations of the primitive are reproduced by the neurotic on a subjective and antisocial basis. Perhaps Kafka's conception of destiny may be understood in part as an example of this type of neurotic regression. His depiction of the Court, despite the modernity of its bureaucratic procedures, recalls us to remote and primordial ideas of fate. This is even truer of his novel *The Castle*, where the sense of fate is expressed in spatial rather than in temporal terms. By this I mean that the Castle, which is the abode of divinity, as well as the village, which is the community of men —

the crowd of celestial functionaries as well as the crowd of peasants — are all subordinate to an even more primary power which has no personification and no rationale but which is simply the necessary and eternal disposition of things. This conception of fate is older than religion and antedates the birth of the gods. It originated in the magical and animistic stage of tribal life. The Greek word *Moira* — fate as F. M. Cornford has shown in his book *From Religion to Philosophy*, once possessed spatial significance. It refers back to a cosmogony which was developed prior to the Homeric theogony. *Moira* was an impersonal potency dominating both gods and humans whose real meaning was portion, allotment, province, domain. To sin meant to encroach, to cross a sacred frontier, to expose oneself to Nemesis — the avenger of trespass. This "separation of the world into elemental provinces" can be traced back, according to Cornford, to the sanctification of "status," namely, to the projection into myth of the social and economic organization of the tribe.

In this sense it can be said that what is represented in *The Castle* is *Moira* rather than fate working itself out according to modern conceptions of it. Unable to establish himself in the "village," which is the province of man, the pathos of K. in this novel is the pathos of an alien whose pursuit of status ends in failure. Status is synonymous with the state of grace; and he who has a home has status. This home, this cosmic security, this sacred order of status, is not a mythical or psychological but a historical reality. It persisted as a way of life, despite innumerable modifications, until the bourgeois era, when the organization of human life on the basis of status was replaced by its organization on the basis of free contract. The new, revolutionary mode of production sundered the unity of the spiritual and temporal, converting all things into commodities and all traditional social bonds into voluntarily contracted relations. In this process man was despiritualized and society atomized; and it is against the background of this vast transformation of the social order that the meaning of the death of Ilyich and K. becomes historically intelligible.

What should be clearly understood about Ilyich and K. is that they typify the average man of modern society. Tolstoy was much more conscious of this than Kafka, who in picturing society as a fabulous totality confounded this world with the kingdom of heaven.

4

But Tolstoy was socially motivated; his "conversion" was prompted by the dissolution of the centuries-old feudal ties, the breakdown of the ancient patriarchal relations, and the protest of the bewildered peasantry and nobility against the transformation of Russia into a capitalist country. His preoccupation with religion mirrored a utopian social program which has been defined as "feudal socialism"; and the historically reversed socialism of an aristocracy which bankers and tradesmen threaten to evict or have evicted from power cannot but assume idealist and religious forms.

Ilyich is the man of the city — the anonymous commodity-materialist who sweeps away the simple and transparent social relations of the past. His energy, the depersonalized energy of the modern man, subverts the idyllic world of sanctified status. In this connection it is characteristic that the only positive figure in Tolstoy's story should be the peasant Gerasim, a domestic in Ilyich's household, whose health and heartiness, in contrast to that of the city people, not only does not offend but soothes the sick man. And as to the mysterious catastrophe which destroys Ilyich, what is it in historical reality if not the ghost of the old idealism of status returning to avenge itself on its murderer? Through Ilyich's death the expropriators are expropriated.

But Kafka's religious preoccupation, you will say, is devoid of social meaning, since it seems purely psychological and even neurotic in origin. Yes, but let us not confuse origin with content. While it is true that Kafka's religious feelings were fed by a neurosis, there is however a sense, I believe, in which one might speak of the modern neurotic as the victim of the destructive triumph of "psychology" over nature, of the city over the country. He might be described as a casualty of a collective neurosis, of an illness of society.

What is K. if not, again, the blank man of the city, the standard *Teilmensch* cut off from all natural ties? He lives in the agitated, ever-changing world of modern relationships, a world in which the living man, destitute of individuality, has forgotten the ancient poetry of status, the hallowed certitudes that once linked law and destiny, justice and necessity, rights and duties. It is this dry world and himself in it that Kafka represents in the person of K. Against him, who embodies the present, Kafka directs his irony by entangling him with the banished past, with the ancient poetry. This happens when K. is suddenly arrested by the agents of an unknown Court, and when he finds himself under the jurisdiction of an inaccessible Castle. The Court and the Castle are sinister symbols of the old idealism; and K.'s entanglement with it effects a fantastic reversal of past and present, or dream and reality. It is now the dream of the past which is installed as master, and reality — the present — is banished. Naturally, everything is now turned upside down for K. He, the perverted modern man, can never adapt himself to the conditions of the absolute; he commits the most ludicrous errors and, though guilty, he thinks himself innocent. As he enters the Court he feels stifled in its pure air; its magnificent chambers he mistakes for dingy tenement rooms. Blinded by the fierce light of *Moira,* he can never experience the unity of justice and necessity but must ever divide the one from the other. K. dies of his contact with the past. His fate bears witness to a conflict of past and present, a conflict out of which the past emerges victorious. But the victory is wholly metaphysical.

This analysis by no means implies that Kafka was in any way conscious of the hidden historic reference of his symbols. On the contrary, no one among modern writers seems more deficient in a sense of history. The conflict between past and present is rendered in his work as a conflict between the human and divine orders. K. is allowed to live out his illusions; in fact, on the human level he is justified, for on that level the Court inevitably appears to be no more than an arbitrary and amoral power. Nevertheless, since the divine disposition of things cannot ultimately be questioned, man is destined to be ever in the wrong. Yet this abstract and mystical idea cannot be taken at face value. The time-spirit enters art without waiting for the permission of the artist. Kafka was writing under an obscure and irresistible compulsion, and his attitude toward his work, which he seldom felt the need to publish, was contradictory: on the one hand he thought of it as a form of transcendental communion with his fellowmen, and on the other as an effort strictly personal in function. It would be shortsighted, however, to limit its application to its subjective origin and purpose.

So far as Kafka's religiosity is concerned, it is clear that he was not religious in any traditional sense. His imagination excluded dogmas, systems of theology, and the concept of time-hallowed institutions as a bulwark. He was not looking to religion to do the work of politics: to effect a new synthesis or restore an old one, to make culture coherent or to impose order upon society. His religious feeling was of a pristine nature, essentially magical and animistic; and he attempted to rematerialize the soul thousands of years after religious thought had dematerialized it.

Unlike novelists like Dostoevsky and even Tolstoy in some of his moods, who are seldom at a loss for directions to the divine, Kafka makes the unknowability of God his chief postulate and the lack of communication between man and the powers that rule him its first corollary. Whereas Dostoevsky does not at all hesitate to describe a saint, Kafka cannot even imagine saintliness, for that would imply familiarity with the divine — precisely what, in his view, is unattainable. He asked, What is God like? as if the conception of the deity is utterly without a history. And the fantasy of his interrogations on this theme is deepened by his turning the empirical method inside out in applying it to the investigation of a nonempirical hypothesis, to the rationalization of the irrational.

Moreover, to postulate a God without a history has its consequences: it means that one is also lifting the world out of history. And, indeed, in Kafka history is abolished; there is only one time, the present; his people are not characters but simply bundles of human behavior, as immutable as a dream, rendered instantaneously, their inner and outer selves confounded. Character, individuation, are after all a proof of some measure of adjustment to the environment; the Kafkan man, however, is deprived of the most elementary requisites of adjustment: he moves within the dimension of fate, never within the dimension of personality, and the necessary link between the two is sprung.

Yet in spite of the profoundly unhistorical character of Kafka's art there are certain qualities in K., the chief protagonist of his narratives, that cannot be perceived except on the plane of historical interpretation. Thus historically his death, as that of Ilyich, signifies the disappearance of the hero from the drama of fate; their death falls outside the framework of the traditional tragic scheme. Tragedy implies that the hero, though vanquished by fate, commemorates in his very defeat the greatness and importance of man. The hero is always sharply individualized; his is an ample character. The opposite is true of K. and Ilyich, however. They are characterless in the sense indicated by Dostoevsky when he wrote in *Notes from Underground* that "the man of the nineteenth century must be, is morally obliged to be, a characterless individual," and by Marx when he remarked that the advantages of progress are paid for by the loss of character.

K. and Ilyich are heroes neither on the classic nor on the romantic level. Romanticism made of the self the primary criterion of values and its hero relived the past in terms of the new, critical, self-conscious bourgeois individuality. But in time the abstract modes of modern life undermined the self-confidence of the romantic hero and, stripped of his hopes and ambitions, he sank into anonymity. It is this historic depletion of man which is brought to light in the fate of K. and Ilyich alike.

But whereas the pathos of Tolstoy is that of a heroic struggle for a better life and for a constructive, even if utopian, rationality in the perception of man's enterprises and fate, the pathos of Kafka is that of loneliness and exclusion. In him the tradition of Western individualism regards itself with self-revulsion; its joyous, ruthless hero is now a victim; he who once proudly disposed of many possessions is now destitute, he has neither woman nor child; in his conflict with society he has suffered an utter rout, and his fate no longer issues from his own high acts but from the abstract, enigmatical relations that bend him to their impersonal will.

Despite his longing for positive values, Kafka never resolved his perplexity. Considered in purely subjective terms, his myth of the Law is clearly the idealized impasse of his experience. If in the past of humanity the *unknown* — God, Destiny, the law — served in the hands of kings and prophets as a collective and collectivizing formula, as an instrument of ordering and controlling life, in Kafka it manifests itself in an exhausted condition, no longer a means of mythically unifying reality but of decomposing it. The pious emotion is here being reabsorbed into its primordial origins. Again the gods are taboo, that is, both holy and unclean. Moreover, even they are unable to retrace their steps and go back to their ancient home in nature. Once the lively and fertile emanations of primitive fear, of tribal need and desire, they now exist only as dead letters in a statute book.

Believing as he does in the spirituality of life, in the "indestructible," Kafka nevertheless replies to his own query about the coming of the Messiah by declaring that he will appear only "when he is no longer needed, he will arrive the day after his arrival, he will not come on the last of the days, but on the day after the last." So out of his reach is human fulfillment that it has become unreal. Even his hope for salvation is ambiguous. He fears it as the final betrayal, the ironic confirmation of his despair.

1940

THE DARK LADY OF SALEM

Because I seek an image not a book . . .
— W. B. Yeats

HAWTHORNE is generally spoken of as a novelist of sin, but the truth is that he is not a novelist, at least not in the sense in which the term is commonly used, nor is sin wholly and unequivocally his subject. What that subject is remains to be defined, though by way of introduction it might be said that it is less a subject than a predicament. Or, better still, the predicament is the subject.

What is the intention of the novel as we have come to know it? In the broadest sense, it is to portray life as it is actually lived. Free access to experience is the necessary condition of the novel's growth as well as the objective guaranty of its significance; experience is at once its myth and its reason; and he who shuns experience is no more capable of a convincing performance in its sphere than a man unnerved by the sight of blood is capable of heroic feats on the battlefield. Now Hawthorne lived in an age when it was precisely experience — or, at any rate, those of its elements most likely to engage the interests of an artist — that was least at the disposal of the imaginative American, whose psychic resistance to its appeal was everywhere reinforced by the newness and bareness of the national scene, by its much-lamented "paucity of ingredients." It is this privation that accounts for Hawthorne's chill ideality, for his tendency to cherish the fanciful at the expense of the substantial and to reduce the material world to the all-too-familiar abstractions of spiritual law and the moral conscience. Two strains mingle in his literary nature: the spectral strain of the Gothic tale and the pietistic strain of Christian allegory, and both contribute to his alienation from the real.*

Yet there is in this writer a submerged intensity and passion — a tangled imagery of unrest and longing for experience and regret at its loss which is largely ignored by those of his critics who place him too securely within the family circle of the New England moralists. His vision of evil carries something more than a simple, one-way assertion of traditional principles; it carries its negation as well. He was haunted not only by the guilt of his desires but also by the guilt of his denial of them. The puritan in him grappled with the man of the nineteenth century — historically a man of appetite and perspective; and the former did not so easily pacify and curb the latter as is generally assumed.

The whole tone and meaning of Hawthorne's work, it seems to me, turns on this conflict.

In his own estimate he was a "romancer," and his insistence on designating himself as such should not be overlooked. Time and again he admonished his readers not to expect from him that "fidelity, not merely to the possible, but to the probable and ordinary course of man's existence" which is the mark of the novelist. He took pains to distinguish between the romance and the novel in order to lay claim, though not without due apologies, to the latitude inherent in the earlier genre. Yet he was fully aware of its defi-

* In his *American Prose Masters,* W. C. Brownell observes that Hawthorne's particular genius took him out of the novelist's field altogether. "His novels are not novels. They have not the reality of novels, and they elude it not only in their personages but in their picture of life in general." But the fact is that Hawthorne's particular genius cannot be assessed apart from the forces that shaped its expression. If we accept Brownell's definition of the novel as the medium of the actual, it can be stated flatly that neither Hawthorne nor any of his contemporaries succeeded in mastering it.

ciencies, aware that the freedom it afforded was more apparent than real, committing him to all sorts of dodges and retreats to which his artist's conscience could not be reconciled. This explains his habit of referring to his own compositions in a disparaging manner as "fancy-pictures" that could not survive a close comparison with the actual events of real lives.

Even while writing *The Scarlet Letter*, the theme of which suited him perfectly, he publicly regretted the "folly" of flinging himself back into a distant age and attempting to create "a semblance of a world out of airy matter." He would have been far better served, he goes on to confess in that superb essay, *The Custom House*, had he sought his themes in the "warm materiality" of the daily scene. "The fault," he concludes, "was mine. The page of life that was spread out before me seemed dull and commonplace, only because I had not fathomed its deeper import. A better book than I shall ever write was there . . . At some future day, it may be, I shall remember a few scattered fragments and broken paragraphs, and write them down, and find the letters turn to gold upon the page." But he was fated to be disappointed. The golden flow of reality never suffused his pages. Instead of entering the waking world of the novel, he remained to the last a "romancer" under the spell of that shadowy stuff which he at once loved and hated.

In the development of narrative-prose his place is decidedly among the pre-novelists — a position which he holds not alone but in the company of Poe and Melville and virtually the entire clan of classic American writers who, at one time or another, turned their hand to the making of fiction. The fact is that no novels, properly speaking, were produced in America until late in the nineteenth century, when the moralistic, semiclerical outlook which had so long dominated the native culture-heroes finally began to give way. The freedom promised by the Transcendentalist movement of the mid-century had not gone beyond a certain philosophical warmth and ardor of purpose. Though this movement expanded American thought, in itself this did not suffice to release the novelistic function. The release was effected only after the Civil War, when the many-sided expansion of American life created a new set of circumstances more favorable to artists whose business is with the concrete manifestations of the real and with its everyday textures. Then it was that James and Howells, susceptible, in different degrees, to the examples of European writing, came forward with new ideas, plans, and recipes.

Hawthorne's isolation from experience incapacitated him as a novelist. Yet he longed to break through this isolation, searching for the key that would let him out of the dungeon and enable him to "open intercourse with the world." "I have not lived," he cried, "but only dreamed of living . . . I have seen so little of the world that I have nothing but thin air to concoct my stories of . . ." Even the moderately candid biographies of him show that such protests were typical of his state of mind. And since these protests also inform his fiction, even if only in a tortuous and contradictory fashion, it can be said that his basic concern as a writer, though expressed in the traditional-moral terms of the problem of sin, was at bottom with the problem of experience — experience, however, not in the sense of its open representation in the manner of a novelist, but simply in the sense of debating its pros and cons, of examining good and evil, its promise and threat.

This preparatory scrutiny of experience constitutes his real subject, which is obscured by his creative means of allegoric construction and lavish employment of fantasy. His subject and the method he adopted to give it fictional form are incongruously related, but it was the only method available to him in his situation and, despite its faults, it permitted the growth of a novelistic embryo in each of his romances. That which is most actual in his work is comprised in these embryos; the rest — coming under the head of "romance" — is composed by his Gothic machinery and fed by the ceaseless pullulations of the sin-dogma. Knowingly or not, he indicated his own practice in remarking: "Realities keep in the rear, and put forward an advance-guard of show and humbug."

But the split in his emotional and intellectual nature prevented him from ever resolving the conflict of value and impulse implicit in his subject. All he could do was reproduce his predicament within his creations. On the one hand he thought it desirable "to live throughout the whole range of one's faculties and sensibilities" and, on the other, to play the part of a spiritualized Paul Pry "hovering invisible around men and women, witnessing their deeds, searching into their hearts, borrowing brightness from their felicity and shade from their sorrow, *and retaining no emotion peculiar to himself.*" In other words, he wanted the impossible — to enjoy the warmth and vitality of experience without exposing himself to its perils. His entire heritage predisposed him to regard a welcoming and self-offering attitude to experience as the equivalent of a state of sin; and though he was inclined to doubt the justice and validity of this cruelly schematic equation, its sway over him nevertheless told in the end. It barred him from any patent commitment to that program of personal liberation which his successors in the American creative line were later to adopt and elaborate into peculiarly indigenous forms of literary art. Is experience identical with sin? — and if so, is sin the doom of man or his salvation? To these queries he provided no clear rejoinder, but his bent was to say one thing on the surface of his work, on the level of its manifest content, while saying something else in its depths, in its latent meanings. He tried to serve at once the old and the new gods, and in the main it is within the active play of this ambivalence, of this sundered devotion, that he achieved his unique color and interest. His incubus he taught to poetize.

The constraint under which he labored had its source, of course, in the old Calvinist faith, but he was born too late to know it for what it once was. Of religion, indeed, he knew little beyond its fears. Originally a powerful vision of man's relation to God, the puritan orthodoxy was now reduced to a narrow moral scheme with clerical trappings. And Hawthorne's dilemma was that though the supernatural hardly existed for him in any realm save that of the fanciful, he was nonetheless unable to free himself from the perception of human destiny in terms of sin and redemption, sacrilege and consecration. The sacramental wine had turned to poison in his cup. His dreams abounded in images of his ancestors rising from their graves and of himself walking down Main Street in a shroud. No wonder, then, that he tended to conceive of the past as a menace to the living, as a force the ghastly fascination of which must be resisted.

The House of the Seven Gables is one long symbolization of this feeling. "In this age," preaches Holgrave, the young man who stands for the renovation of life, "the moss-grown and rotten Past is to be torn down, and lifeless institutions to be thrust out of the way, and their dead corpses buried, and everything to begin anew . . . What slaves we are to bygone times — to Death . . . We live in dead men's houses . . . as in this of the Seven Gables . . . The house ought to be purified with fire, — purified till only its ashes remain." Still, at the same time as Hawthorne abused the past and remonstrated against its morbid influences, he continued to indulge his taste for gloom and moldiness — for "old ideals and loitering paces and muffled tones." And as the years passed he yielded more and more to this tendency, with the result that in his last phase his mind faltered — it had lost, as he himself admitted, its fine edge and temper — and he could produce nothing but such fragmentary and essentially pointless allegories as *Septimius Felton* and *The Dolliver Romance.*

The conflict in him is clearly between a newborn secular imagination, as yet untried and therefore permeated with the feeling of shock and guilt, and the moribund religious tradition of old New England. It is a conflict which has seldom been detected by his critics, who have for the most part confounded his inner theme of experience with the all-too-apparent theme of sin. Yet the two themes, regardless of their mutual relation from a theological standpoint, are quite distinct as life-elements — though Hawthorne could not but confuse them. Perhaps it is this that was intuitively sensed by D. H. Lawrence, when he spoke of the duplicity of that "blue-eyed *Wunderkind* of a Nathaniel," thus construing as double-dealing a double-mindedness the roots of which lie deep in American history. But the melodramatic twist of Lawrence's insights is scarcely a valid reason for discounting them. He accurately noted the split in Hawthorne between his outward conformity and the "impeccable truth of his art-speech," between his repressed under-meanings and the moonshiny spirituality of his surface.

The evidence, of course, is in the tales and romances. There is one heroine they bring to life who is possibly the most resplendent and erotically forceful woman in American fiction. She dominates all the other characters because she alone personifies the contrary values that her author attached to experience. Drawn on a scale larger than reality, she is essentially a mythic being, the incarnation of hidden longings and desires, as beautiful, we are repeatedly told, as she is "inexpressibly terrible," a temptress offering the ascetic sons of the puritans the "treasure-trove of a great sin."

We come to know this dark lady under four different names — as Beatrice in the story *Rappaccini's Daughter*, Hester in *The Scarlet Letter*, Zenobia in *The Blithedale Romance*, and Miriam in *The Marble Faun*. Her unity as a character is established by the fact that in each of her four appearances she exhibits the same physical and mental qualities and plays substantially the same role. Hawthorne's description of her is wonderfully expressive in the fullness of its sensual imaginings. He is ingenious in devising occasions for celebrating her beauty, and conversely, for denigrating, albeit in equivocal language, her blond rival — the dovelike, virginal, snow-white maiden of New England. But the two women stand to each other in the relation of the damned to the saved, so that inevitably the dark lady comes to a bad end while the blonde is awarded all the prizes — husband, love, and absolute exemption from moral guilt. There is obviously an obsessive interest here in the psycho-sexual polarity of dark and fair with its symbolism of good and evil — a polarity which in Fenimore Cooper's treatment (in *The Last of the Mohicans* and *The Deerslayer*) is little more than a romantic convention but which both in Hawthorne and in Melville (Hautia and Yillah in *Mardi* and Isabel and Lucy in *Pierre*) acquires a newly intensive meaning.

Beatrice, of *Rappaccini's Daughter*, is as luxuriant as any of the gemlike flowers in her father's garden of poisonous plants. She looks "redundant with life, health, and energy . . . beautiful as the day, with a bloom so deep and vivid that one shade more would have been too much"; her voice, "rich as a tropical sunset," makes her lover Giovanni "think of deep hues of purple or crimson and of perfumes heavily delectable." Hester, of *The Scarlet Letter*, is "tall, with a figure of perfect elegance on a large scale. She had dark and abundant hair, so glossy that it threw off the sunshine with a gleam, and a face which besides being beautiful from regularity of feature and richness of complexion, had the impressiveness belonging to a marked brow . . . She had in her nature a rich, voluptuous, Oriental characteristic." In the redundancy of her charms Zenobia, of *The Blithedale Romance*, is fully the equal of Hester Prynne. "Zenobia was an admirable . . . a magnificent figure of a woman, just on the hither verge of her maturity . . . her hand, though very soft, was larger than most women would like to have . . . though not a whit

62/Literature and the Sixth Sense

too large in proportion with the spacious plan of her development
. . . the native glow of coloring in her cheeks, and even the flesh-
warmth of her round arms, and what was visible of her full bust —
in a word, her womanliness incarnate — compelled me sometimes to
close my eyes . . . One felt an influence breathing out of her such as
we might suppose to come from Eve, when she was just made . . . a
certain warm and rich characteristic . . . the whole woman was alive
with a passionate intensity in which her beauty culminated. Any
passion would have become her well; and passionate love, perhaps,
best of all." And Miriam, of *The Marble Faun*, also had "a great
deal of color in her nature . . . a beautiful woman . . . with dark eyes
. . . black, abundant hair . . . a dark glory."

It is plain that the physical characteristics of these four heroines
are interchangeable, and this cannot be due to poverty of invention
on Hawthorne's part. What it suggests, rather, is a strong fixation on
a certain type of woman, in every way the opposite of the sexually
anesthetic females to whom he officially paid homage.° The dark
lady is above all an ambivalent love-object†; but beyond that she
makes visible that desire for an open-handed conduct of life and individual fulfillment which was in later years to become the major
concern of American writing. Reduced to more realistic proportions

° In this connection a revealing passage from W. D. Howells' *Literary Friends
and Acquaintance* is worth citing. Howells is telling of his first meeting with
Hawthorne in 1860: "With the abrupt transition of his talk throughout, he
[Hawthorne] began to speak of women, and said he had never seen a woman
whom he thought quite beautiful. In the same way he spoke of the New
England temperament, and suggested that the apparent coldness in it was also
real, and that the suppression of emotion for generations would extinguish it at
last." Psychologically speaking, the second remark might be taken as a sufficient
explanation of the first. On the other hand, perhaps Hawthorne meant to say
that no woman he had ever met in the flesh was quite as resplendent as his
imagined dark lady.

† Her type is not unknown of course in Victorian fiction, from Trollope to
Hardy. She also enters the folklore of the Anglo-Saxon countries as the vil-
lainous "dark vampire" of the early American films and popular romances. It
is interesting to note that in the 1920s the glamorous (the "hot") blonde re-
places the mysterious and voluptuous brunette as the carrier of the sexually
potent and dangerous. In Anita Loos's *Gentlemen Prefer Blondes* the usurpation
has already gone so far that it is taken for granted. This reversal of roles may
well be due to the newly won sexual freedom of the postwar era, a freedom
which brought the sexual element to the light of day and thus ended its hitherto
exclusive identification with the secrets of the night.

but nonetheless still invested with mythic powers, she reappears, in such novels as Sherwood Anderson's *Dark Laughter* and *Many Marriages*, in the part of the ideal love partner for whom thwarted husbands desert their wives; and a character like Hemingway's Maria (*For Whom the Bell Tolls*) — likewise not a "real" person but a dream-image of sexual bliss — is clearly in her line of descent. In her latter-day mutations, however, the sinister side of this heroine has been obliterated. She is now wholly affirmed.

But insofar as they no longer threaten us, these idealized modern women have also ceased to be thoughtful. The Anderson and Hemingway girls leave us without any distinct impression of their minds, whereas the dark lady of Salem displays mental powers that are the counterpart of her physical vitality. Invariably she dominates, or seeks to dominate, the men she loves, and her intellectual range equals and at times even exceeds theirs. She not only acts but thinks passionately, solving the problem of the relation between the sexes in a radical fashion and subverting established values and standards. After being cast out by the community, Hester, we are told, "assumed a freedom of speculation . . . which our forefathers, had they known it, would have held to be a deadlier crime than that stigmatized by the scarlet letter"; Zenobia, who is something of a *littérateur* and a crusader for women's rights,* has an aptitude for extreme ideas that fill her interlocutors with dismay; and Miriam evolves a conception of sin which amounts to a justification, for she takes the view that sin is a means of educating and improving the personality.

The dark lady is a rebel and an emancipator; but precisely for this reason Hawthorne feels the compulsion to destroy her. *He thus converts the principle of life, of experience, into a principle of death.* Incessantly haunted by the wrongs of the past, by the memory of such brutal deeds directly implicating the founders of his family as the witchcraft trials and the oppression of the Quakers, this repentant puritan is nevertheless impelled by an irresistible inner need to reproduce the very same ancestral pattern in his work. Roused by

---

* This is the basis of the widespread impression that she is modeled after Margaret Fuller. Henry James thought there was no truth in the legend. Hawthorne's references to the Boston sibyl in his notebooks are uniformly unkind; he describes her as devoid of the "charm of womanhood" and as a "great humbug" to boot.

long-forgotten fears and superstitions, he again traces the footprints of the devil and hears demonic laughter in the woods as darkness falls. His story of the dark lady renews, in all essentials, the persecution of the Salem witches. Beatrice is "as lovely as the dawn and gorgeous as the sunset," yet the "rich perfume of her breath blasts the very air" and to embrace her is to die. Passionate love becomes Zenobia best, yet through insinuating symbols she is pictured as a sorceress. She wears an exotic flower in her hair, and perhaps if this talismanic flower were snatched away she would "vanish or be transformed into something else." Miriam, too, has the "faculty of bewitching people." When her nerves give way and she fancies herself unseen, she seeks relief in "fits of madness horrible to behold." Such is the twice-told tale of the dark lady. The victim, in her earlier incarnations, of grim black-browed puritan magistrates, she is now searched out by a secluded New England author who condemns her because she coerces his imagination.

Her figure is first evoked by Hawthorne in *Rappaccini's Daughter* (1844), an entirely fantastic tale generally ranked among the most brilliantly effective of his earlier writings. Beatrice is the daughter of a malignant old professor, who, in his search of fearsome secrets, is experimenting with the medicinal properties of poisonous plants. On coming to Padua, the student Giovanni rents a room the window of which overlooks Rappaccini's garden. Though unaware of the real nature of the flowers in this garden, he is at once troubled by their strange and rampant bloom. — "The aspect of one and all of them dissatisfied him; their gorgeousness seemed fierce, passionate, and even unnatural. There was hardly an individual shrub which a wanderer, straying by himself through a forest, would not have been startled to find growing wild, as if an unearthly face had glared at him out of the thicket." His initial impression of Beatrice is that she is but another flower — "the human sister of these vegetable ones, as beautiful as they, more beautiful than the richest of them, but still to be touched only with a glove, nor to be approached without a mask"; and when night closes in, he dreams of a rich flower and a lovely girl. "Flower and maiden were different and yet the same, and fraught with some peculiar peril in either shape." In time, as Giovanni ventures into the garden, he learns that the flowers are deadly. But he is now in love with Beatrice and tormented by the suspicion that she possesses the same fatal attributes. Can such dreadful peculiarities in her physical nature exist, he asks himself, without some corresponding "monstrosity of soul"? The day comes when after many tests he is at last sure that not only is she poisonous but that she had begun to instill her poison into his system. He procures an antidote which he forces her to drink. But it is too late to save her, for "so radically had her earthly part been wrought upon by Rappaccini's skill, that as poison had been her life, so the powerful antidote was death; and thus the poor victim of man's ingenuity and of thwarted nature . . . perished there, at the feet of her father and Giovanni."

No summary can give an adequate sense of the exotic light in which this story is drenched, nor of the extravagantly erotic associations of its imagery. It opens with the "peephole" motif, so typical of Hawthorne. ("Sometimes through a peephole I have caught a glimpse of the real world . . ." he wrote to Longfellow.) At first it is only from the outside — through a window — that Giovanni dares to peer into this "Eden of poisonous flowers," which Freudians would have no trouble at all translating into a garden of genitalia. But whether interpreted in a Freudian manner or not, its mystery is easily unraveled. What is this Eden if not the garden of experience, of the knowledge of good and evil. Giovanni is tempted to enter it, only to discover that its gorgeous flowers are emblems of sin and that the gorgeous Beatrice embodies all that is forbidden. She has succeeded in enticing him into a "region of unspeakable horror," but it is she who is doomed, while he, being innocent, escapes. The wages of sin is death.

To be sure, there are other readings of this story. The traditional one simply takes at face value Hawthorne's stated intention, his "message" warning against such unscrupulous love of power and knowledge as is manifested in Rappaccini. The old professor, who is a shadow character, is thus put in the foreground, while Beatrice, who is the real protagonist, is reduced to the role of a mere passive victim of her father's monomaniacal ambition. Needless to say, this approach ignores the story's specific content for the sake of its abstract and, it should be remarked, utterly commonplace moral. It fails to account for the mystic sensuality, the hallucinated at-

5

mosphere, and the intertwining symbolism of flower and maiden. No, this business of the wizard Rappaccini and his poisons is just so much flummery and Gothic sleight-of-hand. Its use is that of an "alibi" for the author, who transforms Beatrice into a monster in order to punish her for tempting Giovanni. Actually it is her beauty that Hawthorne cannot forgive her.

The flower-symbolism of this tale is repeated in the later romances of the dark lady. So resplendent is the scarlet token of shame worn by Hester Prynne that it might well be a flower in Rappaccini's garden formed to spell the letter A. ("On the breast of her gown, in fine red cloth, surrounded with an elaborate embroidery and fantastic flourishes of gold thread, there appeared the letter A. It was so artistically done, and with so much fertility and gorgeous luxuriance of fancy . . .") And, again, much is made in *The Blithedale Romance* of the single flower that adorns Zenobia's hair. — "It was a hot-house flower, an outlandish flower, a flower of the tropics, such as appeared to have sprung passionately from a soil the very weeds of which would be fervid and spicy . . . so brilliant, so rare, so costly . . ." It is manifestly a flower of a preternatural order, a kind of *mana*-object, an instrument of magic and witches' work.

As compared to the subsequent full-length versions of the same theme, the story of Beatrice is but a primitive fantasy. There is a gap between *Rappaccini's Daughter* and *The Scarlet Letter*, which was written six years later and which is the most truly novelistic of Hawthorne's romances. Its concrete historical setting gives it greater density of material and sharpness of outline; and largely because of this gain in reality, Hester Prynne is the least symbolically overladen and distorted of the four heroines who share in the character of the dark lady. There is nothing satanic about her motives and she is the only one who, far from being ultimately spurned, is justified instead.

There are ambiguities in *The Scarlet Letter*, as in all of Hawthorne, yet it is possible to say that it represents his furthest advance in affirming the rights of the individual. Known as a story of the expiation of a sin, it is quite as much an analysis of this sin as a "kind of typical illusion." It is the Reverend Mr. Dimmesdale, his brain reeling from ghostly visions, who in his repentance plies a bloody scourge on his own shoulders; Hester, on the other hand, is ready to reject the puritan morality altogether, to make a clean sweep of the past and to escape from the settlement in order to fulfill her love without shame or fear. Her pariah-status in the community is not productive of remorse and humility. On the contrary, we are told that "standing alone in the world . . . the world's law was no law for her mind . . . In her lonesome cottage, by the seashore, thoughts visited her, such as dared enter no other dwelling in New England."

This is best shown in Chapters XVII and XVIII of the novel when Hester finally persuades the minister that the only way he could rid himself of Chillingsworth's persecution is to desert his congregation and return to England. At first he thinks that she bids him go alone, whereupon he protests that he has not the strength or courage to embark on such a venture. At this point she reveals her plan, proving that she does not recognize her guilt, that for her nothing has changed, that in fact "the whole seven years of outlawry and ignominy had been little other than a preparation for this very hour." — But some of the passages that follow are worth quoting at length.

> He repeated the word.
> "Alone, Hester!"
> "Thou shalt not go alone!" answered she, in a deep whisper.
> Then all was spoken!
> Arthur Dimmesdale gazed into Hester's face with a look in which hope and joy shone out, indeed, but with fear between them, and a kind of horror at her boldness, who had spoken what he vaguely hinted at but dared not speak.
> But Hester Prynne, with a mind of native courage and activity, and for so long a period not merely estranged, but outlawed from society, had habituated herself to such latitude of speculation as was altogether foreign to the clergyman . . . For years past she had looked from this estranged point of view at human institutions, and whatever priests or legislators had established . . . The tendency of her fate has been to set her free.
> "Thou wilt go," said Hester, calmly, as he met her glance.
> The decision once made, a glow of strange enjoyment threw its flickering brightness over the trouble of his breast. It was the exhilarating effect — upon a prisoner just escaped from the dungeon of his own heart — of breathing the wild, free atmosphere of an unredeemed, unchristianized, lawless region . . .
> "Do I feel joy again?" cried he, wondering at himself. "Methinks the

germ of it was dead in me! O, Hester, thou art my better angel! I seem to have flung myself — sick, sin-stained, and sorrow-blackened — down upon these forest-leaves, and to have risen up all made anew, and with new powers to glorify Him that hath been merciful! This is already the better life. Why did we not find it sooner?"

"Let us not look back," answered Hester Prynne. "The past is gone! . . . See! With this symbol I undo it all, and make it as it had never been!"

So speaking, she undid the clasp that fastened the scarlet letter, and taking it from her bosom, threw it to a distance among the withered leaves . . . The stigma gone, Hester heaved a deep, long sigh, in which the burden of shame and anguish departed from her spirit. O exquisite relief! . . . By another impulse she took off the formal cap that confined her hair; and down it fell upon her shoulders, dark and rich . . . There played around her mouth and beamed out of her eyes, a radiant and tender smile, that seemed gushing from the very heart of womanhood. A crimson flush was glowing on her cheeks, that had been long so pale. Her sex, her youth, and the whole richness of her beauty, came back from what men call the irrevocable past, and clustered themselves, with her maiden hope and a happiness before unknown, within the magic circle of this hour.

This unregenerate temptress knows her power, but in the end Dimmesdale cheats her of her triumph by publicly confessing his sin on the scaffold; and that, of course, is *his* triumph. This thin-skinned clergyman is the ancestor of all those characters in Henry James who invent excruciatingly subtle reasons for renouncing their heart's desire once they are on the verge of attaining it. But in James there are also other characters who, while preserving Dimmesdale's complex qualities of conscience and sensibility, finally do succeed in overcoming this tendency to renunciation. Lambert Strether of *The Ambassadors* and Milly Theale of *The Wings of the Dove*, whose ideal aim is "to achieve a sense of having lived," are plainly cases of reaction against Hawthorne's plaint: "I have not lived but only dreamed of living!"

This link with James is further evidence that, though in no position to show his hand and not even fully conscious of what was at stake, Hawthorne dealt with the problem of sin mainly insofar as it served him as a mold for the problem of experience. It is difficult to believe in the sins committed by his characters for the simple reason that he hardly believes in them himself. Consider how he stacks the cards, how he continually brings up extenuating circumstances and even lapses into telltale defensive statements, so that before long we cannot but lose the conviction of evil and corruption. Who, actually, are his sinners? The minor figures cannot, of course, be taken into account in this respect, for, like Chillingsworth, Westervelt, Miriam's model and even Judge Pyncheon, they are nothing more than conventional villains, and at that most of them are so unreal that their conduct is of little consequence. It is only the protagonists, then, who count. But of these, with the exception of Dimmesdale, there is scarcely one who can be objectively regarded as a wrongdoer. Among the women only Hester's guilt is definitely established, yet even she is shown to have so many rights on her side that it is impossible to see in her anything more portentous than a violator of the communal *mores*. It is not, however, by their flouting of the communal *mores* that we judge the great transgressors pictured in literature. These big biters into the apple inevitably sin against the Holy Ghost.

Zenobia and Miriam wholly exemplify Hawthorne's bias against the dark lady, a bias which, instead of being supported and objectified by a credible presentation of her misdeeds, is limited in its expression to atmospheric effects, insinuations, and rumors. He wants to destroy the dark lady at the same time that he wants to glorify her; hence his indictment of her is never really driven home. This divided intention cannot but impair the dramatic structures of *The Blithedale Romance* and *The Marble Faun*, and these two narratives are in fact much inferior to *The Scarlet Letter*.

But the *Romance*, with its marvelous sense of place and weather and with its contrasted tableaux of town and country, has a unique appeal of its own. Both James and Lawrence have testified to its attraction. The former speaks of it as "leaving in the memory an impression analogous to that of an April day — an alternation of brightness and shadow, of broken sun-patches and sprinkling clouds." James also thought that in Zenobia Hawthorne made his nearest approach to the complete creation of a character. But this vivid brunette is treated with much less sympathy than Hester — and perhaps the reason is that since she exerts greater sexual power she must needs be subjected to firmer measures of control. At any rate, his attitude toward her is markedly more subjective, and this note of subjectivity is one of the charms of the *Romance,* the unfailing charm of the confessional tone and of the personal modulation. The story is told through a narrator by the name of Miles Coverdale, a minor Boston poet in whom one easily discerns many features of the author.

No sooner does Coverdale come upon Zenobia in Blithedale — a utopian colony inhabited by a "little army of saints and martyrs" — than her beauty moves him to rhapsodic appreciation; he is in a fever of susceptibiltiy, and the very next day a fit of sickness lays him low. His illness and exhaustion render him even more sensitive — morbidly so — to what he calls "Zenobia's sphere." (What a master stroke, this episode of Coverdale's illness, with its suggestions of a rite of passage from one mode of life to another!) Obviously infatuated with her, he is not the man to submit to such a feeling. By what is plainly a psychological detour — analysts would see in it an example of protective displacement — he persuades himself that his real attachment is to Zenobia's half-sister, the mediumistic, shadowy snow-maiden who is the Prissy of the tale. This convenient self-deception permits him to covet Zenobia and to pry into her affairs without in any way committing himself to her — for how could he, a paleface poet with overcharged scruples, make up to a woman who is "passionate, luxurious, lacking simplicity, not deeply refined, incapable of pure and perfect taste"? Moreover, as if to spare him further trouble, both females fall in love not with him but with the fanatical reformer Hollingsworth, who is a mere stick of a character, a travesty as a reformer and even worse travesty as a lover. The emotional economy of this story is throughout one of displacement. It is evident on every page that the only genuine relationship is that of Coverdale to Zenobia; the rest is mystification. But the whole point of Coverdale's behavior is to avoid involvement. As Zenobia tells him in one of the final bang-up scenes, his real game is "to grope for human emotions in the dark corners of the heart" — strictly in the hearts of other people, to be sure. He plays perfectly the role of the ideal Paul Pry that Hawthorne envisaged for himself in the earlier passages of his journals.

Though vowing that he adores the ethereal Priscilla, Coverdale is nevertheless quite adept at belittling her by means of invidious comparisons that strike home despite their seemingly general reference. Some finicky people, he reflects after his first encounter with Zenobia, might consider her wanting in softness and delicacy, but the truth is that "we find enough of these attributes everywhere; preferable . . . was Zenobia's bloom, health, and vigor, which she possessed in such overflow that a man might well have fallen in love with her for their sake only." And again: "We seldom meet with women nowadays, and in this country, who impress us as being women at all; — their sex fades away and goes for nothing . . . a certain warm and rich characteristic seems to have been refined away out of the feminine system." Finally, in view of these frequent digs at Prissy, there can be no doubt that Westervelt, the villain of the piece, is really speaking for Coverdale when he describes her as "one of those delicate, young creatures, not uncommon in New England, and whom I suppose to have become what we find them by the gradual refining away of the physical system among young women. Some philosophers chose to glorify this habit of body by terming it spiritual; but in my opinion, it is rather the effect of unwholesome food, bad air, lack of outdoor exercise, and neglect of bathing, on the part of these damsels and their female progenitors, all resulting in a kind of hereditary dyspepsia. Zenobia, with her uncomfortable surplus of vitality, is far the better model of womanhood."

But this "better model of womanhood" commits suicide for want of love, while the obstreperous Hollingsworth is collared by Prissy and dragged to the altar. The puritan morality of predestination takes its toll as the story closes. Humanity is divided into the damned and the saved, irretrievably so, and never the twain shall meet. Yet the *Romance*, despite its mechanically enforced moral lessons, stands out among Hawthorne's works for its outspokenness and for its bold and free characterization of Coverdale and Zenobia. In its painful doubleness, in its feeling of combined attraction and repulsion, the relationship between these two characters is one of the most meaningful and seminal in American literature. It is intrinsically the relationship between New England and the world, and again the connection with James comes to mind. Zenobia can be understood as an earlier and cruder version of Madame de Vionnet (of *The Ambassadors*), whose worldly motives and passionate nature Lambert Strether finally comes to understand and to accept; and Coverdale, too, is reproduced in James, and not in one type alone. One recognizes his kinship with Strether, who has overcome the obsession with sin and is priming himself to enter forbidden territory, no less than with such a curious figure as the spying, eavesdropping protagonist of *The Sacred Fount*, whose neurotic fear and envy of life find an outlet in a mania of snooping and prying into the lives of his neighbors. In this nameless Jamesian snooper the "peephole" motif reaches its culmination: it has become his medium of existence and his intellectual rationale besides.

In *The Marble Faun* Hawthorne resumes his story of the dark lady, and his attitude to her is now formulated in more logical terms. The conception of sin as an "instrument most effective in the education of intellect and soul" is openly expounded and affirmed by Miriam, whereas the snow-maiden Hilda, who is a purist and perfectionist, defends to the last the old puritan ethic. What Miriam advocates is the right of the personality to that self-knowledge and self-development which only the process of experience can provide. But she too, like Hester, is in the end sentenced by the author to life-long suffering and expiation of her sin. Unlike Hester's sin, however, Miriam's is utterly chimerical, fabricated out of whole cloth by the Gothic machinery of horror; what alone is real is her defiance of the ancestral taboos.

The part of the male evildoer in *The Marble Faun* is taken by Donatello, the innocent, faunlike, quasi-mythical Italian who is drawn by Miriam to commit a crime and is thus brought within the confines of "sinful, sorrowful mentality." It is the story, of course, of the fall of man, with the dark lady cast in the dual role of Eve and the serpent. Hilda and the sculptor Kenyon are the onlookers and commentators on the action. Presented as models of virtue, they are actually an insufferable pair of prigs, especially Hilda, who is in fact one of the grimmest figures in Hawthorne, despite all the proper talk about her dovelike nature. Symbolically enough, this militant virgin dwells in a tower which is continually referred to as the "young girl's eyerie," and from this high vantage point she surveys the conduct of mankind with the self-assurance of a moral millionaire. The sculptor, to be sure, tends to sympathize with Miriam, but

Hilda never fails to pull him up short. The whole issue is summed up perfectly in the following dialogue between them:

"Ah, Hilda," said Kenyon, "you do not know, for you could never learn it from your own heart, which is all purity and rectitude, what a mixture of good and evil there may be in things evil; and how the greatest criminal, if you look at his conduct from his own point of view, or from any side-point, may seem not so unquestionably guilty, after all. So with Miriam, so with Donatello. They are, perhaps, partners in what we must call awful guilt; and yet, I will own to you, — when I think of the original cause, the motives, the feelings, the sudden concurrence of circumstances thrusting them onward, the urgency of the moment, and the sublime unselfishness on either part, — I know not well how to distinguish it from much that the world calls heroism. Might we not render some such verdict as this? — 'Worthy of Death, but not unworthy of Love!'"

"Never!" answered Hilda, looking at the matter through the clear crystal medium of her own integrity. "This thing, as regards its causes, is all a mystery to me, and must remain so. But there is, I believe, only one right and only one wrong; and I do not understand, and may God keep me from understanding, how two things so totally unlike can be mistaken for one another; nor how two mortal foes, such as Right and Wrong surely are, can work together in the same deed . . ."

"Alas for human nature, then!" said Kenyon, sadly . . . "I have always felt you, my dear friend, a terribly severe judge, and have been perplexed to conceive how such tender sympathy could coexist with the remorselessness of a steel blade. You need no mercy, and therefore know not how to show any."

"That sounds like a bitter gibe," said Hilda, with the tears springing to her eyes. "But I cannot help it. It does not alter my perception of the truth. If there be any such dreadful mixture as you affirm — and which appears to me almost more shocking than pure evil, — then the good is turned to poison, not the evil to wholesomeness."

It is against such pharisaical moralism as Hilda displays that Hawthorne reacted in creating the figure of the dark lady, yet he could never muster the resolution to repudiate Hilda openly. Hence the dark lady, too, is inevitably stricken down by the same minatory code. Miriam pleads that the crime joining her to Donatello was "a blessing in disguise" in that it brought "a simple and imperfect nature to a point of feeling and intelligence which it could have reached under no other discipline." But her pleas are of no avail — in the end she is destroyed. And how illusory is the crime of which she is accused, with its horror-romanticism of the murder of a timeless wizard who has in some inexplicable way gained an ascendancy over her. And this in what is presumably a serious novel of crime and punishment! One might claim, of course, that the failure of actuality at this crucial turn of the plot is nothing more than a defect in the storyteller's art, a carryover from the obsolescent Gothic technique. But it is precisely Hawthorne's persistent reliance on this technique which is so revealing of his real situation. It seems to me that he is unable to authenticate Miriam's guilt for the quite obvious reason that her beauty and love of life already sufficiently condemn her in his eyes. In other words, it is not her deeds but her very existence which is the supreme provocation and the supreme crime.

The critics of the school of "original sin" have for some years now tried to present Hawthorne as a kind of puritan Dostoevsky. But this comparison will not stand the test of analysis. In their eagerness to make ideological capital out of Hawthorne's "traditionalism," these critics overlook one vital distinction: whereas in Dostoevsky's case the awareness of sin flows from a mighty effort to regain a metaphysical and religious consciousness, in Hawthorne this awareness is at the point of dissolution. What is behind it is no genuine moral passion nor a revival of dogma but a fear of life induced by narrow circumstances and morbid memories of the past. The faith of his forefathers had lost its rational appeal, yet psychologically it still ruled and confined him. Hence the inherited beliefs appear in his work as specters rather than as convictions.

A literature of sin is more naturally developed in a society suffering from a surfeit of experience — an excess which it cannot control because of a derangement of values. This was the condition of Russian society in Dostoevsky's time; and it is this unlimited availability of experience, amounting almost to anarchy, which enabled the Russian novelist to materialize his themes of sin and evil. We believe in the sins of Stavrogin, Raskolnikov, and the Karamazovs because they are actualized within the experiential realm, the only realm in which significant actions can be truly confirmed. Now if regarded from this point of view, the American romancer must be placed at the opposite pole from the Russian novelist. The society to which he belonged suffered not from a surfeit but from poverty of experience; and, far from being too fluid, its values were altogether too rigid. His problem was simpler than Dostoevsky's as well as radically different in nature. It was not an exceptional but necessarily a typical problem — typical, despite all variations, of America's creative writers in the nineteenth century and in the early decades of the twentieth. It can be defined as the problem of the reconquest, of the reacquisition of experience in its cultural, aesthetic, and, above all, subjective aspects. For this is the species of experience which had gradually been lost to the migrant European man in the process of subjugating and settling the new world.

Van Wyck Brooks has described Hawthorne as the "most deeply planted of American writers." But this is true only in the sense that he is the most deeply and vividly local. He rifled the hive of New England honey, but he was quite indifferent to the wider ranges of the national scene. His is the "sweet flavor," to use one of his own similes, of "a frost-bitten apple, such as one picks up under the tree in December." It is the chill yet mellow flavor of the Salem centuries. On this side of him he indeed sums up and closes the puritan cycle; but from another angle of vision he can be seen to be precursive of the later and more positive interests of American letters. Times past are mirrored in the dark lady's harsh fate, yet in her mystic sensuality she speaks of things to come.

1941

NOTES ON THE DECLINE OF
NATURALISM

QUITE A FEW protests have been aired in recent years against the sway of the naturalist method in fiction. It is charged that this method treats material in a manner so flat and external as to inhibit the search for value and meaning, and that in any case, whatever its past record, it is now exhausted. Dissimilar as they are, both the work of Frank Kafka and the works of the surrealist school are frequently cited as examples of release from the routines of naturalist realism, from its endless bookkeeping of existence. Supporting this indictment are mostly those writers of the younger group who are devoted to experimentation and who look to symbolism, the fable, and the myth.

The younger writers are stirred by the ambition to create a new type of imaginative prose into which the recognizably real enters as one component rather than as the total substance. They want to break the novel of its objective habits; some want to introduce into it philosophical ideas; others are not so much drawn to expressing ideas as to expressing the motley strivings of the inner self — dreams, visions, and fantasies. Manifestly the failure of the political movement in the literature of the past decade has resulted in a revival of religio-aesthetic attitudes. The young men of letters are once again watching their own image in the mirror and listening to inner promptings. Theirs is a program calling for the adoption of techniques of planned derangement as a means of cracking open the certified structure of reality and turning loose its latent energies. And surely one cannot dispose of such a program merely by uncovering the element of mystification in it. For the truth is that the artist of the avant-garde has never hesitated to lay hold of the instruments of mystification when it suited his purpose, especially in an age such as ours, when the life about him belies more and more the rational ideals of the cultural tradition.

It has been remarked that in the long run the issue between naturalism and its opponents resolves itself into a philosophical dispute concerning the nature of reality. Obviously those who reject naturalism in philosophy will also object to its namesake in literature. But it seems to me that when faced with a problem such as that of naturalist fiction, the critic will do well not to mix in ontological maneuvers. From the standpoint of critical method it is impermissible to replace a concrete literary analysis with arguments derived from some general theory of the real. For it is plainly a case of the critic not being able to afford metaphysical commitments if he is to apply himself without preconceived ideas to the works of art that constitute his material. The art-object is from first to last the one certain datum at his disposal; and in succumbing to metaphysical leanings — either of the spiritualist or materialist variety — he runs the risk of freezing his insights in some kind of ideational schema the relevance of which to the task in hand is hardly more than speculative. The act of critical evaluation is best performed in a state of *ideal aloofness* from abstract systems. Its practitioner is not concerned with making up his mind about the ultimate character of reality but with observing and measuring its actual proportions and combinations within a given form. The presence of the real affects him directly, with an immediate force contingent upon the degree of interest, concreteness, and intensity in the impression of life conveyed by the literary artist. The philosopher can take such impressions or leave them, but luckily the critic has no such choice.

Imaginative writing cannot include fixed and systematic definitions of reality without violating its own existential character. Yet in any imaginative effort that which we mean by the real remains the basic criterion of viability, the crucial test of relevance, even if its specific features can hardly be determined in advance but must be *felt anew* in each given instance. And so far as the medium of fiction is concerned, one cannot but agree with Henry James that it gains its "air of reality" — which he considers to be its "supreme virtue" — through "its immense and exquisite correspondence with life." Note that James's formulation allows both for analogical and realistic techniques of representation. He speaks not of copies or reports or transcripts of life but of relations of equivalence, of a "correspondence" which he identifies with the "illusion of life." The ability to produce this illusion he regards as the storyteller's inalienable gift, "the merit on which all other merits . . . helplessly and submissively depend." This insight is of an elementary nature and scarcely peculiar to James alone, but it seems that its truth has been lost on some of our recent catch-as-catch-can innovators in the writing of fiction.

It is intrinsically from this point of view that one can criticize the imitations of Kafka that have been turning up of late as being one-sided and even inept. Perhaps Kafka is too idiosyncratic a genius to serve as a model for others, but still it is easy to see where his imitators go wrong. It is necessary to say to them: To know how to take apart the recognizable world is not enough, is in fact merely a way of letting oneself go and of striving for originality at all costs. But originality of this sort is nothing more than a professional mannerism of the avant-garde. The genuine innovator is always trying to make us actually experience his creative conflict. He therefore employs means that are subtler and more complex: *at the very same time that he takes the world apart he puts it together again.* For to proceed otherwise is to dissipate rather than alter our sense of reality, to weaken and compromise rather than change in any significant fashion our feeling of relatedness to the world. After all, what impressed us most in Kafka is precisely this power of his to achieve a simultaneity of contrary effects, to fit the known into the unknown, the actual into the mythic and vice versa, to combine within one framework a conscientiously empirical account of the visibly real with a magical decomposition of it. In this paradox lies the pathos of his approach to human existence.

A modern poetess has written that the power of the visible derives from the invisible; but the reverse of this formula is also true. Thus the visible and the invisible might be said to stand to each other in an ironic relation of inner dependence and of mutual skepticism mixed with solicitude. It is a superb form of double-talk; and if we are accustomed to its exclusion from naturalistic writing, it is all the more disappointing to find that the newly evolved "fantastic" style of the experimentalists likewise excludes it. But there is another consideration, of a more formal nature. It seems to me a profound error to conceive of reality as merely a species of material that the fiction writer can either use or dispense with as he sees fit. It is a species of material, of course, and something else besides: it also functions as the *discipline of fiction*, much in the same sense that syllabic structure functions as the discipline of verse. This seeming identity of the formal and substantial means of narrative prose is due, I think, to the altogether free and open character of the medium, which prevents it from developing such distinctly technical controls as poetry has acquired. Hence even the dream, when told in a story, must partake of some of the qualities of the real.

Whereas the surrealist represents man as immured in dreams, the naturalist represents him in a continuous waking state of prosaic daily living, in effect, as never dreaming. But both the surrealist and the naturalist go to extremes in simplifying the human condition. J. M. Synge once said that the artist displays at once the difficulty and the triumph of his art when picturing the dreamer leaning out to reality or the man of real life lifted out of it. "In all the poets," he wrote, and this test is by no means limited to poetry alone, "the greatest have both these elements, that is they are supremely engrossed with life, and yet with the wildness of their fancy they are always passing out of what is simple and plain."

The old egocentric formula, "Man's fate is his character," has been altered by the novelists of the naturalist school to read, "Man's fate is his environment." (Zola, the organizer and champion of the school, drew his ideas from physiology and medicine, but in later years his disciples cast the natural sciences aside in favor of the social sciences.) To the naturalist, human behavior is a function of its social environment; the individual is the live register of its qualities; he exists in it as animals exist in nature.* Due to this emphasis the naturalist mode has evolved historically in two main directions. On the one hand it has tended toward passive documentation (milieu-panoramas, local-color stories, reportorial studies of a given region or industry, etc.), and on the other toward the exposure of socio-economic conditions (muckraking). American fiction of the past decade teems with examples of both tendencies, usually in combination. The work of James T. Farrell, for instance, is mostly a genre-record, the material of which is in its very nature operative in producing social feeling, while such novels as *The Grapes of Wrath* and *Native Son* are exposure-literature, as is the greater part of the fiction of social protest. Dos Passos' trilogy, *U.S.A.*, is thoroughly political in intention but has the tone and gloss of the methodical genre-painter in the page-by-page texture of its prose.

I know of no hard and fast rules that can be used to distinguish the naturalist method from the methods of realism generally. It is certainly incorrect to say that the difference is marked by the relative density of detail. Henry James observes in his essay *The Art of Fiction* that it is above all "solidity of specification" that makes for the illusion of life — the air of reality in a novel; and the truth of this dictum is borne out by the practice of the foremost modern inno-

---

* Balzac, to whom naturalism is enormously indebted, explains in his preface to the *Comédie Humaine* that the idea of that work came to him in consequence of a "comparison between the human and animal kingdoms." "Does not society," he asks, "make of man, in accordance with the environment in which he lives and moves, as many different kinds of man as there are different zoological species? . . . There have, therefore, existed and always will exist social species, just as there are zoological species."

Zola argues along the same lines: "All things hang together: it is necessary to start from the determination of inanimate bodies in order to arrive at the determination of living beings; and since savants like Claude Bernard demonstrate now that fixed laws govern the human body, we can easily proclaim . . . the hour in which the laws of thought and passion will be formulated in their turn. A like determination will govern the stones of the roadway and the brain of man. . . . We have experimental chemistry and medicine and physiology and later on an experimental novel. It is an inevitable evolution." (*The Experimental Novel*)

vators in this medium, such as Proust, Joyce, and Kafka. It is not, then, primarily the means employed to establish verisimilitude that fix the naturalist imprint upon a work of fiction. A more conclusive test, to my mind, is its treatment of the relation of character to background. I would classify as naturalistic that type of realism in which the individual is portrayed not merely as subordinate to his background but as wholly determined by it — that type of realism, in other words, in which the environment displaces its inhabitants in the role of the hero. Theodore Dreiser, for example, comes as close as any American writer to plotting the careers of his characters strictly within a determinative process. The financier Frank Cowperwood masters his world and emerges as its hero, while the "little man" Clyde Griffiths is the victim whom it grinds to pieces; yet hero and victim alike are essentially implements of environmental force, the carriers of its contradictions upon whom it stamps success or failure — not entirely at will, to be sure, for people are marked biologically from birth — but with sufficient autonomy to shape their fate.

In such a closed world there is patently no room for the singular, the unique, for anything in fact which cannot be represented plausibly as the product of a particular social and historical complex. Of necessity the naturalist must deal with experience almost exclusively in terms of the broadly typical. He analyzes characters in such a way as to reduce them to standard types. His method of construction is that of accretion and enumeration rather than of analysis or storytelling; and this is so because the quantitative development of themes, the massing of detail and specification, serves his purpose best. He builds his structures out of literal fact and precisely documented circumstance, thus severely limiting the variety of creative means at the disposal of the artist.

This quasi-scientific approach not only permits but, in theory at least, actually prescribes a neutral attitude in the sphere of values. In practice, however, most naturalists are not sufficiently detached or logical to stay put in such an ultraobjective position. Their detractors are wrong in denying them a moral content; the most that can be said is that theirs is strictly functional morality, bare of any elements of gratuity or transcendence and devoid of the sense of personal freedom.* Clearly such a perspective allows for very little self-awareness on the part of characters. It also removes the possibility of a tragic resolution of experience. The world of naturalist fiction is much too big, too inert, too hardened by social habit and material necessity, to allow for that tenacious self-assertion of the human by means of which tragedy justifies and ennobles its protagonists. The only grandeur naturalism knows is the grandeur of its own methodological achievement in making available a vast inventory of minutely described phenomena, in assembling an enormous quantity of data and arranging them in a rough figuration of reality. *Les Rougon-Macquart* stands to this day as the most imposing monument to this achievement.

But in the main it is the pure naturalist — that monstrous offspring of the logic of a method — that I have been describing here. Actually no such literary animal exists. Life always triumphs over methods, over formulas and theories. There is scarcely a single novelist of any importance wearing the badge of naturalism who is all of a piece, who fails to compensate in some way for what we miss in his fundamental conception. Let us call the roll of the leading names among the French and American naturalists and see wherein each is saved.

The Goncourts, it is true, come off rather badly, but even so, to quote a French critic, they manage "to escape from the crude painting of the naked truth by their impressionistic mobility" and, one might add, by their mobile intelligence. Zola's case does not rest solely on our judgment of his naturalist dogmas. There are entire volumes by him — the best, I think, is *Germinal* — and parts of volumes besides, in which his naturalism, fed by an epic imagination, takes on a mythic cast. Thomas Mann associates him with Wagner in a common drive toward an epic mythicism:

> They belong together. The kinship of spirit, method, and aims is most striking. This lies not only in the ambition to achieve size, the propensity to the grandiose and the lavish; nor is it the Homeric leitmotiv alone that is common to them; it is first and foremost a special kind of naturalism, which develops into the mythical . . . In Zola's epic . . . the

* Chekhov remarks in one of his stories that "the sense of personal freedom is the chief constituent of creative genius."

characters themselves are raised up to a plane above that of every day. And is that Astarte of the Second Empire, called Nana, not symbol and myth? (*The Sufferings and Greatness of Richard Wagner*)

Zola's prose, though not controlled by an artistic conscience, overcomes our resistance through sheer positiveness and expressive energy — qualities engendered by his novelistic ardor and avidity for recreating life in all its multiple forms.* As for Huysmans, even in his naturalist period he was more concerned with style than with subject matter. Maupassant is a naturalist mainly by alliance, i.e., by virtue of his official membership in the School of Médan; actually he follows a line of his own, which takes off from naturalism never to return to it. There are few militant naturalists among latter-day French writers. Jules Romains is sometimes spoken of as one, but the truth is that he is an epigone of all literary doctrines, including his own. Dreiser is still unsurpassed so far as American naturalism goes, though just at present he may well be the least readable. He has traits that make for survival — a Balzacian grip on the machinery of money and power; a prosiness so primary in texture that if taken in bulk it affects us as a kind of poetry of the commonplace and ill-favored; and an emphatic eroticism which is the real climate of existence in his fictions — Eros hovering over the shambles. Sinclair Lewis was never a novelist in the proper sense that Zola and Dreiser are novelists, and, given his gift for exhaustive reporting, naturalism did him more good than harm by providing him with a ready literary technique. In Farrell's chronicles there is an underlying moral code which, despite his explicit rejection of the Church, seems to me indisputably orthodox and Catholic; and his Studs Lonigan — a product of those unsightly urban neighborhoods where youth prowls and fights to live up to the folk-ideal of the "regular guy" — is no mere character but an archetype, an eponymous hero of the street-myths that prevail in our big cities. The naturalism of Dos Passos is most completely manifested in *U.S.A.*, tagged by the critics as a "collective" novel recording the "decline of our business civilization." But what distinguishes Dos Passos from other novelists of the same political animus is a sense of justice so pure as to be

---

* Moreover, it should be evident that Zola's many faults are not rectified but merely inverted in much of the writing — so languidly allusive and decorative — of the literary generations that turned their backs on him.

almost instinctive, as well as a deeply elegiac feeling for the intimate features of American life and for its precipitant moments. Also, *U.S.A.* is one of the very few naturalist novels in which there is a controlled use of language, in which a major effect is produced by the interplay between story and style. It is necessary to add, however, that the faults of Dos Passos' work have been obscured by its vivid contemporaneity and vital political appeal. In the future, I think, it will be seen more clearly than now that it dramatizes social symptoms rather than lives and that it fails to preserve the integrity of personal experience. As for Faulkner, Hemingway, and Caldwell, I do not quite see on what grounds some critics and literary historians include them in the naturalist school. I should think that Faulkner is exempted by his prodigious inventiveness and fantastic humor. Hemingway is a realist on one level, in his attempts to catch the "real thing, the sequence of motion and fact which made the emotion"; but he is also subjective, given to self-portraiture and to playing games with his ego; there is very little study of background in his work, a minimum of documentation. In his best novels Caldwell is a writer of rural abandon — and comedy. His Tobacco Road is a sociological area only in patches; most of it is exotic landscape.

It is not hard to demonstrate the weakness of the naturalist method by abstracting it, first, from the uses to which individual authors put it and, second, from its function in the history of modern literature. The traditionalist critics judge it much too one-sidedly in professing to see in its rise nothing but spiritual loss — an invasion of the arcanum of art by arid scientific ideas. The point is that this scientific bias of naturalism was historically productive of contradictory results. Its effect was certainly depressive insofar as it brought mechanistic notions and procedures into writing. But it should be kept in mind that it also enlivened and, in fact, revolutionized writing by liquidating the last assets of "romance" in fiction and by purging it once and for all of the idealism of the "beautiful lie" — of the long-standing inhibitions against dealing with the underside of life, with those inescapable day-by-day actualities traditionally regarded as too "sordid" and "ugly" for inclusion within an aesthetic framework. If it were not for the service thus rendered in vastly increasing the store of literary material, it is doubtful whether such works as *Ulysses* and even *Remembrance of Things Past* could have been

written. This is not clearly understood in the English-speaking countries, where naturalism, never quite forming itself into a "movement," was at most only an extreme emphasis in the general onset
of realistic fiction and drama. One must study, rather, the Continen-
tal writers of the last quarter of the nineteenth century in order to
grasp its historical role. In discussing the German naturalist school of
the 1880s, the historian Hans Naumann has this to say, for instance:

> Generally it can be said that to its early exponents the doctrine of
> naturalism held quite as many diverse and confusing meanings as the
> doctrine of expressionism seemed to hold in the period just past. Imagi-
> native writers who at bottom were pure idealists united with the dry-
> as-dust advocates of a philistine natural-scientific program on the one
> hand and with the shameless exploiters of erotic themes on the other.
> All met under the banner of naturalism — friends today and enemies
> tomorrow . . . But there was an element of historical necessity in all
> this. The fact is that the time had come for an assault, executed with
> glowing enthusiasm, against the epigones . . . that it was finally possible
> to fling aside with disdain and anger the pretty falsehoods of life and
> art (*Die Deutsche Dichtung der Gegenwart, Stuttgart,* 1930, p. 144).

And he adds that the naturalism of certain writers consisted simply
in their "speaking honestly of things that had heretofore been
suppressed."

But to establish the historical credit of naturalism is not to refute
the charges that have been brought against it in recent years. For
whatever its past accomplishments, it cannot be denied that its
present condition is one of utter debility. What was once a means
of treating material truthfully has been turned, through a long
process of depreciation, into a mere convention of truthfulness, devoid of any significant or even clearly definable literary purpose or
design. The spirit of discovery has withdrawn from naturalism; it
has now become the common denominator of realism, available in
like measure to the producers of literature and to the producers of
kitsch. One might sum up the objections to it simply by saying that
it is no longer possible to use this method *without taking reality for
granted.* This means that it has lost the power to cope with the ever
growing element of the problematical in modern life, which is precisely the element that is magnetizing the imagination of the true

artists of our epoch. Such artists are no longer content merely to question particular habits or situations or even institutions; it is reality itself which they bring into question. Reality to them is like that "open wound" of which Kierkegaard speaks in his *Journals*: "A healthy open wound; sometimes it is healthier to keep a wound open; sometimes it is worse when it closes."

There are also certain long-range factors that make for the decline of naturalism. One such factor is the growth of psychological science and, particularly, of psychoanalysis. Through the influence of psychology literature recovers its inwardness, devising such forms as the interior monologue, which combines the naturalistic in its minute description of the mental process with the anti-naturalistic in its disclosure of the subjective and the irrational. Still another factor is the tendency of naturalism, as Thomas Mann observes in his remarks on Zola, to turn into the mythic through sheer immersion in the typical. This dialectical negation of the typical is apparent in a work like *Ulysses*, where "the myth of the *Odyssey*," to quote from Harry Levin's study of Joyce, "is superimposed upon the map of Dublin" because only a myth could "lend shape or meaning to a slice of life so broad and banal." And from a social-historical point of view this much can be said, that naturalism cannot hope to survive the world of nineteenth-century science and industry of which it is the product. For what is the crisis of reality in contemporary art if not at bottom the crisis of the dissolution of this familiar world? Naturalism, which exhausted itself taking an inventory of this world while it was still relatively stable, cannot possibly do justice to the phenomena of its disruption.

One must protest, however, against the easy assumption of some avant-gardist writers that to finish with naturalism is the same as finishing with the principle of realism generally. It is one thing to dissect the real, to penetrate beneath its faceless surface and transpose it into terms of symbol and image; but the attempt to be done with it altogether is sheer regression or escape. Of the principle of realism it can be said that it is the most valuable acquisition of the modern mind. It has taught literature how to take in, how to grasp and encompass, the ordinary facts of human existence; and I mean this in the simplest sense conceivable. Least of all can the novelist dispense with it, as his medium knows of no other principle of coherence. In Gide's *Les Faux-Monnayeurs* there is a famous passage in which the novelist Édouard enumerates the faults of the naturalist school. "The great defect of that school is that it always cuts a slice of life in the same direction: in time, lengthwise. Why not in breadth? Or in depth? As for me, I should like not to cut at all. Please understand: I should like to put everything into my novel." "But I thought," his interlocutor remarks, "that you want to abandon reality." Yes, replies Édouard, "my novelist wants to abandon it; but I shall continually bring him back to it. In fact that will be the subject; the struggle between the facts presented by reality and the ideal reality."

1942

HENRY MILLER

IF HENRY MILLER'S STATUS in our literary community is still so very
debatable, it is probably because he is the type of writer who
cannot help exposing himself to extreme appraisals with every page
that he adds to his collected works. He is easily overrated and with
equal ease run down or ignored altogether. Consider his present
situation. With few exceptions the highbrow critics, bred almost
to a man in Eliot's school of strict impersonal aesthetics, are bent on
snubbing him. What with his spellbinder's tone, bawdy rites, plebeian rudeness and disdain of formal standards, he makes bad copy
for them and they know it. His admirers, on the other hand, are so
hot-lipped in praise as to arouse the suspicion of a cultist attachment. They evade the necessity of drawing distinctions between the
art of exploiting one's personality and the art of exploiting material,
from whatever source, for creative purposes. And in Miller's case
such distinctions are very much in order. His work is so flagrantly
personal in content that in moments of acute irritation one is tempted
to dismiss it as so much personality-mongering. Repeatedly he has
declared that his concern is not with writing as generally understood
but with telling the "more and more inexhaustible" story of his life

— a story stretched to include a full recital of his opinions, philosophic rhapsodies, intuitions, hunches, and buffooneries. All too often he plunges into that maudlin boosting of the ego to which the bohemian character is generically disposed. Yet at his best he writes on a level of true expressiveness, generating a kind of all-out poetry, at once genial and savage.

Unfortunately, since finishing off his expatriation and returning to his native country he has given more and more free rein to his worst tendency, that of playing the philosopher on a binge and the gadabout of the California avant-garde. The last book of his in which his great talent is shown to best advantage is *The Colossus of Maroussi*, published in 1942. It is a travel book on Greece of a very special type. Though containing some plain information about the country and its inhabitants, it intrinsically belongs to the modern tradition of the fugitives from progress — from the lands ravaged by the machine, the salesman, and the abstract thinker — the tradition of Melville and Gauguin in Tahiti and D. H. Lawrence in Mexico and Taos. Miller went to Greece to purge himself of his long contact with the French and to make good his hope for spiritual renewal. "In Greece," he writes, "I finally achieved coordination. I became deflated, restored to proper human proportions, ready to accept my lot and to give of all that I have received. Standing in Agamemnon's tomb I went through a veritable rebirth." He speaks of the Greeks as "aimless, anarchic, thoroughly and discordantly human," thus identifying them closely with his own values; and though confessing that he never read a line of Homer, he nonetheless believes them to be essentially unchanged.

Where he shows an unusual aptitude for descriptive prose is in the account of his visits to Mycenae, Knossus, Phaestos, and other sites of antiquity. Some of the passages are very good examples of his rhetorical prowess. Hyperbolic statement is his natural mode of communication, yet he has a vital sense of reference to concrete objects and symbols which permits him to gain a measure of control over his swelling language. He is particularly addicted to using terms and images drawn from science, especially biology and astronomy; and his unvarying practice is to distribute these borrowings stylistically in a manner so insinuating as to produce effects of incongruity and alarm. It is a device perfectly expressive of his fear of science and all its works. For Miller belongs to the progress-hating and machine-smashing fraternity of contemporary letters, though lacking as he does the motive of allegiance to tradition, it is open to question whether his co-thinkers would ever assent to his company. Of late, too, he has increasingly yielded to his mystical leanings, and his mysticism is of the wholesale kind, without limit or scruple. Thus there is a curious chapter in *The Colossus of Maroussi* describing his interview with an Armenian soothsayer in Athens, who confirms Miller in his belief that he is never going to die and that he is destined to undertake missions of a messianic nature that will "bring great joy to the world." Now this is the sort of thing that can be taken, of course, either as a fancy piece of megalomania or as a legitimate aspiration to which every human being is entitled.

But if Miller's recent work has been disappointing, the one way to recover a sense of his significance is to go back to his three early novels — *Tropic of Cancer, Black Spring,* and *Tropic of Capricorn.* These novels are autobiographical, and he appears in them in the familiar role of the artist-hero who dominates modern fiction. Where he differs from this ubiquitous type is the extremity of his destitution and estrangement from society. Reduced to the status of a lumpenproletarian whom the desolation of the big city has finally drained of all illusions and ideals, he is now an utterly declassed and alienated man who lives his life in the open streets of Paris and New York.

In these novels the narrator's every contact with cultural objects serves merely to exacerbate his anarchic impulses. There no longer exists for him any shelter from the external world. Even the idea of home — a place that the individual can truly call his own because it is furnished not only with his belongings but with his very humanity — has been obliterated. What remains is the fantasy of returning to the womb, a fantasy so obsessive as to give rise to an elaborate intra-uterine imagery as well as to any number of puns, jokes, imprecations, and appeals.

It is precisely in his descriptions of his lumpenproletarian life in the streets that Miller is at his best, that his prose is most resonant and alive — the streets in which a never ending array of decomposed and erratic phenomena gives his wanderings in search of a woman or a meal the metaphysical sheen of dream and legend. In every shop window he sees the "sea-nymph squirming in the maniac's arms," and everywhere he smells the odor of love "gushing like sewergas" out of the leading mains: "Love without gender and without lysol, incubational love, such as the wolverines practice above the treeline." In these novels food and sex are thematically treated with such matter-of-fact exactitude, with such a forceful and vindictive awareness of rock-bottom needs, that they cease to mean what they mean to most of us. Miller invokes food and sex as heroic sentiments and even generalizes them into principles. For the man who is down and out has eyes only for that which he misses most frequently; his condition makes of him a natural anarchist, rendering irrelevant all conventions, moral codes, or any attempt to order the process of experience according to some value-pattern. The problem is simply to keep alive, and to that end all means are permissible. One turns into a desperado, lurking in ambush in hallways, bars, and hotel rooms in the hope that some stroke of luck will enable one "to make a woman or make a touch." He literally takes candy from babies and steals money from prostitutes. As for obtaining regular work, he was always able "to amuse, to nourish, to instruct, but never to be accepted in a genuine way . . . everything conspired to set me off as an *outlaw*."

The fact that the world is in a state of collapse fills him with deep gratification ("I am dazzled by the glorious collapse of the world") because the all-around ruin seems to justify and validate what has happened to him personally. His particular adjustment he accomplishes by accepting the collapse as a kind of apocalyptic show from which the artist who has been rejected by society, and whose role is to revive the primeval, chaotic instincts, might even expect to gain the resurgence of those dreams and myths that the philistines have done their utmost to suppress. It is senseless to interfere, to try to avert the catastrophe; all one can do is to recoil into one's private fate. "The world is what it is and I am what I am," he declares. "I expose myself to the destructive elements that surround me. I let everything wreak its own havoc with me. I bend over to spy on the secret processes to obey rather than to command." And again: "I'm neither for nor against, I'm neutral . . . If to live is the paramount thing, then I will live even if I become a cannibal." And even in his own proper sphere the artist is no longer free to construct objective forms. He must abandon the "literary gold standard" and devote himself to creating biographical works — human documents rather than "literature" — depicting man in the grip of delirium.

And Miller's practice fits his theory. His novels do in fact dissolve the forms and genres of writing in a stream of exhortation, narrative, world-historical criticism, prose-poetry and spontaneous philosophy, all equally subjected to the strain and grind of self-expression at all costs. So riled is his ego by external reality, so confused and helpless, that he can no longer afford the continual sacrifice of personality that the act of creation requires, he can no longer bear to express himself implicitly by means of the work of art as a whole but must simultaneously permeate and absorb each of its separate parts and details. If everything else has failed me, this author seems to say, at least this book is mine, here everything is fashioned in my own image, here I am God.

This is the meaning, I think, of the "biographical" aesthetic that Miller at once practiced and preached in his early work and which an increasing number of writers, though not cognizant of it as a program, nevertheless practice in the same compulsive manner, not necessarily for reasons as personal as Miller's or with the same results, but because the growing alienation of man in modern society throws them back into narcissistic attitudes, forces them to undertake the shattering task of possessing the world that is now full of abstractions and mystifications through the instrumentality of the self and the self alone. Not "Know Thyself!" but "Be Yourself!" is their motto. Thomas Wolfe was such a writer, and his career was frustrated by the fact that he lacked sufficient consciousness to understand his dilemma. Miller, on the other hand, was well aware of his position when writing his early fictions. Instead of attempting to recover the lost relation to the world, he accepted his alienated status as his inexorable fate, and by so doing he was able to come to some kind of terms with it.

If freedom is the recognition of necessity, then what Miller gained was the freedom to go the whole length in the subversion of values, to expose more fully perhaps than any other contemporary novelist in English the nihilism of the self which has been cut off from all social ties and released not only from any allegiance to the past but also from all commitments to the future. The peculiarly American affirmation voiced by Whitman was thus completely negated in Miller. Total negation instead of total affirmation! No wonder that like Wolfe and Hart Crane and other lost souls he was continually haunted by Whitman as by an apparition. In *Tropic of Cancer* he speaks of him as "the one lone figure which America has produced in the course of her brief life . . . the first and last poet . . . who is almost undecipherable today, a monument covered with rude hieroglyphs for which there is no key." And it is precisely because he had the temerity to go the whole length that Miller is important as a literary character, though his importance, as George Orwell has observed, may be more symptomatic than substantial, in the sense that the extreme of passivity, amoralism, and acceptance of evil that his novels represent tends to demonstrate "the impossibility of any major literature until the world has shaken itself into a new shape."

In all his books Miller apostrophizes the Dadaists, the Surrealists, and the seekers and prophets of the "marvelous," wherever they may be found. Perhaps because he discovered the avant-gardists so late in life, he is naive enough to take their system of verbal ferocity at its face value and to adopt their self-inflationary mannerisms and outcries. At the same time he likes to associate himself with D. H. Lawrence, who was not at all an avant-gardist in the Parisian group sense of the term. He apparently regards himself as Lawrence's successor. But the truth is that they have very little in common, and there is no better way of showing it than by comparing their approaches to the sexual theme.

Miller is above all morally passive in his novels, whereas Lawrence, though he too was overwhelmed by the alienation of modern man, was sustained throughout by his supreme gift for moral activity; and he was sufficiently high-visioned to believe that a change of heart was possible, that he could reverse the current that had so long been running in one direction. Hence his idea of sexual fulfillment as a means of reintegration. Miller, however, in whose narratives sex forms the main subject matter, presents sexual relations almost without exception in terms of fornication, which are precisely the terms that Lawrence simply loathed. The innumerable seductions, so casual and joyless, that Miller describes with such insistence on reproducing all the ribald and obscene details, are almost entirely on the level of street encounters. He has none of Molly Bloom's earthiness, nor does he ever quake with Lawrence's holy tremors. He treats erotic functions with a kind of scabrous humor, for there is scarcely any feeling in him for the sex partner as a human being. What he wants is once and for all to expose "the conjugal orgy in the Black Hole of Calcutta." Not that he is open to the charge of pornography; on the contrary, behind his concentration on sexual experience there is a definite literary motive, or rather a double motive: first, the use of this experience to convey a sense of cultural and social disorder, to communicate a nihilist outlook, and second, an insatiable naturalistic curiosity. It is plain that Miller and Lawrence are opposites rather than twins.

Miller's claims as a guide to life and letters or as a prophet of doom can be easily discounted. In his three novels, however, he is remarkable as the biographer of the hobo-intellectual and as the poet of those people at the bottom of society in whom some unforeseen or surreptitious contact with art and literature has aroused a latent antagonism to ordinary living, a resolve to escape the treadmill even at the cost of hunger and degradation. In dealing with this material, Miller has performed a new act of selection. There is in his fiction, also, a Dickensian strain of caricature which comes to the surface again and again, as in the riotously funny monologues of the journalists Carl and Van Norden in *Tropic of Cancer*. The truth is that his bark is worse than his bite. He strikes the attitudes of a wild man, but what he lacks is the murderous logic and purity of his European prototypes. Though he can be as ferocious as Céline, he is never so consistent; and the final impression we have of his novels is that of a naturally genial and garrulous American who has been through hell. But now that he has had a measure of recognition and has settled down at home to receive the homage of his admirers he seems to have entered a new phase, and his work only occasionally reminds us of the role of bohemian desperado which in his expatriate years he assumed with complete authority and conviction.

1942

ATTITUDES TOWARD HENRY JAMES

HENRY JAMES is at once the most and least appreciated figure in American writing. His authority as a novelist of unique quality and as an archetypal American has grown immeasurably in the years since his death, and in some literary circles his name has of late been turned into the password of a cult. But at the same time he is still regarded, in those circles that exert the major influence on popular education and intelligence, with the coldness and even derision that he encountered in the most depressed period of his career, when his public deserted him and he found himself almost alone.

To illustrate the extent to which he is even now misunderstood, let me cite the opening gambit of the section on James in *The College Book of American Literature*, a text currently used in many schools. "It is not certain that Henry James really belongs to American literature, for he was critical of America and admired Europe." The attitude so automatically expressed by the editors of this academic volume obviously borders on caricature. The responsibility for it, however, must be laid at the door of all those critics and historians who, in response to a deep anti-intellectual compulsion or at the service of some blindly nationalistic or social creed, or not content merely to say no to the claims made in James's behalf but must ever try to despoil him utterly. The strategy is simple: James was nothing but a self-deluded expatriate snob, a concocter of elegant if intricate trifles, a fugitive from "reality," etc., etc. Professor Pattee, a run-of-the-mill historian of American writing, permits himself the remark that James's novels "really accomplish nothing." Ludwig Lewisohn is likewise repelled by the novels — "cathedrals of frosted glass" he calls them; in his opinion only the shorter narratives are worth reading. In his *Main Currents* Parrington gives two pages to James as against eleven to James Branch Cabell, and he has the further temerity (and/or innocence) to round out his two pages by comparing James — much to his disadvantage, of course — to Sherwood Anderson. And Van Wyck Brooks does all he can, in *New England: Indian Summer,* to promote once more the notoriously low estimate of the later James to which he committed himself in *The Pilgrimage.* Brooks may well believe that the Jamesian attachment is to be counted among the fixed ideas of our native "coterie-writers" — and plainly the best cure for a fixed idea is to stamp on it.

This depreciation of James is prepared for by some of the leading assumptions of our culture. The attitude of Parrington, for example, is formed by the Populist spirit of the West and its open-air poetics, whereas that of Brooks is at bottom formed by the moralism of New England — a moralism to which he has reverted, even though in practice he applies it in a more or less impressionistic and sentimental manner, with all the vehemence of a penitent atoning for his backsliding in the past. And the difference between such typical attitudes is mainly this: that while Parrington — like Whitman and Mark Twain before him — rejects James entirely, Brooks at least recognizes the value and fidelity to life of his earlier novels. Yet if James can be named, in T. S. Eliot's phrase, "a positive continuator of the New England genius," then surely Brooks must be aware of it as well as any of us; for he is nothing if not a pious servitor of this genius; after all, he, too, is a paleface. But still he scoffs at the more complex and, so to speak, ultimate James. And this Brooks does essentially for the same reasons, I think, that the Boston public of the 1870s scoffed at the works he now admits into his canon. We know that when the first of James's books appeared in America, they were actively disliked in Boston: Mrs. Fields (the wife of the publisher) relates that they were thought "self-conscious, artificial, and shallow." A like animus is now betrayed in Brooks's judgment of such novels as *The Spoils of Poynton, The Wings of the Dove,* and *The Golden Bowl:*

> Magnificent pretensions, petty performances! — the fruits of an irresponsible imagination, of a deranged sense of values, of a mind working in a void, uncorrected by any clear consciousness of human cause and effect. (*The Pilgrimage of Henry James*)
>
> There was scarcely enough substance in these great ghosts of novels . . . What concerned him now was form, almost regardless of content, the problems of calculation and construction . . . His American characters might be nobler, but, if the old world was corrupt, its glamor outweighed its corruption in his mind . . . so that he later pictured people, actually base, as eminent, noble and great. (*New England: Indian Summer*)

What are such extreme statements if not critical rationalizations of the original Boston prejudice? Brooks begins by magnifying the distinctions between James's early and late manner into an absolute contradiction, and ends by invoking the charge of degeneracy. But the fact is that the changes in James's work mark no such gap as Brooks supposes but are altogether implicit in the quality of his vision, flowing from the combined release and elaboration of his basic tendency. Moreover, these changes, far from justifying the charge of degeneracy, define for a good many of his readers the one salient example in our literature of a novelist who, not exhausted by his initial assertion of power, learned how to nourish his gifts and grow to full maturity. To me he is the only really fine American writer of the nineteenth century who can truly be said to have mastered that "principle of growth," to the failure of which in our creative life Brooks has himself repeatedly called attention in his earlier preachments.

For what is to be admired in a late narrative like *The Wings of the Dove* is James's capacity to lift the nuclear theme of his first period — the theme of the American innocent's penetration into the "rich and deep and dark" hive of Europe — to a level of conscious experience and aesthetic possession not previously attained. James orders his world with consummate awareness in this narrative, applying successfully his favorite rule of an "exquisite economy" in

7

composition. There are brilliant scenes in it of London and Venice, and strongly contrasted symbols of social glamor and decay; it is invigorated, too, by an unflagging realism in the plotting of act and motive and by the large movement of the characters. No literary standpoint that allows for the dismissal of this creation as a "petty performance" can possibly be valid. Is its heroine, Milly Theale, a character without reality? She remains in our mind, writes Edmund Wilson, "as a personality independent of the novel, the kind of personality, deeply felt, invested with poetic beauty and unmistakably individualized, which only the creators of the first rank can give life to."

James suffers from a certain one-sidedness, to be sure. This tends to throw off balance such readers as are unable to see it for what it is — the price he paid, given the circumstances of his career, for being faithful to his own genius. For James could continue to develop and sustain his "appeal to a high refinement and a handsome wholeness of effect" only through intensively exploiting his very limitations, through submitting himself to a process of creative yet cruel self-exaggeration. The strain shows in the stylization of his language, a stylization so rich that it turns into an intellectual quality of rare value, but which at times is apt to become overwrought and drop into unconscious parody. It is further shown in his obsessive refinement — a veritable delirium of refinement — which again serves at times to remove us from the actuality of the represented experience. This should be related to his all-too-persistent attempts, as Yvor Winters has observed, to make the sheer *tone* of speech and behavior "carry vastly more significance than is proper to it." It is true that, for instance, in novels like *The Sense of the Past* and *The Awkward Age,* he pushes his feelings for nuances and discriminations to an unworkable extreme. But such distortions, inflated into awful vices by his detractors, are of the kind which in one form or another not only James but most of the considerable modern artists are forced to cultivate as a means of coping with the negative environment that confines them. To regard such distortions as the traits of a willful coterie is utterly naive. They are the traits, rather, of an art which, if it is to survive at all in a society inimical to all interests that are pure, gratuitous, and without cash value, has no other recourse save constantly to "refine its singularities" and expose itself more and more to the ravages of an unmitigated individualism.

But in all this I do not mean to imply that I agree with those enthusiasts who see no moral defects whatever in James. From the
viewpoint of social criticism, there is a good deal of justice in Ferner
Nuhn's mordant analysis of *The Golden Bowl.** This novel is one
of the much debated items in the James canon, for in it James applied his spellbinding powers as never before to the creation of
a line of illusory value for his wealthy Americans in Europe and
their sponging aristocratic friends with whom they conduct a romantic historical liaison. Not a few critics have been provoked by
this quality of the novel. One instance is Stephen Spender, who,
flying in the face of the Jamesian specifications, describes Prince
Amerigo as "an unknown, well-bred scoundrel." Some have argued,
weakly, I think, that the picture of the Ververs and their bought-
and-paid-for Prince is to be taken in an ironical sense. In *Henry
James: the Major Phase* F. O. Matthiessen takes the story as given,
and his interpretation coincides in many respects with Ferner Nuhn's
reading of it. I agree entirely with their approach, but one cannot
go along with Matthiessen in his conclusion that the novel is "with
all its magnificence . . . almost as hollow of real life as the chateaux
that had risen along Fifth Avenue and that had also crowded out
the old Newport world that James remembered." To say that *The
Golden Bowl* is morally decadent is one thing, but to claim that for
this reason it is empty of life and, by implication, an inferior work
of art is something else again. To my mind, this is an example of
moral overreaction at the expense of literary judgment. I can think
of other novels, say Dostoevsky's *The Possessed,* which are thoroughly distorted from the standpoint of any radical social morality
but which are nonetheless supreme works of fiction. *The Golden
Bowl* must be placed, I believe, among the dozen or so great novels
of American literature; there is one section in it — the second, third,
and fourth chapters of the fifth "Book" — which for vividness, directness, and splendidly alive and spacious imagery is without counterpart in the American novel. Ferner Nuhn has defined *The Golden
Bowl* as a dream story. He is right of course, since the indicated
position of its characters and the idea they have of themselves are
not in correspondence with reality. Yet as a dream story it is far

* In his book, *The Wind Blows from the East,* 1942.

from being a mere invention. It has the enormous vitality which springs from the actual dreamlife of a social class — a dream of the "loot of empire," an imperial dream full of "real" objects and "real" life. One can object to its content on ideological grounds, and on those grounds James is indeed vulnerable; but one cannot deny that it is historically meaningful and that it has interest and artistry and a kind of meditated though cruel beauty.

Furthermore, whatever one may think of the millionaire self-indulgence of the Ververs, this is a far cry from the charge that James's long exile put him into such a bad state that he could no longer distinguish between the noble and the base. This sort of charge is answered once and for all, it seems to me, by Stephen Spender in his study, *The Destructive Element*:

> The morality of the heroes and heroines [in the last great novels] is to "suffer generously." What they have to suffer from is being more intelligent than the other characters. Also, there are no villains. It is important to emphasize this, because in these really savage novels the behavior of some of the characters is exposed in its most brutal form. But the wickedness of the characters lies primarily in their situation. Once the situation is provided, the actors cannot act otherwise. Their only compensation is that by the use of their intelligence, by their ability to understand, to love and to suffer, they may to some extent atone for the evil which is simply the evil of the modern world.

As against the sundry moralizers and nationalists who belittle James, there are the cultists who go to the other extreme in presenting him as a kind of culture-hero, an ideal master whose perfection of form is equaled by his moral insight and staunch allegiance to "tradition." This image is no doubt of consolatory value to some high-minded literary men. It contributes, however, to the misunderstanding of James, in that it is so impeccable, one might say transcendent, that it all but eliminates the contradictions in him — and in modern literature, which bristles with anxieties and ideas of isolation, it is above all the creativity, the depth and quality of the contradictions that a writer unites within himself, that gives us the truest measure of his achievement. And this is not primarily a matter of the solutions, if any, provided by the writer — for it is hardly the writer's business to stand in for the scientist or philosopher —

but of his force and integrity in reproducing these contradictions as felt experience. Very few of us would be able to appreciate Dostoevsky, for instance, if we first had to accept his answer to the problem of the Christian man, or Proust if we first had to accept his answer to the problem of the artist. We appreciate these novelists because they employ imaginative means that convince us of the reality of their problems, which are not *necessarily* ours.

T. S. Eliot was surely right in saying that the soil of James's origin imparted a "flavor" that was "precisely improved and given its chance, not worked off" by his living in Europe. Now James differs radically in his contradictions from European novelists — that is why readers lacking a background in American or at least Anglo-Saxon culture make so little of him. And the chief contradiction is that his work represents a positive and ardent search for "experience" and simultaneously a withdrawal from it, or rather, a dread of approaching it in its natural state. Breaking sharply with the then still dominant American morality of abstention, he pictures "experience" as the "real taste of life," as a longed-for "presence" at once "vast, vague, and dazzling — an irradiation of light from objects undefined, mixed with the atmosphere of Paris and Venice." Nevertheless, to prove truly acceptable, it must first be Americanized as it were, that is to say, penetrated by the New World conscience and cleansed of its taint of "evil." This tension between the impulse to plunge into "experience" and the impulse to renounce it is the chief source of the internal yet astonishingly abundant Jamesian emotion; and because the tension is not always adequately resolved, we sometimes get that effect, so well described by Glenway Wescott, of "embarassed passion and hinted meaning in excess of the narrated facts; the psychic content is too great for its container of elegantly forged happenings; it all overflows and slops about and is magnificently wasted." On this side of James we touch upon his relationship to Hawthorne, whose characters, likewise tempted by "experience," are held back by the fear of sin. And Hawthorne's ancestral idea of sin survives in James, though in a secularized form. It has entered the sensibility and been translated into a revulsion, an exasperated feeling, almost morbid in its sensitiveness, against any conceivable crudity of scene or crudity of conduct. (The trouble with American life, he wrote, is not that it is "ugly" — the ugly can be strange and grotesque — but that it is "plain"; "even nature, in the western world, has the peculiarity of seeming rather crude and immature.") Any failure of discrimination is sin, whereas virtue is a compound of intelligence, moral delicacy, and the sense of the past.

And Hawthorne's remembrance of the religious mythology of New England and his fanciful concern with it is replaced in James — and this too is a kind of transmutation — by the remembrance and fanciful concern with history. It was for the sake of Europe's historical "opulence" that he left his native land. Yet this idea is also managed by him in a contradictory fashion, and for this reason W. C. Brownell was able to say that he showed no real interest in the "course of history." Now as a critic Brownell had no eye for James's historical picture of the American experience in Europe; but it is true that on the whole James's sense of history is restricted by the point of view of the "passionate pilgrim" who comes to rest in the shade of civilization. Above all, he comes to enrich his personality. Thus there is produced the Jamesian conception of history as a static yet irreproachable standard, a beautiful display, a treasured background, whose function is at once to adorn and lend perspective to his well-nigh metaphysical probing of personal relations, of the private life. There never was a writer so immersed in personal relations, and his consistency in this respect implies an antihistorical attitude. This helps to explain the peculiarities of his consciousness, which is intellectual yet at the same time indifferent to general ideas, deeply comprehensive yet unattached to any open philosophical motive.

These contradictions in James — and there are others besides those I have mentioned — are chiefly to be accounted for in terms of his situation as an American writer who experienced his nationality and the social class to which he belonged at once as an ordeal and as an inspiration. The "great world" is corrupt, yet it represents an irresistible goal. Innocence points to all the wanted things one has been deprived of, yet it is profound in its good faith and not to be tampered with without loss. History and culture are the supreme ideal, but why not make of them a strictly private possession? Europe is romance and reality and civilization, but the spirit resides in America. James never faltered in the maze of these contraries; he knew how to take hold of them creatively and weave them into the web of his art. And the secret of their combination is the secret of his irony and of his humor.

1943

THE HEIRESS OF ALL THE AGES

Henry James is not fully represented in his novels by any one single character, but of his principal heroine it can be said that she makes the most of his vision and dominates his drama of transatlantic relations. This young woman is his favorite American type, appearing in his work time and again under various names and in various situations that can be taken as so many stages in her career. Hence it is in the line of her development that we must study her. Her case involves a principle of growth which is not to be completely grasped until she has assumed her final shape.

This heroine, too, is cast in the role, so generic to James, of the "passionate pilgrim," whose ordinary features are those of the "good American bewildered in the presence of the European order." But bewilderment is not a lasting motive in this heroine's conduct; unlike most of her fellow pilgrims in James's novels, she soon learns how to adjust European attitudes to the needs of her personality. Where she excels is in her capacity to plunge into experience without paying the usual Jamesian penalty for such daring — the penalty being either the loss of one's moral balance or the recoil into a state of aggrieved innocence. She responds "magnificently" to the beauty of the Old-World scene even while keeping a tight hold on her native virtue: the ethical stamina, goodwill, and inwardness of her own provincial background. And thus living up to her author's idea both of Europe and America, she is able to mediate, if not wholly to resolve, the conflict between the two cultures, between innocence and experience, between the sectarian code of the fathers and the more "civilized" though also more devious and dangerous code of the lovers. No wonder James commends her in terms that fairly bristle with heroic intentions and that in the preface to *The Wings of the Dove* he goes so far as to credit her with the great historic boon of being "that certain sort of young American," exceptionally endowed with "liberty of action, of choice, of appreciation, of contact . . . who is more the 'heir of all the ages' than any other young person whatsoever."

If James's relation to his native land is in question, then more is to be learned from this young woman's career than from any number of discursive statements quoted from his letters, essays, and autobiographies. "It's a complete fate being an American," he wrote. Yes, but what does this fate actually come to in his work? The answer, it seems to me, is mostly given in his serial narrative of the heiress of all the ages.

The initial assignment of this heroine is to reconnoiter the scene rather than take possession of it. As yet she is not recognized as the legitimate heiress but merely as a candidate for the inheritance. Such is the part played by Mary Garland, for instance, a small-town girl from New England who herself feels the pull of the "great world" even as she tries to save her errant lover from its perils (*Roderick Hudson*, 1875). Daisy Miller, a young lady whose friends are distressed by the odd mixture of spontaneous grace, audacity, and puerility in her deportment, is also cast in this role, though with somewhat special and limited intentions. Bessie Alden (*An International Episode*, 1878), a more cultivated and socially entrenched figure than the famous Daisy, voyages to England — inevitably so — for the sake of enjoying its picturesque associations; and she is noteworthy as the first of the James girls to reap the triumph of turning down the proposal of an Old-World aristocrat. But it is in Isabel Archer (*The Portrait of a Lady*) that we first encounter this heroine in a truly pivotal position, comprising the dramatic consequences of a conflict not merely of manners but of morals as well. In Isabel her heretofore scattered traits are unified and corrected in the light of James's growing recognition of the importance of her claims. Two decades later, at the time when his writing had settled into the so portentously complex style of his ultimate period, she reappears as the masterful though stricken Milly Theale of *The Wings of the Dove* and as the impeccable Maggie Verver of *The Golden Bowl*, to whom all shall be given. These last displays of her age are by far the most accomplished, for in them her function as "princess" and "heiress" is fully defined and affirmed.

The evolution of our heroine thus gives us the measure of James's progressively rising estimate of that American fate to the account of which he devoted the greater part of his work. The account opens with the simple, almost humble, instances of Mary Garland and Daisy Miller, who are baffled and shamed by Europe, and closes with the "prodigious" success of Maggie Verver, to whom Europe offers itself as a dazzling and inexhaustible opportunity. What is the heiress, then, if not a character-image of aggrandizement on every level of meaning and existence? She is that in her own right, as the representative American mounting "Europe's lighted and decorated stage"; but she also serves James as the objective equivalent of his own increase and expansion as man and artist. This is all the more striking when we consider that both author and heroine entered upon their careers under seemingly inauspicious circumstances. At the start they are beset by the traditional scruples of their race, by fits of enervation and recurrent feelings of inferiority; yet as both mature he achieves a creative dignity and consciousness of well-nigh lordly dimensions, while she comes to value herself and to be valued by the world at large as the personage appointed by history to inherit the bounty of the ages. Francis Fergusson has aptly summed up this entire process of growth in remarking that James "developed a society manner into a grand manner much as he developed a rich American girl into a large, sober, Bérénice-like stage queen."

Such exceptional prosperity is hardly to be explained in terms of individual aptitude alone. Certain large conditions make it possible, such as America's precipitant rise as a national power in the late nineteenth century; its enhanced self-knowledge and self-confidence;

and, more particularly, the avid desire of its upper classes to obtain forthwith the rewards and prerogatives of high civilization. The truth is that for qualities of a surpassingly bourgeois and imperial order James's heiress is without parallel in American fiction. Note that this millionaire's daughter is an heiress in moral principle no less than in material fact, and that James, possessed of a firmer faith in the then existing structure of society than most novelists and wholly sincere in his newly gained worldliness, tends to identify her moral with her material superiority.* Yet in the long run she cannot escape the irony — the inner ambiguity — of her status. For her wealth is at once the primary source of her so lavishly pictured "greatness" and "liberty" and the source of the evil she evokes in others. There is no ignoring the consideration, however, that in the case of the heiress, as in the case of most of James's rich Americans, money is in a sense but the prerequisite of moral delicacy. What with her "higher interests" and pieties, the rigor of her conscience

---

* Some critics writing about James in the early 1930s sought to put him in line with the Leftist trend of the times. This sort of intention is evident in Robert Cantwell's several essays of that period and to a lesser extent in Stephen Spender's study, *The Destructive Element*. These critics overlook, it seems to me, a depth of the conservative idea in James, and that is why they are forced to exaggerate the meaning of novels like *The Ivory Tower* and *The Princess Casamassima*. Even though in the latter the atmosphere of class conflict is genuine enough, its revolutionary theme cannot be taken at face value. For imbedded in this novel is the more familiar theme of the passionate pilgrim — the pilgrim being the hero, Hyacinth Robinson, who sees the "immeasurable misery of the people" but who also sees, even more clearly and passionately, "all that has been, as it were, rescued and redeemed from it: the treasures, the felicities, the splendors, the successes of the world"; and in the end, when the final choice is put to him, he takes his stand not with the people but with the "world" resting upon their misery. Thus Robinson is enticed by the same image that draws the Jamesian Americans to Europe. The one variation is that he constructs this image out of class rather than national or, so to speak, hemispheric differences.

So far as the political estimate of James is concerned, one cannot but agree with Joseph Warren Beach that he is basically a "gentleman of cultivated and conservative, not to say, reactionary instinct, who will generally be found to favor the same line of conduct as that favored by the ecclesiastical and civil law, as far as the law goes" (*The Method of Henry James*). So blunt a characterization is likely to offend the James-cultists, but I think it can stand so long as we take it in a strictly political sense, not as a judgment of his moral realism. On that score Spender is closer to the truth in observing that James "saw through the life of his age" but that he "cherished the privilege that enabled him to see through it."

and the nicety of her illusions, what is she really if not a graduate of the school of Boston Transcendentalism? Her author's imagination operated according to the law of the conversion of the lower into the higher, and by means of this ideal logic his heroine's debut in the "social successful worldly world" is transformed into a kind of spiritual romance. What James knew best of all is, of course, how to take things immensely for granted; and not to appreciate the wonder of his beguilement is to miss the poetry, the story, the very life of his fictions.

To grasp the national-cultural values implicit in the progress of his heroine is to be done once and for all with the widely held assumption that to James the country of his birth always signified failure and sterility. Edmund Wilson is surely right in contending that it is America which really "gets the better of it in Henry James." Such an interpretation is consistent with his return to the theme of the heiress at the turn of the century, with his honorific treatment of her, his enamored tone and laudatory report of her aims and prospects — her aims and prospects being not merely those of a typical Jamesian aspirant but of an American emissary endowed with a character "intrinsically and actively ample . . . reaching southward, westward, anywhere, everywhere." As the years passed James's awareness of the American stake in the maintenance of civilization grew increasingly positive and imposing. In his later writings old Europe serves once more as the background for young America, and his restored interest in the nuclear fable of the passionate pilgrim is now worked out on a more ambitious scale and with more intricate artistic intentions. His last great novels are remarkable, too, for the resurgence in them of that native idealism — that "extraordinary good faith" — the effect of which in his early fiction was to link him with the classic masters of American literature. In *The Wings of the Dove, The Ambassadors,* and *The Golden Bowl* the motives and standards of this idealism are applied to the mixed disorder and splendor of the "great world," now no longer simply admired from afar but seen from within.

But the question whether the ultimate loyalty of James is claimed by Europe or America is hardly as meaningful as it has appeared to some of his interpreters. For actually his valuations of Europe and America are not the polar opposites but the two commanding centers of his work — the contending sides whose relation is adjusted so as to make mutual assimilation feasible. It is the only means by which the Jamesian idea of heritage can be brought to fruition. What his detractors can never forgive him, however, is his bursting the bounds of that autarchic Americanism of which Whitman is the chief exponent. Never having fallen into the habit of "glowing belligerently with one's country," he is able to invest his characters with a historic mission and propel them into spheres of experience as yet closed to them at home. They are the people named as the Ambassadors — and the nationalist critics who make so much of his expatriation should be reminded that there is a world of difference between the status of an ambassador and the status of a fugitive.

James's all-inclusive choice is dramatized in his recurrent story of the marriage of an eminent New-World bride to an equally eminent Old-World groom. The marriage is symbolic of the reconciliation of their competing cultures; and if it sometimes turns out badly, as in *The Portrait of a Lady*, or if it fails to come off altogether, as in *The Wings of the Dove*, James still holds fast to his scheme, continuing his experiments in matchmaking till finally, in *The Golden Bowl*, all the parts fall into their proper place, the marriage is consummated and bears luxurious fruit. Observe, though, that this happy ending is postponed again and again until the American wife, in the person of Maggie Verver, has established herself as the ruling member of the alliance.

The advancement of this heroine takes on historical form against the period background of the American female's rise to a position of cultural prestige and authority. She it was who first reached out for the "consummations and amenities" of life while her male relatives were still earnestly engaged in procuring its "necessities and preparations." No wonder W. D. Howells declared that "the prosperity of our fiction resides in the finer female sense." Now James's so-called feminine orientation is to be explained partly by this social fact and partly by his instinct, the most exquisite possible, for private relations and for their latent refinement of fact and taste. So estranged was he from typical masculine interests that he could not but fall back more and more on the subject of marriage, a subject dominated, in his treatment of it, by the "social" note and meeting the "finer female sense" on its own preferred ground.* Moreover, he could have found no better framework of realistic detail for his picture of "young American innocence transplanted to European air." And if his stories of marriage are mostly stories, as he himself once put it, about "very young women, who, affected with a certain high lucidity, thereby become characters," it is because all the conditions of his art made for such a choice.

His male figures are, generally speaking, to be identified with his less masterful side, with the negative component of his sense of experience and the masochistic tendency to refuse the natural gifts of life. It is in deviating from this code of refusal that Roderick Hudson goes to pieces. In *The Ambassadors* Lambert Strether learns the lesson of *not* refusing, but his adventure in Paris gains its point from the sheer process of his learning that lesson rather than from his application of it. Nor can one overlook the repeated appearance in James of certain sad and uncertain young men who vie with each other in devising painfully subtle motives for renouncing their heart's desire once it is within their grasp. One such specimen is the young man (Bernard Longmore in *Madame de Mauves*) who is revolted by the idea of making love to the woman whose happiness he tries to save. Another is the incredibly appealing though emotionally dense Mr. Wendover, who has "no more physical personality than a consulted thermometer" and who, courting the girl he loves with more propriety than imagination, fails her when she needs him most (*A London Life*). In point of fact, the heiress is the one native Jamesian who knows exactly what she wants. She, too, is confronted, to be sure, with "beautiful difficulties," but they are never of the kind that spring from some crucial frustration or of the kind that can be translated into some moral issue, which is then to be carefully isolated and solved in a chessboard fashion. In her case the "beauti-

* In *The Point of View*, a story published in the early eighties, James inserts the following ironic reference to himself into the Paris-bound letter of a French visitor to New York: "They have a novelist here with pretensions to literature, who writes about the chase for the husband and the adventures of the rich Americans in our corrupt old Europe, where their primeval candor puts the Europeans to shame. *C'est proprement écrit;* but it's terribly pale." In later years he would hardly have enjoyed any such ironic play at his own expense, for with age self-depreciation gave way to portentousness in his estimate of himself.

ful difficulties" spring out of her very search for self-fulfillment and impetuosity in "taking full in the face the whole assault of life."

It is with a bright and sudden flutter of self-awareness that Mary Garland reveals, in a brief passage of dialogue, the state of mind of the heiress as she sets out to meet her fate. The occasion for it is a night scene in *Roderick Hudson*, when Mary confesses to Rowland Mallet that her stay in Italy has induced a change in her conception of life:

> Mary: "At home . . . things don't speak to us of enjoyment as they do here. Here it's such a mixture; one doesn't know what to believe. Beauty stands here — beauty such as this night and this place and all this sad strange summer have been so full of — and it penetrates one's soul and lodges there and keeps saying that man wasn't made, as we think at home, to struggle so much and to miss so much, but to ask of life as a matter of course some beauty and some charm. This place has destroyed any scrap of consistency that I ever possessed, but even if I must say something sinful I love it!"

> Rowland: "If it's sinful I absolve you — insofar as I have power. We should not be able to enjoy, I suppose, unless we could suffer, and in anything that's worthy of the name of experience — that experience which is the real *taste* of life, isn't it? — the mixture is of the finest and subtlest."

The pathos of this dialogue is the pathos of all the buried things in the American past it recalls us to. It recalls us, moreover, to one of the most telling and precise relations in our literature, that of the early James to Hawthorne.* Consider how this relation is at once contained and developed in Mary's vision of what life holds for those bold enough to ask for it as a matter of course "some beauty and some charm." For Mary is essentially a figure from a novel such as *The Blithedale Romance* or *The Marble Faun* brought forward into a later age; and because of the shift of values that has occurred

---

* Among the first to notice the connection was William James. In 1870 he wrote to his brother: "It tickled my national feeling not a little to note the resemblance of Hawthorne's style to yours and Howells's. . . . That you and Howells, with all the models in English literature to follow, should involuntarily have imitated (as it were) this American, seems to point to the existence of some real mental American quality."

in the meantime, she is able to express in a mundane fashion those feelings and sentiments that in Hawthorne are still somewhat hidden and only spoken of with a semiclerical quaver, as if from under a veil. In Mary's confession the spectral consciousness of the perils of beauty, of the evil it hides, is at long last being exorcised, the mind is being cleared of its homegrown fears and mystifications. The reality of experience can no longer be resisted: "Even if I say something sinful I love it!" And having said it, she is absolved of her "sin" by Rowland, who in this scene is manifestly acting for the author. It is Rowland, too, who describes experience as the "real *taste* of life," thus disclosing its innermost Jamesian sense. For in this sense of it the idea of experience is emptied of its more ordinary meanings, of empirical reference, and made to correspond to pure consummation, to that "felt felicity" so often invoked by James, to something lovingly selected or distilled from life — all of which is perfectly in line with the indicated function of the heiress as the prime consumer of the resources, material and spiritual, of both the Old and the New World. And though it is not within the power of even this superior brand of experience to exempt one from suffering, still the risk is well worth taking so long as "the mixture is of the finest and subtlest."

But in Mary the ferment of experience is as yet more potential than actual. At this stage James is already sure of his heroine's integrity and liveliness of imagination, knowing that in this fine flower of a provincial culture he had gotten hold of a historical prodigy admirably suited to his purpose as a novelist. He is still doubtful, however, of her future, uncertain as to the exact conditions of her entry into the "great world" and of the mutual effect thus created. Daisy Miller and Bessie Alden represent his further experiments with her character. Daisy's social adventures make for a superb re-creation of manners and tones and contrasts and similitudes. Spontaneity is her principal quality — a quality retained by the heiress through all her mutations and invariably rendered as beautifully illustrative of the vigor and innocence of the national spirit. But Daisy is altogether the small-town, the average American girl; and by virtue of this fact she lays bare the lowly origin of the heiress in the undifferentiated mass of the New-World democracy.

Winterbourne, Daisy's admirer and critic, observes that "she and her mamma have not yet risen to the stage — what shall I call it? — of culture, at which the idea of catching a count or a *marchesse* begins."

Bessie, on the other hand, seizes upon this conception only to rise above it. This "Bostonian nymph who rejects an English duke" combines the primal sincerity of her forebears with a Jamesian sensitivity to the "momentos and reverberations of greatness" in the life of ancient aristocracies — and this amalgam of values proves to be beyond the comprehension of Lord Lambeth's simple matter-of-fact mind. Bessie's behavior was resented, of course, by English readers, just as Daisy's was resented by American readers. But the so-challenged author, far from being flustered by the protests that reached him, took it all in with gloating satisfaction, delighted by the contrast, with its "dramas upon dramas . . . and innumerable points of view," thus brought to light. He felt that the emotion of the public vindicated his faith in the theme of the "international situation."

As the 1870s come to a close, James is done with the preliminary studies of his heroine. Now he undertakes to place her in a longer narrative — *The Portrait of a Lady* — the setting and action of which are at last commensurate with the "mysterious purposes" and "vast designs" of her character. In the preface to the New York edition (written nearly a quarter of a century later) he recalls that the conception of a "certain young woman affronting her destiny had begun with being all my outfit for the large building of the novel"; and he reports that in its composition he was faced with only one leading question: "What will she 'do'?" But this is mainly a rhetorical question, for naturally "the first thing she'll do will be to come to Europe — which in fact will form, and all inevitably, no small part of her principal adventure." *The Portrait* is by far the best novel of James's early prime, bringing to an end his literary apprenticeship and establishing the norms of his world. Its author has not yet entirely divorced himself from Victorian models in point of structure, and as a stylist he is still mindful of the reader's more obvious pleasure, managing his prose with an eye to outward as well as inward effects. It is a lucid prose, conventional yet free, marked by aphoristic turns of phrase and by a kind of intellectual gaiety in the

8

formulation of ideas. There are few signs as yet of that well-nigh
metaphysical elaboration of the sensibility by which he is to become
known as one of the foremost innovators in American writing.

Isabel Archer is a young lady of an Emersonian cast of mind, but
her affinity as a fictional character is rather with those heroines of
Turgenev in whose nature an extreme tenderness is conjoined with
unusual strength of purpose.* No sooner does Isabel arrive at the
countryhouse of her uncle Mr. Touchett, an American banker re-
siding in England, then everyone recognizes her for what she is —
"a delicate piece of human machinery." Her cousin Ralph questions
his mother: "Who is this rare creature, and what is she? Where did
you find her?" "I found her," she replies, "in an old house at Albany,
sitting in a dreary room on a rainy day . . . She didn't know she was
bored but when I told her she seemed grateful for the hint . . . I
thought she was meant for something better. It occurred to me it
would be a kindness to take her about and introduce her to the
world." The American Cinderella thus precipitated from the town
of Albany into the "great world" knows exactly what she must look
forward to. "To be as happy as possible," she confides in Ralph,
"that's what I came to Europe for." It is by no means a simple
answer. On a later and more splendid occasion it is to be repeated
by Maggie Verver, who proclaims her faith, even as the golden
bowl crashes to the ground, in a "happiness without a hole in it . . .
the golden bowl as it *was* to have been . . . the bowl with all our
happiness in it, the bowl without a crack in it." This is the crowning
illusion and pathos, too, of the heiress, that she believes such happiness to be attainable, that money can buy it and her mere good
faith can sustain it. And even when eventually her European en-
tanglements open her eyes to the fact that virtue and experience are
not so charmingly compatible after all, that the Old World has a
fierce energy of its own and that its "tone of time" is often pitched
in a sinister key, she still persists in her belief that this same world
will yield her a richly personal happiness, proof against the evil

* The influence may well be conscious in this case, though in the preface
to the novel James admits to being influenced by the Russian novelist only
on the technical plane, with respect to the manner of placing characters in
fiction. James's critical essays abound with favorable references to Turgenev,
whose friendship he cultivated in Paris and of whom he invariably spoke with
enthusiasm.

spawned by others less fortunate than herself; and this belief is all the more expressive because it is wholly of a piece with the psychology of the heiress as a national type. The ardor of Americans in pursuing happiness as a personal goal is equaled by no other people, and when it eludes them none are so hurt, none so shamed. Happiness, one might say, is really their private equivalent of such ideals as progress and universal justice. They take for granted, with a faith at once deeply innocent and deeply presumptuous, that they deserve nothing less and that to miss it is to miss life itself.

The heiress is not to be humbled by the tests to which life in Europe exposes her. The severer the test the more intense the glow of her spirit. Is she not the child, as Isabel proudly declares, of that "great country which stretches beyond the rivers and across the prairies, blooming and smiling and spreading, till it stops at the blue Pacific! A strong, sweet, fresh odour seems to rise from it . . ." The Emersonian note is sounded again and again by Isabel. She is truly the Young American so grandly pictured by the Concord idealist in his essay of that title, the Young American bred in a land "offering opportunity to the human mind not known in any other region" and hence possessed of an "organic simplicity and liberty, which, when it loses its balance, redresses itself presently . . ." Witness the followowing passage of character analysis, with its revelation of Isabel's shining beneficent Emersonianism:

Every now and then Isabel found out she was wrong, and then she treated herself to a week of passionate humility. After that she held her head higher than ever; for it was of no use, she had an unquenchable desire to think well of herself. She had a theory that it was only on this condition that life was worth living: that one should be the best, should be conscious of a fine organization . . . *should move in a realm of light, of natural wisdom, of happy impulse, of inspiration fully chronic. It was almost as unnecessary to cultivate doubt of oneself as to cultivate doubt of one's best friend.* . . . The girl had a certain nobleness of imagination which rendered her a good many services and played her a good many tricks. She spent half her time in thinking of beauty, and bravery, and magnanimity; *she had a fixed determination to regard the world as a place of brightness, of free expansion, of irresistible action; she thought it would be detestable to be afraid or ashamed.* [Italics not in the original.]

Still more revealing is the exchange between Isabel and the thoroughly Europeanized Madame Merle on the subject of the individual's capacity for self-assertion in the face of outward circumstances:

> Madame Merle: "When you have lived as long as I, you will see that every human being has his shell, that you must take the shell into account. By the shell I mean the whole envelope of circumstances. There is no such thing as an isolated man or woman; we're each of us made up of a cluster of circumstances. What do you call one's self? Where does it begin? Where does it end? It overflows into everything that belongs to me — and then it flows back again. I know that a large part of myself is in the dresses I choose to wear. I have a great respect for *things!*"

> Isabel: "I don't agree with you . . . I think just the other way. I don't know whether I succeed in expressing myself, but I know that nothing else expresses me. Nothing that belongs to me is a measure of me; on the contrary, it's a limit, a barrier, and a perfectly arbitrary one."[*]

In *The Portrait* James is still hesitating between the attitude of Madame Merle and that of Isabel, and his irony is provoked by the excessive claims advanced by both sides. But in years to come he is to be drawn more and more to the "European" idea of the human self, his finer discriminations being increasingly engaged by the "envelope of circumstances" in which it is contained.

Isabel is above all a young lady of principles, and her most intimate decisions are ruled by them. In refusing the proposal of the grandiose Lord Warburton, she wonders what ideal aspiration or design upon fate or conception of happiness prompts her to renounce such a chance for glamor and worldly satisfaction. Never had she seen a "personage" before, as there were none in her native land; of marriage she had been accustomed to think solely in terms of character — "of what one likes in a gentleman's mind and in his talk . . . hitherto her visions of a completed life had concerned themselves largely with moral images — things as to which the question would be whether they pleased her soul." But if an aristocratic marriage is not to Isabel's liking, neither is the strictly hometown alternative of

---

[*] Note the close parallel between Isabel's reply to Madame Merle and the Emersonian text. "You think me the child of my circumstances: I make my circumstances. Let any thought or motive of mine be different from what they are, the difference will transform my condition and economy . . . You call it the power of circumstance, but it is the power of me." (*The Transcendentalist*)

marrying a businessman. The exemplary Gaspar Goodwood, who owns a cotton mill and is the embodiment of patriotic virtue, likewise fails to win her consent — "His jaw was too square and grim, and his figure too straight and stiff; these things suggested a want of easy adaptability to some of the occasions of life."

Isabel having so far lacked the requisite fortune to back up her assumption of the role of the heiress, her cousin Ralph provides what is wanting by persuading his dying father to leave her a large sum of money. "I should like to make her rich," Ralph declares. "What do you mean by rich?" "I call people rich when they are able to gratify their imagination." Thus Isabel enters the uppermost circle of her author's hierarchy, the circle of those favored few who, unhampered by any material coercion, are at once free to make what they can of themselves and to accept the fullest moral responsibility for what happens to them in consequence. Now the stage is set for the essential Jamesian drama of free choice. In this novel, however, the transcendent worth of such freedom is not yet taken for granted as it is in *The Wings of the Dove* and *The Golden Bowl*. There is the intervention, for instance, of the lady-correspondent Henrietta Stackpole, who is no passionate pilgrim but the mouthpiece, rather, of popular Americanism. It is she who questions Isabel's future on the ground that her money will work against her by bolstering her romantic inclinations. Henrietta is little more than a fictional convenience used to furnish the story with comic relief; but at this juncture of the plot she becomes the agent of a profound criticism aimed, in the last analysis, at James himself, at his own tendency to romanticize the values to which privilege lays claim. And what Henrietta has to say is scarcely in keeping with her habitual manner of the prancing female journalist. Characteristically enough, she begins by remarking that she has no fear of Isabel turning into a sensual woman; the peril she fears is of a different nature:

> "The peril for you is that you live too much in the world of your own dreams — you are not enough in contact with reality — with the toiling, striving, suffering, I may even say, sinning world that surrounds you. You are too fastidious, you have too many graceful illusions. Your newly-acquired thousands will shut you up more and more in the society of selfish and heartless people, who will be interested in keeping up those illusions . . . You think, furthermore, that you can lead a ro-

mantic life, that you can live by pleasing others and pleasing yourself. You will find you are mistaken. Whatever life you lead, you must put your soul into it — to make any sort of success of it; and from the moment you do that it ceases to be romance, I assure you; it becomes reality! . . . you think we can escape disagreeable duties by taking romantic views — that is your great illusion, my dear."

The case against the snobbish disposition of the Jamesian culture-seekers and their overestimation of the worldly motive has seldom been so shrewdly and clearly stated. But Isabel is not especially vulnerable to criticism of this sort. It is only in her later incarnations that the heiress succumbs more and more to precisely the illusions of which Henrietta gives warning — so much so that in the end, when Maggie Verver appears on the scene, the life she leads may be designated, from the standpoint of the purely social analyst, as a romance of bourgeois materialism, the American romance of newly got wealth divesting itself of its plebeian origins in an ecstasy of refinement!

Henrietta's words, moreover, are meant to prefigure the tragedy of Isabel's marriage to Gilbert Osmond, an Italianate American, virtually a European, whom she takes to be what he is not — a decent compromise between the moral notions of her American background and the glamor of the European foreground. Osmond, whose special line is a dread of vulgarity, employs a kind of sincere cunning in presenting himself to Isabel as the most fastidious gentleman living, concerned above all with making his life a work of art and resolved, since he could never hope to attain the status he actually deserved, "not to go in for honors." The courtship takes place in Rome and in Florence, where Isabel is swayed by her impression of Osmond as a "quiet, clever, distinguished man, strolling on a moss-grown terrace above the sweet Val d'Arno . . . the picture was not brilliant, but she liked its lowness of tone, and the atmosphere of summer twilight that pervaded it . . . It seemed to speak of a serious choice, a choice between things of a shallow and things of a deep interest; of a lonely, studious life in a lovely land." But the impression is false. Only when it is too late does she learn that he had married her for her money with the connivance of Madame Merle, his former mistress, who had undertaken to influence her in his behalf. This entrapment of Isabel illustrates a recurrent formula of James's fiction.

The person springing the trap is almost invariably driven by mer-
cenary motives, and, like Osmond, is capable of accomplishing his
aim by simulating a sympathy and understanding that fascinate the
victim and render her (or him) powerless.* Osmond still retains
some features of the old-fashioned villain, but his successors are
gradually freed from the encumbrances of melodrama. Merton
Densher (*The Wings of the Dove*) and Prince Amerigo (*The Golden
Bowl*) are men of grace and intelligence, whose wicked behavior is
primarily determined by the situation in which they find themselves.

Osmond reacts to the Emersonian strain in Isabel as to a personal
offense. He accuses her of willfully rejecting traditional values and
of harboring sentiments "worthy of a radical newspaper or a Uni-
tarian preacher." And she, on her part, discovers that his fastidious-
ness reduced itself to a "sovereign contempt for every one but some
two or three or four exalted people whom he envied, and for everything but half-a-dozen ideas of his own . . . he pointed out to her
so much of the baseness and shabbiness of life . . . but this base,
ignoble world, it appeared, was after all what one was to live for;
one was to keep it forever in one's eye, in order, not to enlighten, or
convert, or redeem, but to extract from it some recognition of one's
superiority." Isabel's notion of the aristocratic life is "simply the
unison of great knowledge with great liberty," whereas for Osmond
it is altogether a "thing of forms," an attitude of conscious calculation. His esteem for tradition is boundless; if one was so unfortunate
as not to be born to an illustrious tradition, then "one must immediately proceed to make it."† A sense of darkness and suffocation

* It seems to me that this brand of evil has much in common with the "un-
pardonable sin" by which Hawthorne was haunted — the sin of *using* other
people, of "violating the sanctity of a human heart." Chillingsworth in *The
Scarlet Letter* is essentially this type of sinner, and so is Miriam's model in *The
Marble Faun*. In James, however, the evil characters have none of the Gothic
mystique which is to be found in Hawthorne. Their motives are transparent.

† The significance of Osmond's character has generally been underrated by
the critics of James. For quite apart from his more personal traits (such as his
depravity, which is a purely novelistic element), he is important as a cultural
type in whom the logic of "traditionalism" is developed to its furthest limits.
As a national group the American intellectuals suffer from a sense of inferiority
toward the past, and this residue of "colonial" feeling is also to be detected in
those among them who raise the banner of tradition. It is shown in their one-
sided conformity to the idea of tradition, in their readiness to inflate the mean-

takes hold of Isabel as her husband's rigid system closes in on her. She believes that there can be no release from the bondage into which she had fallen and that only through heroic suffering is its evil to be redeemed. On this tragic note the story ends.

Yet the heiress is not to be turned aside from her quest by such inevitable encounters with the old evils of history. On the lighted stage the bridegroom still awaits his New-World bride.

In few of his full-length novels is James so consummately in control of his method of composition as in *The Wings of the Dove* and *The Golden Bowl*. It is a method all scenic and dramatic, of an "exquisite economy" in the architectonic placing of incidents, which eliminates any "going behind or telling about the figures" save as they themselves accomplish it. Indulgence in mere statement is banned; the motto is: *represent, convert, dramatize*. By means of this compositional economy the story is so organized that it seems to tell itself, excluding all material not directly bearing on the theme. This despite the "complication of innuendo and associative reference," as William James called it, by which the author communicates the vital information needed to understand the action. Complications of this sort so confuse some readers that they see nothing but surplus matter and digression where, in fact, everything is arranged in the most compact order. Nor is the occasional wordiness and vagueness of James's prose germane to our judgment of his novelistic structure. Even the thoughts of his characters are reproduced along exclusive rather than inclusive lines, as in *The Golden Bowl*, where the interior monologues of Maggie and the Prince are in reality a kind of speech which no one happens to overhear, showing none of the rich incoherence, haphazardness, and latitude of Joyce's rendering of the private mind, for example.

The principle of free association is incompatible with the James-

---

ings that may be derived from it. Their tendency is to take literally what their European counterparts are likely to take metaphorically and imaginatively. My idea is that James tried to overcome this bias which he suspected in himself by objectifying it in the portrait of Osmond. To this day, however, the shadow of Gilbert Osmond falls on many a page of American writing whose author — whether critic, learned poet, or academic "humanist" — presents himself, with all the exaggerated zeal and solemnity of a belated convert, as a spokesman of tradition.

ian technique, which is above all a technique of exclusion. One can best describe it, it seems to me, as the fictional equivalent of the poetic modes evolved by modern poets seeking to produce a "pure poetry." In this sense the later James has more in common with a poet like Mallarmé than with novelists like Joyce and Proust, whose tendency is to appropriate more and more material and to assimilate to their medium even such nonfictional forms as the poem and the essay. In Proust the specific experience is made use of to launch all sorts of generalizations, to support, that is, his innumerable analyses — by turn poetic and essayistic — of memory, love, jealousy, the nature of art, etc. In Joyce this impulse to generalization finds other outlets, such as the investing of the specific experience with mythic associations that help us to place it within the pattern of human recurrence and typicality. James tightens where Joyce and Proust loosen the structure of the novel. In their hands the novel takes on encyclopedic dimensions, surrendering its norms and imperialistically extending itself, so to speak, to absorb all literary genres. It might be claimed, in fact, that *the novel as they write it ceases to be itself, having been transformed into a comprehensive work from which none of the resources of literature are excluded.* Not that they abandon the principle of selection; the point is rather that they select material to suit their desire for an unrestricted expansion of the medium, whereas James selects with a view to delimiting the medium and defining its proper course. He confirms, as very few novelists do, Goethe's observation that the artistic effect requires a closed space. It is true that at bottom it is culture and the history of culture, which constitute the inner theme of all three writers, but while Joyce and Proust express it by continually revealing its universality, James expresses it by limiting himself, through an extraordinary effort of aesthetic calculation, to its particularity.

One need not go so far as to say that the formal character of the Jamesian novel is determined by its social character in order to emphasize the close relation between the two. Both manifest the same qualities of particularity and exclusiveness. But why, it might be asked, is Proust's work so different in form, given the fact that he, too, is drawn by the resplendent image of the "great world" and, presumably, is quite as responsive to some of the values attributed to

James? The answer would be that even on this ground the American and the French novelist are more at variance than would seem at first glance.

Proust's picture of society contains elements of lyricism as well as elements of objective analysis. He is a more realistic painter of social manners than James, perhaps for the reason that he permits no ethical issues to intervene between him and the subject, approaching the world *ab initio* with the tacit assumption that ethics are irrelevant to its functions. By comparison James is a traditional moralist whose insight into experience turns on his judgment of conduct. If sometimes, as in *The Golden Bowl*, we are made to feel that he is withholding judgment or judging wrongly, that may be because he is either conforming, or appears to conform, to certain moral conventions of the world's making by which it manages to flatter itself. In Proust such conventions are brought out into the open, but not for purposes of moral judgment. The sole morality of which the protagonist of his novel is conscious grows out of the choice he faces between two contrary ideals. He must decide whether to pursue the art of life or the life of art, and the novel can be said to be an epical autobiography of his effort to come to a decision. But it is not until the end-volume that the world is finally renounced; and through a kind of optical illusion induced by the novel's astonishing unfoldment, we seem to participate in this renunciation of the world at the precise moment when its alternative — i.e., the work of art — actually comes into being, or, more accurately, is at last fully realized. Since in this work the world is overcome only after it has been possessed, the unity of life and art is affirmed in it despite the author's attempt to divorce them by closing with a purely subjective account of the artistic process. No matter what Proust intended this account to mean, taken in its context it affects us as an ironic expression of the artist's triumph over his material, a mocking valediction addressed to that recalcitrant angel — the objective spirit of reality — with whom the artist grappled through the long night of creation and, having gotten the better of him, can now treat with disdain.

But if in Proust art and life are unified by the contradiction between them, in James they are initially combined in his root-idea of experience. His passionate pilgrims, such as the heiress, are driven, despite all vacillations and retractions, by their need to master the world (which is identified with experience and the "real *taste* of life"), and in art they recognize the means by which the world becomes most richly aware of itself. As Americans they have come to it so belatedly that they can ill afford either the spiritual luxury or spiritual desperation of looking beyond it. This is the reason, I think, that except for the early example of *Roderick Hudson* and later of *The Tragic Muse,* the theme of art and artists enters significantly and independently only into some of James's short stories, in which he deals not with his representative figures but with his own case as a professional writer somewhat estranged from society by his devotion to his craft. Though these stories testify to the artistic idealism of their author, they can scarcely be taken as a serious challenge to the authority of the world.

Now at this point it should be evident that James's inability to overcome the world, in the sense that most European writers of like caliber overcome it, is due not to his being too much of it, but, paradoxically enough, to his being too little of it. And for that the explanation must be sought in his origins. For he approaches the world with certain presumptions of piety that clearly derive from the semireligious idealism of his family background and, more generally, from the early traditions and faith of the American community. But in James this idealism and faith undergo a radical change, in that they are converted to secular ends. Thus one might venture the speculation that his worldly-aesthetic idea of an elite is in some way associated, however remotely and unconsciously, with the ancestral-puritan idea of the elect; hence the ceremoniousness and suggestions of ritual in the social display of a novel like *The Golden Bowl.* So with the ancestral ideas of sin and grace. Is it not possible to claim that the famous Jamesian refinement is a trait in which the vision of an ideal state is preserved — the state of grace to be achieved here and now through mundane and aesthetic means? It is the vision by which Milly Theale is transported as she rests in her Venetian garden — the vision of "never going down, of remaining aloft in the divine dustless air, where she could but hear the plash of water against the stone." And through the same process, as I have already had occasion to remark, the fear of sin is translated in James into a revulsion, an exasperated feeling, almost morbid in its sensitiveness, against any conceivable crudity of scene or crudity of conduct.

Yet whatever the sources and implications of the social legend in James, I have no doubt that it enabled him as nothing else could to formulate his creative method and to remain true, even on his lower levels, to the essential mood and sympathy of his genius. There is an essay on Proust by Paul Valéry in which he speaks of the French novelist's capacity "to adapt the potentialities of his inner life" to the aim of expressing "one group of people . . . which calls itself Society," thus converting the picture of an avowedly superficial existence into a profound work. But I have always felt that what Valéry is saying in this essay could more appropriately be said about the later James than about Proust:

> The group which calls itself Society is composed of symbolic figures. Each of its members represents some abstraction. It is necessary that all the powers of this world should somewhere meet together; that *money* should converse with *beauty,* and *politics* become familiar with *elegance;* that *letters* and *birth* grow friendly and serve each other tea . . . Just as a banknote is only a slip of paper, so the member of society is a sort of fiduciary money made of living flesh. This combination is extremely favorable to the designs of a subtle novelist.
> . . . very great art, which is the art of simplified figures and the most pure types; in other words, of essences which permit the symmetrical and almost musical development of the consequences arising from a carefully isolated situation — such art involves the existence of a conventional milieu, where the language is adorned with veils and provided with limits, where *seeming* commands *being* and where *being* is held in a noble restraint which changes all of life into an opportunity to exercise presence of mind. (*A Tribute*)

This is, however, a peculiarly one-sided view of the Proustian scene, as Valéry allows himself to be carried away by the comparison between the old French literature of the Court and *À la recherche du temps perdu.* Proust balances his poetic appreciation of the Guermantes way with a more than sufficient realism in portraying the rages of Charlus, the passions of Saint-Loup, the schemes of Mme. Verdurin, Bloch, Morel, Jupien, etc.; nor is he averse to showing the pathological condition of that "group which calls itself

Society"; he, too, is infected, after all, with the modern taste for excess, for speaking out with inordinate candor. The truth is that it is in James, rather than in Proust, that we often find it difficult to make certain of the real contours of *being* behind the smooth mask of *seeming*. It is *his* language which is "adorned with veils and provided with limits," and it is the conversation of *his* characters which is so allusive that it seems more to spare than to release the sense.

And Valéry continues: "After a new power has gained recognition, no great time passes before its representatives appear at the gatherings of society; and the movement of history is pretty well summarized by the successive admissions of different social types to the salons, hunts, marriages, and funerals of the supreme tribe of a nation." What an apt description of the rise of the heiress — of, say, Milly Theale entering a London drawing room and being greeted by Lord Mark as the first woman of her time, or of Maggie Verver gravely telling the prince to whom she has just become engaged that he is an object of beauty, a *morceau du musée,* though of course she hasn't the least idea of what it would cost her father to acquire him, and that together they shall possess the "world, the beautiful world!"

1943

KOESTLER AND
HOMELESS RADICALISM

I T IS ABOVE ALL the quality of relevance in Arthur Koestler that
makes for the lively interest in him. This quality is not to be
equated with the merely topical or timely. What enters into it,
chiefly, is something far more difficult to capture — a sense of the
present in its essence, a sense of contemporaneity at once compelling
and discriminating. It is precisely for lack of this quality that most
current writing in the tradition of radical journalism is so dull and
depressing, putting our intelligence to sleep with its fatal immersion
in backward problems; and where the problems are politically not
backward, it is usually the approach that makes them so.

Koestler, on the other hand, has taken hold with dramatic force
of a large historical theme. He is at once the poet and ideologue of
the homeless radical, and his unflagging analysis of this significant
latter-day type — of his dilemma and pathos — has a tonic value
compared to which the "positive contributions" featured in our liberal weeklies seem puerile and inane. Nothing is ultimately so enervating as unreal positiveness, whether it takes the form of the ultra-
leftist's faith in the imminence of the ideal revolution or the liberal's

acceptance of the Soviet myth in accordance with all the precepts of "wave of the future" romanticism. Koestler, despite certain bad slips in the past, is one of the very few writers of the Left not intimidated by the demand for easy affirmations. He understands the positive function of precisely those ideas that help, in Kierkegaard's phrase, "to keep the wound of the negative open."

Koestler is, of course, neither a systematic nor an original thinker. What he exemplifies, rather, is the finest type of European journalism, whose chief advantage over the best American brand lies in its capacity to move with ease within a cultural framework (ours is more efficient in the assembly and organization of facts). Thus Koestler's prose, in which the sensibility of politics is combined with that of literature in what might be described as a psycho-political style, is far superior to anything comparable in American journalism, whether of the straight or fictional variety. Admirable, too, is Koestler's capacity to invent new terms and to order his thought in pithy formulations that sum up an entire period or the experience of an entire generation. His verbal sense is not unlike Trotsky's; the writing of both is distinguished by epigrammatic speed and wit. But Koestler is apt to sacrifice precision for the sake of startling effects or romantic contrasts. His language is occasionally too showy for comfort; and an element of the meretricious is to be detected in his all too easy use of dashingly advanced metaphors drawn from the natural sciences and the tantalizing vocabularies of the newer psychology. It might be said that in his books the phrase often goes beyond the content; that is the price he pays for his facile brilliance.

To my mind, Koestler's best work is to be found in *Spanish Testament* and *Scum of the Earth*, which are accounts of personal experience unmarred by the opportunistic turns his imagination takes when endowed with the freedom of the novelist to order his world as he pleases. For as a novelist Koestler has very little real feeling for existence as texture and pattern or for his characters as human beings over and above their assigned roles and settings. The truth is that these characters are efficient mouthpieces rather than people on their own account. Koestler is able to create an air of reality but scarcely the conviction of it, and none of his novels has that fictional density and integral control of experience by which we know the true artist in the narrative medium. To say, however, that Koestler is not a novelist to the manner born means less in his case than in the case of almost any other popular writer of fiction. Consider a writer like John Steinbeck, for instance. If one says of a novel by Steinbeck that it is without appreciable literary merit one is actually dismissing it *in toto*, for it certainly offers us nothing else by way of intelligence or relevant meaning. Most of our practicing novelists are aware of the age only at a very low level, and their patterns of meaning are tissues of banalities because their power of consciousness is only slightly above that of the mass that reads them. If Koestler, on the other hand, is mainly a novelist of the *Zeitgeist*, he is at least responsive to its virulence and mindful of its mystifications.

Thus Koestler's *Darkness at Noon* is the best study so far written of the mystifications let loose upon the world by the Moscow exhibition-trials. The dialectic of this novel, a dialectic that reveals the psychology of capitulation by which the old Bolshevik leadership was laid low, has a force and tension seldom equaled in the literature of the Russian Revolution. In Koestler's next novel, *Arrival and Departure*, the scene shifts from Russia to the West, and in this work, too, the author takes hold with beautiful candor of the world-historical theme of the breakdown of the revolutionary cause as reflected in the disillusionment and frustration of its intellectual adherents. Thus the hero is the intellectual disarmed by the loss of his faith, the crusader in search of a new cross. Both the panic and promise of our age are concentrated in the several great political faiths that dominate it; and this can only mean that the political-minded individual who is so unfortunate as to have been deprived of his faith is sure to find himself in the predicament of having virtually lost his historical identity.

Such exactly is the situation of Peter Slavek, the young fugitive from a Nazi-occupied country in Central Europe, when he turns up in the capital of "Neutralia," the land without blackout. Peter is a veteran of the Communist movement who in prison had stood up heroically to beatings and torture. Yet now he has renounced the movement, having come to realize that it is but a tool of "utopia betrayed," and that despite its apparent readiness to furnish sound reasons for its vertiginous changes of front the idea behind it is dead. Peter tries to enlist in the British army, but at this initial stage his action is lacking in conviction, being more or less mechanically determined by his anti-fascist past. There can be no escape for Peter from his ordeal. He must pay the penalty of his lost illusions by going through the supremely painful experience of locating himself anew in a world now strangely drained of value. To survive he must discover a way of life other than that of the socialist militant — a way of life that will enable him to redefine his true identity.

Of course, this young man is fated to play the hero to the end, for when last seen he is pulling the rip cord of a parachute and hurtling through space on a secret mission to enemy country. The main substance of the novel, however, is to be found in his recital of his experiences to Dr. Sonia Bolgar, a female likened to a "carnivorous flower" who is at the same time a specialist in the modern branches of psychology and "dream-surgery." Part of Peter's recital is an account of the Nazi terror which is a truly inspired piece of writing. Especially fine is the chapter entitled "Mixed Transports." The rest consists of psychological disputation and analysis of the motives of the middle-class intellectual as a revolutionary type. This is the element in the novel for which the author has been sharply criticized, a criticism that is correct, of course, insofar as Koestler appears to call into question the social value of revolutionary action by attributing to it a neurotic origin. Such procedure is an obvious example of the genetic fallacy. It has likewise been said that Koestler traduces the psychoanalytic profession by depicting Sonia, its representative in the story, as an image of polymorphous sexuality and the surrender to purely instinctual life. Through this maneuver psychoanalysis is censured for its unflattering picture of human nature much in the same way that right-wing polemicists have at times gratuitously censured Marxism for the evils of the class struggle. It seems to me, however, that Koestler's attitude to Freudian ideas is not in the least hostile; and I would explain his fancy picture of Sonia by his tendency to sensationalize his material even at the cost of obscuring his meaning. This novelist is enough of a journalist not to be able to resist a scoop. Also, one should keep in mind that Sonia is cast in the role of a proponent of the nonpolitical life. Now a writer as thoroughly political as Koestler cannot but identify the nonpolitical life with a lower form of existence, that is to say, with the subhistorical. It is in this sense, I think, that we should interpret his dislike of Sonia, voiced by one of the characters who speaks of her as an "opu-

9

lent Amazon" maintaining an "odious intimacy with the forbidden regions where archaic monsters dwelt . . ."

But Koestler's treatment of the Freudian motive is not nearly so dubious as his resolution of the political problem in this novel. The problem facing his hero is that of reconciling his radical convictions with his enlistment in the British army, in the service of values gone musty, "whose force is the power of inertia." The answer given by Koestler is that even if in the dynamics of history the bourgeois democracies act not as the engine but the brake, there is real need for a brake when the engine begins running wild. This is good enough, perhaps, as a reason for a policy of strategic expediency in supporting a democratic war against totalitarianism in order to obtain a second chance for the socialist cause. There is so little pathos, however, in such calculations that Koestler makes every effort to lay hold of something more profound. Hence we are told that, furthermore, "reasons do not matter," and that "he who accepts in spite of his objections . . . he will be secure." The latter argument is wholly unrelated to the first argument, and by bringing it forward the way he does Koestler appears to capitulate to the irrational drives of present-day politics. Yet even this turns out to be not sufficiently "profound," for later on it is asserted that the age of science is over and that salvation will come through a "new god" who is about to be born. Here we are finally consoled with the rhetoric of the new religiosity, whose ambition it is to replace the newly lost illusions with illusions lost long ago. If a new god is about to be born and as yet we know, as Koestler admits, neither his message nor his cult, then why not let the world go hang while we wait for this unknown god to reveal himself?

It is worth noting, however, that in *The Yogi and the Commissar*, a volume of essays brought out shortly after the appearance of *Arrival and Departure*, Koestler seems to have overcome his mystical yearnings, for here he speaks of his refusal to join the "exotic hermitage fit for Yogi exercises." The title piece of this volume strikes me as of small consequence insofar as its key terms, Yogi and Commissar, merely describe the polarization of belief between the concepts of change from without and change from within; and in another sense these terms come to little more than a rather sensational restatement of the old *divertissement* of the psychologists that divides all of us into introverts and extroverts. But if not meaningful in the way of uncovering a permanent human contradiction, these terms do have meaning in their application to present-day realities. For it is the vileness of what Koestler calls "Commissar-ethics," whether of the fascist or Stalinist variety, that has created the historical situation determining the movement of so many intellectuals to the ultraviolet pole of the Yogi. The Yogis in our midst are continually gaining prestige and new recruits, with sorry results, however, so far as creative ideas are concerned. Auden, for instance, neglecting his splendid gifts as satirist and observer of the external world, has gone to school to Kierkegaard and Barth only to emerge as an exponent of stylized anxiety. Marx saw in the spirit of spiritless conditions the social essence of religion, and it may well be said that except for this sentiment of wretchedness the present appeal of supernaturalism has quite literally no other objective content.

What is of considerable value in Koestler's essay on the intelligentsia is the contrast drawn between the historical roles of the Russian and Western intellectuals. In the intellectuals Koestler sees a social group driven by "an aspiration to independent thought" — a group now declining in all countries, debilitated by its political experiences and gradually penned in by the growing power of the State. — "Thus the intelligentsia, once the vanguard of the ascending bourgeoisie, becomes the lumpenbourgeoisie in the age of its decay." This last seems particularly applicable to America. Not so long ago a good many of our intellectuals were economically no better off than lumpenproletarians, a position which allowed them to assume attitudes of cultural intransigence toward society, whereas of late, what with the prosperity of the last war and the proliferation of jobs, both in the government and in educational institutions, the once impoverished intellectuals have been converted almost to a man into lumpenbourgeois. And lumpenbourgeois, who combine an inherent sense of insecurity with sufficient status and revenue to make them pine for more, are notoriously feeble in their aspirations to independent thought.

When it comes, however, to Koestler's imputation of neuroticism to the intelligentsia as a group, one cannot agree with him quite so easily. In his view neuroticism is the "professional disease" of the intellectuals because of the pathological pattern produced by the hostile pressure of society. Koestler may be right, but I cannot say that I found his argument convincing. Precise etiological data are missing; without a controlled Freudian analysis the Freudian conclusions hang in the air; and in general the kind of observation that Koestler brings to bear is literary rather than scientific. It seems to me that he assimilates the intellectuals far too readily to the artist-types among them, who are after all but a minority within a minority. The personality structure of the artist is quite different from that of most members of the intelligentsia, whose connection is with the more technical and less estranged forms of culture and who are not noted in any special way for the vulnerability, complication or perversity of their subjective life.

Equally schematic, to my mind, are the arguments advanced in some of Koestler's essays that deal directly with literature. Thus in "The Novelist's Temptations" he makes the point that to function properly the novelist must possess "an all-embracing knowledge of the essential currents and facts (including statistics), of the ideas and theories (including the natural sciences) of his time." The saving proviso is that "this knowledge is not for actual use . . . It is for use by implication." Even with this proviso, however, this appears to be an excessively rationalistic view of the literary process. The movements of the imagination are tortuous and obscure; great works of fiction have often been created by compulsive and extremely one-sided talents (consider the cases of Gogol or Kafka). The element of knowledge in imaginative literature is easily overestimated. What is important in writing as in art generally is the quality of relevance —a quality perhaps synonymous with that "sense of modernity" which Baudelaire stressed so frequently and for which he praised artists like Courbet and Manet. This modernity can take various and contradictory forms, some of them unrecognizable to those above all concerned with being up to date. Kafka, for instance, is deeply modern not because the latest acquisitions of the social and natural sciences are embodied in his work but because it is reverberant with the feelings of loss and unreality characteristic of modern man. Being *au courant* with the latest facts and theories is desirable in itself and can certainly do the novelist a lot of good. There is no need, however, to elevate such useful knowledge to a prerequisite of the creative life.

1946

TOLSTOY: THE GREEN TWIG AND
THE BLACK TRUNK

The critic's euphoria in the Tolstoyan weather. Tolstoy and literature. The green twig and the black trunk. The art of Tolstoy is of such irresistible simplicity and truth, is at once so intense and so transparent in all of its effects, that the need is seldom felt to analyze the means by which it becomes what it is, that is to say, its method or sum of techniques. In the bracing Tolstoyan air, the critic, however addicted to analysis, cannot help doubting his own task, sensing that there is something presumptuous and even unnatural, which requires an almost artificial deliberateness of intention, in the attempt to dissect an art so wonderfully integrated that, coming under its sway, we grasp it as a whole long before we are able to summon sufficient consciousness to examine the arrangement and interaction of its component parts.

Tolstoy is the exact opposite of those writers, typical of the modern age, whose works are to be understood only in terms of their creative strategies and design. The most self-observant of men,

Written as an introduction to *The Great Short Novels of Tolstoy*, published in the Permanent Library series of The Dial Press in 1946.

whose books are scarcely conceivable apart from the ceaseless introspection of which they are the embodiment, Tolstoy was the least
self-conscious in his use of the literary medium. That is chiefly because in him the cleavage between art and life is of a minimal nature.
In a Tolstoyan novel it is never the division but always the unity of
art and life which makes for illumination. This novel, bristling with
significant choices and crucial acts, teeming with dramatic motives,
is not articulated through a plot as we commonly know it in fiction;
one might say that in a sense there are no plots in Tolstoy but simply
the unquestioned and unalterable process of life itself; such is the
astonishing immediacy with which he possesses his characters that
he can dispense with manipulative techniques, as he dispenses with
the belletristic devices of exaggeration, distortion, and dissimulation.
The fable, that specifically literary contrivance, or anything else
which is merely invented or made up to suit the occasion, is very
rarely found in his work. Nor is style an element of composition of
which he is especially aware; he has no interest in language as such;
he is the enemy of rhetoric and every kind of artifice and virtuosity.
The conception of writing as of something calculated and constructed — a conception, first formulated explicitly in startlingly
modern terms by Edgar Allan Poe, upon which literary culture has
become more and more dependent — is entirely foreign to Tolstoy.

All that is of a piece, of course, with his unique attitude toward
literature, that is, for a writer of modern times. For Tolstoy continually dissociated himself from literature whether considered mat-
ter-of-factly, as a profession like any other, or ideally as an autonomous way of life, a complete fate in the sense in which the French
writers of Flaubert's generation conceived of it. In his youth a soldier who saw war at first hand, the proprietor and manager of Yasnaya Polyana, a husband and father not as other men are husbands
and fathers but in what might be described as programmatic and
even militant fashion, and subsequently a religious philosopher and
the head of a sect, he was a writer through all the years — a writer,
but never a *littérateur,* the very idea repelled him. The *littérateur*
performs a function imposed by the social division of labor, and inevitably he pays the price of his specialization by accepting and even
applauding his own one-sidedness and conceit, his noncommitted
state as witness and observer, and the necessity under which he

labors of preying upon life for the themes that it yields. It is with pride that Tolstoy exempted Lermontov and himself from the class of "men of letters" while commiserating with Turgenev and Goncharov for being so much of it; and in his *Reminiscences of Tolstoy* Gorky remarks that he spoke of literature but rarely and little, "as if it were something alien to him."

To account for that attitude by tracing it back to Tolstoy's aristocratic status, as if he disdained to identify himself with a plebian profession, is to take much too simple a view of his personality. The point is, rather, that from the very first Tolstoy instinctively recognized the essential insufficiency and makeshift character of the narrowly aesthetic outlook, of the purely artistic appropriation of the world. His personality was built on too broad a frame to fit into an aesthetic mold, and he denied that art was anything more than the ornament and charm of life. He came of age at a time when the social group to which he belonged had not yet been thoroughly exposed to the ravages of the division of labor, when men of his stamp could still resist the dubious consolations it brings in its train. Endowed with enormous energies, possessed of boundless egotism and of an equally boundless power of conscience, he was capable, in Leo Shestov's phrase, of destroying and creating worlds, and before he was quite twenty-seven years old he had the audacity to declare his ambition, writing it all solemnly down in his diary, of becoming the founder of "a new religion corresponding with the present state of mankind; the religion of Christ but purged of dogmas and mysticism — a practical religion, not promising future bliss but giving bliss on earth." No wonder, then, that while approaching the task of mastering the literary medium with the utmost seriousness, and prizing that mastery as a beautiful accomplishment, he could not but dismiss the pieties of art as trivial compared with the question he faced from the very beginning, the question he so heroically sought to answer even in his most elemental creations, in which he seems to us to move through the natural world with splendid and miraculous ease, more fully at home there than any other literary artist. Yet even in those creations the very same question appears now in a manifest and now in a latent fashion, always the same question: How to live, what to do?

In 1880, when Turgenev visited Yasnaya Polyana after a long

estrangement, he wrote a letter bewailing Tolstoy's apparent deser-
tion of art. "I, for instance, am considered an artist," he said, "but
what am I compared with him? In contemporary European literature he has no equal . . . But what is one to do with him. He has
plunged headlong into another sphere: he has surrounded himself
with Bibles and Gospels in all languages, and has written a whole
heap of papers. He has a trunk full of these mystical ethics and of
various pseudo-interpretations. He read me some of it, which I
simply do not understand . . . I told him, 'That is not the real thing';
but he replied: 'It is just the real thing' . . . Very probably he will
give nothing more to literature, or if he reappears it will be with
that trunk." Turgenev was wrong. Tolstoy gave a great deal more
to literature, and it is out of that same trunk, so offensive in the eyes
of the accomplished man of letters, that he brought forth such masterpieces as *The Death of Ivan Ilyich* and *Master and Man*, plays
like *The Power of Darkness*, also many popular tales which, stripped
of all ornament, have an essential force and grace of their own, and
together with much that is abstract and overrationalized, not a few
expository works, like *What Then Must We Do?*, which belong with
the most powerful revolutionary writings of the modern age. For it
is not for nothing that Tolstoy was always rummaging in that black
trunk. At the bottom of it, underneath a heap of old papers, there
lay a little mana-object, a little green twig which he carried with
him through the years, a twig of which he was told at the age of five
by his brother Nicholas — that it was buried by the road at the edge
of a certain ravine and that on it was inscribed the secret by means
of which "all men would cease suffering misfortunes, leave off quar-
reling and being angry, and become continuously happy." The legend of the green twig was part of a game played by the Tolstoy children, called the Ant-Brothers, which consisted of crawling under
chairs screened off by shawls and cuddling together in the dark.
Tolstoy asked to be buried on the very spot at the edge of the ravine
at Yasnaya Polyana which he loved because of its association with
the imaginary green twig and the ideal of human brotherhood. And
when he was an old man he wrote that "the idea of ant-brothers lovingly clinging to one another, though not under two arm-chairs cur-
tained by shawls but of all mankind under the wide dome of heaven,
has remained unaltered in me. As I then believed that there existed

a little green twig whereon was written the message which would destroy all evil in men and give them universal welfare, so I now believe that such truth exists and will be revealed to men and will give them all it promises." It is clear that the change in Tolstoy by which Turgenev was so appalled was entirely natural, was presupposed by all the conditions of his development and of his creative consciousness. In the total Tolstoyan perspective the black trunk of his old age represents exactly the same thing as the green twig of his childhood.

Even the crude heresies he expounded in *What Is Art?* lose much of their offensiveness in that perspective. In itself when examined without reference to the author's compelling grasp of the central and most fearful problems of human existence, the argument of that book strikes us as a willful inflation of the idea of moral utility at the expense of the values of the imagination. But actually the fault of the argument is not that it is wholly implausible — as a matter of fact, it is of long and reputable lineage in the history of culture — as that it is advanced recklessly and with a logic at once narrow and excessive; the Tolstoyan insight is here vitiated in the same way as the insight into sexual relations is vitiated in *The Kreutzer Sonata*. Still, both works, the onslaught on modern love and marriage as well as the onslaught on the fetishism of art to which the modern sensibility has succumbed, are significantly expressive of Tolstoy's spiritual crisis — a crisis badly understood by many people, who take it as a phenomenon disruptive of his creative power despite the fact that, in the last analysis, it is impossible to speak of two Tolstoys, the creative and the noncreative, for there is no real discontinuity in his career. Though there is a contradiction between the artist and the moralist in him, his personality retains its basic unity, transcending all contradictions. Boris Eichenbaum, one of the very best of Tolstoy's Russian critics, has observed that the spiritual crisis did not operate to disrupt his art because it was a crisis internally not externally determined, the prerequisite of a new act of cognition through which he sought to rearm his genius and to ascertain the possibility of new creative beginnings. Thus *My Confession*, with which Tolstoy's later period opens and which appeared immediately after *Anna Karenina*, is unmistakably a work of the imagination and at the same time a mighty feat of consciousness.

Six years after writing *What Is Art?* Tolstoy finished *Hadji Murad* (1904), one of the finest *nouvelles* in the Russian language and a model of narrative skill and objective artistry. Is not the song of the nightingales, that song of life and death which bursts into ecstasy at dawn on the day when Hadji Murad attempts to regain his freedom, the very same song which rises in that marvelous sensual scene in *Family Happiness*, a scene bathed in sunlight, when Masha, surprising Sergey Mikhaylych in the cherry orchard, enjoys for the first time the full savor of her youthful love? *Hadji Murad* was written not less than forty-five years after *Family Happiness*. It can be said of Tolstoy the man that he was a rationalist who was usually at odds with human beings; nor did he especially love them. As a novelist, however, he was not merely exceptionally aware of them but was capable of investing them with a heroic sympathy that broke the barriers to their inner being. In the portrait of Hadji Murad we at once sense the author's love of the warrior chieftain who is fated, by his tribal code and indeed the whole weight of the past, to be crushed like a lone thistle flower in a plowed field. The twin images that recur through the story — that of the nightingales' song of love and death and that of the crimson thistle plant tenaciously clinging to its bit of soil — serve both as a musical motif drawing together the narrative parts and as a symbol, wonderful in its aptness and simplicity, of the inviolable rhythm of nature and human destiny. Nature and human destiny! — that their rhythm is eternally one in the very essence of Tolstoy's vision of life. His religious conversion forced him to modify his central idea or intuition, and it is wholly appropriate that in *Hadji Murad*, a late work written many years after his renunciation of the objective art of his great novels, he should have reverted to the vision of his major creative period. To himself Tolstoy might have explained away the lapse by claiming that this work of his old age conformed to his notion of "good universal art," which he of course placed in a category below that of religious art; still it is worth noting that he refrained from publishing *Hadji Murad* and that it appeared in print only after his death.

And in *The Devil* — a moral tale, the product, like *The Kreutzer Sonata*, of Tolstoy's most sectarian period and extremest assertion of dogmatic asceticism — what we remember best is not Eugene Irtenev's torments of conscience, his efforts to subdue his passion, but precisely the description of his carnal meetings in the sun-drenched woods with Stephanida, the fresh and strong peasant girl with full breasts and bright black eyes. The truth is that in the struggle between the old moralist and the old magician in Tolstoy both gave as good as they got.

The rationalist and anti-Romantic in Tolstoy. Sources in the eighteenth century. Divergence from the intelligentsia. Creative method. Tolstoy has been described as the least neurotic of all the great Russians, and by the same token he can be said to be more committed than any of them to the rational understanding and ordering of life and to the throwing off of romantic illusions. Unlike Dostoevsky, he owes nothing either to the so-called natural school of Gogol or to the Romantic movement in Western literature. The school of Gogol is a school of morbidity, whereas Tolstoy is above all an artist of the normal — the normal, however, so intensified that it acquires a poetical truth and an emotional fullness which we are astounded to discover in the ordinary situations of life. Analysis is always at the center of the Tolstoyan creation. It is the sort of analysis, however, which has little in common with the analytical modes of such novelists as Dostoevsky and Proust, for example, both characteristically modern though in entirely different ways. While in their work analysis is precipitated mainly by deviations from the norm, from the broad standard of human conduct, in Tolstoy the analysis remains in line with that standard, is in fact inconceivable apart from it. Dostoevsky's "underground" man, who is a bundle of plebeian resentments, is unimaginable in a Tolstoyan novel. Even in Tolstoy's treatment of death there is nothing actually morbid — certainly not in the descripiton of the death of Prince Andrey in *War and Peace* and of Nikolay Levin in *Anna Karenina.* As for *The Death of Ivan Ilyich,* that story would be utterly pointless if we were to see Ivan Ilyich as a special type and what happened to him as anything out of the ordinary. Ivan Ilyich is Everyman, and the state of absolute solitude into which he falls as his life ebbs away is the existential norm, the inescapable realization of mortality. Nothing could be more mistaken than the idea that Tolstoy's concern with death is an abnormal trait. On the contrary, if anything it is a supernormal trait, for the intensity of his concern with death is proportionate to the intensity of his concern with life. Of Tolstoy it can be said that he truly lived his life, and for that very reason he was so tormented by the thought of dying. It was a literal thought, physical through and through, a vital manifestation of the simplicity with which he grasped man's life in the world. This simplicity is of a metaphysical nature, and in it, as one Russian critic has remarked, you find the essence of Tolstoy's world-view, the energizing and generalizing formula that served him as the means unifying the diverse motives of his intellectual and literary experience. It is due to this metaphysical simplicity that he was unable to come to terms with any system of dogmatic theology and that in the end, despite all his efforts to retain it, he was compelled to exclude even the idea of God from his own system of rationalized religion. Thus all notions of immortality seemed absurd to Tolstoy, and his scheme of salvation was entirely calculated to make men happy here and now. It is reported of Thoreau that when he lay dying his answer to all talk of the hereafter was "one world at a time." That is the sort of answer with which Tolstoy's mentality is wholly in accord.

The way in which his rationalism enters his art is shown in his analysis of character, an analysis which leaves nothing undefined, nothing unexplained. That systematization of ambiguity which marks the modern novel is organically alien to Tolstoy. Given the framework in which his characters move we are told everything that we need to know or want to know about them. The tangled intimate life, the underside of their consciousness, their author is not concerned with: he sets them up in the known world and sees them through their predicaments, however irksome and baffling, without ever depriving them of the rationality which supports their existence. For just as in Tolstoy's religiosity there is no element of mysticism, so in his creative art there is no element of mystery.

Unlike most of his contemporaries, Tolstoy did not pass through the school of Romanticism, and perhaps that is the reason he never hesitated to strike out the dark areas in the place in which he outlined his leading figures. He has few links with the literary culture evolved in Russia after 1820; the fact is that he has more in common with his literary grandfathers than with his literary fathers. Insofar as he has any literary affiliations at all they go back to the eighteenth century, to Rousseau, to Sterne, to the French classical writers, and in Russia to the period of Karamzin, Zhukovsky, Novikov, and Radichev. He has their robustness and skepticism. His quarrels with Turgenev, his inability to get on with the liberal and radical writers grouped around the *Contemporary*, a Petersburg periodical edited by the poet Nekrasov in which Tolstoy's first stories were published, are explained not so much by personal factors, such as his intractability of temper, as by the extreme differences between the conditions of his development and those of the Russian intelligentsia, whose rise coincides with the appearance of the plebeian on the literary scene. Tolstoy's family background was archaistic, not in the sense of provincial backwardness, but in the sense of the deliberate and even stylized attempt made by his family — more particularly his father — to preserve at Yasnaya Polyana the patriarchal traditions of the Russian nobility of the eighteenth century. It was a conscious and militant archaism directed against the "new" civilization of Petersburg, with its state-bureaucracy and merchant princes. The young Tolstoy was scornful of the "theories" and "convictions" held by the writers he met in Petersburg in the 1850s; instead of putting his trust in "theories" and "convictions" he relied on those Franklinesque rules and precepts of conduct with which he filled his diaries — rules and precepts he deduced from his idea of unalterable "moral instincts." In Nekrasov's circle he was regarded as a "wild man," a "troglodyte"; and in the early 1860s, when he set out on his second European tour, Nekrasov and his friends hoped that he would return in a mood of agreement with their notions of education and historical progress. Nothing came of it, of course, for he returned armed with more of those "simplifications" that cut under their assumptions. But if the Westernizers found no comfort in Tolstoy, neither did the Slavophils. The latters' ideology, with its forced and artificial doctrine of superiority to the West, was also aligned with plebeian social tasks; at bottom it represented the discomfiture of a small and weak plebeian class in a semifeudal society, a discomfiture idealized through national messianism. It was an obscurantist ideology incompatible with Tolstoy's belief in self-improvement and in the possibility of human perfection. Moreover, in Tolstoy's approach to Western culture there was no distress, no anger, no hostility. He was never put off by it, for he considered European culture to be a natural sphere the products of which he could appropriate at will, and in any order he pleased, without in the least committing himself to its inner logic. He felt no more committed by his use of Western ideas than the French-speaking gentry in *War and Peace* feel obligated to import the social institutions of France along with its language. Thus Tolstoy was able to sort out Western tendencies to suit himself, as in *War and Peace*, where he is to some extent indebted for his conception of Napoleon to certain French publicists of the 1850s and sixties, who in their endeavor to deflate the pretensions of Napoleon III went so far in their polemics as also to blot out the image of his illustrious ancestor. Again, in that novel he is partly indebted for his so-called organic idea of war to Proudhon's book *La Guerre et la Paix*, which came out in a Russian translation in 1864. (Tolstoy had met Proudhon in Brussels in March 1861.) And the arbitrary way in which he helped himself to the ideas of Western thinkers is shown by the fact that he entirely ignored Proudhon's enthusiastic affirmation of Napoleon's historical role. The West was the realm of the city, a realm so strange to Tolstoy that he could regard it as neutral territory. The city was essentially unreal to him; he believed in the existence solely of the landowners and of the peasants. The contrast between Dostoevsky and Tolstoy, which Merezhkovsky and after him Thomas Mann have presented in terms of the abstract typology of the "man of spirit" as against the "man of nature," is more relevantly analyzed in terms of the contradiction between city and country, between the alienated intellectual proletariat of the city and the unalienated patriciate-peasantry of the country.

Much has been written concerning the influence of Rousseau on Tolstoy, but here again it is necessary to keep in mind that in Western literature we perceive the Rousseauist ideas through the colored screen of Romanticism while in Tolstoy Rousseau survives through his rationalism no less than through his sensibility. In point of fact, the Rousseauist cult of nature is operative in Tolstoy in a manner that leads toward realism, as is seen in his Caucasian tales, for instance. If these tales now seem romantic to us, it is largely because of the picturesque material of which they are composed. A narrative like *The Cossacks* is actually turned in a tendencious way against the tradition of "Caucasian romanticism" in Russian literature — the tradition of Pushkin, Lermontov, and Marlinsky. Olenin, the protagonist of *The Cossacks,* is so little of a Romantic hero that he is incapable of dominating even his own story; the impression of his personality is dissipated as the attention shifts to the Cossack lad Lukashka, to Daddy Eroshka, and to the girl Marianka. Think what Chateaubriand would have made of a heroine like Marianka. In Tolstoy, however, she is portrayed in an authentically natural style, with all the calm strength, unawareness of subjective values, and indifference of a primitive human being. Though she is a "child of nature" and therefore an object of poetical associations, she is seen much too soberly to arouse those high-flown sentiments which "nature" inspires in Romantic poets like Novalis or even the Goethe of *Werther.* Where the Romantics convert nature into a solace for the trials of civilization, into a theater of lyrical idleness and noble pleasures, Tolstoy identifies nature with work, independence, self-possession.

Compared with Pierre, Prince Andrey, or Levin, Olenin is a weak hero, but he is important in that in his reflections he sums up everything which went into the making of the early Tolstoy and which was in later years given a religious twist and offered as a doctrine of world-salvation. The primacy which the issue of happiness assumes in Olenin's thoughts is the key to his Tolstoyan nature. "Happiness is this," he said to himself, "happiness lies in living for others. That is evident. The desire for happiness is innate in every man; therefore it is legitimate. When trying to satisfy it selfishly — that is, by seeking for oneself riches, fame, comforts, or love — it may happen that circumstances arise which make it impossible to satisfy these desires. It follows that it is these desires which are illegitimate, but not the need for happiness. But what desires can always be satisfied despite external circumstances? What are they? Love, self-sacrifice." In these few sentences we get the quintessence of the Tolstoyan mentality: the belief that ultimate truth can be arrived at through common-sense reasoning, the utilitarian justification of the values of love and self-sacrifice and their release from all otherworldly sanctions, the striving for the simplification of existence which takes the form of a return to a life closer to nature — a return, however, involving a self-consciousness and a constant recourse to reason that augurs ill for the success of any such experiment.

Tolstoy's art is so frequently spoken of as "organic" that one is likely to overlook the rationalistic structure on which it is based. This structure consists of successive layers of concrete details, physical and psychological, driven into place and held together by a generalization or dogma. Thus in *The Cossacks* the generalization is the idea of the return to nature; in *Two Hussars* it is the superiority of the older Turbin to the younger, that is to say, of the more naive times of the past to the "modern" period. (The original title of the story was *Father and Son.*) The binding dogma in *Family Happiness* is the instability and deceptiveness of love as compared with a sound family life and the rearing of children in insuring the happiness of a married couple. Yet the didacticism of such ideas seldom interferes with our enjoyment of the Tolstoyan fiction. For the wonderful thing about it is its tissue of detail, the tenacious way in which it holds together, as if it were a glutinous substance, and its incomparable rightness and truthfulness.

Parallelism of construction is another leading characteristic of the Tolstoyan method. In *War and Peace*, in the chronicle of the lives of the Bolkonsky and Rostov families, this parallelism is not devised dramatically, as a deliberate contrast, but in other narratives it is driven toward a stark comparison, as between Anna and Vronsky on the one hand and Kitty and Levin on the other in *Anna Karenina*, or between two generations in *Two Hussars*, or between Lukashka and Olenin in *The Cossacks*. One writer on Tolstoy put it very well when he said that in the Tolstoyan novel all ideas and phenomena exist in pairs. Comparison is inherent in his method.

His early *nouvelles* can certainly be read and appreciated without reference to their historical context, to the ideological differences between him and his contemporaries which set him off to confound them with more proofs of his disdain for their "progressive" opinions. Still, the origin of *Family Happiness* in the quarrels of the period is worth recalling. At that time (in the 1850s) public opinion was much exercised over the question of free love and the emancipation of women; George Sand was a novelist widely read in intellectual circles, and of course most advanced people agreed with George Sand's libertarian solution of the question. Not so Tolstoy, who opposed all such tendencies, for he regarded marriage and family life as the foundations of society. Thus *Family Happiness*, with its denigration of love and of equal rights for women, was

conceived, quite apart from its personal genesis in Tolstoy's affair
with Valerya Arsenev, as a polemical rejoinder to George Sand, then
adored by virtually all the Petersburg writers, including Dostoevsky.

The faith in family life is integral of Tolstoy. It has the deepest
psychological roots in his private history, and socially it exemplifies
his championship of patriarchal relations. It is a necessary part of
his archaistic outlook, which in later life was transformed into a
special kind of radicalism, genuinely revolutionary in some of its
aspects and thoroughly archaistic in others. *War and Peace* is as
much a chronicle of certain families as a historical novel. The historical sense is not really native to Tolstoy. His interest in the period
of 1812 is peculiarly his own, derived from his interest in the story
of his own family. He began work on *Anna Karenina* after failing
in the attempt to write another historical novel, a sequel to *War and
Peace*. And *Anna Karenina* is of course the novel in which his inordinate concern with marriage and family life receives its fullest
expression.

*The existential center of the Tolstoyan art. Tolstoy as the last of the
unalienated artists.* So much has been made here of the rationalism
of Tolstoy that it becomes necessary to explain how his art is saved
from the ill effects of it. Art and reason are not naturally congruous
with one another, and many a work of the imagination has miscar-
ried because of an excess of logic. "There may be a system of logic;
a system of being there can never be," said Kierkegaard. And art is
above all a recreation of individual being; the system-maker must
perforce abstract from the real world while the artist, if he is true to
his medium, recoils from the process of abstraction because it is precisely the irreducible quality of life, its multiple divulgements in all
their uniqueness and singularity, which provoke his imagination.

Now there is only one novel of Tolstoy's that might be described
as a casualty of his rationalism, and that is *Resurrection*. The greater
part of his fiction is existentially centered in a concrete inwardness
and subjectivity by which it gains its quality of genius. In this sense
it becomes possible to say that Tolstoy is much more a novelist of
life and death than he is of good and evil — good and evil are not
categories of existence but of moral analysis. And the binding
dogmas or ideas of Tolstoy's fiction are not in contradiction with its

existential sense; on the contrary, their interaction is a triumph of creative tact and proof of the essential wholeness of Tolstoy's nature. The Tolstoyan characters grasp their lives through their total personalities, not merely through their intellects. Their experience is full of moments of shock, of radical choice and decision, when they confront themselves in the terrible and inevitable aloneness of their being. To mention but one of innumerable instances of such spiritual confrontation, there is the moment in *Anna Karenina* when Anna's husband begins to suspect her relation to Vronsky. That is the moment when the accepted and taken-for-granted falls to pieces, when the carefully built-up credibility of the world is torn apart by a revelation of its underlying irrationality. For according to Alexey Alexandrovitch's ideas one ought to have confidence in one's wife because jealousy was insulting to oneself as well as to her. He had never really asked himself why his wife deserved such confidence and why he believed that she would always love him. But now, though he still felt that jealousy was a bad and shameful state, "he also felt that he was standing face to face with something illogical and irrational, and did not know what was to be done. Alexey Alexandrovitch was standing face to face with life, with the possibility of his wife's loving someone other than himself, and this seemed to him very irrational and incomprehensible because it was life itself. All his life Alexey Alexandrovitch had lived and worked in official spheres, having to do with the reflection of life. And every time he stumbled against life itself he had shrunk away from it. Now he experienced a feeling akin to that of a man who, while calmly crossing a precipice by a bridge, should suddenly discover that the bridge is broken, and that there is a chasm below. That chasm was life itself, the bridge that artificial life in which Alexey Alexandrovitch had lived. For the first time the question presented itself to him of the possibility of his wife's loving someone else, and he was horrified at it."

It is exactly this "standing face to face with life," and the realization that there are things in it that are irreducible and incomprehensible, which drew Tolstoy toward the theme of death. Again and again he returned to this theme, out of a fear of death which is really the highest form of courage. Most people put death out of their minds because they cannot bear to think of it. Gorky reports that Tolstoy once said to him that "if a man has learned to think, no matter what he may think about, he is always thinking of his own death. All philosophers were like that. And what truths can there be, if there is death?" That is a statement of despair and nihilism the paradox of which is that it springs from the depths of Tolstoy's existential feeling of life; and this is because the despair and nihilism spring not from the renunciation but from the affirmation of life; Tolstoy never gave up the search for an all-embracing truth, for a rational justification of man's existence on the earth.

The fact is that Tolstoy was at bottom so sure in his mastery of life and so firm in his inner feeling of security that he could afford to deal intimately with death. Consider the difference in this respect between him and Franz Kafka, another novelist of the existential mode. In Kafka the theme of death is absent, not because of strength but rather because of neurotic weakness. He was ridden by a conviction, as he himself defined it, of "complete helplessness," and baffled by the seeming impossibility of solving even the most elementary problems of living, he could not look beyond life into the face of death. He wrote: "Without ancestors, without marriage, without progeny, with an unbridled desire for ancestors, marriage, and progeny. All stretch out their hands towards me: ancestors, marriage, and progeny, but from a point far too remote from me." That is the complaint of an utterly alienated man, without a past and without a future. Tolstoy, on the other hand, was attached with the strongest bonds to the patrician-peasant life of Yasnaya Polyana, he was in possession of the world and of his own humanity. His secret is that he is the last of the unalienated artists. Hence it is necessary to insist on the differences not so much between him and other artists generally as between him and the modern breed of alienated artists. It is thanks to this unalienated condition that he is capable of moving us powerfully when describing the simplest, the most ordinary and therefore in their own way also the gravest occasions of life — occasions that the alienated artist can approach only from a distance, through flat naturalistic techniques, or through immense subtleties of analysis, or through the transportation of his subject onto the plane of myth and fantasy.

But, of course, even Tolstoy, being a man of the nineteenth century, could not finally escape the blight of alienation. In his lifetime

Russian society disintegrated; he witnessed the passing of the old society of status and its replacement by a cruelly impersonal system of bourgeois relations. Tolstoy resisted the catastrophic ruin of the traditional order by straining all the powers of his reason to discover a way out. His so-called conversion is the most dramatic and desperate episode in his stubborn and protracted struggle against alienation. His attack on civilization is essentially an attack on the conditions that make for alienation. The doctrine of Christian anarchism, developed after his conversion, reflects, as Lenin put it, "the accumulated hate, the ripened aspiration for a better life, the desire to throw off the past — and also the immaturity, the dreamy contemplativeness, the political inexperience, and the revolutionary flabbiness of the villages." Still, the point of that doctrine lies not in its religious content, which is very small indeed, but rather in its formulation of a social ideal and of a utopian social program.

1946

FREUD AND THE LITERARY MIND

DIFFICULTIES SOMETIMES leading to the sharpest disagreements and controversy are likely to arise in any literary-critical discourse of our time in which the word "literature" is emphatically and purposely followed by the word "and." The conjunction is invariably disputed. Whether speaking of literature and ideas, or literature and politics, or literature and psychoanalysis, one at once comes up against the standard objections drawn from the arsenal of the art for art's sake doctrine — a doctrine so protean in its manifestations and ravaging in its effects that there is no knowing in what quarter it will be encountered next. For the fact is that the inner drive of the modern creative process toward autonomy has encouraged the literary artist to belittle, if not altogether to deny the conjunctive relations of his medium and to resent any emphasis placed upon them; and these attitudes are of course shared by many literary critics.

But first of all, before discussing such issues, I would like to pay tribute to Freud as a writer, a master of expository as well as nar-

Text of a lecture given at the School of Letters of Kenyon College in July 1949.

rative prose, who brought superb literary resources to bear upon the expression of his ideas. Consider, for instance, the effect of the prodigious case histories compiled in the third volume of his *Collected Papers*. These narratives, built up not of imagined but real life-experiences, are composed without any sort of artistic intent; nevertheless they yield a distinct and unusual novelistic pleasure. It is as if in setting down these histories Freud unwittingly discovered a new literary form which creative writers might someday adapt to their own uses; and this can be said of these case histories without disputing the validity of the research methods of which they are the product. Or consider the grand imaginative power of Freud's experimental myths, such as the myth of the primal sire and the brother-horde that you find in *Totem and Taboo*. (I call this myth experimental to indicate its cognitive function and by way of distinguishing it from traditional mythology which is a collective creation.) This myth of the primal sire is at once a scientific hypothesis and an epical poetic construction which, regardless of its degree of historical truth, presents us with an unforgettable image of the origins and destiny of the human psyche — a mythic tale of fathers and sons, of the familial relationships of gods and men, that our culture must cope with because for better or worse it has already been irrevocably caught up in it.

I scarcely think that I am claiming too much in observing that to readers of literary temper the appeal of Freud's writings is to be explained not only by their substance but also by their form and style, their clarity of design and firmness of structure holding and controlling an infinitely suggestive, infinitely provocative and malleable content. Surely Thomas Mann is right to speak of Freud as "an artist of thought, like Schopenhauer, and like him a writer of European rank." There is in the work of Freud a union of sensibility and analytic power, of imagination and reality-mindedness, of humanistic pathos and the pathos of his patient and indomitable search for empirical knowledge, which permits him to transcend the confines of scientific inquiry in the narrow sense of the term and to engage a great many of our most vital responses, including the response that we call aesthetic without quite knowing what we mean by it.

To say this is but one way of focusing upon the fact that there

exists a close affinity between the Freudian and the literary mind —
an affinity natural, immediate, and indefeasible. Its secret is that
both these minds are in different ways impelled to divine the riddle
of the sphinx, to penetrate, that is, into the inner recesses of human
nature and to know man as he truly is, to know him not as that
theoretical projection which philosophers call an essence but as a
being living at one and the same time a biological and historical
life, and living it here and now, within the real world in which man
is at once placed and displaced. Freud understood this affinity very
well, and frequently paid his debt to literature, as when he credited
poets and writers with discovering the unconscious before him,
speaking of them as "those few to whom it is given . . . to salvage
from the whirlpool of their emotions the deepest truth to which
we others have to force our way, ceaselessly groping among torturing uncertainties." And in *Delusion and Dream,* the essay analyzing
the novel *Gradiva,* he wrote that storytellers are valuable allies, "for
they usually know many things between heaven and earth that are
not yet dreamed of in our philosophy. In psychological insights,
indeed, they are far ahead of us ordinary people, because they draw
from sources that are not yet accessible to science."

There is nonetheless great hostility among literary critics and
scholars to the introduction of Freudian ideas into the study of literature, their chief objection being that art is an autonomous process. Now no matter how sympathetic one may be to this conception,
it is still necessary to insist on the distinction, so often overlooked
by the latter-day fetishists of art, between autonomy and total independence. And insofar as here is a measure of agreement, even if
only in theory, that the literary process is by no means entirely independent, that it in fact stands in a conjunctive relation to other
modes of knowing and describing the world, we cannot without
obvious and obdurate inconsistency refuse to recognize the existence
of a significant linkage between psychoanalysis and literature. At
this stage of the argument I am not so much concerned with what
exactly is to be made of that linkage as with its existence pure and
simple; and I would say that among the critics and scholars refusing
to recognize that linkage the only ones exempt from the charge of
methodological confusion are the practitioners of pure formalism.

As an example one may cite the extreme wing of the Russian

formalists, a critical school that came into being in the second decade of this century and which, alas, has long since been liquidated, as they say, by the Soviet regime. The Russian formalists, with Victor Shklovsky as the most prominent of their leaders, proclaimed imaginative creation to be no more than the sum of its methods, subsuming all content, of whatever sort, under the heading of "raw material." Thus their critical position was clear and self-contained because it represented a clean break with all of literature's conjunctive relations. Though it is rather easy to dismiss their theories of the nature and history of art as extravagant fallacies, still it is impossible to deny that, being in full command of the virtues of their defects, they were able to accomplish a good deal in the matter of the technical investigation of craft and style. It is a pity that so little is known of their work outside of Russia, for in many ways it is a model of critical integrity.

Perhaps the chief factor in their success, however limited, was their readiness to practice in their texts what they preached in their theories. Having denied the relevance of beliefs and values in the study of literature, they evolved a strategy of excluding all "extrinsic" references from critical discourse. Unfortunately, that cannot be said of what is taken for formal criticism among us; for here it is the rule rather than the exception that critics pluming themselves on their "intrinsic" approach (like Cleanth Brooks, for instance) nevertheless manage to introduce all sorts of unanalyzed and unacknowledged ideological themes and motives into their criticism, thus inevitably distorting the self-imposed and beautifully clear limits of the formal analysis of literary art. I would call the ideological activity of such critics a form of "rhetoric," in Kenneth Burke's sense of the term, in that they produce what is seemingly a value-neutral elucidation of literary works while indirectly engaging in the war of ideas. I do not mean to say that the elucidation is necessarily unreal. It is there for all to see; but other things are also there, not so easy to spot.

So far as I know the Russian formalists had no occasion to encounter the claims of psychoanalysis. Freud and his school never really became a cultural issue in Russia. However, there can be no doubt that the formalists would have rejected the Freudian claims for the same reasons that they rejected the larger claims of Marxism;

and their repulse of all extra-aesthetic pressures on the discipline of literary scholarship and criticism was entirely in line with their stated aims and professions. What is incongruous, though, and contrary to all procedures at all logically organized, is to admit and even to promote relations between literature and, say, history or philosophy or theology, while at the same time denying that the critic can make profitable use of certain psychoanalytic principles and insights.

The incongruity, however, is scarcely due to naiveté; and if there is an element of naiveté in it, it is largely of that unconsciously willed kind that proves so serviceable in polemical situations. But be that as it may, the fact is that not a few literary critics (such as Leavis, Tate, Ransom, and the late R. P. Blackmur) react against psychoanalysis with an intensity of distaste which suggests an animus far removed from any purely literary determination. What is to be noted is that the objections of these critics, even if logically inconsistent, are nonetheless quite consistent with their general outlook and scheme of values. The conclusion is inescapable that these objections are mainly of an ideological character. In Anglo-American criticism it is in particular the critics of the school of Eliot who are most squeamish in their references to psychoanalysis, refusing any application of it to the literary object; and, to be sure, to concede the possibility of a friendly commerce between psychoanalysis and literary studies is basically incompatible with the values of traditionalism. Thus the rejection of Freud's thoughts by some of our foremost critics, who until very recently exerted great influence both in and out of the academy, is understandable and even in a certain sense legitimate. It is legitimate, however, so long as it is out in the open. What is not legitimate at all from the standpoint of method is a falling back to arguments against psychoanalysis borrowed from the formalists and, at one remove, from the art for art's sake doctrine — a doctrine in no sense consonant with the traditionalist position.

It is tempting to avail oneself of Freud's theory of the "resistance" to his teaching as a means of disclosing the hidden meaning of the animus displayed by certain literary types. But I must admit that it would scarcely be fair to bring to bear Freudian considerations to explain the "resistance" to Freud. In the psychoanalytic texts the word "resistance" appears as a loaded term, for in their deployment of it the exponents of depth-psychology tend to assume exactly what is their business to prove. However, there is another form of "resistance," ideological in nature, on the nature of which Freud is well worth quoting, because of the brilliant suggestiveness of his argument. Thus more than once he speaks of the "resistance" to his insights as motivated by the "general narcissism of man, the self-love of humanity, that has up to the present been three times wounded by the researches of science." The first blow to humanity's self-love was the cosmological revolution, that is the Copernican revolution in astronomy; the second blow was delivered by Darwin in the realm of biology; and the third is of course the Freudian revolution in psychology. Now it is hardly to be expected that literary men who have so far failed to make their peace with either the cosmological or biological revolution would not stubbornly oppose the psychological one — the latest and perhaps the most telling blow so far administered to man's self-esteem.

In another work, in recounting the history of the psychoanalytic movement, Freud observes that "very soon it was discovered that the dreams invented by writers stand in the same relation to psychoanalysis as genuine dreams . . . Naturally, here also, in the sphere of art and literature, opposition was not lacking . . . and expressed itself with the same lack of understanding and passionate rejection as on the native soil of psychiatry. For it was to be expected that everywhere psychoanalysis penetrated it would have to go through the same struggle with the natives." Yet despite the effort of most members of the English departments of our universities as well as of certain sections of the literary world to retain exclusive possession of their domain, the psychoanalytic mode of thought has immensely influenced the contemporary literary mind. The natural affinity between them makes any prolonged estrangement inconceivable.

It is true that psychoanalysis is an affront to gentility in all fields, in psychiatry no less than in literary criticism. The affront lies chiefly in the libidinal emphasis of the Freudian teaching. But psychoanalysis, scientifically considered, should be characterized not so much by its principal subject matter as by its methods of research. These methods are applicable, though of course with different degrees of relevance, to many fields of study, and not least to the study of works of art. The main achievement of psychoanalysis has been the discovery of unconscious mental life, or the primary process, as some analysts call it. And since the primary process is no doubt very much involved in the making of works of art, the critic wishing to gauge this involvement cannot fashion his tools either *ex nihilo* or from purely traditional materials but must look to psychoanalysis for a good part of his equipment. Of course, it is always possible for the critic to ignore the primary process and to stay on the level of the cultural overtones of literature. But then he lays himself open to the stricture of which Freud made such fine use in his polemic against Adler and Jung, disciples who fell away from him, when he said that "they have caught a few cultural overtones from the symphony of life but once more they have failed to hear the powerful melody of the impulses." Poetry, for example, resounds with this powerful melody, but most critics of poetry content themselves with catching some of its cultural overtones. Think of W. B. Yeats's *Last Poems and Plays*, in which the melody of the senses sets astir the old poet's soul:

> What hurts the soul
> My soul adores,
> No better than a beast
> On all fours.

And again:

> You think it horrible that lust and rage
> Should dance attention upon my old age;
> They were not such a plague when I was young;
> What else have I to spur me into song?

And from "the foul rag-and-bone shop of the heart" he fashioned the following audacious quatrain:

> Whence did all that fury come?
> From empty tomb or virgin womb?
> Saint Joseph thought the world would melt
> But liked the way his finger smelt.

According to Freud, then, the creative writer has for his special domain the portrayal of the psychic life of human beings, and this of course forms the bond between the writer and the scientific psychologist, who enters this sphere by another route, his object being not to depict psychic life but to investigate its workings with the aid of rational methods subject to control and verification. The difference is important, and it will not do to obscure it. Psychology is a science, or rather it tries hard to become one, and its task is to deal with its subject in a manner largely deterministic, in terms of laws and probabilities. The writer, on the other hand, such as the novelist for instance, is concerned with the individual in his uniqueness, indeterminateness, and spontaneity, with the individual, that is, so envisaged that he can on no account be denied the freedom and the responsibility of decision, of choosing either the good or evil courses open to him. The novelist's insight into character is thus not really of the same order as that of the specialist in psychology, though the two orders of insight may run parallel and meet at some point beyond their specific and separate contexts, a point where it becomes possible to formulate the novelist's perceptions into general ideas regarding the nature of the self and its articulation through a concrete historical and social medium. Still, this distinction in no way invalidates Freud's view of the writer as an intuitive psychologist and as a precursor of analytic knowledge.

At the same time, however, that Freud seems to estimate so highly the psychological truth that literature contains, he also has another theory of it, developed in the course of analyzing the fantasy-life of the individual — a theory for which he has been repeatedly taken to task because it appears to reduce literary art to the level of a substitute gratification, a socially organized indulgence in wish-thinking, a narcotic mainly. Thus Lionel Trilling, who is so exceedingly appreciative of the Freudian doctrine as to say of it that it makes "poetry indigenous to the very constitution of the mind," has severely criticized this hedonistic theory in his well-known essay "Freud and Literature." And it is indeed true that at times Freud does compare the writer with one who dreams "in broad daylight" and his creations with "daydreams."

However, let us keep in mind that at such times Freud is speaking almost exclusively of writers, as he himself remarks, who are "not highly esteemed by critics," namely writers of popular novels, romances and stories addressed to a mass audience. He shows that all these productions have one leading trait in common, in that in all of them the center of interest is a hero for whom "the author tries to win our sympathy by every possible means, and whom he places under the protection of a special providence." This hero (or heroine) is apparently immune to the blows of fate, he engages in hard and spectacular struggles but somehow always wins out at the end, nothing can really touch him, success is from the outset his allotted portion, he gains riches, fame, and the love of women through exertions more simulated than real. The accounts of this hero given in fiction as well as in other mass media are easily recognized as being essentially the constituents of a daydream. This hero's significant mark, as Freud observes, is his "invulnerability," and that clearly betrays him as a stand-in for "His Majesty the Ego," who is in fact the one authentic protagonist of actual daydreams and of those contrived or constructed daydreams on which popular fiction bases its appeal. By a process of natural identification the reader of such fiction merges his own ego with that of the hero, thus satisfying in fantasy and in a socially permissible manner his cravings for pleasure and power.

Now this theory is obviously true as far as it goes, and it goes only so far as to explain the appeal of art in its aspect as a mass medium rather than in its qualitative differentiation. As a theory it is more plausibly applied to best sellers, radio and television serials and movies than, say, to the novels of George Eliot and Henry James, Tolstoy and Dostoevsky, Flaubert and Proust. Perhaps Freud is at fault here for not sharply discriminating, in an essay such as "The Relation of the Poet to Daydreaming," between upper and lower levels in art. But that he is perfectly aware of the diversity of levels is shown by the high tribute he frequently paid to literary artists for their psychological insight. Thus it would seem that the contradiction between Freud's two ideas of literature is more apparent than real. It is a matter of different perspectives, of what questions he was undertaking to answer at different times.

Let us not lose sight of the fact that when literary critics think of literature they usually have in mind its finest examples (bad writing they simply dismiss as a fraud, which is a nonsensical procedure because it exists and performs a social role), while Freud, in the essay I mentioned above, was thinking of literature in its broad generic sense, from the standpoint of its psychological effect on the public, and without any special regard for standards of quality. And in this respect he is indeed right: for most literature is bad literature and most writers do in fact succumb to the temptation of playing up to the weaknesses, the passivity and immersion in self-glorifying fantasies of their readers, instead of appealing to their strength, maturity, and cultivated reality-sense.

It is necessary to emphasize, however, that no Chinese wall separates high art from low art, the permanent from the ephemeral, the superior work of literature from the inferior one. The process of identification on the reader's part is equally present in both instances, though on entirely different planes of understanding and discrimination; and the processes of disguise and distortion, of condensation, displacement, visual representation and symbolic reference — processes so startlingly similar to those by which Freud has shown the dream-work transforming latent dream-thoughts into manifest dream-images — are as operative in the superior as in the inferior work, though operative to different ends and with different results. Both the high-level and the low-level artist are equally engaged in socializing the life of fantasy. The psyche of both has the attribute of what Freud calls "flexibility of repressions," a flexibility enabling them to liberate psychosexual energy for creative purposes; and both possess the capacity to elaborate their inner life in seemingly objective constructions purged of those embarrassing personal notes "which grate upon strange ears and prevent their becoming enjoyable to others." What then, speaking strictly from a psychological point of view, does the distinction between good and bad art come to finally? I would say that what it comes to chiefly is this: that while good art makes use of the pleasure principle only to find its way back into the sphere of the reality principle, bad art panders to the pleasure principle all the way through and never leaves its protective domain.

I do not mean to say that good art accepts the reality principle unchanged, that it makes no amends for it. We know that reality offers cold comfort, that at all times men find it hard to endure, and that more often than not its true nature is such as to repel and horrify them. How, then, does art reconcile us to it? To answer this

question we might at this point draw on an insight of Nietzsche's
to supplement that of Freud's. In *The Birth of Tragedy* Nietzsche
tells us that when the will of man is imperiled by the awfulness of
reality "art approaches as a healing and redeeming enchantress; she
alone may transform . . . horrible reflections on the terror and absurdity of existence into representations with which men may live.
These are the representations of the *sublime* (the tragic) as the artistic conquest of the terrible and of the *comic* as the artistic release
from the nausea of the absurd." So it would appear that art, however high its reach and whatever its excellence, is ultimately inseparable from pleasure, though not in the sense of banishing the
real for the sake of pleasure but rather in the sense of gaining a
pleasure peculiar to itself from the very act of boldly coping with
the real and at last coming to terms with it by means of the relief
afforded by the exercise of the powers of understanding, intelligence, sympathy and compassion, and by the assertion of human
worth even in the face of defeat and extinction.

Freud has much to tell us about the inner mechanism of creative
projection, also about the relation between a writer's biography and
his work, the relation between that work and fantasy-life in all its
forms, and about the recurrence in mythology and tradition of themes
and symbols by which writers are preoccupied. Freud admits, however, that his theory can do nothing, as he once put it, "to elucidate
the nature of the artistic gift nor can it explain the means by which
the artist works — artistic technique." We would do well to distinguish between what the Freudian teaching does and does not contribute to our understanding of art. If in this teaching the artistic
endowment as such is regarded as not subject to analysis, then speculations about the artist as a neurotic type are scarcely as profitable
as they seem to many people who delight in expatiating on this
theme.

For to say that most artists have exhibited neurotic traits is by no
means the same thing as laying down neurosis as the pre-condition of
the artistic function. The psychologist Otto Rank, who in the earlier
phase of his career was a close collaborator of Freud's, put it even
more thoroughly than his master in writing that

> the latest statements in the field of psychology show with astonishing
> frankness and unanimity that the psychology of personality has helped

little or not at all in the understanding of genius, or as it is termed scientifically, the productive or creative personality. Moreover, that it will probably never contribute anything, since ultimately we are dealing with dynamic factors which remain incomprehensible in their specific expression in the individual personality. This implies that they can be neither predetermined nor wholly explained *ex post facto* . . . In any event, the notion of art has always proved too narrow to include under one aspect the varieties of creative personality or their manifold achievements; and on the other hand the psychological idea of the creative personality was too broad to explain artistic production . . . and again the poet may be so different from the plastic artist, the musician or the scientifically productive type, that it is impossible to bring them all under one head.

It seems to me that this is an extremely perspicacious formulation, disposing once and for all of the innumerable attempts to define the nature of the artist as a psychic type. It is clear that psychoanalytic observation does not throw light on the puzzling question of natural gifts for art. At bottom psychoanalysis cannot really explain why one child will suffer certain deprivations and hardships without damage to his mental health, while identical deprivations and hardships will permanently affect another child sharing the same environment. No, the Freudian doctrine cannot specify the psychic state and conditions that will make one person an artist, another person a scientist, and a third person a doctor or an engineer or an actor. It appears to me that the literary critic would do well to keep away from all such speculations, the aim of which is usually either to absolve the artist entirely of neurotic tendencies and thus assimilate him to normality or else to glorify neurosis by identifying it with the power and prestige of artistic achievement.

One thing, however, we can say, and that is that even if many artists are neurotic, art is surely not a neurotic formation — we must differentiate between art and artists. Freud has indicated that there is a correspondence between what he called the "great social productions of art, religion and philosophy" on the one hand, and the neuroses on the other. Thus Freud remarks that hysteria seems like a caricature of artistic creation, the compulsion neurosis seems like a caricature of a religion and the paranoiac delusion like the caricature of a philosophic system. The element of caricature originates in the fact that the neuroses are essentially asocial formations seeking to

11

accomplish "by private means what arose in society through collective labor." Hence cultural creation differs radically from neurosis in that it rests on social impulses and needs, converting personal fantasies, wishes, and perceptions into publicly negotiable values.

In the world of antiquity creative inspiration was very commonly spoken of as a form of madness. But what kind of madness is it? It is a state of productive madness in which the rational ego controls the unconscious processes, pressing them into its service. It is thus the diametrical opposite of the state of real madness in which the rational ego is overwhelmed by unconscious strivings. Freud recognized this when he observed that there is in fact "a path leading from fantasy back again to reality, and that is the path of art . . ." It is true that the artist is urged on "by instinctual needs that are clamorous," but unlike most people he has a way of transforming those clamorous needs into the kind of energy required for creative work. The power which the ancients attributed to the Muses and which they called inspiration or possession is explained by Freud as the power of gaining direct access to the primary process of the unconscious mind and converting psychosexual energy to creative ends.

Freud's idea of the artist as a man driven by clamorous instinctual needs is in part at least confirmed by Thomas Mann in one of his most perspicuous essays, the essay on "Goethe as a Man of Letters," where he states that the artist "as poet and man of letters is connected *through the senses* with the idea of human dignity . . . His very being is based upon a union — which is not without its perils — between dignity and sensuality . . . Two forces are above the average strong in him: his sexual life and his intellectual life; the two together make him a revolutionary, a disturbing, upsetting, even an undermining force . . ." In this passage, which among other things is to be valued for its plain speaking, Mann at once corroborates and corrects Freud who, in putting so much stress on the unconscious sources of literary art, tended to underestimate its intellectual intensity and pressure. The Elizabethan poet George Chapman wrote that the Muses sing of "love's sensual empery," to which we might add that they simultaneously sing of its intellectual sway.

If we compare the poet not to a madman, as Plato did, but to a dreamer, as we are tempted to do by psychoanalysis, we can see that he differs radically from the dreamer in that he plays a double role:

that of the dreamer as well as that of the interpreter of dreams, that of the neurotic as well as that of the analyst. Even fictions dealing with extreme pathological states, such as for instance Melville's *Pierre* and "Bartleby the Scrivener," Gogol's "The Overcoat," Dostoevsky's "The Double," and Kafka's "Metamorphosis," reveal this dual function of the writer, this combination of neurotic expression with analytic labor. Of course, the analysis in such stories is not brought to scientific formulation — doing so would turn the stories into clinical documents and, moreover, such procedures are entirely outside their authors' real interest, and where these authors differ even more radically from analysts is that they identify themselves with their protagonists by investing them with their own anxiety, guilt, and power of fantasy-making. Yet even in such literary cases of direct entanglement with the morbid and abnormal the writer continues to function in his double capacity, his instinctual side predominating in the first and his intellectual side in the second. Hence it might be said that good literature depends on balancing, however precariously, these two sides, the instinctual and intellectual, as against literature which fails in this essential task and pays the penalty of forfeiting the reader's attention because of shallowness or distortion, sensationalism or obsession, boredom or even sheer unintelligibility.

So far I have spoken only of the Freudian approach to the literary mind. What about the literary mind's approach to Freud? It is evident that his influence on that mind has been enormous on all levels, and in ways both positive and negative. It is unfortunately true that even in the literary world the Freudian theory is better known through the vulgarizations of it than through its subtleties and refinements. There have been literary critics who imagined that they were applying Freudian conceptions to literature when actually all they were doing was to locate phallic references and sexual puns. But that is a trivial use of psychoanalysis, for the existence of such references and puns may be safely taken for granted. Another vulgarization is the production of clinical studies of behavior and quasi-analytic confessions in the guise of fiction. These productions are of course negligible as literature, for obviously a writer is misusing Freud when he

takes his work as a source book of ready-made, prefabricated interpretations of human motivation and conduct. Fiction produced in
this fashion is but thinly disguised autobiography and for the most
part a proof of a radical insufficiency of novelistic talent. For in this
respect I cannot but agree with Coleridge's dictum that "one of the
promises of genius is the choice of subjects very remote from the private interests and circumstances of the writer himself." But, on the
other hand, the positive effect of Freud's doctrine has also been
great, though this effect is not always to be perceived in a manner
enabling us to identify it directly and unequivocally. In American
literary criticism the work of Edmund Wilson and Lionel Trilling
clearly exhibits an intense engagement with Freudian ideas, while in
the writings of Leslie Fiedler these ideas are mostly presented with a
crassness and grossness that utterly belie this critic's claim to analytic
perspicacity.

But in speaking of psychology and literature, in the very act of
connecting them, it at once becomes necessary to insist on certain
distinctions. If the minimal definition of criticism is that it is "the
valuation, by some standard, of the worth of literature," then psychoanalytic statements about it are not *as such* criticism. Such statements are a species of research, analogous in value to historical or
formal research. But of course research, all forms of it, is the indispensable material on the basis of which the critic forms his judgments. I do not believe that there is any such thing as pure criticism,
any more than I believe that there is any such thing as pure poetry.
Even the best and most reputable literary criticism contains all sorts
of observations drawn from diverse spheres of human interest. Manifestly, the value of psychoanalysis to criticism is simply a matter of
its relevance to the particular text under examination. For essentially the task of appraising the worth of a poem or a novel is independent of psychoanalysis or any other scientific, philosophical, or
political doctrine; there can be no substitute for the act of evaluation; and when the Freudian approach is used in isolation from other
methods and other approaches it tends to become an end in itself
and to displace the art-object by turning it into a document.

One must distinguish, to be sure, between writings on literature by
analysts and writings by literary critics influenced by them. The
analysts have written more about the lives and complexes of writers

than about their work, and a good example of this is Freud's essay on Dostoevsky. This essay is in the first place a biographical analysis and only secondarily a commentary on the novels. But it is an analysis that the literary student of the Russian novelist would be ill-advised to ignore. Another example of the psychoanalyst writing about literature is Dr. Ernest Jones's by now famous study of *Hamlet*. As a study it is suggestive and illuminating, but it does exemplify the reductive fallacy. I agree with Francis Fergusson's criticism of Dr. Jones in his book *The Idea of a Theatre*. Fergusson does not in the least deny that the Oedipus complex plays its part in *Hamlet*, but he objects to the reduction of the drama to this single motivation, contending that "the disease which is killing the state of Denmark is not to be explained in purely psychological terms." His discussion of Dr. Jones's study is a fine example of the way in which the literary critic can utilize psychoanalytic research without allowing it to usurp his function. The critic modifies and corrects the inevitable one-sidedness of the professional psychologist, who easily falls into the error known as psychologism. It is the error of enlisting psychology to provide the answers to questions that are outside its sphere, questions that are in essence philosophical or political or religious or historical, and which can be dealt with adequately only on their own ground. In other words, psychologism is an attempt to construct a *Weltanschauung* out of psychological material alone, and this cannot but lead to an impasse. As the philosopher Gilson once put it: "Psychology is a science, while psychologism is a sophistry. It substitutes the definition for the defined, the description for the described, the map for the country."

My view is that the literary critic can benefit from the Freudian discipline if he turns it to account in a strictly empirical fashion, without attempting to construct an exclusive system out of it. It can aid him in analyzing the emotional economy of a work of art and in locating its emotional origin and goal, which sometimes cannot be detected through ordinary methods of study. Of course, not all modes of art are equally open to psychoanalytic investigation. The least open is that type which is realistic, rational, and impersonal, deeply social in import and integrated with the ruling ideals and norms of the society of which it is a product. The art most accessible to psychoanalysis is the type which is strongly individualistic and marked by the range and depth of its unconscious reference and meaning. Thus in the novel the Freudian approach is rewarding when made use of in situations of psychic conflict arising out of what Freud calls the family romance; and by analogy one cannot but observe that works of a religious content often stand in some disguised but indubitably significant relation to the theme of the family romance. The fiction of Franz Kafka, for instance, provides the perfect example of writing that virtually demands a Freudian gloss. But to say that is not the same thing as claiming a monopoly for psychoanalysis in the interpretation of Kafka. There is a metaphysical level of meaning in his work which is vulgarized when reduced to purely psychological terms, and the critics must know how to distinguish between the two levels of meaning while at the same time keeping open a line of communication between them.

One of the worst vulgarizations of the Freudian doctrine — a vulgarization to which critics of a religious-traditionalist bent are especially prone — is the conception of it as an immoral doctrine, and of Freud as one of the grand immoralists of the modern age. This is a conception very hard to uproot, for in this chaotic age an idea of that sort plays in perfectly with what people actually want to believe. But the fact is that Freud, in spite of his positivist bias, was a firm believer in the capacities of the mind and in control of the unruly instincts through knowledge. For analysis is knowledge. It is Freud who wrote that "according to the conclusions we have reached so far, neurosis would be the result of a kind of ignorance, a not-knowing of mental processes which should be known." This approaches very closely the well-known Socratic teaching in which even vice is conceived as the product of ignorance. An enemy of morbid asceticism and of the excessive demands of the super-ego or cultural ego-ideal for exclusive control of human conduct, Freud is at the same a theorist evaluating civilization as the fruit of the renunciation of total instinctual satisfaction. The idea of sublimation is basic to Freud's notion of the origin and evolution of culture. And in one of his last essays he wrote that we must make up our minds that "renunciation and suffering are not to be eluded by the race of men." This corresponds in all essentials to the insight of the great poets of the Western tradition.

Also, Freud offers no support or solace whatever to proponents of authoritarian outlooks, both of the theological and orthodox Marxist variety. In his book, *Inhibitions, Symptoms and Anxiety,* there is a statement that beautifully sums up his attitude to the demand for certainty, for an overall and absolute truth that will once and for all explain the nature of the universe and the meaning of man's life. It is a statement aimed specifically at dogmatic philosophers, but it is equally applicable to literary men looking to some kind of orthodoxy for salvation:

> I must confess that I am not at all partial to the fabrication of *Weltanschauungen.* Such activities may be left to philosophers who avowedly find it impossible to make their journey through life without a Baedeker of some kind to tell them about everything . . . But . . . even such "Guides to Life" soon grow out of date, and it is precisely such shortsighted, narrow and finicky work as ours which obliges them to appear in new editions . . . even the most up-to-date of such Guides are nothing but attempts to find a substitute for the ancient, useful and all-embracing catechism. We know well enough how little science has so far been able to throw light on the problems surrounding us. Only patient, persevering research . . . can gradually bring about a change. The benighted traveler may sing aloud in the dark to deny his own fears; but, for all that, he will not see an inch further beyond his nose.

1949

RELIGION AND THE INTELLECTUALS

T HE BACK-TO-RELIGION MOVEMENT among the intellectuals is scarcely to be understood without reference to the permutations of the *Zeitgeist* — and the *Zeitgeist* makes fools of us all. In the 1930s the key term was "revolution" while now it is "tradition." And it is tradition which provides the leading motive, not belief in God.

There are currently but two positions among us worth talking about: that of the secular radicals at one pole and that of the traditionalists at the other. Secular radicalism, in its multiple variations, is in a state of extreme crisis brought on by the cumulative historical frustrations and calamities of the twentieth century. Having lost confidence in the doctrine of progress, it is now more than ever exposed to the criticism of its opponents. The traditionalists, who attempted very little on the plane of historical action and who mostly stayed put in their dusty corners, have now come forward to speak their piece, with "I told you so" as the leitmotif of their quite unoriginal presentation. This is their privileged moment, and they are

A contribution to the *Partisan Review* symposium of 1950 on the growth of religiosity among American intellectuals.

bound to make the most of it. And why not? Still, if it is the new religiosity that we are to discuss, then the first thing to be remarked about it is that it is hardly distinguishable from the world-view of traditionalism, with which it is far more deeply involved than with the primary and crucial commitments of genuine belief.

What, concretely, does it mean to believe? When Stephen Dedalus, in *Ulysses*, is asked whether he believes in "creation from nothing and miracles and a personal God," that is to say, whether he believes "in the narrow sense of the word," his reply is that there is only one sense of the word. It might be said of Stephen that he is a casuist in everything but the essential: in all essential matters his sincerity is unconditional. Unable to accept what is required of all true believers, i.e., required in no strict sense perhaps by all the established churches though surely both by the mind of conscience and the conscience of mind, Stephen confesses to being "a horrible example of free thought."

Of course, some modern thinkers tell us that one can be religious without believing, so to speak, in anything in particular, certainly not in the particulars of dogmatic theology. All that is necessary is to reinterpret the concept of the divine as pure transcendence, or as the absolute ground of existence (an absolute of which nothing, however, can be demonstrably known), or, more mildly still, as a perspective uniting the real and the ideal. All such notions are wretched substitutes for the *mysterium tremendum* of a dying and rising god. Though notions of that kind may serve the modernizing dialectician bent on saving something of religion by cutting its losses, they starve the religious imagination by depriving it of its major assets in ritual, myth, and dogma. It seems to me that Stephen Dedalus, in his stubborn innocence, is aware of the ineluctable facts of religion in a way that eludes the subtle dialecticians; and I have no doubt that in this respect Stephen is wholly at one with his author. Another "horrible example of free thought" in modern fiction is Kirillov, of *The Possessed*, who commits suicide because he will settle for nothing less than God's actual existence. All his life long, the author of *The Possessed* said of himself, he was tormented by the problem of the existence of God.

Such stubborn innocence is alien, however, to the partisans of tradition, who have learned not only how to by-pass Dostoevsky's "problem" but also how to make it appear that the very formulation of it is somehow in bad taste. Their way is simply to restore God to His heaven by means of a mental operation speciously pragmatic so as to secure for tradition its indispensable metaphysical basis. In other words, if they believe in God it is mainly because such belief is logically implicit in their traditionalist alignment. One further step in this analysis and we discover that it is not they, as individuals, in the aloneness of their existential subjectivity, who have come to have faith in God but, rather, that it is the tradition which is possessed of that faith. The tradition does everything; they merely feed on its heavenly manna.

What this suggests is that at bottom traditionalism is really a form of perverted historicism, in the sense that it is fixated on some period of the past idealized through the medium of the historical imagination, that uniquely modern product. (The neo-classicist and traditionalist school of Maurras was fixated on the period of Louis XIV, for instance.) Whitehead once remarked that there are two ways of reading history, backwards and forwards, and that thinking requires both methods. The traditionalists, however, are committed to reading history only backwards, for they tend to regard nearly everything that has happened since the elected period to be part of a process of degeneration, as nothing less, in fact, than a falling away from grace.

But is it actually possible to believe traditionally while living in an untraditional society dominated by secular forces? Belief of that kind is vulnerable both on objective and subjective grounds. It neither offers new and challenging motives for effecting the reconciliation of faith and knowledge; nor does it yield itself to immediacy and the inescapable hazards of unqualified subjectivity as did the faith of a rebel Christian like Kierkegaard, who, differentiating radically between the Christianity of the New Testament and that of Christendom, sought to anchor his desperate and paradoxical belief not in tradition, hierarchy, and authority but in God and the revelation in Christ. Piety toward the past is what traditionalism offers instead. Christendom is its all, while of Christianity it conceives in a formal and remote fashion as an unattainable ideal, an ideal so strictly divorced from all natural and historical processes that it can be safely tucked away in eternity.

The center of gravity of traditionalism is seldom in religious ex-

perience. Its center, clearly, is in the attachment to the social and cultural order of some past age in which religion, in a highly developed institutionalized form, played an integral part. Thus the locus of value is displaced from the sacred or supernatural object to the institutional factor. One might put it another way by saying that to the traditionalists, whether of the Anglo-American school of Eliot or the French school of Maurras, religion is merely the theory of which certain social and ecclesiastical institutions are the practice.*
But long ago it was written that "he who cometh to God must believe that He is"; and the proposition that "He is" is scarcely to be deduced from the plain historical fact, which no one has ever questioned, that the men of past societies have believed in Him.

Since nobody has gone so far as to claim that a new revelation is at hand, or that a prophetic *pneuma* is sweeping the world, as it swept the Christian world in the era of the Reformation or the Jewish world with the rise of Hasidism, one is perhaps justified in summing up the so-called religious revival as the high talk of literary men and journalists about the necessity of returning to traditional Christianity. (Here again one is struck by the fact that the emphasis in all this talk is not so much on the truth of traditional Christianity as on the allegedly beneficent consequences of its restoration. The argument from consequences, so grossly pragmatic, is thus inevitably laid hold of by the very same people who ostensibly reject the pragmatic mode of thought as philosophically vulgar and spiritually inadmissible.) There have also been a number of conversions — a fact not very important as a sign of cultural change if it were not for the attitudes of ingratiation and appeasement toward the converts and the entire phenomenon of conversion now manifest in intellectual circles. Not so long ago this phenomenon was generally regarded with amused bafflement or unconcern. That is a difference worth noting, as it is

---

* It is necessary to distinguish here between Eliot the poet and Eliot the ideologue of tradition in such prose writings as *Notes towards the Definition of Culture*. In Eliot's later poetry there is a strain of mystical religion the actuality of which is not open to question. As an ideologue, however, he inclines toward socio-historical formulations that bring him close to the position of Maurras. It is particularly among the followers of Eliot, some of whom have performed the remarkable feat of taking over his ideas on culture and society without an equivalent commitment to religious belief, that the archaistic social attitudes of traditionalism become the center of value.

exactly the *Zeitgeist* which accounts for it. It is noteworthy, too, that among the new converts there is no exigent religious individualism à la Tolstoy, no prophets or visionaries, no grand and courageous reformation of ethical demands. Nothing of that sort is to be expected, for nearly all the converts have reached their present state through a process of historical retrospection which has apparently brought home to them the power and sublimity of the traditions and institutions of Christendom.

As usual, it is the literary men who are in the vanguard of the movement. In certain literary quarters the idea of tradition has lately taken on an honorific meaning that empties it of all empirical content. Thus *"the* tradition" — as it is spoken of in some of our literary reviews, with the definite article stressing an exclusiveness staggering in its presumption and historical naiveté — has been transmogrified into a patent ideological construction. It has come to stand for a special kind of higher reality, no less, bristling with magico-religious associations on the one hand and promises of aristocratic investiture on the other. Of course, the number of intellectuals now taking up tradition is much smaller than the number that took up revolution in the thirties. Still the trend is unmistakable, particularly among the intellectuals migrating into the academy, who easily discern a desirable connection between tradition, in its purely ideological aspects to be sure, and their newly acquired social function and status.

The pity of it is that not a few gifted writers are plunging from one debauch of ideology into another without giving themselves time to sober up. Actually, what they need is not more of the same medicine but a dose of skepticism so strong as to make them stand fast against the solicitations of ideologies whose chief function is that of mythicizing the world — the essential prerequisite of subjecting the mind to some form of authoritarian discipline. The intellectual converts to myth and dogma, some of whom formerly adhered to a social-revolutionary position, fondly imagine that they have undergone a total change of outlook. That is the typical error of abstract unhistorical thinking.

What was it, in fact, that disillusioned those people with Soviet Communism, for so long the dominant version of the secular-revolutionary outlook? It was the discovery that Soviet Communism had nothing in common with the classic socialist ideals but that, like fascism, it was a form of revolutionary reaction, that is, a form of reaction devoid of norms and standards, arbitrary in its violence and boundless in its hankering for power and mastery. Yet this discovery, however painful, has not led them to reject the authoritarian approach, no matter what its source. To accomplish such a rejection is beyond either their need or desire, for what they want above all is to be possessed by the spirit of consolation and to be lured by the promise of metaphysical certainty and social stability. Hence if they abjured revolutionary reaction it was only to go over to the traditional reaction of ideologies much older than Communism, a reaction richly endowed with norms and standards, embellished with the achievements, real or imaginary, of past generations, and institutionalized in the Roman Church and other conservative organizations. The difference between the two types of reaction must appear to them like the difference noted by Hegel between the shockingly bare and matter-of-fact social relationships of modern society and those of the ancient city-states, where "the iron bond of necessity was still garlanded with roses." But Hegel's insight is not applicable to the realities of our epoch. The iron bond of necessity is what we must think of, not the withered roses; and for that it is essential that we introduce into our thought, to quote Hegel again, "the seriousness, the suffering, the patience and the labor of the negative." Then we shall realize soon enough that in reality there is no Chinese wall separating the two types of reaction. They share a common secret, in that the appeal of both is to "miracle, mystery, and authority" — the three forces that Dostoevsky's Grand Inquisitor found indispensable for holding captive the conscience and loyalty of mankind.

The reactionary implications of traditionalism in the social and political sphere are of course inevitably lost on the majority of its partisans, who tend to think in high-falutin' romantic-literary categories that fall short of any possibility of application in the real world. In those circles a high tone is invariably taken toward the disciplines of the political mind, as if politics, denoting those facts of power from which there is no longer any escape and by which our fate is increasingly determined, comprised some inferior form of reality with which no person of really fine sensibilities would seriously concern himself.

It is curious, too, that those people, who in literature urge upon us the adoption of a neo-classicist aesthetic to replace the muddle of Romanticism, should remain so strangely unaware of the extent to which they are indebted for their leading ideas to Romanticism, particularly the German brand of Romanticism, with its strivings to reenchant the world, its idealization of Christendom, its nostalgic remembrance of the feudal-agrarian past, its archaizing social attitudes generally, and the conversion of its chief spokesmen to Catholicism. In Novalis' essay *Die Christenheit oder Europa* you will find most of the generative ideas of traditionalism, expressed with a beautiful poetic abandon inconceivable in our time, which has produced texts belonging to the same order of thought, such as Eliot's *Ideal of a Christian Society* and *Notes toward the Definition of Culture,* that are marked by a painful though futile effort to achieve precision and relevance.

I may be overstating the case but it seems to me that there is a connection between the present slump in creative writing and the ascendancy of traditionalist ideas in this decade. It is a fact that in the forties writing fell far below the level attained in the twenties or even in the thirties. And literary discourse has again become cluttered with a modish phraseology nearly as obnoxious as the class-struggle phraseology of the thirties. There is the term "original sin," for instance, which has lately taken on a flavor definitely avant-gardist, like the word "marvelous" in the lingo of the surrealists. Altogether there is far too much manipulation of the notions of guilt, evil, and sin, notions drawn from theological sources at second or third hand and converted, under cover of the religious revival, into a kind of aesthetic demonology which is really little more than a mid-century version of the "Satanism" that prevailed in the advanced literary circles of Paris at the time of Baudelaire's youth.

All that is but a symptom of the appalling disinclination on the part of the new literary converts to make anything more of the Christian ethic of love and goodness than the world will allow. What they make much more of is the orthodox doctrine of evil — a doctrine the ambiguities of which have baffled many a theologian but which for that very reason perhaps suits the literary faculty in its present state of privation. It is a doctrine that can be worked with facility both as a mystification of magical import and as a prefabricated motive to be pressed into service wherever concrete and specific insight into human nature and conduct is missing. To be sure, there is no denying the reality of evil. But it is precisely its reality which is obscured and dissipated when turned into an all sufficing explanation and then made the object of aesthetic play-acting with modern ideas of the irrational and the demonic, ideas as ubiquitous as they are indeterminate. One recalls that in *Faust* Mephistopheles observes with his characteristic shrewdness that

> *Auch die Kultur, die alle Welt beleckt,*
> *Hat auf den Teufel sich erstreckt.*

Since that verse was written Faust has been virtually eclipsed by Mephistopheles in the role of protagonist of the higher productions of *Kultur;* and being exceedingly practiced in beating the high-minded at their own game, Mephistopheles is no doubt far from displeased by his rise to a position of glamor in the cultural hierarchy.

Moreover, the free play now given to the doctrine of evil and sin has more than an aesthetic resonance. The moral implications are not to be overlooked. If the Utopians on the Left (the futurists, as Toynbee calls them) disastrously assume the innate goodness of man in their social schemes, the Utopians on the Right (the archaists, in Toynbee's phrase) are ever inclined to assume a fixed human nature that is innately evil, an assumption which has always served as one of the principal justifications of man's inhumanity to man. It is the permanent alibi of those unconcerned with justice. Futurism and archaism are a pair of alternative reactions produced by the schism in the soul of the members of a disintegrating society. Insofar as the American intellectuals are abandoning futurism in favor of archaism they are once more choosing an easy alternative and engaging themselves in a pursuit of Utopia that will again end in frustration and disillusion.

1950

AMERICAN INTELLECTUALS IN THE
POSTWAR SITUATION

I T IS TRUE of course that of late American artists and intellectuals
have largely come to terms with the realities of the national life.
Hence, if they no longer feel "disinherited" and "astray," neither for
that matter are they attached any longer to the attitudes of dissidence and revolt that prevailed among them for some decades. As
their mood has gradually shifted from opposition to acceptance, they
have grown unreceptive to extreme ideas, less exacting and "pure" in
ideological commitment, more open to the persuasions of actuality.
This far-reaching change has by no means run its course. It is of a
complexity not to be grasped by a simple approach, whether positive or negative; and it is easy to fall into one-sided constructions in
discussing it.

Among the factors entering into the change, the principal one, to
my mind, is the exposure of the Soviet myth and the consequent
resolve (shared by nearly all but the few remaining fellow travelers)
to be done with utopian illusions and heady expectations. In their

A contribution to the *Partisan Review* symposium, "Our Country and Our
Culture," May–June 1952.

chastened mood American democracy looks like the real thing to the intellectuals. Its incontestable virtue is that, for all its distortions and contradictions, it actually exists. It is not a mere theory or a deduction from some textbook in world salvation. Whether capitalist or not, it has so far sustained that freedom of expression and experiment without which the survival of the intelligence is inconceivable in a modern society — a society lacking any organic basis, social or religious, for unity of belief or uniformity of conduct. In the palmy days when it was possible to take democracy for granted — that is, before the rise to global power of Hitlerism and then of Stalinism — the intellectuals were hardly aware of the very tangible benefits they derived from it. Now, however, only the most doctrinaire types would be disposed to trade in those benefits for some imaginary perfection of good in the remote future.

This change of perspective has inevitably made for a greater degree of identification with American life, with its traditions and prospects; and to suppose that this is simply a regression to nationalism is a mistake. (The nationalist motive is in fact far more strongly operative among European than among American intellectuals.) What has happened, rather, is that we have gained a sense of immediate relatedness to the national environment, a sense of what is concretely even if minimally our own. In these terms one can indeed speak of a "reconciliation" of the intellectuals.

Another factor, relating to the arts proper, is that the passage of time has considerably blunted the edge of the old Jamesian complaint as to the barrenness of the native scene. James was surely right in drawing the moral that "the flower of art blooms only where the soil is deep, that it takes a great deal of history to produce a little literature, that it needs a complex social machinery to set a writer in motion." But since 1879, when that severe sentence was written, much has happened to modify the conditions James deplored. For one thing, the time is past when "business alone was respectable" in America and when many of its artists were therefore forced into a state of dreary and dreamy isolation. The businessman, though still a most formidable figure, is no longer looked up to as the one and only culture-hero of the country: not since the debacle of 1929, at any rate. Moreover, the national literature has now accumulated a substantial tradition and the dynamism of our historical life in this

12

century has brought into existence a social machinery more than sufficiently complex for literary purposes. This is not to say that this machinery works beneficently; there is no necessary relation between beneficence and literary purpose. If anything, the machinery has now become so prodigious, so vast in operation and prodigal in performance, that the writer is just as likely to be thrown back as to be set into motion by it.

As for the Jamesian vision of Europe as the "rich, deep, dark Old World," its appeal has been markedly reduced by a series of social upheavals, revolutions, and two world wars. The historical richness is still there, though what it comes to at present is hardly more than a combination of décor and recollection; it is the depths and the darkness of the Old World that are almost intolerably actual at present, and in that oppressive atmosphere the Jamesian vision pales and dissolves. It is hard to believe that Western Europe has lost its cultural priority for good, even if for the time being the social and political strains are too great to permit the exercise of leadership. Its past is not in question here, since we cannot but appropriate it as our past too. What is in question is the effort of contemporaries, and that effort is of a scale and intensity insufficient to compel our attention or to provoke meaningful reactions in American culture. Existentialism was, I suppose, the last consequential movement to engage our interest, but the literary work that it produced turned out to be of small consequence. Moreover, the impression is that much of the culture-building energy of Europe's intellectuals is now dissipated in political adventurism; that in their thinking both of their position and ours they are apt to fall into disastrous oversimplifications. And some have plunged into the abyss of Stalin's Utopia.

But if among us that fatal temptation has been largely overcome, it is scarcely because we have been especially endowed with good sense or idealism. The difference lies in the more fortunate, more spacious American environment. Thus it is imperative not to overlook so direct and concrete a factor as the long spell of prosperity that America has enjoyed since the war. It has at long last effected the absorption of the intellectuals into the institutional life of the country. The prosperity that followed the First World War had no such result, the game being strictly business and the intellectuals remaining mostly on the outside looking in, while this time their status has been strikingly improved by the phenomenal expansion of the economy. Writers and artists have succeeded in breaking down the scholastic barriers that kept them out of university teaching, and many economists and sociologists have made their way into government bureaus. In particular it has been the many-sided extension of the educational system which has furnished the greater opportunity. Consider that the intellectual bohemian or proletarian has turned into a marginal figure nowadays, reminding us in his rather quixotic aloneness of the ardors and truancies of the past. We are witnessing a process that might well be described as that of the *embourgeoisement* of the American intelligentsia. In the main, it accounts for the fact that the idea of socialism, whether in its revolutionary or democratic reference, has virtually ceased to figure in current intellectual discussion.

Yet the material security so newly gained must be seen as an achievement of the American system not under normal conditions but under the stress of war and preparation for war. We have been drawn, as Reinhold Niebuhr recently put it, into "an historic situation in which the paradise of our domestic security is suspended in a hell of global insecurity." "Suspended" is the key word, for a good many other satisfactions of American life similarly exist in a state of insecure suspension. The fact is that the Cold War has reduced social tensions within the nation even as it has increased international tension. The war-geared economy has made for conditions of prosperity which again are typically taken to mean that "good Americanism" contains within itself the secret of overcoming the hazards of history. The illusion that our society is in its very nature immune to tragic social conflicts and collisions has been revived, and once more it is assumed that the more acute problems of the modern epoch are unreal so far as we are concerned. And in their recoil from radicalism certain intellectuals have now made that easy assumption their own. Not that they say so openly, but their complacence and spiritual torpor quite give them away.

Especially vulnerable in this respect are some of the ex-radicals and ex-Marxists, who have gone so far in smoothly readapting themselves, in unlearning the old and learning the new lessons, as to be scarcely distinguishable from the common run of philistines. In their narrow world anti-Stalinism has become almost a professional stance.

It has come to mean so much that it excludes nearly all other concerns and ideas, with the result that they are trying to turn anti-Stalinism into something which it can never be: a total outlook on life, no less, or even a philosophy of history. Apparently some of them find it altogether easy to put up with the vicious antics of a political bum like Senator McCarthy, even as they grow more and more intolerant of any basic criticism of existing social arrangements.

The old anti-Stalinism of the independent Left had the true pathos and conviction of a minority fighting under its own banner for its own ends; but that was back in the thirties and early forties. Its function then was to warn — and though the warning was not heeded the anti-Stalinists of that period played a vanguard role in that they were the first to discern the totalitarian essence of the Soviet myth. Since then, however, that minority political grouping has lost its bearings, continuing to denounce the evils of Communism with deadly sameness and in apparent obliviousness of the fact that in the past few years anti-Stalinism has virtually become the official creed of our entire society. What is needed is not more and more demonstrations of the badness of Stalinism but some workable ideas as to how to go about preparing its defeat. The locus of political action has shifted to the sphere of foreign policy, and it is precisely in the formulation and discussion of foreign policy that the deconverted radicals, with very few exceptions, have displayed no special aptitude or initiative or grasp of the immensely perplexing problems that will have to be solved before American leadership of the "free world" can be made to yield positive results.*

* Characteristic of the petrified anti-Stalinists is their inability to distinguish between Communism as an external and as an internal danger. For Communism, though surely a grave danger *to* America — perhaps the gravest that the nation has had to cope with since the Civil War — is hardly so grave a danger *in* America. The local Party has lost its power in the trade unions, it has been deserted by nearly half its membership, and it has only a residual hold on some sections of liberal opinion. The Kremlin's postwar strategy has all but destroyed the influence of the American Communists, an influence almost wholly due to their success in deceiving people as to their real allegiance and intention. In the period of the People's Front and later of the war-alliance with Russia, conditions were extremely favorable to the Stalinist strategy of deception and infiltration. These conditions no longer exist in this country, and the nation as a whole has now been able to take the measure of the party-liners and their assorted dupes and stooges. No doubt they still have a nuisance value to the Kremlin, but to regard them on that account as the main danger *inside* the U.S.

"It is difficult to change gods," says Shatov to Stavrogin in *The Possessed*. Shatov, who turns from "nihilism" to orthodoxy and national messianism, knows whereof he is speaking. One wishes that more people among us confessed to the difficulty, instead of engaging themselves with unseemly haste to positions so safe and sound as to be devoid of all moral or intellectual content. There is the emergent group of parvenu conservatives, for instance, who, having but lately discovered the pleasures of conformity, are now aggressively intent on combating all dissent from the bourgeois outlook and devaluating the critical traditions of modern thought. Thus it has become fashionable to dismiss ideas of cultural or social insurgence by relating them, with a facility all too suspect, to the Russian experience, while at the same time all sorts of heretofore unsuspected plausibilities — if not profundities — are read into the standard notions of the ideologues of reaction; and a new magazine like *The Freeman*, with its boosting of laissez-faire and hero-worship of Taft and McCarthy, is by no means an untypical phenomenon.

In our literary culture there is a more complicated play of forces. The rout of the left-wing movement has depoliticalized literature — which is not necessarily a bad thing in itself if the political motive had been not simply abandoned but creatively displaced by a root-idea of a different order. No such idea has emerged so far; what is to be observed now is a kind of detachment from principle and fragmentation of the literary life. Also to be observed is the rise of a neo-philistine tendency, an oddly belated growth of the mood of acceptance and of the defensive reaction to Communism, which, if unchecked by the revival of the critical spirit, threatens to submerge the tradition of dissent in American writing.

The neo-philistines make an opportune kind of optimism their credo; they are impatient to assume the unchallengeable reality of the "world," and while reconciled to mass-culture they are inclined to deprecate the traditional attitudes of the literary and artistic avant-garde — attitudes said to arise out of negativism pure and

---

is to escape from actualities into the shadow-world of political sectarianism and sheer obsession. Of course, so long as the Soviet power exists its propagandists and spies will circulate among us, and it is up to the intelligence agencies of the government to deal with them. It is scarcely the function of political-minded intellectuals, however, to serve as an adjunct to the F.B.I.

simple and willful indulgence in "alienation." Now the avant-garde is of course open to criticism. It has the typical faults of its incongruous position in a mass-society, such as snobbery and pride of caste. It is disposed to take a much too solemn and devotional view of the artist's vocation. Its distortions of perspective result from its aloofness and somewhat inflexible morality of opposition. But to accuse it of having invented alienation is ludicrous. For what the avant-garde actually represents historically, from its very beginnings in the early nineteenth century, is the effort to preserve the integrity of art and the intellect amidst the conditions of alienation brought on by the major social forces of the modern era. The avant-garde has attempted to ward off the ravages of alienation in a number of ways: by means of developing a tradition of its own and cultivating its own group norms and standards, by resisting the bourgeois incentives to accommodation and perforce making a virtue of its separateness from the mass. That this strategy has in the main been successful is demonstrated by the only test that really counts — the test of creative achievement. After all, it is chiefly the avant-garde which must be given credit for the production of most of the literary masterpieces of the past hundred years, from *Madame Bovary* to the *Four Quartets;* and the other arts are equally indebted to its venturesome spirit.

If the artists of the avant-garde are alienated, as it is said, then at least they are free to convert their consciousness of that unhappy state into an imaginative resource. This cannot be claimed for the artists in mass-culture, whose function literally depends on their capacity to cultivate a kind of strategic unawareness of meaning and consequence. Of course, there are certain elements in mass-culture, some types of jazz and the folklore of sport for instance, that have a positive value. On the whole, though, the proliferation of kitsch in this country under the leveling stimulus of the profit-motive is a liability of our society which is not to be wished away by pious appeals to democracy and the rights of the "common man." But if under present conditions we cannot stop the ruthless expansion of mass-culture, the least we can do is to keep apart and refuse its favors.

1952

AN INTRODUCTION TO KAFKA

Franz Kafka is today firmly linked in the literary mind to such names as Joyce and Proust and Yeats and Rilke and Eliot — the sacred untouchables, as they have been rightly called, of the modern creative line. Among them he is exceptional in that he enjoyed no public recognition of consequence in his lifetime, for he withheld his longer narratives from publication and was scarcely known beyond a narrow circle of German writers. His posthumous world fame came to him only in the past two decades.

The first translation of one of his books appeared in this country in 1930, six years after his death. That book was *The Castle*, a novel that ranks high in the Kafka canon. Few readers were then able to gauge its true worth, and even as late as 1937, when *The Trial* was brought out here, it was chiefly Kafka's apparent mystifications rather than his pattern of meaning and basic motives that aroused interest. Readers were astonished by his work but hardly convinced of its importance. Since then his idiosyncratic but powerful sensibility has entered into the blood stream of twentieth-century litera-

Written as an introduction to the *Selected Tales of Franz Kafka* in the Modern Library edition.

ture. He has been made the subject of numerous critical studies in many languages; and everywhere the more sensitive younger writers, conscious of the static condition of the prevailing fictional techniques and seeking creative renewal, have taken his example to heart. There can be little doubt any longer of his stature as an artist in the metaphysical mode, whose concern is with the ultimate structure of human existence, or of his surpassing originality as an innovator in creative method. Like Rilke in the *Duino Elegies* he asked the supreme question: *Was war wirklich im All?* (What was real in the world?)

A master of narrative tone, of a subtle, judicious, and ironically conservative style, Kafka combines in his fiction the real and the unreal, extreme subjectivity of content with forms rigorously objective, a lovingly exact portrayal of the factual world with dreamlike dissolution of it. By unifying these contrary elements he was able to achieve a fundamentally new appropriation of the resources of the prose medium. This much can be said, I think, without attempting to give an integrated critical estimate of his work, which may well be premature even now. The analysis and description of its qualities will suffice. Thus it is clear that if Kafka so compellingly arouses in us a sense of immediate relatedness, of strong even if uneasy identification, it is because of the profound quality of his feeling for the experience of human loss, estrangement, guilt, and anxiety — an experience increasingly dominant in the modern age.

That Kafka is among the most neurotic of literary artists goes without saying. It accounts, mainly, for the felt menace of his fantastic symbolism and for his drastic departure from the well-defined norms of the literary imagination. For all its obviousness, however, the fact of Kafka's neuroticism presents a danger, if not a vulgar temptation, to the unliterary mind, which tends to confuse a fact so patent with critical judgment and appraisal. No greater error is possible in our approach to literary art. To avoid that common error it is above all necessary to perceive that Kafka is something more than a neurotic artist; he is also an artist of neurosis, that is to say, he succeeds in objectifying through imaginative means the states of mind typical of neurosis and hence in incorporating his private world into the public world we all live in. Once that is accomplished, the creative writer has performed the essential operation which is the secret of his triumph as an artist, if not as a man; he has exorcised his demon, freed himself of his personal burden, converting us into his accomplices. And we, as good readers, as willing accomplices, have no real reason to complain. Neurosis may be the occasion but literature is the consequence. Moreover, the creative writer is the last person we may look to if our concern is with drawing a line between the normal and the abnormal. For whatever the practicing psychologist may make of that crude though useful distinction, the artist cannot attend to it without inhibiting his sense of life in its full concreteness and complexity.

The novelist Graham Greene has remarked that "every creative writer worth our consideration, every writer who can be called in the wide sense of the term a poet, is a victim: a man given over to an obsession." Kafka's obsession was an inordinate sense of inadequacy, failure, and sinfulness — a sinfulness corresponding to nothing he had actually done or left undone, but lodged in the innermost recesses of his being. "The state in which we find ourselves is sinful, quite independently of guilt," he wrote in his notebook. The clue to *The Trial* is the reflection that "only our concept of time makes it possible for us to speak of the Day of Judgment by that name; in reality it is a summary court in perpetual session." And in the same sequence of reflections we find the perfectly typical sentence: "The hunting dogs are playing in the courtyard, but the hare will not escape them, no matter how fast it may be flying already through the woods." The identification here is plainly with the hare; and with the hunting dogs, too, insofar as they represent the hare's longing for self-punishment, his inner wish to be cornered, to be hurt and torn to pieces so as to atone for the guilt that fills him from top to bottom. In this one short sentence about the hare and the dogs you have the gist of the typical Kafkan narrative, the obsessive theme, the nuclear fable concerning the victim of an unappeasable power to which he returns again and again, varying and complicating its structure with astonishing resourcefulness, and erecting on so slender a foundation such marvelous superstructures as that of the myth of the Old Commander in "In the Penal Colony," the myth of the Law in *The Trial*, and of the celestial bureaucracy in *The Castle*.

The simplicity of the nuclear fable in Kafka should not lead us, however, to disregard the qualities that make him one of the most enigmatic figures in world literature. It does no good to speak of him as an author of religious allegories. Unlike such religious allegorists as Dante or Bunyan he does not depend on the definitive logic of a generally known system of theology; his creative mode presupposes no body of knowledge external to itself; he is not allegorical in any accepted sense but rather an innovator so deeply individualistic as to fit none of the familiar categories. Also, the difficulty of understanding him is on a different plane from that encountered in reading a novelist like James Joyce, for example. Whereas the obscurities of the latter are inherent in the elaborate stylization of his material and in his complex structural designs, in Kafka's case it is the meaning alone that baffles us. Both in language and construction he is elementary compared to Joyce, yet many readers have been mystified by his fictions. But the mystification is gradually cleared up once we learn to listen attentively to his tone and become accustomed to the complete freedom with which he suspends certain conventions of storytelling when it suits his symbolic purpose. Thus when we read in the first sentence of "The Metamorphosis" that the clerk Gregor Samsa awoke one morning to find himself changed into a gigantic insect, it is a mistake to think that by means of this bold stroke Kafka intends to call into question the laws of nature. What he calls into question, rather, is the convention that the laws of nature are at all times to be observed in fiction; and having suspended that convention in the very first paragraph of the story, from that point on he develops it in a logical and realistic manner. The clerk's metamorphosis is a multiple symbol of his alienation from the human state, of his "awakening" to the full horror of his dull, spiritless existence, and of the desperate self-disgust of his unconscious fantasy-life, in which the wish to displace the father and take over his authority in the family is annulled by the guilt-need to suffer a revolting punishment for his presumption.

Another type of symbolism, far less psychologically charged, is found in stories like "The Great Wall of China." What is the Great Wall? It is likewise a multiple symbol — of human solidarity, of earthly fulfillment and of mankind's effort to obtain supernatural guidance. But why was the wall built in a piecemeal fashion, thus permitting the nomads of the North to slip through the gaps? The reply is that it is in the nature of man to achieve only limited ends. He cannot comprehend the Whole; his vision is discontinuous, his security always incomplete; his aims he can realize only in fragmentary fashion. No doubt the "high command" is ultimately responsible for the apparently inexpedient method of the wall's construction; yet it would never do to question its decrees. Not that such questioning is blasphemous in itself but rather that in the long run it is useless. Logic can bring us only to a certain point. Beyond that an answer of a sort is given by the beautiful parable of the river in spring. And as the story continues, the theme of the wall is dialectically converted into a series of poetic speculations concerning the relationship between the Chinese and the imperial court at Pekin, that is between God and man. While in "Investigations of a Dog" the remoteness of God is represented as a remoteness in time, in this story the imagery is chiefly spatial. Pekin is so far away from the villagers of the South that they can hardly imagine its existence. They worship dynasties long since dead; news arriving from the imperial court is obsolete by the time it reaches them. This inability of the "Chinese" to possess their Emperor in his vital contemporaneity appears to be a reflection on the idea of God as known to modern man — an idea ill-defined, nebulous and, above all, archaic. Man is now unaware of the real powers that govern his life; insofar as he has any knowledge of divinity it is as of something purely historical.

The quarrel between the religious and the psychoanalytic interpreters of Kafka is of no great moment, as his work is sufficiently meaningful to support some of the "truths" of both schools. Thus the father who condemns his son to death by drowning (in "The Judgment") can be understood as the tyrannical father of Freudian lore and at the same time as the God of Judgment rising in His wrath to destroy man's illusion of self-sufficiency in the world. At bottom there is no conflict between the two interpretations. For one thing, they are not mutually exclusive; for another, the reading we give the story depends as much on our own outlook — within certain limits of course — as on that of the author. There was in Kafka's character an element of radical humility not permitting him to set out to "prove" any given attitude toward life or idea about it. This he plainly tells us in some of the aphorisms that he wrote about him-self in the third person: "He proves nothing but himself, his sole proof is himself, all his opponents overcome him at once, not by refuting him (he is irrefutable) but by proving themselves."

That Kafka was a man of religious temper I have no doubt. Though the creator of a surpassing imagery of human failure and frustration, inclined to feel imprisoned on this earth, afflicted with "the melancholy, the impotence, the sicknesses, the feverish fancies of the captive," he never abandons his trust in the spirituality of existence, in the "indestructible," and is disheartened by his literary effort because he wants his writing to attain the power of lifting the world into the realm of "the pure, the true, the immutable." Yet there is nothing either in his private papers or in his fiction to war-rant the claim that he was a believer in a personal God who gave his assent to any of the dogmatic systems associated with institu-tional religion. Even original sin, the dogma closest to the thematic center of his work, he interprets speculatively as "consisting of the complaint, which man makes and never ceases making, that a wrong had been done to him, that the original sin was committed upon him." From the standpoint of the theologian that is sheer heresy, gentle, self-incriminating heresy, to be sure, but heresy nevertheless. The German critic Franz Blei, who was personally acquainted with Kafka, speaks of him as "the servant of a God not believed in." A piety so paradoxical, so immune to categorical definition, so removed from the fixed and traditional, refusing the consolation of revealed religion yet intent on winning through to "a faith like a guillotine, as heavy, as light," could never have found expression in general ideas or logical thought but only in the language of art, the one language capable of offering everything while claiming nothing, asserting nothing, proving nothing.

Born in 1883 of middle-class Jewish parents, Kafka appears to have lost his self-confidence early in life, exchanging for it, as he himself put it, "a boundless sense of guilt." Moods of loss and fail-ure, and the idea of the insolubility even of the most ordinary human problems, depressed his youth and later inspired his art. In the center of his life stands the father, a figure fully corresponding to that Freudian terror, the Primal Sire. Energetic, overbearing, capricious, successful, respectable, the father, not so much by malicious intention as by being simply what he was, exposed to ridicule his son's impractical inclinations and spiritual wanderings. The mother, though solicitous for her son, was far too much absorbed in her husband to play an independent role; and young Franz was thus driven to extremes of loneliness and introspection that continually negated themselves in the idea of integration through marriage, children, and the practice of an honorable profession ("a true calling . . . the right vocation"). The effect on him of his father was such that though he usually talked exceedingly well, in the presence of the formidable parent he took to stuttering. "For me," he wrote to his father in later life, "you began to have that mysterious quality which all tyrants have, whose privilege is based on their personality, not on reason." It is clear that the source of the principle of authority so characteristic of his art is to be traced to his ambivalent attitude to his father, an attitude of strong repulsion as well as identification. Constructed out of elements of his own personality, the protagonist of his major fictions is coerced by extranatural powers who are continually justified and exalted even as they are made to manifest themselves in the guise of a menacing and arbitrary bureaucracy. Max Brod, Kafka's lifelong friend, biographer, and editor of his posthumous writings, relates that in many talks he attempted to demonstrate to him the foolishness of his self-contempt and chronic overestimation of his father. These talks were useless, for Kafka produced a "torrent of arguments" that shattered and repelled his friend, who soon realized that only from the standpoint of an outsider could it be asked: "What difference could his father's approval make to Kafka?" His need for that approval was obviously "an innate, irrefutable feeling" that lasted to the end of his life.

In 1906 he took his degree in law at the German University in Prague and soon afterwards obtained a post in an accident insurance office. But his real interest was in writing, which he approached with the utmost moral earnestness, regarding it as a sacred expenditure of energy, an effort at communion with one's fellowmen, the reflected splendor of religious perception. However, it could never serve as his means of livelihood; aside from his objection in principle to turning literary talent into a source of material benefits, there were other obstacles. He wrote at a pace altogether his own, filled with a raging discontent; at the same time there was the drastic need to stand on his own feet, to win immediate independence from the family. Yet the work at the insurance office disintegrated him; the two occupations were incompatible.

In his letters he writes of literature as his only hope for happiness and fulfillment; and telling of trancelike states when he felt himself at the boundary of the human, he adds that they lacked the serenity of inspiration and were not conducive to the best writing. He speaks of himself as having been on the way to create "a new secret doctrine, a Kabala," but his replies as to the meaning of that doctrine are as diverse as they are contradictory. (His precision, Brod rightly says, was moral, not intellectual.) "I represent," we read in his diary, "the negative elements of my age . . . Unlike Kierkegaard, I was not guided in life by the new heavily sinking hand of Christianity, nor have I caught hold, like the Zionists, of one of the ends of the flying prayer-shawl of the Jews." The one break in his relationship with Brod seems to have been caused by his coolness to Zionism. "What have I in common with the Jews," he wrote, "when I have scarcely anything in common with myself?" In later years, however, he developed a lively interest in the aspirations of the Zionists, studied Jewish folk literature, the Hebrew language, and read the Talmud (to which his style, by the way, in its reasoning, argumentative quality, in its movement through assertion and contradiction, statement and refutation, bears some resemblance.)

It was in 1912 — a fateful year in his life — that he met Felice B., the young woman from Berlin whom he wanted to marry but was forced to renounce, suffering terrible anguish in twice breaking off his engagement to her. He felt that for a man in his uprooted condition, lacking independent status and a secure orientation in life, marriage was an impossible task. But that was the year, too, in which his literary intentions and continual probing of his own predicament came together in a way enabling him to forge decisively ahead in his work. Compared to what he wrote in the fall of that year everything he had previously written seems sketchy and unfinished. On the night of September 22 of that seminal fall he wrote "The Judgment" in one sitting, remarking afterwards that during that long stretch between ten o'clock in the evening and six o'clock the next morning he more than once carried his weight on his own back. "The Judgment" is the first Kafkan story which is all of a piece and the first in which the characteristic theme of the struggle between father and son is sounded to the depths. That same month and the next he wrote the long opening chapter of *Amerika,* his first novel, and in November he completed "The Metamorphosis," certainly his greatest story, in which he achieves an overpowering effect through his consummate handling of the factual detail that supports and actualizes the somber fantasy of the plot. This story is the very embodiment of that quality of the exigent and the extreme, that sense of a human being hemmed in by his own existence and absolutely committed to it, which touches us so deeply in Kafka because it is at once method and content, entreaty and response, the goal and the way. It is mainly through this "existential" quality that Kafka *substantiates* his world for us, imparting the unmistakable appeal of reality to those elements in it that might otherwise appear to be little more than the products of a bizarre or erratic imagination. In "The Metamorphosis," I would say, Kafka for the first time fully realized his own innermost conception of writing — a conception of inexpressible urgency and inwardness. Long before the composition of the story, he attempted to explain what writing meant to him when he said, in a letter to his friend Oskar Pollak, that "the books we need are of the kind that act upon us like a misfortune, that make us suffer like the death of someone we love more than ourselves, that make us feel as though we were on the verge of suicide, or lost in a forest remote from all human habitation — a book should serve as the ax for the frozen sea within us."

In October of the same year Max Brod notes in his diary: "Kafka in ecstasy. Writes all night long . . ." And again: "Kafka in incredible ecstasy." There is something more to this ecstatic state than elation and the sense of freedom a writer normally experiences when making visible progress in his work. The patently compulsive nature of "The Judgment" and "The Metamorphosis," no less than Kafka's own comment upon them in his diaries, suggest that these stories served as "the ax for the frozen sea" within him — in other words, that the process of their creation involved a breakthrough to layers of repressed material which had heretofore proven inaccessible. It is as if in these psychodynamic fictions the neurotic sufferer in Kafka and the artist in him locked hands and held on for dear life. Precisely of works such as these one can say with Yeats that "the more unconscious the creation the more powerful."

The novel *Amerika*, begun in that period, stands somewhat apart from the bulk of Kafka's work. The extranatural plays no part in it; there is no evocation of mysterious powers or any derangement of the known and recognizable world for the sake of injecting into it the menace of the irrational and unfathomable. It is the only one of Kafka's longer narratives in which he fully indulged his flair for comedy. The intention behind it, however, is not the exposure of specific foibles but the portrayal of the typical human condition. "If sufficiently systematized comedy turns into reality," he wrote in his notebooks. And this statement can stand as the motto of this picaresque tale of the adventures of the sixteen-year-old boy Karl Rossmann, a native of Prague, in the mechanized cities of the United States, a country which Kafka had never seen but of which he had a definite image in his mind.

Steeped as he was in moods of loss and failure, he tended to regard with astonishment and inordinate admiration all examples of constructive will, of the ability of men to discover their true calling and achieve that integration in the community to which he attached the highest value but which he believed to be beyond his own reach. His constant plaint was the same as that of the character in Hawthorne's story "The Intelligence Office," who never ceases to cry out: "I want my place, my own place, my proper sphere, my thing to do, which nature intended me to perform when she fashioned me thus awry, and which I have vainly sought all my lifetime!" For this reason Benjamin Franklin, who was singularly successful in all his undertakings, was among Kafka's favorite historical figures; and Franklin's *Autobiography* is one of the sources of *Amerika*. Let no one think, however, that Kafka was charmed by Poor Richard's opinion of himself or by his general philosophy; what interested him in this exemplary American career was its inexplicable element of fate, which in this case had manifested itself in a positive guise. He probably read Poor Richard's recommendations of virtue, his list of proverbs on frugality, temperance, moderation, tranquility, and the like, as one reads a work on strategy, interpreting those dismally sagacious sayings as so many moves in the complicated game of ingratiating oneself with the nameless authorities whose law, though its intent and meaning are unknown and unknowable, prevails nonetheless. It was the Ulysses-like aspect of Franklin that attracted Kafka, and he conceived of America as his Mediterranean. Americans, he thought, wore perpetual smiles on their faces, for somehow they had managed, perhaps through the protection afforded them by the extraordinary dimensions of the New World, to beat fate to the draw.

Karl Rossmann is truly innocent, and in this respect he differs radically from K., the protagonist of *The Trial* and *The Castle*. Whereas K., who is thoroughly impregnated with rationality, approaches the problem of guilt largely in a legalistic fashion, reacting vindictively to the misfortunes that befall him and seeking to prove by logical processes that he has committed no crime and should therefore be let alone, Karl suffers persecution without dreaming of vengeance or unduly dwelling on the wrongs that have been done him. When his rich uncle willfully turns him out of his house for virtually no reason at all, he utters no word of protest but calmly goes about the business of adjusting himself to his new situation. He is not a subjective character; his energy is of that benign kind which flows congenially even into the narrowest channels of reality.

The Kafkan irony expends itself on Karl by entangling him in a series of accidents, errors, and misunderstandings that are as circumstantially precise as they are magical in arrangement. His first steps in America — whose bewildering and immense bureaucratic mechanisms he dare not examine too closely — are attended by good fortune, but after a few months he is suddenly overtaken by disaster and compelled to take to the road in search of work in the company of the unemployed and thievish mechanics Delamarche and Robinson. After many trials he is befriended by a woman, a kind of Athene in the shape of a hotel manager. But this position too is soon lost to him, when he is abducted by the thievish mechanics with the design of forcing him into the service of Brunelda, a great slob of a Circe who had transformed them both into swinish lechers. (The seventh chapter, called "The Refuge," describing the Chaplinesque chase of Karl by a policeman, his encounter with the incomparable Brunelda, the election parade, and his conversation with the coffee-nourished student, is to my mind one of the finest single pieces of

13

writing in modern fiction.) In the end he escapes from Brunelda's household to find work in the "Nature Theatre of Oklahoma," a beneficent and fantastic enterprise miraculously welcoming the unemployed into its almost limitless spaces, where they are provided with jobs and reconciled to the inscrutable purposes of the powers ruling the life of man.

Kafka makes no attempt to give a realistic account of America. He is quite inaccurate in every detail, yet the picture as a whole has uncanny symbolic truth. And if on its existential side this story is a sort of good-humored parody of the career of Poor Richard, on its literary side it derives from Dickens. David Copperfield, who is also a good boy with the wit to make the most of his virtue in his trials and tribulations, is Karl's prototype. But this "imitation" of Dickens' novel is in its way a burlesque treatment of it and is analogous to Joyce's use of Homer in his *Ulysses*.

One misses in *Amerika* the profound implications of Kafka's other work. Plainly his imagination did not wholly support this one effort to guide the life of a human being to a happy outcome. He was more at home in the dread castles and courts where K. wanders in search of justice, only to discover at the very last that justice is as meaningless as it is inescapable. *Amerika* belongs to what one might call the psychological phase of Kafka's art. The movement of this art is from psychology to experimental mythology, from the immediate appropriation of personal states to their projection into the world at large. Thus the principle of authority on which his work is grounded is at the outset, as in "The Judgment" and "The Metamorphosis," represented in the figure of a "real" father, a father whom it is not very difficult to identify in terms of the Freudian "family romance," while in the later and longer fictions the father is no longer recognizable as a figure in the world we know. He has been removed from the family circle and generalized into an institutional power — hierarchic, remote, mysterious — such as the Law, the Court and the order of officials that reside in the Castle.

In respect to this line of development "In the Penal Colony" can be regarded as a transitional story. It was written in November 1914, when Kafka had already begun working on *The Trial*. Perhaps because it shows the influence of Kierkegaard, upon whom Kafka first came in 1913, the religious analogues of this story are clearer than in the earlier tales. The Old Commander, whose dread memory is invoked in "In the Penal Colony," retains some of the individual traits of the "real" father, at the same time as he is mythicized in the manner of the images of authority projected in the later novels.

But in the long run in the early breakthrough in his writing to the deeper layers of his psychic life failed to free Kafka of his nerve-destroying fears and sense of unworthiness. He continued to quarrel with himself, plotting self-punishment, thinking even of suicide. "Balzac carried a cane on which was carved the legend: I smash every obstacle; my legend reads: Every obstacle smashes me." The constant seesaw between writing and his job affected his health. He suffered from headaches and insomnia, finally tuberculosis set in and he was compelled to spend years in sanitariums. His illness he considered to be psychically determined — "My head conspired with my lung behind my back." It was not until 1923, when he met Dora Dymant, a girl brought up in an orthodox Jewish family in Poland, and he found himself well enough to move with her to Berlin, that he at long last realized his longing for independence. But, as it turned out, it was already too late to obtain the restitution he sought for the lost years of sickness and misery. In June 1924, at the age of forty-one, he died in a hospital near Vienna of laryngeal tuberculosis.

During his lifetime he published only some of his shorter works, and he never quite finished any of his three novels. Before his death he wrote to Max Brod requesting him to burn all the manuscripts he was leaving behind. Fortunately, his friend took upon himself the honourable responsibility of disregarding that desperate last instruction.

1952

GOGOL AS A MODERN INSTANCE

IN REFLECTING ABOUT GOGOL while preparing my remarks for this commemorative occasion I found myself thinking of him first of all as a peculiarly modern instance of the literary artist. This may surprise those who see him entirely in terms of the Russian background, placing him all too securely within a nearly self-sufficient national tradition. There is no denying, to be sure, that the Russian background is of primary importance for the understanding of Gogol's creative course. He crosses the frontiers of language far less easily than writers like Turgenev and Dostoevsky and Tolstoy and Chekhov, whose creations exercise an appeal unconfined by differences of nationality and cultural setting. Gogol's work, with the possible exception of his story "The Overcoat," cannot be said to have become an intimate possession of the Western world; only in the Russian milieu is it an indispensable part of a literary education. But the reason for that is quite simple. Gogol's characters, like Chichikov and Khlestakov, are no less universal than the characters of Tolstoy and Dostoevsky. What hinders us in our appropria-

Text of a talk at a public meeting in Columbia University commemorating the one-hundredth anniversary of Gogol's death.

tion of them is the fact that Gogol is so great a master of style and verbal orchestration that his power to move us is virtually indissoluble from his language.

Another approach to Gogol is by way of his creative psychology, in which one recognizes certain traits that recall us to the fate of modern literature. It is above all our sense of the deeply problematic character of this literature that impels us to conceive of Gogol as our contemporary. His creative psychology is so tortuous and obsessive, so given over to moods of self-estrangement and self-loathing, so marked by abrupt turns from levity to despair, that one cannot but see it as a tissue of contradictions from top to bottom. These contradictions are at once the secret of his poetic power and the cause of his ruin as a man — his tragic renunciation of the creative life in mid-career and the frightful end that came to him under the stress of a spiritual crisis of a surpassingly primitive and even savage nature. It is easy enough to expatiate on the neurotic components in his makeup, or, to put it more precisely, on the unmistakable pathology of his life-experience. Let us keep in mind, however, that in the case of great artists neuroticism is never in itself a sufficient explanation. For the neuroticism of such artists tends to assume a symbolic meaning, taking on the suprapersonal significance of a general state of mind or of a radical change in consciousness. In this sense it becomes possible to relate the discontinuities and discords in Gogol to the problematical character of the modern artist as a type. Gogol's dilemma was that he was incapable of reconciling the meaning of his art with the meaning of his life. This discord, to which the artists of the modern epoch are peculiarly open, was scarcely operative in the classic ages of literature when life and art were not at war with each other but were integrated by common presuppositions and a common faith.

The problem of the separation of art and life has an objective historical import that is not to be grasped if analyzed solely from the standpoint of the artist's personal character and disposition. It is exactly from this point of view that Arnold Hauser discusses the struggles and sufferings of Flaubert. Hauser attributes Flaubert's lack of a direct relationship to life, his dogmatic aestheticism and his turning away with disdain from human existence as a symptom of "the gulf that has opened up in the modern artistic career between the possession of life and the expression of it." Gogol, too, wanted to possess his life in a manner quite incompatible with his expression of it; and there is still another way in which we might link these two novelists in spite of the obvious differences between them. Both are leading protagonists in the extremely complex and perilous passage of European literature from romanticism to realism. Like Flaubert, Gogol is an inverted Romantic trying to resolve the tension between actuality and romance, between the deflation and inflation of life's vital illusions, by the most rigorous application of rhetorical and stylistic force, by exploiting the necromantic properties of language so as to establish some kind of psychic control and a measure of moral poise, however precarious. In wholly different ways both of these literary artists used language as a shield against chaos and as a therapeutic resource; and both were compelled to create prodigious images of negation even as they inwardly yearned to utter the saving, the positive, the loving word. Thus Flaubert, who began as a Romantic, was inclined from the outset to idealize love; yet what he actually wrote is novels about the destructive effects of love and its power to entangle us in fatal illusions. The theme of love was of course closed to Gogol by his prohibitive fear of sexuality, but in his own chosen themes he too was compulsively driven to expose precisely that which he would have liked to portray in glowing colors. Starting from the invulnerably naive premise that it was his task to idealize the feudal-bureaucratic order of imperial Russia and to paint an idyllic picture of the rural squires, what he in fact produced is a picture so grotesquely satiric that it could easily be made to serve as an instrument of social disruption. Flaubert found his ideal enemy in the bourgeois, whom he tirelessly berated, while Gogol, inasmuch as in his time the Russian bourgeois existed as no more than an embryo in the body politic, seized on the government official and on the parasitic landlord as types whom he could paralyze with his satiric virus and then fix forever in the monstrous tableau his imagination constructed. Even Flaubert's statement, "*Madame Bovary, c'est moi,*" has its parallel in Gogol's remark that in laughing at his characters the reader was really laughing at their author, for he had impregnated them with his own looseness and "nastiness."

It is not difficult to recognize in Gogol some of the features of

Dostoevsky's underground man, in particular the split between sickly, spiteful vanity on the one hand and aspirations toward truth and goodness on the other. Some Russian scholars have surmised that Dostoevsky had Gogol in mind in his portrayal of Foma Fomich, the buffoon-like protagonist of his long story *The Friend of the Family*. Whether this surmise is correct or not, there is indeed something in Foma Fomich's insufferably didactic tone, in his outrageous preaching of virtue and uplift that reminds us irresistibly of Gogol's vainglorious and clownish bombast in that incredible book, *Selected Passages from the Correspondence with Friends,* probably the most implausible work ever produced by a writer of genius.

The truth is that Gogol was quite aware of his own "underground" traits, and he spoke more than once of "the terrible mixture of contradictions" of which his nature was composed. This master of language, the first truly important artist of Russian prose, strove with might and main to overcome what he regarded as the morbid negativism of his relationship to life, a striving pitiful in its futility; for as he himself admitted in "The Author's Confession," his real predilection was "for bringing out the trivialities of life, describing the vulgarity of mediocrity . . . and all those small things which generally remain unobserved." What is missing, however, in this self-analysis of Gogol's is any hint of the astonishing comic sense that enabled him to invest mediocrity and smallness of soul with a super-real quality that ultimately acts to liberate us and restore us to our humanity. The one thing that Gogol failed to believe in is that laughter cures. His conviction of guilt and unworthiness forced him to hold out obstinately against that catharsis of laughter for which his readers are immensely grateful to him.

Gogol was in no sense a cultivated man of letters. He appeared on the literary scene like an utterly unexpected and rude guest after whose departure life at home could never again be the same. It does not matter that the rude guest's performance was not quite understood for what it was, that a critic like Belinsky, for instance, could cite this performance as an overriding example of the writer's assumption of responsibility to society, of his civic consciousness and fidelity to the factually real. What was then chiefly overlooked in Gogol was the fantastic gratuity of his humor and his transcendence of the limited social motive through the unearthly and well-nigh metaphysical pathos of a supreme creation like "The Overcoat." For in truth Baschmatskin, the little copying clerk who is the hero of that story, attains a stature far greater than that of any mere victim of an unjust social system. He is a timeless apparition of humanity *in extremis,* of man homeless not only in his society but in the universe. There is one story in American literature, Melville's "Bartelby the Scrivener," which has a spiritual affinity with "The Overcoat." But it is no more than affinity. Melville's story, for all its profound overtones, lacks the inner coherence, the resonance, and marvelous stylization of Gogol's masterpiece.

But having allowed for the period prejudices of a critic like Belinsky and discounted the narrowly sociological approach to Gogol, I still cannot accept the aesthetic-modernist reading of his work that we get in Vladimir Nabokov's critical study of him. Brilliantly appreciative as Nabokov is of the grotesque side of Gogol and, indeed, of all that side of him relating to the poetry of the irrational and the spirit of incongruity and mystification, he has no eye whatever for his subject's place in literary history and social and national peculiarities. Nabokov seems to suffer from something like a phobic fear of all interpretive techniques not strictly literary in reference — a fear driving him toward the extremely one-sided emphasis which takes the literary act to be a phenomenon solely "of language and not of ideas." And Nabokov reduces his formalist bias to sheer absurdity when he goes so far as to state that "Gogol's heroes happen to be Russian squires and officials; their imagined surroundings and social conditions are perfectly unimportant." He is equally vehement in denying that Gogol can in any way be characterized as a realist. It is true, of course, that Gogol never deliberately set out to describe his social environment; but the fact is that his subjective method of exaggeration, of caricature and farce, produced an imagery of sloth, ugliness, and self-satisfied inferiority which, if not directly reflective, is nonetheless fully expressive of the realities of life in Czarist Russia. Moreover, Nabokov ignores the dynamic plebeianism of Gogol's genius. For that is what enabled him to make a radically new selection of material and to assimilate to his medium elements of everyday existence, with their lowlife and vulgar details, heretofore excluded by the aristocratic conventions of literature in Russia as elsewhere. Even if the creatures of his imagination are not so much "real people" as caricatures, he nonetheless contributed greatly to the development of realism by opening up the lower reaches and underside of life to literary portraiture.

It is impossible to abstract Gogol from his historical moment and to dissociate the necessary and contingent elements of his creative personality so as to arrive at the pure substance of Gogolism. Nabokov's rite of purification converts Gogol into the ghost of his own work. I do not object to Nabokov's Gogol because he bears so little resemblance to the Gogol of Belinsky and Dobroluibov but rather because Nabokov's Gogol is too pure to be true, too literary and abstract to be genuine. The poet who inserted into *Dead Souls* epic apostrophes to Holy Russia — apostrophes infused with messianic hope in which love and despair are inextricably mingled — was not a purist writing in a vein of exclusive subjectivity and dedicated to the tormenting refinements of his solitary dreams. He too, like all of Russia's great writers, suffered with his country and its people. It is exactly this meaningful aspect of the Russian classic tradition that was impassionedly recalled by the symbolist poet Alexander Blok in his essay "The Intelligentsia and the Revolution" (1918) when he wrote that "the great Russian artists — Pushkin, Gogol, Dostoevsky, Tolstoy — were submerged in darkness, but it was never their will to stay hidden in it; for they believed in the light. Each one of them, like the whole nation which carried them under its heart, ground its teeth in the darkness seized by despair and fury. Yet they knew that sooner or later life will be renewed because life is beautiful."

1952

THE MYTH AND THE POWERHOUSE

One must know how to ask questions: the question is
who was Ariadne and which song did the sirens sing? —

FRIEDRICH GEORG JUENGER

MUCH HAS BEEN WRITTEN of late about myth. What it is and what it will do for us has been widely debated, yet I cannot see that any clear statement of the intrinsic meaning of present-day mythomania has emerged from the discussion. The exponents of myth keep insisting on its seminal uses, appealing indiscriminately to Yeats and Joyce and Mann and other exemplars of the modern creative line, while the opponents point to the regressive implications of the newfangled concern with myth, charging that at bottom what it comes to is a kind of nebulous religiosity, a vague literary compromise between skepticism and dogma, in essence a form of magico-religious play with antique counters in a game without real commitments or consequences.

To be sure, not all exponents of myth are of one type. Some make no excessive claims; others have turned into sheer enthusiasts who blow up myth into a universal panacea, proclaiming that the "reintegration of the myth" will not only save the arts but will lead to no less than the cure of modern ills and ultimate salvation. So extravagant have been their claims that even Jacques Maritain, who is hardly to be accused of a naturalistic view of myth, has been moved to rebuke them, primarily for confusing metaphysical and poetic myths, that is, confusing the fictions composed by the poet *qua* poet (which may be called myths, if at all, only in a loose analogical sense) with the great myths deriving their power solely from the belief that men have in them.* For myth actually believed in is not understood as a symbolic form, competing with other such forms, but as truth pure and simple.

Now why should a distinction so elementary be generally overlooked by the cultists of myth? For the very good reason, obviously, that it is this very cultism which enables them to evade the hard choice between belief and unbelief. After all, now that the idea of myth has been invested in literary discourse with all sorts of intriguing suggestions of holiness and sacramental significance, one can talk about it as if it were almost the same thing as religion, thus circumventing the all too definite and perhaps embarrassing demands of orthodoxy even while enjoying an emotional rapport with it. At the same time, myth having been somehow equated with the essence of poetry, it becomes possible to enlist its prestige along with that of religion. The mythomaniac puts himself in the position of speaking freely in the name both of poetry and religion without, however, making himself responsible to either. But it should be evident that in the long run neither benefits from so forced a conjunction. It deprives them equally of specific definition and commitment, and this, I take it, is the implicit point of M. Maritain's critical remarks.

The discussion of myth has led some literary men to undertake interpretations of it in terms of its origins and fundamental import in the history of culture. Such interpretations are in the main more wishful than accurate, running counter to the findings at once of such noted philosophical students of myth as Ernst Cassirer and anthropologists and ethnologists like Malinowski, Jane Harrison, Lord Raglan, A. M. Hocart, S. M. Hooke, and others. The fact is that the current literary inflation of myth is not in the least sup-

* Jacques Maritain: *Creative Intuition in Art and Poetry* (New York, 1953), pp. 18off.

ported by the authoritative texts in this field of study. Typical is the approach of a distinguished literary critic, who on the subject of myth proceeds entirely without discretion. Myth is for him "the cartograph of the perennial human situation," and he contends that in myth alone can we hope to encounter "a beckoning image of the successful alliance of love and justice, the great problems of the race from its dark beginnings." In other words: Back to myth if you want to be saved! It leaves one wondering how that sort of thing can possibly be squared with anything to be found, for instance, in the late Professor Cassirer's numerous, painstaking, and truly imaginative inquiries into myth. What we do realize in reading Cassirer, however, is that contemporary mythomania makes for the renewal in our time of the symbolic-allegorical treatment of myth favored by the romantics, who saw in myth a source of higher teachings and ultra-spiritual insights, converting it into a magic mirror that reflected their heart's desire. As Cassirer observes, the romantic philosophers and poets in Germany were the first to embrace myth with rapture, identifying it with reality in the same way as they identified poetry with truth: from then on "they saw all things in a new shape. They could not return to the common world — the world of the *profanum vulgus.*"* The cultism of myth is patently a revival of romantic longings and attitudes.

It seems as if in the modern world there is no having done with romanticism — no having done with it because of its enormous resourcefulness in accommodating the neo-primitivistic urge that pervades our culture, in providing it with objects of nostalgia upon which to fasten and haunting forms of the past that it can fill with its own content. And the literary sensibility, disquieted by the effects of the growing division of labor and the differentiation of consciousness, is of course especially responsive to the vision of the lost unities and simplicities of times past. Now myth, the appeal of which lies precisely in its archaism, promises above all to heal the wounds of time. For the one essential function of myth stressed by all writers is that in merging past and present it releases us from the flux of temporality, arresting change in the timeless, the permanent, the ever-recurrent conceived as "sacred repetition." Hence the mythic is the polar opposite of what we mean by the historical,

* Ernst Cassirer: *The Myth of the State* (New Haven, 1946), p. 5.

which stands for process, inexorable change, incessant permutation and innovation. Myth is reassuring in its stability, whereas history is that powerhouse of change which destroys custom and tradition in producing the future — the future that at present, with the fading away of the optimism of progress, many have learned to associate with the danger and menace of the unknown. In our time the movement of history has been so rapid that the mind longs for nothing so much as something permanent to steady it. Hence what the craze for myth represents most of all is the fear of history. But of that later. First let us turn to the genetic approach to myth developed by the scholars in this field, comparing it with some of the literary notions which, by infusing myth with the qualities that properly belong to art, have brought about widespread confusion as to the differences between the mythic and the aesthetic mode of expression.

The most commonly accepted theory among scholars is the so-called ritual theory defining myth as a narrative linked with a rite. The myth describes what the ritual enacts. A mode of symbolic expression objectifying early human feeling and experience, the myth is least of all the product of the reflective or historical consciousness, or of the search for scientific or philosophical truth. Though satisfying "the demands of incipient rationality . . . in an unfathomed world,"* it arises, basically, in response to ever-recurrent needs of a practical and emotional nature that are assumed to require for their gratification the magical potency of a sacral act. Its originators, as S. M. Hooke writes, "were not occupied with general questions concerning the world but with certain practical and pressing problems of daily life. There were the main problems of securing the means of subsistence, of keeping the sun and moon doing their duty, of ensuring the regular flooding of the Nile, of maintaining the bodily vigor of the king who was the embodiment of the prosperity of community . . . In order to meet these needs the early inhabitants of Egypt and Mesopotamia developed a set of customary activities directed toward a definite end. Thus the coronation of a king . . . consisted of a regular pattern of actions, of things prescribed to be done, whose purpose was to fit the king

* A. N. Whitehead: *An Anthology* selected by F. S. C. Northrop and Mason Gross (New York, 1953), p. 475.

completely to be the source of the well-being of the community. This is the sense in which we shall use the term 'ritual.' "* Cassirer uses the term in much the same sense, as for example, in his comment on the mythic tale of Dionysus Zagreus: "What is recalled here is neither a physical nor historical phenomenon. It is not a fact of nature nor a recollection of the deeds or sufferings of a heroic ancestor. Nevertheless the legend is not a mere fairy tale. It had a *fundamentum in re;* it refers to a certain 'reality.' . . . It is *ritual.* What is seen in the Dionysiac cult is explained in the myth." As for the Greek myths with which we are most familiar, Hooke sees them as the fragments of a very antique pattern that in becoming separated from ritual gradually acquired an independent life through poetic formulation. Thus both the Minotaur and Perseus myths manifestly involve an underlying ritual pattern of human sacrifice developed in a stage when myth and ritual were still one. And to comprehend that unity one must keep in mind, as Lord Raglan puts it, that "in the beginning the thing said and the thing done were inseparably united, although in the course of time they were divorced and gave rise to widely differing literary, artistic and religious forms." It is clear that both *epos* and *logos* evolved out of *mythos.* But that this evolution is irreversible the literary expatiators of myth fail to grasp.

The primitive significance of myth is not to be disclosed by scrutinizing ancient poetry. "It is as vain to look to Homer for the primitive significance of myth," writes A. M. Hocart, "as it would be to seek it in Sir Thomas Malory." The epic, though a medium of mythological lore, is at the same time, as Susanne M. Langer observes, "the first flower, or one of the first, of a new symbolic mode — the mode of art. It is not merely a receptacle of old symbols, namely, those of myth, but is itself a new symbolic form, great with possibilities, ready to take meaning and express ideas that have had no vehicle before."† Poetic structure transforms the mythic material, disciplining and subjecting it to logical and psychological motives that eventually alienate it from its origins. To take the fact that myth is the common matrix of many literary forms as an indication that myth is literature or that literature is myth is a simple instance

---

* S. M. Hooke: *Myth and Ritual* (London, 1949), p. 6.
† Susanne M. Langer: *Philosophy in a New Key* (New York, 1948), pp. 16off.

of the genetic fallacy. Myth is a certain kind of objective fantasy to which literature has had frequent recourse for its materials and patterns; but in itself it is not literature. The literary work is mainly characterized by the order and qualitative arrangement of its words; myths, on the other hand, as Miss Langer notes, are not bound to "any particular words, nor even to language, but may be told or painted, acted or danced, without suffering degradation or distortion . . . They have no meter, no characteristic phrases, and are just as often recorded in vase-paintings and bas-reliefs as in words. A ballad, however, is a composition . . ." We know that *Oedipus Rex* is based on a mythic ritual. But the question is, what chiefly affects us in the play? Is it the myth, as such indifferent to verbal form, serving as Sophocles' material, or his particular *composition* of it? The Oedipus myth has its own power, to be sure, but one must distinguish between this power and that of the dramatic embodiment the poet gave it. And by confusing these different powers the inflaters of myth are able to credit it with properties that really belong to art.

Moreover, the mythic imagination is a believing imagination. Attaching no value to fictions, it envisages its objects as actually existing. Conversely, the imagination of art, a relatively late development in the history of human mentality, is marked above all by its liberation from the sheerly actual and material. Art achieves independence as it gradually detaches itself from myth. The poetic image, Cassirer notes, attains "its purely representative, specifically 'aesthetic' function only as the magic circle with which mythical consciousness surrounds it is broken, and it is recognized not as a mythico-magical form, but as a particular sort of *formulation*." Then what is meant by saying that not only the great epic and dramatic poets but even the best lyric poets seem to be possessed by a kind of mythic power? Cassirer's reply is that in those poets "the magic power of insight breaks forth again in its full intensity and objectifying power. But this objectivity has discarded all material constraints. The spirit lives in the world of language and in the mythical image without falling under the control of either." Word and image, which once affected the mind as awesome external forces, have now cast off effectual reality, becoming for the literary artist "a light, bright ether in which the spirit can move without let or hindrance. This liberation is achieved not because the mind throws aside the sensuous forms of word and image, but because it uses them both as organs of its own, and thereby recognizes them for what they really are: forms of its own self-revelation."*

This type of historical analysis of the relation between art and myth is unlikely to interest the cultists. For what is the mind's recognition of its own creations if not an advance toward freedom? But it is freedom which is refused by those who wish to remystify the world through myth or dogma. This new-fashioned freedom is still largely untried by the generality of men. Why not keep it so, thus saving them from its perils? In literature this has prompted the endeavor to establish what might well be called a poetics of restitution — restitution for the disenchantment of reality carried through by science, rationality, and the historical consciousness. It is only natural that in such a poetics, ruled by schematic notions of tradition, the liberation of art from the socio-religious compulsions of the past should be taken as a calamity — a veritable expulsion from Eden. And how is Eden to be regained? Inevitably some of the practitioners of this poetics discovered that myth answered their purpose much better than tradition. After all, the supra-temporality of myth provides the ideal refuge from history. To them, as to Stephen Dedalus in *Ulysses,* history is a nightmare from which they are trying to awake. But to awake from history into myth is like escaping from a nightmare into a state of permanent insomnia.

But if the road back to genuine mythic consciousness is closed, what is still open is the possibility of manipulating ideas of myth. And that is precisely the point of my objection. For myth is not what its ideologues claim it to be. Though the common matrix of both, it is neither art nor metaphysics. In fact, both art and metaphysics are among those superior forces which culture brought to bear in its effort to surmount the primitivism of myth. Dialectical freedom is unknown to myth, which permits no distinction between realities and symbols. The proposition that "the world of human culture . . . could not arise until the darkness of myth was fought and overcome"† is no doubt historically valid. Witness the struggle against it in Greek philosophy, as for instance in the animadversions

* Ernst Cassirer: *Myth and Language,* pp. 97ff.
† Ernst Cassirer: *The Myth of the State,* p. 298.

on mythic tales in the *Phaedrus*. Socrates, walking with his companion by the banks of the Ilissus, calls those tales "irrelevant things," declining to put his mind to them by reason of their uselessness in his search for self-knowledge. Even if instructive in some things, the one thing they cannot impart is ethical enlightenment: the question of good and evil is beyond myth and becomes crucial only with the emergence of the individual, to whom alone is given the capacity at once to assent to the gift of self-knowledge and to undergo its ordeal.

Individuality is in truth foreign to myth, which objectifies collective rather than personal experience. Its splendor is that of the original totality, the pristine unity of thought and action, word and deed. The sundering of that unity is one of the tragic contradictions of historical development, which is never a harmonious forward movement but "a cruel repugnant labor against itself," as Hegel described it with unequaled insight. It is the paradox of progress that humanity has proven itself unable to assimilate reality except by means of "the alienation of human forces." In order to recover the potency of myth civilized man would first have to undo the whole of his history; and when some literary intellectuals dream of this recovery they are manifestly reacting against the effects of self-alienation at the same time that they exemplify these effects with appalling simplicity. What Marx once called "the idiocy of the division of labor" must have gone very far indeed if people can so drastically separate their theories of life from their concrete living of it! (The "idiocy" results from the fragmentation of vital human functions, since, as Marx said, "together with the division of labor is given the possibility, nay, the actuality, that spiritual activity and material activity, pleasure and work, production and consumption, will fall to the lot of different individuals.")

It is not unimaginable that in the future the paradox of progress will be resolved and acting and thinking reintegrated. We can be certain, however, that a conquest so consummate will take place not within our civilization but beyond it, on the further shore of historical necessity, when man, at long last reconciling nature and culture within himself, will no longer be compelled to purchase every gain in freedom with the loss of wholeness and integrity. Admittedly that too is probably a dream, but it is at least a possible dream and

14

so long as civilization lasts perhaps an indefeasible one. The fulfillment it promises is the hope of history — and its redemption. And inconceivable as that fulfillment may seem to us at present, it will be brought about through the real processes of history or not at all — never through the magic potion of myth.

I said above that the craze for myth is the fear of history. It is feared because modern life is above all a historical life producing changes with vertiginous speed, changes difficult to understand and even more difficult to control. And to some people it appears as though the past, all of it together with its gods and sacred books, were being ground to pieces in the powerhouse of change, senselessly used up as so much raw material in the fabrication of an unthinkable future. One way certain intellectuals have found of coping with their fear is to deny historical time and induce in themselves through aesthetic and ideological means a sensation of mythic time — the eternal past of ritual. The advantage of mythic time is that it is without definite articulation, confounding past, present, and future in an undifferentiated unity, as against historical time which is unrepeatable and of an ineluctable progression. The historical event is that which occurs once only, unlike the timeless event of myth that, recurring again and again, is endlessly present.

The turn from history toward myth is to be observed in some of the important creative works of this period, as Joseph Frank has shown in his remarkable essay "Spatial Form in Modern Literature." He quotes Allen Tate as saying that Ezra Pound's *Cantos* in their "powerful juxtapositions of the ancient, the Renaissance, and the modern worlds reduce all three elements to an unhistorical miscellany, timeless and without origin." Frank analyzes *The Waste Land*, *Ulysses*, *Nightwood*, and other literary works along the same lines, establishing that while on one level they seem to be dealing with "the clash of historical perspectives induced by the identification of contemporary figures and events with various historical prototypes," in practice they made history unhistorical in that it is sensed as "a continuum in which distinctions of past and present are obliterated . . . past and present are seen spatially, locked in a timeless unity which, even if accentuating surface differences, eliminates any feeling of historical sequence by the very act of juxtaposition. The objective historical imagination, on which modern man has prided himself, and which he has cultivated so carefully since the Renaissance, is transformed in those writers into the mythical imagination for which historical time does not exist." Frank offers no social-historical explanation of this retreat from history; he is simply concerned with it as an aesthetic phenomenon expressing itself in "spatial form."

Perhaps for that very reason he too readily assumes that the mythic imagination is actually operative in the writers he examines. But the supplanting of the sense of historical by the sense of mythic time is scarcely accomplished with such ease; the mere absence of the one does not necessarily confirm the presence of the other. For my part, what I perceive in Pound and Eliot are not the workings of the mythic imagination but an aesthetic simulacrum of it, a learned illusion of timelessness. We should not mistake historical retrospection, however richly allusive and organized in however "simultaneous" a fashion, for mythic immediacy and the pure imaginative embodiment of a perpetual present. In point of fact, the polemical irony which the poems both of Pound and Eliot generate at the expense of modern society in itself attests to a marked commitment toward history. Are not these poets conducting a campaign against history precisely in the name of history, which they approach, however, with mythic prepossessions, that is to say without either dynamism or objectivity, responding to its archaistic refinements while condemning its movement? The truth is that they are as involved in historicism as most contemporary writers sensitive to the "modern situation," but in their case the form it takes is negative. Willy-nilly they express the age, that few would deny is historicist through and through.* As Eliot

---

* "Historicism," writes Karl Mannheim, "has developed into .an intellectual force of extraordinary significance . . . The historicist principle not only organizes, like an invisible thread, the work of the cultural sciences (*Geisteswissenschaften*) but also permeates everyday thinking. Today it is impossible to take part in politics, even to understand a person . . . without treating all those realities we have to deal with as having evolved and as developing dynamically. For in everyday life, too, we apply concepts with historicist overtones, for example, 'capitalism,' 'social movement,' 'cultural process,' etc. These forces are grasped and understood as potentialities, constantly in flux, moving from some point in time to another; already on the level of everyday reflection we seek to determine the position of our present within such a temporal framework, to tell by the cosmic clock of history what the time is." — *Essays on the Sociology of Knowledge* (New York, 1952), p. 84.

himself once wrote, if a poet is "sincere, he must express with in-dividual differences the general state of mind — not as a duty, but because he cannot help participating in it." Eliot is plainly a more "sincere" poet than Pound, and he is also a religious man; and it is necessary to uphold the distinction between religion and myth. His religiousness, which has temperamental as well as deep social roots, hardly disallows the cultivation of historical awareness. This may well explain why he has always been able to curb his "mythicism," so that it is but one of the several tendencies in his work rather than its motive-power. As a literary critic he is seldom inclined to hunt for mythological patterns, whose task it seems to be to reduce the history of literature to sameness and static juxtaposition; more typically he searches for those alterations of sensibility that are historically illumi-nating and productive of significant change.

It is Pound who in his later phase is wholly in the throes of "myth-icism." But, far from being a reincarnation of an ancient imaginative mode, it is really but another sample of modern ideology, applied to poetry with frenetic zeal in an effort to compensate for loss of co-herence. In the *Cantos* time neither stands still as in myth nor moves as in history; it is merely suspended. As for Joyce's *Ulysses*, it seems to me that the mythological parallels it abounds in provide little more than the scaffolding for the structure of the novel; and only critics fascinated by exegesis would mistake it for the structure itself. Those parallels do not really enter substantively into the presentation of the characters. The manner in which Bloom is identified with Odysseus and Stephen with Telemachus is more like a mythic jest or conceit, as it were, than a true identification. To be sure, it reflects the somewhat scholastic humor of the author; but its principal func-tion is that of helping him organize his material. In that sense it has more to do with the making of the novel than with the reading of it — for as readers we find both Stephen and Bloom convincing be-cause they are firmly grounded in the historical actualities of Joyce's city, his country, and Europe as a whole. It is in *Finnegans Wake*, far more than in *Ulysses*, that the mythic bias is in the ascendant, the historical element recedes, and the language itself is converted into a medium of myth.

Finnegans Wake is the most complete example of "spatial form" in modern literature. Joseph Frank's definition of that form is extremely plausible, yet I cannot agree that it is a mythic form in any but a very limited analogical sense. It is best understood, to my mind, as the aesthetic means devised for the projection of a nonhistorical or even antihistorical view of history. The most one can say of this form is that it reflects a mythic bias. But this bias is by no means independent of historicism, of which it is a kind of reactionary distortion or petrifaction.

There is a good deal of evidence supporting this conception of "spatial form." Thus in his book, *The Protestant Era,* Paul Tillich lists the main premises of the nonhistorical interpretation of history, and we find that one such premise is that "space is predominant against time; time is considered to be circular or repeating itself infinitely." What is the inner meaning of this spatializing of time? From Tillich's philosophical standpoint it means that time is being detached from history and yielded back to nature. In other words, the contradiction between history and nature is resolved in favor of the latter. Tillich defines time, in terms reminiscent of Schelling and Bergson, as the dimension of the dynamic, creative, and qualitative, whereas space he defines as the static quantitative. If this contrast is valid, then one can only conclude that the attempt to respatialize time implies a defeatist attitude toward history, an attitude that in the long run makes for cultural regression.

Further premises of the nonhistorical interpretation of history are that "salvation is the salvation of individuals from time and history, not the salvation of a community through time and history," and that history is to be understood as "a process of deterioration, leading to the inescapable self-destruction of a world era." It is not difficult to recognize here some of the components of "mythicism." As an ideology "mythicism" is of course not to be equated at all points with its artistic practice. One must distinguish between the cultism of myth, which is primarily an ideological manifestation, and the literary works in which myth is made use of in one way or another. In Joyce the ideology is hardly perceptible, but you will find it in Eliot and a somewhat secularized version of it in Pound. Some critics write about Thomas Mann as if he too were enlisted in the service of myth. This is a mistake, I think. *Joseph and His Brothers* is not so much a mythic novel as a novel on mythic themes. In this narrative it is the characters, not at all the author, who confound past and present in their experience of that "pure time" which transcends both. Furthermore, in his re-creation of myth Mann is heavily indebted to the Freudian psychology; and psychology is inherently anti-mythic. The Freudian method is a special adaptation of the historical method in general. Freud's early efforts to fit his theory into a biological framework were of no avail; and now it is clear, as W. H. Auden has so well put it, that Freud "towers up as the genius who perceived that psychological events are not natural events but historical and that, therefore, psychology, as distinct from neurology, must be based on the presuppositions . . . not of the biologist but of the historian."

Not a few characteristics of "mythicism" are brought into Tillich's exposition under the heading of the "mystical" approach to history, against which he argues in the name of historical realism. This is a perspective that he evaluates as a creation of the West, especially insofar as it stands under Protestant influence. "For historical realism the really real appears in the structures created by the historical process," he writes. "History is open to interpretation only through active participation. We can grasp the power of historical being only if we are grasped by it in our historical experience."* His analysis, combining certain Marxist concepts with the religious variant of existential thought, repudiates all attempts to escape the present for the sake of the unreal past of archaism or the equally unreal future of utopianism. It is a view resistant to attitudes of religious pessimism toward the historical world and even more so to the mythic dissolution of it in the eternal past of ritual.

The fear of history is at bottom the fear of the hazards of freedom. Insofar as man can be said to be capable of self-determination, history is the sole sphere in which he can conceivably attain it. But though history, as Tillich affirms, is above all the sphere of freedom, it is also the sphere in which "man *is determined* by fate against his freedom. Very often the creations of his freedom are the tools used by fate against him; as, for instance, today the technical powers created by him turn against him with irresistible force. There are periods in history in which the element of freedom predominates, and there are periods in which fate and necessity prevail. The latter is

* Paul Tillich: *The Protestant Era* (Chicago, 1948), pp. 71ff.

true of our day . . . "* An analysis of this type, largely coinciding with the Hegelian-Marxist idea of historical tension and crisis, sufficiently accounts for the retreat from history toward myth. In our time the historical process is marked far more by loss and extremity than growth and mastery, and this fact is interpreted by the spokesmen of traditionalism as completely justifying their position. The mythic principle appeals to them because of its fixity and profoundly conservative implications. But the hope of stability it offers is illusory. To look to myth for deliverance from history is altogether futile.

In literature the withdrawal from historical experience and creativeness can only mean stagnation. For the creative artist to deny time in the name of the timeless and immemorial is to misconceive his task. He will never discover a shortcut to transcendence. True, in the imaginative act the artist does indeed challenge time, but in order to win he must also be able to meet *its* challenge; and his triumph over it is like that blessing which Jacob exacted from the angel only after grappling with him till the break of day.

In criticism the reaction against history is shown in the search for some sort of mythic model, so to speak, to which the literary work under scrutiny can be made to conform. The critics captivated by this procedure are inclined to take for granted that to identify a mythic pattern in a novel or poem is tantamount to disclosing its merit — an assumption patently false, for the very same pattern is easily discoverable in works entirely without merit. Implicit here is the notion that the sheer timelessness of the pattern is as such a guarantee of value. What is not grasped, however, is that the timeless is in itself nothing more than a pledge waiting for time to redeem it, or to vary the figure, a barren form that only time can make fecund. And Blake said it when he wrote in his "Proverbs of Hell" that "eternity is in love with the productions of time."

1953

* *Ibid.*, p. 186.

THE EDUCATION OF ANTON CHEKHOV

T HE UNDERSTANDING of Chekhov's background and personality is
greatly enhanced by a reading of his *Selected Letters*, edited by
Lillian Hellman and translated by Sidonie K. Lederer. From first to
last the impression conveyed is that of astounding courage and of
heroic manliness and self-possession. Dead at the age of forty-four,
apparently Chekhov knew well enough even before reaching his
mid-twenties that his life would be short and racked with hurt and
pain; and he resolutely kept that knowledge from his family and
friends. The severe and repeated pulmonary hemorrhages and other
afflictions he suffered would surely have laid low anyone more self-
indulgent or open to the not inconsiderable spiritual temptations of
disease and physical debility. Another exacerbating circumstance
was the material pressure he was under since early youth when he
had first undertaken the major responsibility for the support of his
large family, mostly made up of weaklings and ne'er-do-wells. All in
all he had little time for imaginative self-realization, and a good part
of the time he did have was consumed in the study and practice of
medicine as well as in the frequent travels and changes of abode
forced upon him by the state of his health.

Thus what comes through to us most vividly in his letters is a sense of the enormous odds against which Chekhov pitted himself in striving to achieve those rare qualities of his narrative and dramatic art that make it so uniquely his own. This art is at once astringent and poetic, circumstantially exact in a prose-sense yet structurally allied to the lyric mode. It is an art of unmistakable originality though not of the very first order; and if it is known above all for fixing imperishably conditions of human staleness, futility, torpor, and ennui, the explanation is not to be sought in any hidden enervation of the author or covert sympathy for negative states of being — he was no Baudelairean bell with a crack in it — but rather in the passionate even if undemonstrative integrity with which he resisted the denial of life's richer and finer possibilities.

A late child of the fatally belated Russian Enlightenment and the last important figure in the great nineteenth-century line of the masters of Russian prose, he believed that life could be lived with intelligence and love, without coercion and falsehood, at the same time that he concentrated on showing that life as actually lived was sad and boring. But in his expression of this sadness and boredom there is no finality (of acceptance or complicity or mean pleasure in exposure and reduction), such as we find in many similar evocations of negative states in Western literature of the modern period. The petty decadence inherent in such evocations is entirely alien to Chekhov. He is not attacking human nature, saying that this is the way things are and always will be, while calling for some impossible transcendence which is no more than a metaphysical coda to positive despair. The pessimism commonly ascribed to him is one of mood and temperament perhaps, and it no doubt reflects the stalemate reached by Russian society at the time of his emergence on the literary scene; but it never is a pessimism of ultimate belief and vision. The voice that cries out "No, one cannot go on living like that!" at the end of one of his typical anecdotes of wasted existence ("The Man in a Shell") is indubitably that of the writer; and in that somber masterpiece "Ward No. 6" he identifies himself most lucidly and credibly with the standpoint of the madman Gromov, whose madness is of a piece with his refusal to come to terms with "human baseness and oppression trampling up truth" and to renounce his faith that "a splendid life will in time prevail upon the earth." The source of the powerful emotion embodied in this tale is the felt idea that however forlorn the world of men may be, it nevertheless contains within itself the promise of release and change. "Ward No. 6" is of course part and parcel of the literature of protest against the Czarist autocracy. Yet if it were no more than that we would not read it today. The images of staleness it evokes are universally viable in that they disclose some of the permanent traits of human existence. The madness of Gromov is that of a man who, in spite of his weaknesses, has suffered the vertiginous experience of absorbing a great truth into his very flesh and bones. Significantly, it is Gromov who is the irreconcilable foe of quiescence and in whose speeches we catch the authentic voice of his author, who was likewise irreconcilable and likewise firm in his feeling that it is given to men to act upon their own lives and that to stand still is to fall back and eventually to collapse into the mire.

It is the wonder and triumph of Chekhov that the animating principle of his pathos of "lives clipped and wingless" is resistance to slackness and inertia — the seepage of the psyche epitomized in the term Oblomovism. Let us keep in mind, though, that only one form of Oblomovism is represented in Goncharov's famous novel. Chekhov's insight penetrated to other and more complicated forms of it that are perhaps not so easily determinable; and Oblomovism, after all, is a state not merely of Russia but of the soul.

These letters, if read in conjunction with any fairly adequate biography, enforce the conviction of a productive life whose end is for once not in its beginnings but is marked throughout by change, growth, increasing self-development and self-mastery, *Bildung* and *Selbstbildung* in the classic sense. It can justly be said of Chekhov that the sum of what happened to him is that he achieved an education toward freedom. "The sense of personal freedom," he wrote, "is the chief constituent of creative genius," and the freedom he thus invokes is scarcely to be understood without reference to his beginnings, his ancestry, his childhood, the formative years. The grandson of a serf and the son of a petty tradesman, he suffered in his childhood and early youth the ravages of that backwardness, cruelty, and servility which were as much a family as a national inheritance. If all his life he remained immune to the appeal of the Russian versions of traditionalism, if he remained an agnostic and a radical, a resolute friend of the West and advocate of science and the secular intelligence, it is largely because of the lessons absorbed in those formative years. It is with irresistible concreteness that he put his case to a correspondent: "From childhood I have believed in progress and cannot help believing, as the difference between the time when I got whipped and the time when the whippings ceased was terrific."

The perception of this difference is ineluctably one of the great points of the arduous educational process through which he strove to attain his freedom. He literally had to make himself over to undo the stultification brought on by the early influences that played upon him, influences in no way fortuitous but imbedded in Russian life. In this respect the *locus classicus,* from the standpoint of the biographer and the literary critic alike, is the passage in his letter to Suvorin of January 7, 1889, in which he explains why plebian writers must buy at the price of their youth what the writers of the gentry have been endowed with by nature. "Go ahead," he tells Suvorin, "and write about a young man, the son of a serf, an ex-small shopkeeper, a choir boy, high school and university student, brought up on respect for rank, kissing priests' hands, and the worship of others' ideas, offering thanks for every mouthful of bread, often whipped, going to school without shoes, fighting, torturing animals, fond of dining with rich relatives, playing the hypocrite before God and people without any cause, except that of a consciousness of his own insignificance — then tell how this young man squeezes the slave out of himself one drop at a time and how he wakes one fine morning to feel that in his veins flows not the blood of a slave but real human blood . . ." Here we come upon the essence of Chekhov's story and upon the basic Chekhovian theme. In this effort to squeeze the slave out of himself we confront the actuality of his education, the ordeal of it, the struggle, the relapses, the price paid and the victory scored. The meaning of this education, in the sense of its absolute necessity and the consequences of failure to undertake it, forms the sum and substance of the criticism of life contained in his plays and fictions.

Chekhov was intrinsically too modest in his spiritual makeup and too much of a wry realist (no wonder he objected to Dostoevsky's novels on the ground of their "immodesty") to be capable of engaging in momentous affirmations carrying him beyond the experience provided by his time and environment. For this and related reasons it is far from difficult to make out, as some commentators have done, that generally all he leaves us with is a mood of "delicious depression." Such a view is wholly erroneous, to my mind. We cannot gain anything like a full recovery of the import of his work unless we grasp the one surpassing moral intuition controlling it — that man can hope to realize the promise of his humanity only if he succeeds in overcoming the slave within himself in all his guises and disguises. The Rilkean dictum "You must change your life!" is implicit in the entire Chekhovian statement. But to interpret this one fundamental intuition in a bare political sense, as the Soviet critics are instructing their readers to do to the benefit of the official dogma, is patently a gross oversimplification. A slave is not transformed into a man by changing masters. Moreover, the slave in man is a cunning animal that knows not only how to survive changes, however radical, in social institutions but also how to adapt such changes to suit his nature. "People must never be humiliated — that is the main thing," Chekhov wrote in an early letter; and in a later one he wrote: "God's earth is good. It is only we on it who are bad . . . The important thing is that we must be just, and all the rest will be added unto us." It is in the light of such precepts that he is best understood. To take him simply as a critic of Russian society at a certain stage of its development is to limit him intolerably.

In one of her engaging and perceptive introductory notes to the text of this volume, Miss Hellman remarks that Chekhov was without "that final spiritual violence which the very great creative artist has always had. And he knew it as he knew most things about himself." To this I would assent, though with some uneasiness about the use of the word violence as the clincher in her formulation. Ultimate imaginative power need not necessarily be equated with the shock tactics of frenzied and eruptive geniuses. One agrees, nonetheless, that such ultimate power is wanting in Chekhov. Perhaps the crux of the matter is that he expended so much vitality on his exemplary education that what was left could not suffice to carry him beyond the lessons that engrossed him. This too is of course among the lessons he learned, as is implied in his rueful saying that he was forced to buy at the price of his youth what others are endowed with by nature. He was certainly aware that he never really got all he bargained for. Still, taking everything into account, the stricken life and the fashioned work, the price was well worth paying. For his effort to redeem the age he lived in he deserves to be ranked as nearly the equal of his great predecessors in Russian letters.

1955

FICTION AND THE CRITICISM
OF FICTION

THE NOVEL is at the present time universally recognized as one of the greater historic forms of literary art. Its resources and capacities appear to be commensurate with the realities and consciousness of the modern epoch, and its practitioners, having inherited a good many of the functions once exercised by poetry and the drama, no longer feel the slightest need to engage in the kind of apologetics that were quite common even as late as a hundred years ago, when in respectable quarters novel writing and novel reading were still looked upon as activities falling below the level of true cultural aspiration. But if the novel was then still widely regarded as a thing somewhat effeminate and moonshiny, fit mainly for the consumption of young ladies, it was at the same time quickly impressing itself upon the mind of the age as a newfangled form full of rude plebeian energy, unruly, unpredictable, and ungovernable in its appropriation of materials from unprocessed reality — "the conscience of a blackened street impatient to assume the world." Much of the life the novel contains is defined by these contrary reactions, one pointing to its origin in romance and the other to its revitalization through the new principle of realism.

Among the last apologies for the novel — an apology in which we fully sense, however, the surge of confidence and power generated by the phenomenal rise of this relatively new genre — is the preface that the Goncourt brothers wrote for their novel *Germinie Lacerteux* (1864). "Now that the novel," they observed, "is broadening, growing, beginning to be a great, serious, impassioned living form of literary study and social research, now that by means of analysis and psychological inquiry it is turning into contemporary moral history, now that the novel has imposed upon itself the investigations and duties of science, one may again make a stand for its liberties and privileges." This memorable formulation is in the main still acceptable to us. The one dated element in it is of course the reference to science, a reference all too patently of its period and linked to the development of the naturalistic school in French fiction. At the time not a few writers were so impressed by the triumphs of scientific method as to want to borrow some of its magic for themselves, yet at bottom it was not so much a matter of faith in science (though doubtless that played its part too) as of an intention to gain prestige for the novel by means of an honorific association. But apart from that the formulation I have cited has scarcely lost its cogency. The one question arising in connection with it is whether it is still necessary at this late date again to make a stand for the novel's liberties and privileges. So far as the intelligent reader at large is concerned such a stand may well be redundant. But it is not in the least redundant, I think, so far as some present-day critics of fiction are concerned and the reading practices to which they have been habituating us.

My argument rests on a premise that most of us will surely accept, and that is that twentieth-century criticism has as yet failed to evolve a theory and a set of practical procedures dealing with the prose medium that are as satisfactory in their exactness, subtlety, and variety as the theory and procedures worked out in the past few decades by the critics of poetry. It may well be, as is so frequently said, that in art there is no such thing as progress. But then, criticism is only partially an art, so little of an art perhaps as to admit in some periods not only change, as all the arts do, but also gradual development toward a more accurate knowledge. One is certainly disposed to think so when comparing the present state of poetry criticism with its state, say, forty or fifty years ago. The criticism of poetry has of late acquired a rich consciousness which may be defined objectively as the self-consciousness of the medium — a historic acquisition that, acting as a force in its own right, has already considerably affected the writing of poetry and may be expected to affect it even more in the near future.*

In fiction the prevailing situation is quite different. Is it not a curious fact that while we have had in this century novelists as fully accomplished in their métier as the poets we all esteem are in theirs, none of these novelists have made a contribution to the theory of fiction that comes anywhere near what the poets have attained in their critical forays? You can go through all the essays of Thomas Mann, for instance, without finding anything of really clinching interest for students of the novel as a form; and Mann is surely an exceptionally intellectual and self-conscious artist. Nor will you find, in this respect, any truly close insights in Joyce or Proust. Both *A Portrait of the Artist as a Young Man* and *Ulysses* contain some discussions of aesthetic structure on a fairly abstract level, and these are of no help to us if we are on the lookout for the differentia distinguishing the prose narrative from the other verbal arts. In Proust you encounter a metaphysical theory of the aesthetic meaning of time that generalizes the author's creative experience, but it scarcely yields the kind of concrete illumination of the novelistic form that we gain in poetic theory from the discursive writings of poet-critics like Valéry, Eliot, Pound, Empson, Ransom, and Tate. As for American novelists of our time such as Fitzgerald, Wolfe, Faulkner, and Hemingway, they have influenced fictional modes solely through their practice, steering clear of theoretical divagations. Henry James differs of course from the novelists I have mentioned by virtue of his unusual effort to formulate in critical terms his fascination with

* Let us keep in mind, though, that the sway of consciousness is by no means an unmixed blessing. At the heart of consciousness there is always equivocation. One can do no more than hope that this heightened and elaborated awareness of the poetic medium, which is after all a kind of wisdom or self-knowledge, will not soon provide us with another melancholy illustration of Hegel's famous dictum that the owl of Minerva begins its flight only when the shades of night are gathering. Not that I in the least associate myself with Edmund Wilson's thesis that verse is a "dying technique." Still, we know that in this world nothing comes free, and one wonders what the price of so intense a consciousness will turn out to be in this instance.

method and technique. But James, like Flaubert, is not a novelist of our age. Chiefly he belongs to that heroic period of the past century when the novel fought and won its fight for recognition as an auton- omus literary genre making good its claims to the status of high art. At present, however, the practitioners of fiction appear to lack suffi- cient motive to engage in the analytic study of problems specific to their medium. Such studies are mostly left to professional critics and scholars.

The authority of fact often proves irresistible. I am inclined to think that it is precisely the fact of signal progress that we have wit- nessed in the criticism of poetry that accounts in some ways for the observable lag in the criticism of fiction. We must beware of taking a simplistic view of progress. In criticism, as in any other sphere, it is never a unilinear, harmonious forward movement in which every critical concern is equally well served. On the contrary, progress is necessarily an uneven and irregular process: the advantage gained at one point is ordinarily paid for by regress or loss at another point. And to entertain some such notion of what progress comes to in reality is to understand why the very success of the poetry critics has of late begun to exert an influence on the criticism of prose which is far from salutary. For the commanding position assumed by poetic analysis has led to the indiscriminate importation of its characteristic assumptions and approaches into a field which requires generic criti- cal terms and criteria of value that are unmistakably its own. Just as Zola, the Goncourt brothers, and other pioneers of the naturalist school associated the novel with science for the sake of the prestige that this conjunction seemed to confer upon their literary ambitions, so now critics of fiction are attempting to assimilate it to the poem, thus impeding an adequate inspection of the qualities and effects of the prose medium. This effort to deduce a prosaics from a poetics is *au fond* doomed to fail, for it is simply not the case that what goes for a microscopic unit such as the lyric poem goes equally well for the macroscopic compositions of the writer of narrative prose.

In this paper I wish to isolate three biases that can be traced directly or indirectly to this recent infection of the prose sense by poetics. The first bias is manifested in the current obsession with the search for symbols, allegories, and mythic patterns in the novel — a search conducted on the unanalyzed assumption that to locate such

15

symbols in a fictional work is somehow tantamount to a demonstration of its excellence. The fact that the same symbols and patterns are just as easily discoverable in the worst as in the best novels counts for nothing among the pursuers of this type of research. The second bias, even more plainly deriving from the sensibility of poetry, is the one identifying style as the "essential activity" of imaginative prose, an identification that confuses the intensive speech proper to poetry with the more openly communicative, functional, and extensive language proper to prose. The third bias is that of technicism, which may be defined as the attempt to reduce the complex structure and content of the novel to its sum of techniques, among which language is again accorded a paramount place. This third bias, which includes the second and exceeds it, is epitomized in Mark Schorer's well-known essay "Technique as Discovery," presenting in summary form an extreme version of the formalist tendency that has played a leading role in the poetics of our time. Mr. Schorer makes no bones about his indebtedness to the theorists of poetry. In the course of his argument he states this to be the fact, not once but repeatedly, evidently unaware that so large an indebtedness in itself poses a problem and points to a predicament.

In examining this bias toward symbolism, allegory, and mythic patterning in the reading of fiction, one is first of all struck by its debilitating effect on the critical mind. There was a time not so long ago when it was clearly understood among us that allegory is an inferior mode scarcely to be compared to symbolism in imaginative efficacy; it was also understood that myth and symbol are by no means synonymous terms. But by now all such elementary though essential distinctions have gone by the board. The younger critics have taken to using all three terms almost interchangeably and always with an air of offering an irrefutable proof of sensibility, with the result that they have been nearly emptied of specific meaning and turned into little more than pretentious counters of approbation.* But the more these terms lose their reference to anything

* The word "myth" in particular is being put to such multiple and varied use these days — as when people speak of the myth of racial superiority, or of the myth of the proletariat, or of the mythology of Americanism — that if any sense at all is to be made of the mythic concern in literature, then the least a

concrete beyond themselves, the easier becomes their conversion into verbal symbols in their own right, symbols of admission and belonging to a school at present academically and critically dominant. And if you add to this sacred triad the famed pair of paradox and irony your initiation is well-nigh complete.

An example is wanted. There is Mr. Robert W. Stallman, for instance, who rather unnerves one with his literal passion for up-to-date notions in criticism. In an essay on Stephen Crane, he writes that

> like Conrad, Crane puts language to poetic uses, which, to define it, is to use language reflexively and to use language symbolically. It is the works which employ this reflexive and symbolic use of language that constitute what is permanent of Crane. It is the language of symbol and paradox; the wafer-like sun [the reference is to Crane's memorable sentence in *The Red Badge of Courage:* "The red sun was pasted in the sky like a wafer"]; or in "The Open Boat" the paradox of "cold, comfortable sea-water," an image which calls to mind the poetry of W. B. Yeats with its fusion of contradictory emotions. This single image evokes the sensation of the whole experience of the men in the boat . . . What is readily recognizable in this paradox of "cold, comfortable sea-water" is that irony of opposites which constitutes the personality of the man who wrote it.°

And preceding this paragraph with its wholesale disgorgement of shibboleths lifted from contemporary poetry criticism, there is a passage in which Mr. Stallman bares his fixation on the sentence previously quoted ("The red sun was pasted in the sky like a wafer"), in which he professes to see the "key to the symbolism of the whole novel." Why? Because the initials, J. C., of Jim Conklin, the tall, spectral soldier who dies in so grotesque a fashion, ineluctably suggests to Mr. Stallman that he represents Jesus Christ. Thus *The Red Badge of Courage,* which is something of a *tour de force* as a novel and which is chiefly noted for the advance it marks

---

critic can do is to discriminate sharply between the broad, popular, loosely analogical employment of the term and what Robert Graves rightly, I think, calls the "true myth," which he defines as "the reduction to narrative shorthand of ritual mime."

° Cf. "Stephen Crane," p. 269, in *Critiques and Essays in Modern Fiction,* edited by John W. Aldridge (New York, 1952).

in the onset of realism on the American literary scene, is transmogrified into a religious allegory. All that is lacking in this analysis
to give it the final certification of the *Zeitgeist* is the word "myth."
Observe, too, that the evidence for this thesis is drawn, not from a
study of the narrative progression of Crane's novel as a whole, but
from a single image and the amalgam of the initials of the tall soldier's name with the name of Jesus Christ. It is entirely characteristic of Mr. Stallman's approach (and of the critical school to which
he is attached) that it never even occurs to him that to speak of "the
symbolism of the whole novel" is perhaps in this case a piece of
sheer gratuity, that the novel is actually "about" what it seems to
be, war and its impact on human beings moved by pride, bravado,
fear, anxiety, and sudden panic. If it is symbolic, it is in the patent
sense in which all good art, insofar as it opens out to the world at
large by transcending its immediate occasions and fixed, exclusive
meanings, can be said to be symbolic. But to attribute a symbolic
character to Crane's novel in this universal sense has nothing whatever to do with Mr. Stallman's idea of symbolism, an idea indis-
tinguishable from the "fallacy of misplaced concreteness," systematically applied to works of literature.

The absurdity of Mr. Stallman's reading of Crane becomes all too
apparent when you look up the text to check on his quotations.
He professes to see a poetic paradox in the phrase "cold, comfortable
sea-water," but in point of fact within the context of the story the
juxtaposition of "cold" and "comfortable" cannot strike us as paradoxical but rather as wholly natural. The situation is that the four
shipwrecked men in the tiny boat — the captain, the correspondent,
the oiler, and the cook — are dog-tired, not having slept for two
days. It is night, and three of them are sleeping in the water-
drenched bottom of the boat while the correspondent is rowing:

> The wind became stronger, and sometimes a wave raged out like a
> mountain cat, and there was to be seen the sheen and sparkle of a
> broken crest.
> The captain, in the bow, moved on his water-jar and sat erect.
> "Pretty long night," he observed to the correspondent. . . .
> "Did you see that shark playing around?"
> "Yes, I saw him. He was a big fellow all right."
> . . . Later the correspondent spoke into the bottom of the boat.

"Billie!" There was a slow and gradual disentanglement. "Billie, will you spell me?"

"Sure," said the oiler.

As soon as the correspondent touched the cold, comfortable sea-water in the bottom of the boat and had huddled close to the cook's life-belt he was deep in sleep.

Now obviously the water *in* the boat feels "comfortable" as against the waves beating *at* the boat, pictured throughout the story as black, menacing, sinister. In contrast the water at the bottom of the boat, in which the men have been sleeping, seems positively domesticated. Hence the adjective "comfortable." Only by carefully sequestering the phrase "cold, comfortable sea-water" from its context can you make it out to be paradoxical.

As for the sentence ending Chapter IX of *The Red Badge of Courage* — "The sun was pasted in the sky like a wafer" — it would seem to me that the verb "pasted" is quite as important to its effect as the substantive "wafer." Moreover, in the first edition of the novel "wafer" was preceded by "fierce," a modifier hardly suggestive of the Christian communion. Crane liked to speak of himself as an impressionist, and as a stylist he was above all concerned with getting away from the morbidly genteel narrative language of his time; the daring colloquialism "pasted in the sky" must have appealed to him on the well-known avant-garde principle of "make it new." More particularly, this concluding sentence of Chapter IX illustrates perfectly what Conrad described as "Crane's unique and exquisite faculty . . . of disclosing an individual scene by an odd simile." Conrad's remark has the aptitude of close critical observation, whereas Mr. Stallman's farfetched religious exegesis is mere *Zeitgeist* palaver.

No wonder that this critic is quite as partial to allegory as he is to symbolism. Thus in a study of Conrad he claims that "The Secret Sharer" is a double allegory — "an allegory of man's moral conscience and . . . of man's aesthetic conscience. The form of 'The Secret Sharer,' to diagram it, is the form of the capital letter L — the very form of the captain's room. (It is hinted at again in the initial letter of Leggatt's name.) One part of the letter L diagrams the allegory of the captain's divided soul, man in moral isolation and spiritual disunity. The other part of the letter represents the allegory of the artist's split soul. . . . The captain stands at the angle of the two isolations and the two searches for selfhood."* It is the inescapable logic of this obsession with symbols and allegories that it is bound to decline into a sort of mechanistic cabala that scrutinizes each sign and letter of the printed page for esoteric or supernal meanings. The plain absurdity of Mr. Stallman's reading of "The Secret Sharer" should not, however, deter us from recognizing that this mode, which he carries to an extreme, is a fairly representative one nowadays and that it is greatly favored by abler critics who at times still manage to retain some sense of proportion. My concern is not with Mr. Stallman's absurdities as such. I cite him only because his very excess brings to light the fantastication inherent in the approach he shares with a good many other people.†

What, at bottom, is the animating idea behind this exaltation of symbolism in current critical practice? As I see it, its source is not directly literary but is to be traced to an attitude of distaste toward the actuality of experience — an attitude of radical devaluation of the actual if not downright hostility to it; and the symbol is of course readily available as a means of flight from the actual into a realm where the spirit abideth forever. If the typical critical error of the thirties was the failure to distinguish between literature and life, in the present period that error has been inverted into the failure to perceive their close and necessary relationship. Hence the effort we are now witnessing to overcome the felt reality of art by converting it into some kind of schematism of spirit; and since what is wanted is spiritualization at all costs, critics are disposed to purge the novel of its characteristically detailed imagination working through experiential particulars — the particulars of scene, figures, and action: to purge them, that is to say, of their gross immediacy and direct empirical expressiveness. It is as if critics were saying

---

* Cf. "Life, Art, and 'The Secret Sharer,'" p. 241 in *Forms of Modern Fiction*, edited by William Van O'Connor (Minneapolis, 1948).

† The payoff of the rage for symbolism is surely Mr. Charles Feidelson's recent book, *Symbolism and American Literature*, the fundamental assumption of which is that "to consider the literary work as a piece of language is to regard it as a symbol, autonomous in the sense that it is quite distinct both from the personality of the author and the world of pure objects, and creative in the sense that it brings into existence its own meaning." In this curious work the interest in symbolism has quite literally consumed the interest in literature.

that the representation of experience, which is the primary asset of the novel, is a mere appearance; the really and truly real is to be discovered somewhere else, at some higher level beyond appearance. The novel, however, is the most empirical of all literary genres; existence is its original and inalienable datum; its ontology, if we may employ such a term in relation to it, is "naive," commonsensical, positing no split between appearance and reality. "The supreme virtue of a novel," as Henry James insisted, "the merit on which all its other merits . . . helplessly and submissively depend," is its truth of detail, its air of reality or "solidity of specification." "If it be not there, all other merits are as nothing, and if these be there, they owe their effect to the success with which the author has produced the illusion of life." It is an illusion in the sense that what is recounted has not really happened but has been imagined by the author; but this cannot mean that it is an illusion in relation to itself too, that the novel dreams itself, as it were. There is not some other novel, composed of spiritual and moral integers, hovering somewhere behind the illusion of life with which the novelist has sought to infuse his fictive world. We are of course free to interpret that world and to approach it from different angles and on different levels. But to interpret a fiction is one thing; to dissolve it is something else again, and we do dissolve it when treating it as a mere appearance, of the senses only, of interest only to the extent that it provides a domicile for symbols, supersensible forms comparable to Plato's Ideas. Such a notion has little in common with the literary theory of symbolism, though on the surface it may look like a logical extension of it. It belongs rather to metaphysics. The obsession with symbolization is at bottom expressive of the reactionary idealism that now afflicts our literary life and that passes itself off as a strict concern with aesthetic form.

This is not to say, to be sure, that fiction excludes symbolization. On the contrary, works of fiction abound in symbolic devices and the more significant among them have symbolic import. But when we speak of the symbolic import of a novel what we have in mind is nothing more mysterious than its overplus of meaning, its suggestiveness over and above its tissue of particulars, the actual representation of which it is comprised; and that is scarcely the same thing as treating these particulars as "clues" which it is the ingenious critic's task to follow up for hidden or buried meanings that are assumed to be the "real point" of the text under examination. In the long run this procedure cannot but make the text itself dispensable; it ceases to be of use once you have extracted the symbols it contains. The text, however, is not a container, like a bottle; it is all there is; and the symbol-hunting critics are unwittingly reasserting the dichotomy of form and content which they ostensibly reject. *Moby Dick*, for instance, is a work of which certain basic elements, such as the whale, the sea, and the quest, have both symbolic and direct representational value. There is no consensus among commentators as to what the symbolic value of those elements comes to in specific, exact terms; and it is a proof of the merit of this work that no such consensus is in fact possible. The narrative, not being an allegory, has no meanings that can be mentally tabulated and neatly accounted for. Its symbols are integrally a part of its fictive reality, and it is precisely their organic character that renders them immune to purely intellectual specification.

One should also be on the lookout against mistaking the creative intent of the conscious symbolic device employed by many modern writers. A novella like *Death in Venice*, in which the symbolic device is used again and again and always with exemplary control, will serve as a splendid example. One device in it is the introduction of a series of figures playing the part of "messengers" to Aschenbach (e.g., the "stranger with the pilgrim air" who appears at the very opening of the narrative and the gondolier who ferries him like Charon over to the Lido) whose function is at once to warn the hero and to foretell his doom. This function, however, has no independent "meaning"; it falls rather within the sphere of the technique devised to vivify our sense of the basic theme, which is the relationship between Aschenbach and Tadzio. This as well as the other symbolic devices to which Mann has recourse belong more to the compositional than to the thematic element of the novella. Mann succeeds in it to the degree in which he convinces us that the relationship between Aschenbach and Tadzio with its tragic consummation is actual and that it *is* what it appears to be. Hence it can be said that whatever symbolic value we may discover in the story is incremental, so to speak, to its actuality. It is a value, in other words, gained in the process of the story's actualization; it had no prior claim to existence and least of all can it lay claim to being its rationale. Nor is it its "essence," but rather a gift freely offered as the story comes to life, and in this sense it is more gratuitous than necessary. This would explain why it is so tractable, that is, why it is open to varying and contradictory interpretations. For anything a fiction might conceivably be a symbol of is inevitably far less compelling than what it immediately is in its felt unity of reality and appearance. To convert the experience it embodies into a symbol pure and simple is to empty it of its palpable substance. Thus what the objection to the excessive critical emphasis on symbolism comes down to is that, in making for a split between spirit and sense, it goes so far in conceptualizing the literary object as to drain it of its existential qualities.

The second bias in the contemporary idea of the prose medium is that of language, a bias which John Crowe Ransom not so long ago brought out into the open in committing himself to the view that "fiction, in being literature, will have style as its essential activity." In dealing with this view we know exactly where we stand, for Mr. Ransom's candor leaves us in no doubt as to its origin. In his essay, "The Understanding of Fiction," he is quite explicit on that point, declaring that "following that criticism of poetry which has made such a flourish in our time," he brings to fiction "a set of procedural biases gained elsewhere . . ." And he goes on to say that since "the criticism of poetry has been an intensive one, concentrating for the most part upon the linguistic detail of the lyric passage," he would like to begin by citing "a few passages . . . from reputable fictions, as an indication of the sort of fixed images or exempla, which I carry around with me, and from which I must start; they will not be poetry but they will be like fictional analogues of lyrical moments." He then proceeds to quote a paragraph from Jane Austen, several paragraphs from *Daisy Miller*, and a paragraph consisting of just sixteen lines from *War and Peace*, taken from the chapter portraying Napoleon coming upon Prince Andrey as he lies wounded on the battlefield. The conclusion Mr. Ransom implicitly comes to is that Tolstoy is not so good a writer as Jane Austen and Henry James. The author of *War and Peace*, he remarks, "does not possess fully the technical advantages of a style. For concentration he substitutes repetition . . ."

Now quite apart from the fact that the passages from Jane Austen and James are quoted as they wrote them while the passage from Tolstoy is given in translation, the procedure adopted by Mr. Ransom, that of citing sixteen lines from a novel of nearly twelve hundred pages, does not seem to justify itself from the standpoint of critical method. A passage so brief might be cited to illustrate some special usage but scarcely the overall effects of a narrative style, for such effects are secured not locally, in the short run, but in the long run, by accumulation and progression. Moreover, for the purpose of my argument here, it is not in the least necessary for me to dispute Mr. Ransom's judgment of the comparative value of the three prose styles he has examined. Let me grant him his judgment — that Tolstoy is inferior as a stylist. What is not acceptable, however, is the implicit estimate of the three novelists involved in this judgment. We cannot but suspect the relevance of a standard the application of which elevates the author of *Mansfield Park* above the author of *War and Peace*. To my mind, *War and Peace* and *Anna Karenina* are both greater works of literature than any of Jane Austen's or James's novels; and if I am right in this respect (I imagine that most qualified readers of fiction would probably agree with me), then perhaps it is the test chosen by Mr. Ransom, the criterion of language or style in the poetry sense of the term, which is at fault. In applying other criteria — character creation, for instance, or the depth of life out of which a novelist's moral feeling springs, or the capacity in constructing a plot (plot, that is, in the Aristotelian sense as the soul of an action) to invest the contingencies of experience with the power of the inevitable — we shall be persuaded soon enough that Tolstoy far outranks Jane Austen. Plainly the difficulty is with the linguistic criterion, which when applied unilaterally is likely to expose us to false valuations, such as that of ranking Turgenev above both Tolstoy and Dostoevsky (for Turgenev is generally admitted to be a better stylist than either of his coevals), or a storyteller like Ivan Bunin above his contemporary Chekhov. In the same way, if we turn to American fiction for examples, few would deny that Dos Passos is a better writer of prose than Dreiser; but is he on that account also the superior novelist? I think not.

Dreiser's fictive world, for all his sloppiness as a stylist, is far more solid and meaningful than that of Dos Passos.

Mr. F. R. Leavis is another critic who, coming to prose with habits of mind acquired in the study of poetry, adopts a view similar to that of Mr. Ransom. He, too, is a great believer in "exemplifying," as he calls it; and he has noted that while it is easier to cite examples from poetry, prose demands the same approach even if it does not admit it quite so readily. "With the novel it is so much harder to apply in a critical method the realization that everything the novelist does is done with words, here, here, and here, and that he is to be judged as an artist (if he is one) for the same kind of reason as a poet is. Poetry works by concentration; for the most part, success or failure is obvious locally . . . But prose depends ordinarily on cumulative effect, in such a way that a page of a novel that is on the whole significant may appear undistinguished or even bad. . . ." But though Mr. Leavis is fully aware of the hazard involved in transferring the poetry critic's method of local exemplification to the study of narrative prose, he nevertheless comes out in its favor because he sees no alternative. The trouble lies, I think, in his reluctance to draw a sharp enough distinction in principle between prosaic and poetic speech. Is it really the case that language plays the same role in both media? In looking to narrative prose for "fictional analogues of lyrical moments," as Mr. Ransom does, are we not in effect ignoring the crucial differences between the use to which language is put in poetry as against its use in prose and hence denying the latter the status of a separate genre?

The approach to the prose medium I am disputing is not an isolated one. It is deeply imbedded in the history of modern literary criticism and scholarship. More or less the same approach was advocated by the extreme wing of the Russian formalists, who were also inclined to overreact to the undeniable fact that fiction is made up of words, just like poetry. In the controversy that developed around this issue, it was the more moderate formalist Victor Zhirmunsky who was in the right, I believe, when he protested against the superstition of the word by which his colleagues appeared to have been overcome. According to Zhirmunsky's theory, a novel and a lyric poem are not to be equated as works of verbal art because the relation in them between theme and composition is quite different. Words in a novel, say, by Tolstoy, or Stendhal, are closer to everyday speech and openly communicative in function, whereas in a poem the verbalization is wholly determined by the aesthetic design and is in that sense an end in itself. There is such a thing, to be sure, as a purely formal prose, in which the elements of style and composition dominate (as in the work of Leskov, Remizov, and Biely), but it is precisely the "ornamentalism" of such prose that basically differentiates it from the narrative language of novelists like Stendhal, Tolstoy, or Dostoevsky, who achieve expressiveness chiefly through extensive rather than intensive verbal means.

I might add that "ornamental prose" is a technical term in Russian criticism which does not at all mean the same thing as "ornate prose." As D. S. Mirsky explains in his *History of Russian Literature,* "ornamental" prose fiction "is not necessarily marked by conventionally uplifted diction." It may be crudely realistic or even blatantly coarse. It is mainly distinguished by the fact that it keeps the reader's attention fixed on the small detail: the words, their sounds, their rhythm. "It is the opposite of Tolstoy's or Stendhal's analytical prose. It is the declaration of independence by the smaller unit . . . Ornamental prose has a decided tendency to escape the control of the larger unit, to destroy the wholeness of the work." I suppose that in English the work of Virginia Woolf would to some extent correspond to what the Russians mean by "ornamental" prose fiction, as would a novel like *Nightwood;* and among the younger American novelists there are not a few "ornamental" writers of prose to whom the test of local exemplification would apply, for the effects they seek depend almost entirely on stylization, on the perceptibility, to borrow a phrase favored by the formalists, of the mode of expression. But the norms of the novel are scarcely those of ornamentation, or of art-prose, a related term employed by the German critic Ernst Robert Curtius in a fine critical passage comparing Balzac and Flaubert:

> Balzac's creative power equals that of the greatest writers. Is he their equal also as an artist? It is evident that Balzac cannot be weighed in the scale of Flaubert's art-ideal. This ideal is that of art for art's sake. To Flaubert the value of a work hinges upon the quality of style, the faultless purity of language, the rhythms of the paragraphs and the music of the prose. His ideal was to transmute reality into imperishable

verbal substance. He called it: *faire du réel écrit*. Flaubert's language is art-prose in the sense in which one speaks of the art-prose of the Greeks and Romans. That was for Flaubert an inner necessity, which had its psychological grounds. An author like Balzac, in whom a world of living figures strains toward the light, cannot possibly write that way and has no need to do so. The artificial linking of artistry and the novel, for which Flaubert is responsible and which degenerates into a mannerism in the Goncourt brothers, leads to a blind alley.

The norms of the novel cannot accommodate a declaration of independence by the smaller unit, the word, the phrase, the sentence or the paragraph. Normatively the language of the novel does not possess the autonomous value that it has in poetry. It only intermittently lends itself to that verbal play characteristic of poetic speech, a play which uncovers the phonic texture of the word while at the same time releasing its semantic potential. In prose the relation between the word or sign and its referent is more firmly fixed and necessarily conventionalized than in poetry, where this relation is continually maneuvered so as to exploit the discord no less than the concord of sign and referent. Why is it, asks Susanne Langer in her book *Feeling and Form*, that the lyric poem is of all literary genres the one most directly dependent on verbal means — the sound and evocative power of words, meter, alliteration, rhyme, and other rhythmic devices, such as repetition, archaisms, and grammatical distortion? Her answer is that "the motif . . . of a lyric is usually nothing more than a thought, a vision, a mood, or a poignant emotion, which does not offer a very robust framework for the creation of a piece of virtual history . . . The lyric poet uses every quality of language because he has neither plot nor fictitious characters, nor, usually, any intellectual argument to give his poem continuity. The lure of verbal preparation and fulfillment has to do nearly everything . . ." Admitting that Miss Langer somewhat overstates her case, what she is saying on the whole is so self-evident as to be hardly more than a truism. It is a truism, however, which poetry critics, carried away by the simultaneous turn toward dramatic speech and intellectual elaboration in modern verse, are inclined to forget, with the result that they almost never stress the radical difference between the illusion of life or air of reality created in a poem and that created in a story or a novel or a play. Actually, the dramatic as well as the narrative (epic) resources of the modern poetic medium are extremely limited and the imagery it employs, however dramatic its impact on its own chosen ground, is no substitute for the bodying forth of character in action.

The late Christopher Caudwell is the critic who has made the most of the difference between poetic and prosaic language. In his book *Illusion and Reality* he wrote that the "poetic word is the logos, the word-made-flesh, the active will ideally ordering, whereas the novel's word is the sign, the reference, the conversationally pointing gesture." And again: "Painting, poetry and melody all have this in common — the timeless universal quality of the human genus rather than the interesting complications and subcomplications of a group of human individuals." It seems to me that he gets to the bottom of the distinction we are seeking to define when he says that "poetry concentrates on the immediate affective associations of the word," whereas the story goes first to "the object or entity symbolized by the word" in order to draw its associations from that. "The poem and the story both use sounds which awake images or outer reality and affective reverberations; but in poetry the affective associations are organized by the structure of the language, while in the novel they are organized by the structure of the outer reality portrayed. . . . Hence the hero of the novel is not like the 'hero' of poetry, a universal common 'I,' but a real concrete individual." The reader of the poem lives in the words of the poem and identifies with the poet, while the reader of the novel does not identify with the novelist but immerses himself instead in his fictive world, in which he finds "a more or less consistent mock-reality that has sufficient stuff in it" to stand between him and external reality. This means that the emotional associations in the novel are attached not to its words but to the mock-reality which they bring into being. "That is why rhythm, 'preciousness' and style are alien to the novel; why the novel translates so well; why novels are not composed of words. They are composed of scenes, actions, *stuff*, and people, just as plays are. A 'jewelled' style is a disadvantage to the novel because it distracts the eye from the things and people to the words — not as words, as black outlines, but as symbols to which a variety of feeling-tone is directly attached . . ." There are of course poetic passages in novels (as in Melville and Lawrence) as there are novelistic passages in poetry, but that in no way changes the characteristics of the two genres.

It seems to me that in Caudwell's formulation, which I have summed up all too briefly, we get at last to the root of the matter. It is the only theory which brings to bear a fundamental principle of explanation telling us why poetry is the form most indissoluble from its language while fiction is translatable with but minor loss to the integrity of the text. It explains why we are able to recognize Dostoevsky's greatness as a novelist at the same time that we are not in the least impressed by his stylistic powers. He is in fact a most indifferent stylist, but that hardly bothers us in reading him, for once we are caught up by the moving current of mock-reality in his narratives we cease noticing the words as such: the language becomes a kind of transparent envelope or medium through which we watch the action. Stendhal is another novelist of the first order whose stylistic gifts are unimpressive. Valéry goes so far as to speak of his "negligence, the wilful negligence, the contempt for all the formal qualities of style." But if so many of us have been drawn into Stendhal's fictive world and utterly won by it, it must be that the word *stylist,* or even the word *writer,* and the word *novelist* are not really synonymous. Sartre once observed that the poet is a writer who refuses to "utilize" language. An admirable formula, and the obverse of it would be that the novelist is a writer who is more often than not perfectly willing to utilize language. And if he is also a fine stylist, that is something thrown into the bargain. This bargain may inspire us with gratitude, but that is hardly a sufficient basis for an aesthetic of prose.

For the poet the major problem is always style, which it seldom is for the novelist. If you look into the working notebooks of two novelists so vastly different as James and Dostoevsky you are struck by the fact that verbal stylization is never among the difficulties they wrestle with. In their private notebooks both writers are talking to themselves, as it were, talking in an effort to define their subject, that above all, and further to see their way through the plot, the complications of the intrigue, the arrangement of scenes, the temporal sequence, the narrative perspective or point of view, and so on. The language in which all these things are to be embodied they take more or less for granted. In the notebook outlining the scenario of *Crime and Punishment* Dostoevsky is greatly worried by such problems as whether to tell the story in the first or third person, i.e., whether to let Raskolnikov tell the story in the form of a diary or whether to adopt the stance of the omniscient author; he has not as yet made up his mind whether Raskolnikov is to commit suicide or repent and go to Siberia to expiate his crime; and his entire conception of the novel changes upon deciding to introduce the Marmeladov family into the plot. These are clearly problems of theme and structure, exclusively, never of stylization. When he repeatedly complained that because of his poverty, the material pressure he was under to write rapidly in order to meet the monthly schedule of the periodicals in which his work was serialized, he could never turn in a performance as finished as that of Turgenev's for example, he did not mean that given more time he would apply himself to improving his diction and sentence structure. What he had in mind, rather, is that with less pressure on him he would have been able to organize his plots and design his scenes more carefully. He would have been able, in other words, to construct a more powerful and convincing illusion of life, a fictive world of superior consistency drawn more accurately to scale.

All that we can legitimately ask of a novelist in the matter of language is that it be appropriate to the matter in hand. What is said must not stand in a contradictory relation to the way it is said, for that would dispel the illusion of life and with it the credibility of the fiction. A Dostoevskyean story cannot be appropriately told in the style, say, of Dreiser, as that style is too cumbersome and the pace too slow. Dostoevsky's style has a kind of headlong, run-on quality which suits perfectly the speed of narration and the dramatic impetuosity of the action. But in itself, if we set out to examine it in small units, it is not rewarding. The principle of Dostoevsky's language is velocity; once it has yielded him that it has yielded nearly everything that his dramatic structure requires of it. The exact opposite of Dostoevsky is a novelist like Proust, whose themes and structures are undramatic and who must therefore secure his effects primarily through stylization. Proust's themes are essentially poetic-ironic rather than dramatic — memory, the intermittences of the heart, nostalgia for childhood, the vocation of the artist, illusion and disillusion with the great social world. There is of course action in Proust, but this action is rendered undramatically, in a mode shifting from analytic meditation to rhapsody and back again; and meditation and rhapsody are closely allied to the poetic medium. The intrinsic nature of Proust's themes and his conception of them as "enchanted realms," as he put it, in which "the dust of reality is mixed with magic sand," are such that they demand a master of language for their realization. It is pointless, however, to ask of a novelist whose themes do not require such an intensive stylistic effort that he captivate us through language when he is quite capable of captivating us through other means.

So far as Mr. Mark Schorer's essay "Technique as Discovery" is concerned, I think I have already dealt with it to the extent that it uniquely puts emphasis on style as an element of novelistic technique. For the rest, what is mainly to be objected to in Mr. Schorer's approach is his exclusive and almost vindictive emphasis on technique which leads him to say that "when we speak of technique in the novel we speak of nearly everything." His notion is that because technique objectifies the materials of art it also *ipso facto* evaluates them in a moral and intellectual sense. To me this formulation represents a monistic scheme, a violent simplification that leaves out of account any number of problems, such as that of creative personality, of the conditioned historical outlook prompting writers to settle upon some techniques while rejecting others, and the problem of the personal and unforeseen which, as Malraux has noted, is always present in our experience of a masterpiece. If by some chance the text of *Hamlet* had been lost to us, we would plainly be unable to imagine it despite all our accumulated knowledge of Shakespeare's techniques. And how are we to reconcile Mr. Schorer's point of view with Proust's precept that style is essentially a matter not of technique but of vision? The implication of that precept is that the technique of a true artist is dictated by an inner need and can be imitated only superficially. Vision is inimitable.

In a way everything Mr. Schorer says about the importance of technique is true, but true only in the trite sense that the novelist cannot render a single scene without some kind of technique, adequate or inadequate. But does Mr. Schorer really intend us to understand him in this altogether obvious manner? He remarks that if Thomas Wolfe had had the right sort of respect for technique and the ability to pursue it he would have written "a great novel on his true subject — the dilemma of romantic genius." Plausible as this sounds, does it actually mean anything more than if Wolfe had been a different kind of man he would have written different books? Tautologies are not insights. There is something anterior to technique and that is sensibility. Wolfe's sensibility was such that he was unable to conceive of the subject of romantic genius in a genuinely novelistic spirit; all he could do is spill the subject rather than express it; and the sensibility of Wolfe is not something he could alter. Sensibility can be cultivated under the appropriate conditions but it can scarcely be learned as a technique is learned. Let us beware of regarding technique as some sort of gimmick which it takes a certain amount of intelligence to master, after which the writer is at liberty to "create" to the top of his bent. One detects in such ideas an unconscious predisposition toward scientism, toward purely manipulative notions of the creative process and a tendency to subject it to rationalization. Let us recall T. S. Eliot's statement about Massinger — that he was a brilliant master of technique without being in any profound sense an artist. This can only mean that even though without technique we can do nothing in art, technique is not nearly enough.

1956

CRITICISM AND THE IMAGINATION
OF ALTERNATIVES

I

A FEW YEARS AGO Mr. Randall Jarrell announced in a caustic essay that ours is an Age of Criticism, and for all the good he saw in it he might as well have called it an Age of Boredom. His outburst was followed by the protests of other creative writers, who tend to see in the ascendancy of criticism the prime cause of the flatness of our literary life in this period. To be sure, this is an oversimplified view. The inflation of criticism must be understood as in some ways a consequence of the prolonged depression into which new imaginative writing has fallen in the postwar years. Moreover, it is pointless to rail at criticism as such. What is really at issue is not literary criticism in the generic sense but rather the uses to which the critical medium has been put and the purposes it has served.

Clearly, the partnership that criticism has of late effected with university teaching has influenced it in ways both positive and negative. The positive aspect is to be noted in the distinct gains that criticism has made in morale and productivity; the negative aspect is that, in becoming overtly pedagogic, criticism runs the risk of cutting itself off from the creative writer as well as from the general

244/Literature and the Sixth Sense

reader, who not unexpectedly is seldom in a mood to go back to school. "Criticism is the very education of our imaginative life," as Henry James so handsomely defined it; in the Jamesian context, however, the word "education" must be taken in a sense more honorific than literal. Education is primarily a matter of institutional practice, while criticism has by and large functioned as a free medium of literary expression and judgment.

In a notable essay in *The Sacred Wood* T. S. Eliot once defined what he named as "the essentially uncritical state"; and among the ways of reaching that state he singled out that of regarding literature as an institution — "accepted, that is to say, with the same gravity as the establishments of Church and State." Now this is an unfortunate state of mind which criticism in its present mood can scarcely be said to resist with sufficient force. Indeed, not a few of our critic-teachers have lately taken to celebrating the institutional aspects of literature. But the sense in which literary art can be described as an institution is at bottom no more than a paltry truism. Institutions are not only inevitable but necessary. Art too cannot escape the bonds they impose; nor would we want it to escape such bonds and attain a condition of unqualified liberty. Yet to join in solemnizing the institutional aspects of art is gratuitous at best. It is far more refreshing to attest to the fact that art has nearly always been much too restive to have acquired very reliable institutional manners and uses; that in a certain sense art is actually the great counterforce to institutions, in that it cannot without self-betrayal be ultimately reconciled to their rigidity and impersonality.

It is above all necessary to distinguish between the uses and abuses of criticism. Thus Edmund Wilson, perhaps our best critic still, continues to write marvelous literary essays; Lionel Trilling, however one may finally judge the ambiguous, if not wholly conservative, implications of his extreme recoil from radicalism, has maintained a fine dialectical grasp of the relation between values in life and values in literature; and younger men like Richard Chase, Alfred Kazin, and Irving Howe have not allowed themselves to be intimidated by the neo-conservative *Zeitgeist* and are upholding the tradition of dissidence and nonconformity in American writing at the same time as they strive to bring to conscious formulation what is most indigenously real and alive in it.

However, it is scarcely the above-mentioned critics who have of late exercised a dominant influence. For one thing, as they are far more concerned with ideas and the larger and more controversial issues than with "close reading" and textual minutiae, the criticism they write is mostly cast in the synoptic mode. None of them is likely to produce the next exegesis of a single poem by John Donne or even W. B. Yeats, a type of exegesis of which we have had no end of examples in recent decades and in which boredom is by now of the very essence. For another, the perspective in which these critics see literature is basically secular and social; the religious revival has left them cold. Mr. Wilson, in point of fact, is not merely cold but positively hostile; in commenting on our intelligentsia's flopover to religiosity he is regularly seized by the *esprit voltairien*. No wonder that in those graduate schools in literature stressing the "critical" rather than the "historical" approach, Mr. Wilson is dismissed as a literary journalist of impressionistic leanings while Professor Cleanth Brooks is regarded as a paragon of critical insight, discipline, and relevance.

Professor Brooks is indeed the model New Critic. A strict adherent of methodological purity, he shuns such incursions into psychology, biography, and social and political history as Mr. Wilson has so frequently and profitably made in his critical portraits and studies. Furthermore, Professor Brooks believes in the dogma of original sin and endeavors to bind himself as closely as he can to something he and his collaborators solemnly call "the tradition." For it is above all this putting oneself in the right relation to "the tradition" that distinguishes the "new" dispensation in criticism from the old. The idea of "the tradition," taken over from Eliot's earlier essays, has now come to stand in some of our literary-academic circles for a peculiar kind of higher reality, spiritual and social. America is a "new" country, in which the successful promotion of products depends on their being advertised as the latest and most up-to-date. Thus even "the tradition" was promoted among us as a novelty.

The effort of Professor Brooks to impose on the literary mind his triad of "paradox, irony, and ambiguity" as the permanent and ultimate tests of poetic quality has not been for a time without success. It is he who is the real *chef d'école*, in the factional sense, of the

New Criticism, which has so long dominated the literary quarterlies as well as the academic environment in which so much of our literary activity has been confined. Yet for all its ambitious claims and the stir it made in the world,* this school of critics has wholly failed to brace us intellectually or to produce those tonic qualities the want of which is so acutely felt in our literary situation. It has made for a deranged relationship between the critical and creative powers in our literary economy; and, by inhibiting the energy of discovery in criticism, it has brought it to a condition of arid self-sufficiency and self-consciousness.

At present it is generally admitted, even by some of its members of the older generation, that the New Criticism has exhausted its credit and is virtually done for. Actually, whatever good it accomplished goes back to a period when the term New Criticism had not yet come into use, the period of the 1920s, mainly, when a grouping of critics, most of them also practicing poets (Eliot, Pound, Ransom, Tate, Winters, Blackmur, Austin Warren, and Robert Penn Warren) undertook to demonstrate the significance of modern poetry by re-valuating the order of English poetry as a whole. This older generation, coming out of a very different and more seminal time, carried out its mission with success. It is their younger disciples really

* In the main, the many references to the New Criticism I have seen in European books and periodicals have struck me as singularly uninformed. For example, in the July 1958 issue of *Encounter,* the French poet Yves Bonnefoy characterizes the New Criticism in a way that quite converts it into the equivalent — in the explication of poetry — of logical positivism in philosophy. Specifically, M. Bonnefoy mentions Cleanth Brooks and R. P. Blackmur. Now these two critics stand in about as close a relation to positivism as Bertrand Russell stands to Thomism or Jacques Maritain to dialectic materialism. M. Bonnefoy's blunder is due to his ignoring or simply not knowing of the allegiance to orthodoxy and traditionalism to which Professor Brooks and most of the American New Critics are committed. Because he takes their formalist professions at face value, he cannot see that it is only superficially that they can be said to pursue the same ends as the Russian formalists, or even English critics like Empson and Leavis, for that matter. Clearly, some form of positivism is the logical presupposition of the formalist method in criticism. That the American New Critics have failed to discover this, and keep denouncing positivism in any form as "heresy," is one of the contradictions they are unaware of and which is tearing their position apart. And M. Bonnefoy is equally uninformed about Mr. Blackmur. After his first book, *The Double Agent,* he has gone in more and more for large-scale philosophizing about literature in a manner so heady as to stand any positivist's hair on end.

who now compose a school of New Critics *tout court,* busying itself
with the academic consolidation of the "revolution in poetry" long
ago accomplished by their elders. This belatedness and lack of a
separate and independent identity account for the self-induced dullness of the narrow textual-formalistic method of the New Criticism
as currently expounded, as well as for its unacknowledged and unanalyzed commitment to an obscurantist social and historical ideology. At bottom it offered little more than an amalgam of diluted
formalism and diluted traditionalism (Eliot's version of it) — an
amalgam because the two elements were artificially combined, in a
forced congruity; the diluting came about as a means of genteel
accommodation to the academic habitat. And by and large it was
the traditionalist bias that made for its fashionableness in this period,
aligning it implicitly with the conservative reaction to which some
American intellectuals succumbed under the gross pressures and
inducements of the Cold War.

As for the formal principle on which the New Critics plumed
themselves, it cannot be said that they ever applied it with any consistency or finesse; and lately it has been giving way to mythomania
and symbol-hunting. Why involve the meanings and values of literary works in the messiness of our historical life when it is so much
safer to fit them into the fixed and supra-temporal framework of
myth? And it is not Freud but Jung with his frigid, impersonal
archetypes who inspires the myth addicts. A variant of this addiction is the trend to "symbolic" analysis. In his book *The Literary
Symbol,* for instance, William York Tindall writes that "since symbolism is the necessary condition of literature, all novels are symbolic." This statement is by no means as innocuous as it sounds. It
does not take long to discover that Professor Tindall really means
to say that novels are chiefly about symbols pure and simple, not
about such profane matters as human experience, character, and
destiny. In the treatment of the "symbolic" analyst the referents of
symbols nearly always turn out to be dessicated abstractions drawn
from ethics or theology. Operating with a minimum of experiential
testimony, he converts the themes and materials of novels and
poems into mere simulacra; symbolic form becomes the essence of
the creative process, at once its end and means.

In his latest book, *The Power of Blackness,* Professor Harry Levin fully avails himself of these up-to-date procedures. His subject is Hawthorne, Melville, and Poe, and it is astonishing how little of central critical value he has been able to add to our understanding of them. What really counts is Professor Levin's addiction to myth-and-symbol hunting, which affords him the opportunity to indulge once again his flair for learned allusions and references; and the symbolic concept of "blackness" permits him no end of play with the modish phraseology of evil, guilt, and sin. But all this is mere bookishness and essentially evasive of the critical act. His method of combing the work of his three authors for the words "black" and "blackness" and "dark" and "darkness," and producing them for our benefit with an air of triumph, is sheer childishness. Naturally he finds what he seeks, as he would have found the words "green" and "red" had he been looking for them.

Equally disconcerting is Hugh Kenner's last book, *Gnomon: Ten Essays on Contemporary Literature.* Mr. Kenner, who is the leading exponent among us of the cult of Ezra Pound, is an extreme right-wing ally of the New Criticism and surely without peer in the ruthless manipulation of literary evidence to suit his prejudices. Pound, who was certified insane by a board of psychiatrists, he regards as a master not only of poetic diction, which he doubtless is, but also as a master of historical insight and social wisdom, whereas he disposes of Freud as a clinical case. The effrontery of which Mr. Kenner is uniquely capable is illustrated by the opening gambit of his review of Dr. Ernest Jones's biography of Freud, reprinted in *Gnomon:*

> It can very nearly be claimed for the subject of Dr. Jones's biography that he has been the presiding genius of the early twentieth century. That he is already as dated as William Archer or *Trilby,* and may come to seem as quaint as Boehme or Swedenborg, are considerations that don't alter this historical fact. An age in flight from diversity is delighted by one-page explanations of all human phenomena, and Freud has seemed for many years the most plausible of those investigators in whose name such pronouncements can be issued. Since the early nineteenth century the dominant philosophy of the West has been some guise or other of German pessimism: of this Freud's utterances-at-large are a clinical interest.

II
One of the major alternatives proposed to criticism is that it convert itself into a science of literature or at any rate into a discipline rigorous enough to justify its advancement to near-scientific status. Is this a meaningful ambition presenting criticism with a viable alternative? I think not. To be sure, there is a whole array of facts about literature that can be studied in a scientific manner more or less. But such studies belong chiefly to scholarship rather than to literary criticism properly speaking. Since criticism deals more with questions of value than with questions of fact, it is unlikely that it will ever be able so to transform itself in essence as to acquire even so much of seeming objectivity as the social sciences lay claim to. Criticism appears to be inextricably bound up with issues of value, of belief, and ideological conflict; and if we are not deluded by purely theoretical models of criticism but look to its actual practice in the past as in the present, we realize soon enough that the greater part of the criticism of consequence that we know is shot through and through with ideological motives and postulations that remain for the most part unanalyzed and unacknowledged.

Of course, once a given criticism has been completed in the sense of having been brought to its historical consummation, the student of it may well undertake to sort out the ideology it contains from other components that appear to him to have permanent validity. In fact, this sorting out is an activity that we pursue continually in our inspection of past criticism, and we may also attempt to cope the same way with our contemporaries. However, this sorting out is essentially an *ex post facto* operation, performed not by the critic himself but by those coming after him; nor is there any certain method available to us insuring that such latecomers go about their task free of ideological presuppositions of their own. We may think that, for example, we have by now sorted out to our complete satisfaction Dr. Johnson's ideas concerning metaphysical poetry; yet in the future critics may conclude that our altered estimate of this poetry was not quite the act of superior critical discernment that we take it to be but was fully as subject as Dr. Johnson's estimate to the varying ideological pressures and provocations of the historical process. This does not necessarily mean that our judgment of metaphysical poetry will not be vindicated in the future. All it means, rather, is that the historical process may either weaken or strengthen our critical judgment, that it may work in our favor or against us; in other words, that as critics we never exercise our judgment in the perfection of self-determination but within an historically conditioned framework of cultural need and response.

The demand that is being made nowadays for a radical purification of criticism implies something quite unreal, namely, that the literary interest can be advantageously divorced from other interests. Mr. F. R. Leavis has very effectively hit at this notion in remarking that "one cannot seriously be interested in literature and remain purely literary in interests." This he said in the course of questioning Ezra Pound's proposal that poetic technique be studied by itself, impersonally and in splendid isolation as it were, apart, that is, from the sensibility, with its varied and manifold content, engaged in applying that technique. Pound had proposed studying "how the pouring is done," and Leavis' retort was that "how the pouring is done cannot be studied apart from the thing poured . . . We have to speak of technique as something distinct from sensibility, but technique can be studied and judged only in terms of the sensibility it expresses. The technique not studied as the expression of a particular sensibility is an unprofitable abstraction." Surely Leavis is entirely in the right in this matter. And, indeed, if we accept the premise that criticism is ever closely attendant upon sensibility, then we must give due weight to the fact that it invariably resists the effort to systematize it and to predict its development; and there is no science without system and prediction. For that matter, sensibility also resists the effort to institutionalize it. In this respect it has an affinity with love, of which Nietzsche once said that it is the one thing in the world which cannot be institutionalized.

Criticism, I take it, is a discourse of the literary mind, and it is very much a mixed discourse besides. And though the good critic knows that the mixing is inevitable, he is also possessed of sufficient intellectual tact and sense of relevance to know just how to mix and what to mix. Yet at the same time he is under no illusions that criticism can be subjected with any real hope of success to a strict delimitation of function and to a purge of its allegedly "extraliterary" interests. He cannot but regard any such notion as a Utopia of rationalism, growing out of the division of labor and the mania for specialization which are among the least attractive features of modern culture.

But if criticism is not a science, is it proper, then, to speak of it as a literary medium? I would say that it is exactly that in the strict sense of being a department of letters. It is not an artistic medium, however, and for my purpose the distinction between a literary and artistic medium is worth stressing. A critical essay is not a work of art but neither is it a piece of purely objective writing, entirely informative or utilitarian in character. Being involved with the objects of sensibility, criticism necessarily adopts some of its means of expression, such as style and symbolic reference.

Having brought criticism so close to some of the primary processes of literature, I am tempted to proceed even further along the same lines. Is it not possible to maintain that the function of criticism is best understood in conceiving of it as a superstructural form of literature, its generalization into consciousness, or, to put it more directly, as a form of literature about literature? It depends on literature not only for its subject matter but also for its fundamental experience, and if it deals with life, as it is often brought to do, it does so at the remove of its aesthetic incarnation in the basic literary genres. I am offering this idea of criticism not as a rigorous definition or conclusive theory of it but simply as a provisional approach and as a corrective to the fetishism of method to which the critical intelligence has lately been yielding.

The principal objection that presents itself is that in conceiving of criticism as a form of literature, even if only as a form of literature *about* literature, we are in effect abolishing its cognitive function. The critic is, after all, concerned for the most part with discovering and verifying truths about the literary process, while the creative writer is concerned with the invention and formal elaboration of fictions. To this objection the rejoinder would be that it is chiefly in the popular view that the fiction embodied in the poem, novel, or play is something wholly feigned or imagined which offers us the possibility of pleasurable identification at the price of untruth. If we reject, however, this vulgar view of the nature of the imaginative fiction, recognizing that it has a measure of cognitive truth peculiar to itself and gained through its own proper means, then we can see our way clear to retaining the truths of criticism. For we can then put it that criticism has cognitive value in relation to literature to the degree, no more and no less, that literature can be said to have cognitive value in relation to life.

This conception of criticism has, to be sure, little to do with formal aesthetic theorizing. It derives rather from the empirical observation of the behavior of criticism, its actual performance in the sphere of letters, and of the demeanor of the critic as a man of letters. Moreover, this conception has in its favor the appeal of economy in that it reforges the unity of the literary mind, bringing its creative and critical faculties into close accord instead of disconnecting and driving them apart, as is being done nowadays by most theorists of the critical task.

To see criticism in its literary character is to realize that an exclusively valid method of work can no more be prescribed in its field than in poetry or the drama. Not that all methods are equally good. Some are obviously more rewarding than others, but this truism hardly comes to the same thing as the idea of salvation through method — a method single, strict, all-pertinent and alone legitimate. Though this idea may appear to resolve some of the quandaries of criticism by normalizing it, in the long run it leaves it in a worse quandary than ever. In its way this idea is in itself an admission that the imagination of alternatives has failed us, that we are prepared to embrace a narrow specialization that may perhaps satisfy our sense of professional status and enhance our pride in it but only at the expense of the living man in us. In the present literary situation what the critic needs above all is to recover the role of participant in the literary event — a role that can again belong to him if he seizes it; and if nowadays he more often than not prefers to play the part of a disengaged spectator and analyst of the literary event, the reasons for such unheroic renunciation are not to be sought in the nature of criticism per se but in other spheres altogether.

The conception of criticism as a literary medium is a difficult one to sustain. I have discussed one objection to it. Another one, not quite so telling, is that it makes criticism into a medium that has its end within itself. Now the dominant view has been that criticism, unlike the basic literary media, has no such autonomy; only a small minority of critics have maintained that in this respect too it differs hardly at all from literature in general. Thus John Middleton Murry contends that criticism performs the same function as literature itself, that of providing the critic with a means of expression; and Rémy de Gourmont speaks of criticism as a subjective literary form, a perpetual confession on the critic's part. "The critic may think," he writes, "that he is judging the work of other people, but it is himself that he is revealing and exposing to the public." Needless to say, this is a notion I do not subscribe to. In my understanding of criticism, it is a medium first and foremost of the critic's response to literature and only indirectly, by refraction as it were, of his response to life.

It seems possible to transcend these contrary views of criticism by going beyond the particular formulations given them. May we not say that subjectively the critic cannot help but regard his work as an end in itself, for in reacting to art he is expressing his own ideas, elaborating his own meanings, and in fact projecting a vision of life, even if only in an indirect and piecemeal fashion, by actively absorbing and pronouncing upon the visions of the artists that engage him? It is nevertheless true that in the economy of literature as a whole criticism is, objectively speaking, seldom an end in itself but mostly a means toward an end. What that ultimate end is we can define, after acknowledging its immediate ends of elucidating and evaluating works of art, under the double aspect of assimilation and mediation. To elucidate and evaluate a work of art is to assimilate it, and assimilation is in essence an act of mediating — mediating between art and the individual artist, between tradition and novelty, between the parts and the whole, and, in the long run, between art and life. This is culturally a function of the highest value, an indispensable one in fact; but it is in the main a function of cultural service and utility. Criticism exhausts itself in accomplishing it, which explains why it has so low a survival value in comparison with other genres of writing. It would seem as if in the very act of using criticism as liberally as we do we make and unmake it.

III

I would like to propose a distinction between types of criticism, a distinction that has little to do with the arid issues of methodology but is centered rather on the quality and import of the critic's interest in the literary process. In my view, there are chiefly two approaches that critics follow, one being prospective and the other retrospective. An excellent though somewhat one-sided example of the prospective attitude is Wordsworth's famous *Preface*. It is an attitude that asserts itself whenever the critic conceives of literature as something actual and alive in his own time and relates himself to it by trying to affect its course of development here and now. Both Eliot and Pound had this approach in mind when they first made their influence felt, as when Pound said that criticism is at best when it is "definitely shot at new creation, at a reinvigoration of writing." In *The Sacred Wood* Eliot put it that "the important critic is the person who is absorbed in the present problems of art, and who wishes to bring the forces of the past to bear upon the solution of these problems." What is indispensable, he argued in another essay in the same volume, is "a creative interest, a focus upon the immediate future"; and it was exactly that focus, of course, adjusted with beautiful calculation, that made for the extraordinary cogency of Eliot's reassessment of the order of English poetry.

This quality of absorption in the present problems of literary art, this sense of it as continuous and open to the incursions of the sensibility in its dynamic changes and responses to new experience, is missing in the retrospective critic, who tends to take literature as something given once and for all, secure in its pastness and unopen toward the future. Retrospective criticism may be good or bad of its kind, it may be extremely useful or nearly useless, but it is always marked by taking for granted that what matters are not the potentialities of literature but its norms. This type of criticism may be written by professors, by free-lance critics, or by literary journalists; it is the lack of a creative and intentional concern that makes it retrospective. Nor is it in the least a question of the critic's subject matter. Prospective criticism, though preoccupied with present problems, is hardly limited to contemporary literature. It may deal with the literature of the past or of the present or both. But in dealing with the past it does so with a certain intention — so well illustrated, for instance, in Eliot's essays on the Elizabethan dramatists and seventeenth-century poetry — the intention plainly being that of mobilizing the masterpieces of the past as a means of reactivating the creative imagination of its own time. Both Coleridge and Arnold shared this particular intention, if not in all then surely in a good part of their work. It is this relation to the past that makes the literary heritage come alive for us, whereas the retrospective critic makes it available to us as an object of study, of intense professional curiosity or antiquarian pleasure, but seldom as a living experience.

Of present-day criticism one might say many things but scarcely that its impact is of a prospective character. In the work of its finer representatives this criticism displays many assets, such as erudition, virtuosity in the selecting and presenting of literary evidence and other qualities; but it is quite clear that it is incapable of serving even in part as the motive power of new creation. It is much too self-contained and safely adjusted to its limited role to undertake the commitments that a programmatic approach to writing exacts from its partisans. As for "the forces of the past" invoked by Eliot, criticism is now marvelously aware of those forces and has no end of traffic with them, though by and large this is a one-way traffic that gets us past rather than into the present problems of art. To be sure, a plea might be entered in defense of contemporary criticism on the ground that, in the absence of a powerful new impulse among creative writers, it can be hardly expected to strike out on its own to perform a function which the history of literature shows to be more naturally and confidently performed in periods witnessing a renewal of imaginative energy and the emergence of insurgent tendencies in the national culture. It should be recalled, too, that the criticism of the generation of Eliot and Pound that might be described as "definitely shot at new creation" was produced not apart from but in conjunction with its literary practice, the sensibility and techniques of which needed, first, to be defined with precision and then justified in the light both of the rediscovery of tradition and of the revolt against it.

But there is another type of prospective criticism, in its way quite as valuable, I think, as that aimed at the immediate reinvigoration of writing, to which contemporary critics might profitably address themselves. This is the type of which Matthew Arnold gave classic definition in his essay "The Function of Criticism at the Present Time." In that essay Arnold was of course mainly concerned with the relationship between the critical and the creative power, and in particular with the operative meaning of that relationship in uncreative periods; and it is by reason of that emphasis that the argument of Arnold's celebrated essay seems to me to bear closely upon our situation. In his view, literary talent mostly manifests itself not in the unfolding of new ideas, not in "synthesis and exposition" but in "analysis and discovery," its great faculty being that of becoming "happily inspired by a certain intellectual and spiritual atmosphere, by a certain order of ideas, when it finds itself in them." Arnold had a far broader and more flexible notion of the relevance of ideas to the imaginative life than that prevailing in our literary world, where ideas are commonly assumed to exert a devitalizing influence on creative effort. Arnold, on the other hand, perceived that ideas, in his richly suggestive and socially viable sense of the term, composed the very element with which "the creative power works," and he held it as certain that in modern literature especially no display of the creative power in disengagement from that element could prove to be "important or fruitful." The fine concreteness of his historical insight is shown in this last observation, no less than in his further observation that the ideas literature works with cannot be those that are accessible at any time but only those that are "current at the time," that is to say, only those which historical development has made actually and directly available to the imagination. Now the creative power, for its effective exercise, must have the requisite atmosphere, it must dispose of itself amidst an order of fructifying ideas. But this atmosphere and order are not within its control. "This is why the great epochs in literature are so rare . . . for the creation of a masterwork two powers must concur, the power of the man and the power of the moment, and the man is not enough without the moment." It is that "moment" that the applied vigor of criticism can help to bring about through its own means of prefigurement and preparation, since, potentially at least, its aptitudes are scarcely so meager as not to be able to contribute to the making of an intellectual situation of which the creative power can avail itself.

That this account of the interaction that sometimes occurs between the critical and creative faculties is substantially correct can be demonstrated from numerous examples from literary history. It is unnecessary to go far afield into foreign literatures to illustrate this interaction. Consider, for instance, the ferment of ideas that occurred in this country in the 1830s and 1840s, a ferment which can only partially be identified with Transcendentalism and the inner meaning of which is now lost on us. The point is that it is this ferment of ideas which instigated changes in the literary consciousness, without which such masterworks as *The Scarlet Letter, Moby Dick,* and *Leaves of Grass* might conceivably never have been written. Or consider the seminal influence in this century, again in Arnold's sense of establishing a new atmosphere and a new intellectual situation, of critics like Mencken, the early Van Wyck Brooks, Randolph Bourne on the one hand and the group of poetry critics taking their cue from Eliot and Pound on the other. However much those critics differed among themselves, they were alike in the immense stimulus they provided to the national literature by striking boldly, openly, and with exhilarating success, at the forces that had long inhibited its growth.

The type of prospective criticism of which Arnold speaks in his essay is patently criticism only in the broadest sense of the term. Being educative and preparative in intent, it is as much a criticism of the larger context of literature as of its specific texts. Still, that is no reason for belittling it; we misunderstand the critical task if we conceive of it as unvarying from age to age; the changing needs of literature are the goad of criticism. In this period we have gone so far in specificity and formalistic detachment as to neglect the wider and more vital interests of American writing. The impulse that animated this writing in the first half of the century is apparently exhausted. A fresh impulse can arise only from a new quickening of thought reaching out from the life within literature toward the greater life by which it is encompassed on all sides.

1956–58

17

THE NATIVE BIAS

"CHARACTERISTICALLY AMERICAN" is a phrase that crops up with virtually compulsive regularity in a good many of the critical and scholarly texts that concern themselves with literature in America. Inevitably it occurs and recurs in all the intensive discussions of the prospects and conditions of the national letters conducted since the earliest years of the Republic. Quite often the phrase carries with it the suggestion that the user of it is far from certain in his own mind as to what the "characteristically American" actually comes to and that he is in fact looking to the literary expression of his countrymen to provide him with the key to the enigma. Thus it would seem that one of the principal functions of literature in America has been to serve as a guidebook or manual of Americanness, if not of Americanism. The latter term has by now acquired an unction or piety compelling its surrender to the politicians; it is with Americanness, a category more existential than political, that our writers and critics have been concerned.

There is little to be wondered at in the uncertainty that has pre-

Written as an introduction to *Literature in America,* an anthology of literary criticism.

vailed from the start as to the actual constituents of the "character-istically American." Henry James saw complexity in the fate of being an American, and among the recognitions that this complexity entails is the fact that as a national entity we are uniquely composed of diverse and sometimes clashing ethnic and regional strains. Even more important is the fact that as a nation we are afloat in history without moorings in prehistory. Americans have no organic past, only ambiguous memories of European derivation. The decisive factor in the forming of American civilization, as one cultural historian has put it, is that "the American community had a beginning at a particular moment in history in contrast with the traditional communities that, far from having a precise historical origin, rose out of the bottomless darkness of time in that epoch of prehistory which is history, if at all, only in its latent and undeveloped stage." Hence American society has the startling look about it of an artifact, constructed for specific socio-political and economic purposes in a given period, a period well known and thoroughly documented. It is a society established on contractual rather than traditional foundations, the very existence of which makes for the impression that in the New World the legend of "the social contract" has finally been brought to visible life. And this very perceptibility, so to speak, of the national origins is not the least of the elements making for a profound sense of the problematical in the American awareness of cultural identity.

This sense of the problematical, this sense of always verging on a definition yet somehow missing it, enters significantly into many of the critical approaches that Americans have made to their own literature — approaches tending to turn into a search for America that takes on the aura of a spiritual adventure or mythic quest. Now the problematical is surely not so far apart from the fascinating; and the more committed minds among those who embarked on this search form a vital band of native spokesmen to whom the American character presents itself as a fascinating problem. The effects of this devotion and fascination are writ large in our criticism. Most of the famous testaments of our cultural history owe to it their verve in undertaking successively fresh appraisals of the national experience. Its operation is everywhere manifest in such works as Emerson's "American Scholar," Whitman's various prefaces and *Democratic*

Vistas, Henry Adams' *Education,* the letters and essays of Randolph Bourne, and the books full of passionate indictment that Van Wyck Brooks issued year after year before the change of front evident in his *Makers and Finders* series. Yet even this voluminous record of patriotic and pious indulgence is quickened and given its rationale by the lasting fascination with the American character, a fascination which continues to serve at once as the goad and the charm of even such relatively late and sober-minded studies as F. O. Matthiessen's *American Renaissance* and Alfred Kazin's *On Native Grounds.* In the latter work Mr. Kazin alludes with insight to some of the consequences of this absorbing commitment on the part of American critics when he observes that "from Emerson and Thoreau to Mencken and Brooks, criticism has been the great American lay philosophy, the intellectual carryall. It has been a study of literature inherently with ideals of citizenship, and often less a study of literary texts than a search for some imperative moral order within which American writing could live and grow . . . It has even been the secret intermediary . . . between literature and society in America."

Among the earliest tasks that American critics set for themselves was that of locating and defining the differences between American and European writing. All through the past century and, in fact, until the renaissance that transformed the American literary consciousness in the earlier part of this century, this effort at definition met with resistance from the more genteel and agreeable writers and critics. These worthies, from Irving and Lowell to Brownell and Woodberry, entertained expurgated notions of the creative life, and they were unable to countenance "the snapping asunder," in Poe's phrase, "of the leading strings of our British Grandmamma." This prolonged resistance is to be explained by the fear of learning that the differences between the literature of the Old and the New World were indeed acute and real. "It is hard to hear a new voice," wrote D. H. Lawrence, "as hard as it is to listen to a new language; and there is a new voice in the old American classics."

This new feeling originated in the psychic shift that occurred in the movement to the Western Hemisphere. Lawrence called it a displacement, adding that "displacements hurt. This hurts. So we try to tie it up, like a cut finger, to put a rag around it." Whitman and Emerson exalted in the displacement; Hawthorne brooded about it and made what he could of it by searching for its beginnings in the annals of New England; Melville was heroic in striving to do it justice but soon suffered a breakdown because he could not sustain the pitch of intensity at which he expended himself. A more easeful or complacent reaction was evolved by Longfellow, Lowell, Holmes, and the other distinguished authors of a tame reflective literature. They recoiled in paleface fashion from the tensions and hazards of the fresh experience thrown up by the dynamism of American life; and insofar as this experience came within their purview at all they saw it in its crude, exposed state, judging it to be unfit for imaginative treatment.

Barrett Wendell, the Harvard professor who published *A Literary History of America* in 1900, was among the foremost exponents of the genteel tradition and one of those luminaries of the academy in America who could not bring themselves to treat American writers as anything but poor relations of the towering British figures to whom they looked up with reverence. In his *Days of the Phoenix* (1957) Van Wyck Brooks recalls that even as late as 1920, when American writing had come to seem important, it was still "ignored in academic circles where Thackeray and Tennyson were treated as twin kings of our literature and all the American writers as poor relations. It was regarded as a pale and obedient provincial cousin about which the less said the better."

As for Barrett Wendell's *History,* though its author ignores Melville in it and disdains Whitman, yet he somehow hit upon the formula that accounts for the feebleness that affects us so discouragingly in studying the pre-modern period in American letters. (It has become habitual among us to regard Melville and Whitman as the representative creative types of that period. But this view indicates a loss of perspective on the past, for both were signally unsuccessful in gaining the esteem of the public of their time and in influencing the creative practice of their contemporaries.) Wendell's formula is that American literature is a "record of the national inexperience" and its "refinement of temper, conscientious sense of form and instinctive disregard of actual fact" are its most charactereristic traits. Thus Wendell accurately noted, though with no objection on his part, the overriding fault — that of innocuousness —

against which Melville warned in declaring that "the visible world of experience . . . is that procreative thing which impregnates the Muses." And if a novelist like William Dean Howells is virtually unread today, then surely it is because of the lack in him of "that procreative thing" — hence the failure of the recent efforts to stage his "revival." Evidently the absence of the "procreative thing" cannot be made up for by the clarity of design of his fiction and by the considerable intelligence and attractiveness of the personality that informs it. It is plain that whatever interest we may have in Howells today is not actual but lies somewhere on the borderline between the historical and the antiquarian; and that is equally true of Longfellow, Whittier, Simms, and others whose names are still honored in the textbooks.

Now modern American literature has attempted to overcome the fault so fatal to Howells and his predecessors by at long last seizing upon what the native genius had long been deprived of, by finding, in other words, its major stimulus in the urge toward and immersion in experience. American writers were able to accomplish this transformation, however, not merely by accepting experience in all its indigenousness but also by overturning the tradition of the palefaces and by frequently making the most, in true redskin fashion, of experience precisely in its crude, exposed state, thus turning what had long been taken as a defect into a virtue. The law of overcompensation is as operative in art as in life.

It seems to me that it is only by facing up to the fact of the enfeeblement of the greater part of the older American literature by its negative relation to experience that we can properly evaluate the complaint against the native environment typically voiced by many of the worst as well as the best of our nineteenth-century writers. Let us attend only to the best of them, noting the virtual identity of the terms in which they state the case against their country's capacity to provide them with imaginative substance. There is James Fenimore Cooper, for instance, asserting back in 1828 that among the main obstacles against which the native writer has to contend is "poverty of materials." "There is scarcely an ore which contributes to the wealth of the author, that is found here in veins as rich as in Europe. There are no annals for the historians; no follies (beyond the most vulgar and commonplace) for the satirist; no

manners for the dramatist; no obscure fictions for the writer of romance . . . nor any of the rich auxiliaries of poetry . . . no costume
for the peasant . . . no wig for the judge, no baton for the general,
no diadem for the magistrate." This complaint is substantially repeated by Hawthorne some three decades later in the preface to
The Marble Faun, where he remarks upon the difficulty of "writing
a romance about a country where there is no shadow, no antiquity,
no mystery, no picturesque and gloomy wrong, nor anything but a
commonplace prosperity, in broad and simple daylight, as is happily
the case with our dear native land." James, quoting these words in
his biography of Hawthorne, is powerfully moved to enlarge upon
them, and it is at this point in his book that the famous passage
comes in ("no sovereign, no court, no personal loyalty, no aristocracy, no church, no clergy, no army," etc.) enumerating the items of
high civilization absent from American life. It is important to observe that James's version, by stretching Hawthorne's statement to
the limit, no longer refers to "romance" alone but to artistic creation
in general. Essentially he is duplicating Cooper's complaint in a
more elaborate and conscious manner; and where Cooper speaks
of "the poverty of materials" available to the American writer, James
speaks of "the paucity of ingredients."

The justice and pathos of this standing complaint have been more
or less recognized by our critics and historians of letters. No doubt
it is justified insofar as we cannot but accept in some sense the
Jamesian dictum that it takes "an accumulation of history and custom . . . to form a suggestion for the novelist." But there is nonetheless a fallacy in the argument so strikingly concurred in by
Cooper, Hawthorne, and James. For what they are saying, intrinsically, is that it is impossible to write European literature in America:
the necessary ingredients are missing. And so they were if we are
thinking in terms of a Walter Scott romance or a Jane Austen novel
or the poems of Byron; no part of the United States was then a
center of high civilization. Still, what is wrong is the tacit assumption that the ingredients are of a fixed kind, given once and for all.
But is it really true that the relationship between high civilization
and literature is so completely binding? If that were strictly the
case, we would be utterly at a loss to explain the appearance in
backward Russia, and early in the nineteenth century at that, of so

great a poet as Pushkin and a master of narrative prose like Gogol. Whitman's "Song of Myself" is in no sense a poem of high civilization, but it is a magnificent poem nevertheless. Is it not more to the point to acknowledge that the genuinely new and venturesome in literary art emerges from a fresh selection of the materials at hand, from an assimilation, that is, to imaginative forms of that which life newly offers but which the conventions of past literature are too rigid to let through? And in the earlier as well as the latter part of the nineteenth century life in America certainly offered sufficient experience for imaginative treatment, though not the sort of experience marked by richness and complexity of historical reference and safely certified for literary use by past conventions of authorship. Actually, in creating the character of Leatherstocking, Cooper did break through these conventions; as Lowell wrote in his *Fable for Critics:* "He has drawn you one character, though, that is new/ One wildflower he's plucked that is wet with the dew/ Of this fresh, western world"; where Cooper failed in his "Leatherstocking Tales," however, is in being far too obedient to the established conventions in point of style and technique.

As for Hawthorne, he appears to have attached a disproportionate importance to the question of "romance," plainly because of his incapacity to come to terms with the kind of subject matter which is novelistic in essence. The fact is that in his time "romance" was a genre already far gone in obsolescence; it was the novel that was then full of promise and vitality. Let us recall, too, that some of the "follies" disdained by Cooper as much too "vulgar and commonplace" for literary exploitation, served the French novel very well in the work of Balzac, Flaubert, and Zola. In his *Human Comedy* Balzac intended to treat all strata of society, but in practice he assigned the major role to the trading and professional classes. There was no lack of such classes in America, and yet no indigenous version of a novel comparable to *César Birotteau* was ever produced by a writer who knew his New York, Boston, or Philadelphia. A subject so lowly as Balzac tackled in his commercial saga of a Parisian linen draper was entirely at variance with "the abnormal dignity" which then prevailed in American letters. Another example would be *Madame Bovary.* Can it really be claimed that the material fashioned by Flaubert into a work of art was unavailable in

America a hundred years ago? After all, a pretty woman's boredom, adultery, and suicide are scarcely a monopoly of French life. Yet the sort of imaginative transaction represented by the story of Emma Bovary is unthinkable in mid-nineteenth-century America. It was not the absence of materials but the absence of writers prepared to cope with the materials actually at hand that decided the issue, and it is in this sense that the standing complaints cited above were misdirected. Allowing for Whitman and in part for Melville as formidable exceptions, what stood in the way was the fixed stance of the writers, their lack of inner freedom to break with tradition so as to be able to say the seemingly unsayable. "The immense and vague cloud-canopy of idealism," in Brooks's phrase, which then hung over the national culture, made any such attempts prohibitive.

The truth is that there were no real novelists in America until the eighties and nineties, only pre-novelists and romancers. A conspicuous instance attesting to this fact is Melville's *Pierre*, the one work in which he undertook to possess himself of the forms of realism developed by his European contemporaries and in which he failed dismally. In that period American literature was not yet in a position to adapt for itself the vitally new principle of realism by which the art of fiction in Europe was at that time evolving toward a hitherto inconceivable condition of objectivity and familiarity with existence. This principle of realism — which Erich Auerbach defines in his *Mimesis* as "a serious representation of contemporary social reality against the background of constant historical movement" — requires above all a give-and-take relation between the ego and experience. It is only with the appearance of narratives like *Washington Square* (1881) and *The Bostonians* (1886) that we sense that this relation is perceptibly beginning to come into being. And if the former narrative, in its re-creation of old New York focusing on the house in Washington Square with its chintz-colored parlor where Catherine Sloper is courted by Morris Townsend, still puts us under a spell, it is hardly because those young people are especially memorable or their case compelling but because earlier American fiction is so poor in its evocation of the actual in its time and place. It is a matter of the Americanness of a past age coming through as an aesthetic impression by virtue of the precision by which it is conveyed. But James was soon to settle in London, taking his American characters with him. It was to be a question for him of becoming either a novelist of high civilization, even if mainly of its impact on his countrymen, or nothing at all. He removed himself from the scene, exerting an uncertain influence from afar. Not till after the turn of the century, when the qualities of national existence changed radically and a native intelligentsia rose to the surface of social life, did American literature succeed in liberating itself from its past inhibitions.

Of course, all through the nineteenth century the ideologues of nativity bent every effort to nullify the complaint against America's "poverty of materials." Whitman's prose is one long counterargument. And at an earlier date, as in the Young America group in New York, powerful voices were raised in defense of America's creative possibilities. There is Emerson, for instance, writing in 1842 that "we have as yet no genius in America, with tyrannous eye, which knew the value of our incomparable materials, and saw, in the barbarism and materialism of the times, another carnival of the same gods he so much admires in Homer . . . Banks and tariffs, the newspaper and caucus, Methodism and Unitarianism, are flat and dull to dull people, but rest on the same foundations of wonder as the town of Troy and the temple of Delphi . . . Our stumps and their politics, our fisheries, our Negroes and Indians . . . the northern trades, the southern planting, the western clearing, Oregon and Texas, are yet unsung. Yet America is a poem in our eyes; its ample geography dazzles the imagination, and it will not wait long for metres." As usual Emerson is being beautifully eloquent. His catalogue of materials is impressive, a splendid retort to disparagers and complainers. But a catalogue is one thing; the personal appropriation of materials is something else again. Only writers of a truly Balzacian grossness of appetite could conceivably have digested them. What was needed was not a "tyrannous eye" but a strong stomach above all; but unfortunately the men of letters of that period were typically inclined either toward a morbid type of spirituality or toward a propitiatory and at bottom escapist jocosity.

Whitman alone responded in programmatic fashion to Emerson's challenge, though his master was sometimes depressed by his want of metres. Moreover, the master, along with the lesser partisans of nativity, was not content to submit his inventory of materials without at the same time prescribing an attitude of patriotic glow as the conditions of their assimilation. Note that Emerson says of America that it is "a poem in our eyes," just as Whitman was to say in the 1855 preface to *Leaves of Grass* that "the United States are themselves the greatest poem." Thus dogmatic patriotism is turned into a prerequisite of artistic creation. Historically speaking, this is indeed the vulnerable side of nativism in literature, that it cannot advocate the use of American subject matter without at once demanding of the writer that he declare himself in advance to stand in an affirmative relation to it. Nativists can never understand that any attempt to enlist literature "in the cause of America" is bound to impose an intolerable strain on the imaginative faculty. The real issue in the times of Emerson and Whitman was not between love of America and disdain of it. Neither Cooper nor Hawthorne nor James disdained it. The issue was rather the availability at home of creatively usable materials; their availability was the point, and the writer's readiness to benefit from it according to his lights, not the political or moral or philosophical valuation to be put upon them.

It is through his achievement in his own medium that the important writer contributes to the spiritual development of his people. To ask that he commit himself to flattering the national ego is a proceeding as simpleminded as it is vicious. And it is a false idea of what affirmation comes to in the long run to believe that the literary artist who brings to his people not peace but a sword has failed in his spiritual task. As isolable qualities neither pessimism nor optimism are open to definition as values in art.

At the present time, when the issue of "poverty of materials" can no longer arise in America, the habit of demanding affirmation still persists. In many circles so recent a lesson as that taught us in the 1920s, when American writing showed far more creative force than it does now even while engaging in a bitter assault on the national pieties, has been conveniently forgotten. As in the old days, so now the appeal to "the sanely and wholesomely American" is taken up as a weapon against the moral freedom of literature.

It is true, as some critics point out, that a good deal of American writing, in the classic as in the modern period, is dominated by forms of flight from the organized pressures of society. Thus Mr.

H. B. Parkes has brilliantly marshaled the evidence to show that the Leatherstocking type of hero who may be seen as a fugitive from society appears again and again in our fiction, which carries with it a specific emotion of disappointment in the consequences of civilization. In *Huckleberry Finn* as in some of the novels of Anderson, Dos Passos, Hemingway, and Fitzgerald, an antagonism is demonstrated between individual integrity and institutional disciplines and mores. To the texts cited by Mr. Parkes one might add so signal an expression of the same tendency as Faulkner's long story "The Bear," in which the principal character, Isaac McCaslin, relinquishes the land he had inherited in the belief that rapacity was the prime motive power of subduing the wilderness and that civilization represents a fall from goodness and innocence requiring the strictest expiation.

One wonders, however, whether Mr. Parkes is right in the interpretation he puts upon the evidence at his disposal. Is not the pessimism which he perceives to be so strikingly characteristic of modern literature to be found in even stronger ideological doses, though not expressed with the same heedless violence, in modern European writing? Are we justified in absolving civilization of sin and guilt while convicting writers of an impossible idealism derived from a Rousseauistic faith in natural virtue and natural religion? Is not discontent with civilization one of the major sources of the virulence of modernity? Literature, here as in Europe, has so long made a specialty of the depiction of evil in man that it can scarcely be said to tell us that he is good; but neither does it tell us that social institutions are admirable, endowed with "prescriptive" rights which the individual does wrong to challenge. Institutions are made and unmade by particular men under particular circumstances, and to confer a sacrosanct character upon their own handiwork is to turn them into idolaters and slaves.

A close observer of the creative process once finely remarked that the honor of a literature lies in its capacity to develop "a great quarrel within the national consciousness." One has only to think of the outstanding Victorian figures who decried the state of England, or of the French, and particularly the Russian novel in the past century, to realize the truth of that statement. In a somewhat different way the modern American novel is likewise implicated in "the great quarrel within the national consciousness." To my mind, the principal theme of this novel, from Dreiser and Anderson to Fitzgerald and Faulkner, has been the discrepancy between the high promise of the American dream and what history has made of it. The inner feeling of this novel is one of nostalgic love of nativity combined with baffled and sometimes angry disenchantment. That is what comes so tellingly through to us, with plangent force, in the wonderful closing paragraphs of *The Great Gatsby,* when the narrator, Nick Carraway, wanders down to the beach at night:

> Most of the big shore places were closed now and there were hardly any lights except the shadowy, moving glow of a ferryboat across the Sound. And as the moon rose higher the inessential houses began to melt away until gradually I became aware of the old island that flowered once for Dutch sailors' eyes — a fresh, green breast of the new world. Its vanished trees, the trees that made way for Gatsby's house, had once pandered in whispers to the last and greatest of all human dreams; for a transitory enchanted moment man must have held his breath in the presence of this continent, compelled into an aesthetic contemplation he neither understood nor desired, face to face for the last time in history with something commensurate to his capacity for wonder.

> And as I sat there brooding on the old, unknown world, I thought of Gatsby's wonder when he first picked out the green light at the end of Daisy's dock. He had come a long way to this blue dawn, and his dream must have seemed so close that he could hardly fail to grasp it. He did not know that it was already behind him, somewhere back in that vast obscurity beyond the city, where the dark fields of the republic rolled on under night.

> Gatsby believed in the green light, the orgastic future that year by year recedes before us. It eluded us then, but that's no matter — tomorrow we will run faster, stretch our arms further . . . And one fine morning —

Art has always fed on the contradiction between the reality of the world and the image of glory and orgastic happiness and harmony and goodness and fulfillment which the self cherishes as it aspires to live even while daily dying. If reality ever measures up to that image, art would witness its own dissolution in a beautiful world. But the world is what is, in the New as in the Old. And in transposing this reflection into a national key, one feels compelled to say that America, whatever it looked like in its fresh flowering to Dutch sailors' eyes, is far more what its best artists have made it out to be than it is the achieved Utopia invoked in our mass media and by officialdom in politics as in culture. In their relation to their native land those artists have never lost their capacity for wonder, and they are in no danger of losing it so long as they do not degrade wonder into submission, acquiescence or a simple, uniform and thoughtless allegiance.

1957

DOSTOEVSKY: TWO SHORT NOVELS

THOUGH the leading Russian critics of Dostoevsky have long recognized the originality, rare psychological insight, and comic
genius of *The Friend of the Family* and *The Eternal Husband*, to
English-speaking readers they are still among the least known of
his works. That is, they are least known as compared with, say,
Notes from Underground, let alone his world-famous major narratives. To be sure, there are a few Western commentators on Dostoevsky who have fully appreciated these tales. In the estimate of
Thomas Mann, for instance, "the incomparable character of the des-
potic hypocrite Foma Opiskin" (the hero of *The Friend of the Family*) is "a comic creation of the first rank, irresistible, rivaling Shakespeare and Molière"; and, in his study of Dostoevsky, André Gide
singles out *The Eternal Husband* as uniquely a masterpiece. It still
remains true, however, that these tales have by no means obtained
the wide recognition among us that is their due.

The reason may well lie in the approach to Dostoevsky peculiar
to the West. Perhaps we have become so habituated to the role
we have assigned to him as foremost exponent of the so-called mysteries of the Russians spirit — or of the "Slav soul" as people used to

speak of it mystifyingly enough — that unwittingly we have tended to underrate those productions of his into which his "Russianness" does not conspicuously enter, and in which his typical creative obsessions do not emerge from his highly controversial religious and national philosophy. In other words, we are inclined to underestimate those works of his in which his dramatic power is not expended on ideological themes. Nor are we prepared, once we have become convinced of his tragic grandeur as a novelist, to prize his abundant gifts in the comic genre at their full value. This is a mistake, I think, for the imaginative artist in Dostoevsky is sometimes more vitally present in his fiction when he is least portentous and least carried away by metaphysical ardor and visionary nationalism. In both *The Friend of the Family* and *The Eternal Husband* it is his comic sense which predominates, though in the latter narrative not a few notes are sounded reminding us of the more ominous bent of his genius.

One need not think, however, of these novellas as comic interludes. In terms of basic character imagery and basic theme, Dostoevsky's *oeuvre* forms an organic whole, and the thematic lines connecting these two works with his major novels are not difficult to establish. There is the theme, for instance, of the psychology of the "underground man," a psychology much too varied and complex to be reduced to a formula, which the two rival protagonists of *The Eternal Husband* exemplify in antithetical but equally surprising ways. More importantly perhaps, there is the characteristic Dostoevskyean theme of the resentful buffoon, whose boundless vanity is fed by early humiliation and defeat and who is driven to take out upon others the psychic mutilation his ego has suffered. The classic definition of this type is·given in *The Brothers Karamazov* by Alyosha, who speaks of "people of deep feeling who have been somehow crushed." Buffoonery in them is "a form of resentful irony against those to whom they daren't speak the truth, from having been for years humiliated and intimidated . . . Believe me . . . that sort of buffoonery is tragic in the extreme." Though the components that go into the making of this type are varied in each case, at least one such specimen is to be found in almost all of Dostoevsky's novels, such as Lebedev in *The Idiot*, Captain Lebyadkin in *The Possessed*, Snegirev and above all Fyodor Pavlovitch in *Karamazov*. Now in

The Friend of the Family Foma Fomitch Opiskin is the most striking early embodiment of this type, and what is peculiar to him is that he is placed, as never again in Dostoevsky, in a position of total power; he is able to dispense altogether with the protective cover of irony and indulge himself to his heart's content in outright tyranny and hypocrisy. If Foma Fomitch is one of the most remarkable characters in world literature, it is precisely because he so completely precipitates himself into his role that, overstepping all limits and piling one outrageous demand upon another, he will settle for nothing less than becoming the veritable idol of the people who surround him. But there is no pathos in Foma Fomitch — he exists and imposes himself on our imagination solely through the prodigious comicality of his insolence and his consistency in excess. Trusotsky, on the other hand, the ambivalent cuckold, the type of "the eternal husband," is a later and more subtle version of this ever-present Dostoevskyean buffoon. In his creation, humor is tempered by pathos, and biting wit by fellow-feeling.

The Friend of the Family is the English title given by the translator Constance Garnett to the novella called in Russian *The Village of Stepanchikovo and Its Inhabitants.* It appeared in 1859 together with another novella called *Uncle's Dream.* This marked Dostoevsky's second debut, so to speak, in Russian literature. After ten years of prison and exile in Siberia,* his name had nearly been forgotten in the literary world. It was in December 1849 that Dosto-

---

* The sentence against him read: "For taking part in criminal plots, for circulating the letter of the writer Belinsky, full of insolent attacks on the Orthodox Church and the Government, and for endeavoring, along with others, to circulate articles directed against the Government by means of a home-printing press, to be sentenced to eight years of penal servitude." The official language of the above should on no account be taken at face value. At bottom, all that Dostoevsky was really guilty of was reading aloud at the home of Petrashevsky, the leader of a group of so-called intellectual conspirators, the radical critic Belinsky's famous letter denouncing Gogol for his servile backing of the status quo. The rest was merely a matter of loose dissident talk, of vague intention rather than actual deeds. But the autocrat Nicholas I was not one to distinguish between intention and action. Nor did he spare Dostoevsky and his fellow "criminals" the agony of a mock execution on Semyonovsky Square (on December 22, 1849). They were made to go through the entire gruesome ceremony and were actually facing the firing squad when a message was delivered from the Czar commuting the sentence to penal servitude.

evsky was deported in irons to Siberia as a convicted political criminal, and after four years of penal servitude in the prison at Omsk he was permitted to serve out the rest of his sentence as a common soldier in a regiment of the line. It was not until 1856, upon obtaining an officer's commission, that he was able to resume writing. He was then living in the dismally small and isolated town of Semipalatinsk under extremely adverse conditions, penniless and forbidden to leave Siberia. It was there that he began composing *The Friend of the Family*.

A letter to his brother Mikhail of January 1856 shows that he began it as a comic play only to switch later to the narrative form. Thus he wrote: "I jokingly started a comedy and jokingly conjured up so many funny circumstances and comical figures, and grew to like my hero so much that I abandoned the form of comedy, despite the fact that it was going well. I did this to satisfy myself, so as to be able to follow the adventures of my new hero further and laugh over him myself. The hero is somewhat like me. In short, I am writing a comic novel ..." And in truth the novel retains many features of a comic play, and of a classical comedy at that. It is entirely theatrical in structure. The Russian critic K. Mochulsky is quite right in pointing out that it is built up strictly in accordance with the ancient and established usages of comedy. The action is concentrated in one place and within the brief span of two days. Opening with an introductory exposition of the plot and the deft "planting" of the requisite information concerning the principal characters, the narrative is caught up in the swift development of the central dramatic crisis along with the required subsidiary complications. After a catastrophic denouement (the downfall of Foma and his expulsion from his patron's establishment), the story is brought to a genial end (as Foma returns and makes everyone happy) with the loose ends tied up in an epilogue.

The formal mastery exhibited in this work, and even more so in *The Eternal Husband*, essentially a far more modern instance of the resources of technique in shaping the long story or novella, should serve as a sufficient rejoinder to those critics of Dostoevsky (like Henry James, for example) who have professed to see no structure in his work, no technical control, but only an imitation of genius of the flow of amorphous life at its most impetuous and confused.

This is an error due to a somewhat limited schematic notion of form in fiction. In spite of the fact that in some of his novels he is formally unsuccessful (particularly in *A Raw Youth* and to a far lesser extent in *The Idiot*), Dostoevsky is one of the great innovators in the history of narrative prose in the sphere of form as well as content. And whatever artistic failure his work shows is attributable for the most part to the truly onerous conditions under which he worked — poverty, ill health, the unremitting pressure of editors and printers to meet the frequent deadlines of serial publication. While writing *The Eternal Husband* he was stranded in Dresden with his family and was virtually starving. No wonder he cried out in a letter to his friend Maykov: "People demand of me art, pure poetry, without strain, without poison, and point to Turgenev, to Goncharov! Let them look at the conditions under which I work."

There is one curious thing about *The Friend of the Family,* which came to the attention of the literary world as late as 1921, with the publication in Moscow of a scholarly work, *Dostoevsky and Gogol,* by Yuri Tynaynov. In this study Tynaynov shows that the portrait of Foma Fomitch is in certain respects modeled in a caricature fashion on the impression we receive of Gogol in his notorious work, which became something of a *cause célèbre* in Russian literary history, entitled *Selected Passages from a Correspondence with Friends* (1847). This book, perhaps the most implausible ever concocted by a writer of genius, and plainly the product of a pathological state of mind, was by the same author of *The Inspector General* and *Dead Souls,* widely regarded upon their appearance as satirical treatments of the regime of serfdom, corporal punishment, and bureaucratic arbitrariness and corruption. Written in an insufferably didactic tone, and consisting mostly of bombastic preachments of virtue and uplift, *Selected Passages* enjoins landowners, officials, and serfs alike to adhere to "the duty of conforming conscientiously . . . with the present God-ordained order of things." Gogol, as D. S. Mirsky observes in his *History of Russian Literature,* expected it "to be received with awe and gratitude, like a message from Sinai. He actually believed that it would be a signal for the immediate regeneration of all Russians from sin." Of course he was grievously disappointed, for even his Slavophile friends were disgusted, not to mention the Westernizing intelligentsia led by the critic Belinsky.

Now Dostoevsky, who was greatly influenced by Gogol, especially in his early career, appears to have captured in Foma Fomitch's sanctimonious speeches the very essence of Gogol's aberrant production; even the very notion of a book like the *Correspondence with Friends* is parodied, as in this passage (it is the narrator of the story who is speaking): "I know that he seriously assured my uncle that some great work lay before him, Foma, in the future — a work for which he had been summoned into the world and to the accomplishment of which he was urged by some sort of person with wings, who visited him at night, or something of the kind. The great task was to write a book full of profound wisdom in the soul-saving line, which would set the whole world agog and stagger all Russia. And when all Russia was staggered, he, Foma, disdaining glory, would retire into a monastery, and in the catacombs of Kiev pray day and night for the happiness of the Fatherland." Surely this is a conscious parody of the peculiar Gogolesque syndrome of delusions of grandeur combined with grotesque piety; and the novel contains many other passages in which Foma Fomitch reproduces, as it were, the very tone and content of Gogol's exhortations. Dostoevsky was indeed a master of parody, including the parody of his own most cherished ideas and attitudes. Not nearly enough has been made of this by critics and scholars, who, by and large, have been so carried away by his powers as psychologist and dialectician that they overlook other elements of intrinsic literary value in his expressive range.

Foma dominates *The Friend of the Family;* the other characters in it are given a lesser degree of reality, deliberately drawn, that is, in a conventional manner so as to make Foma's outrageous impositions all the more credible. Thus Colonel Rostanev, Foma's patron and victim, is so good-natured as to seem positively simple-minded. But that is precisely his function; the simplification involved must be calculated rather than accidental for the tale to achieve its comic catharsis. We are not to look for "realism" where none is intended. But apart from Foma, there is one remarkable figure in the tale who can be said to acquire a life of his own. That is the valet Vidoplyasov, in whom one recognizes a preliminary sketch of one of Dostoevsky's truly great character creations — Smerdyakov in *The Brothers Karamazov.* Vidoplyasov, the provincial dandy with his straw-colored waistcoat, patent-leather shoes, curled, pomaded hair, and pink tie, is rendered in a light, humorous vein. However, there is already present in him, even if in an embryonic form, the far more complex figure of Smerdyakov, the parricide and sinister flunky of Ivan Karamazov's audacious thought. Dostoevsky's fictional world is seldom inhabited by stray or fugitive people, fortuitous types unassimilable to his fundamental vision of life. His character imagery is mainly continuous from work to work, though subject of course to a process of deepening and elaboration.

The Eternal Husband (1870), published eleven years after *The Friend of the Family,* is wholly representative of Dostoevsky's later or ultimate creative phase, which opens with the appearance of *Notes from Underground* in 1864. Dazzling in its marvelous comic invention, *The Eternal Husband* is built around the stock situation of a French farce reworked with the finesse and profundity of a psychological genius. Indeed, on the psychological plane it is a masterwork of analysis, suggesting some of the ambivalences and dissociations of impulse and motive which some decades later found scientific formulation in the work of Freud and his disciples. No wonder the Viennese analyst Jolan Neufeld was moved to say in his study *Dostojewski: Skizze zur einer Psychoanalyse* that the Russian novelist "pictured the unconscious psychic life of his protagonists as if he had discovered psychoanalysis long before Freud, for his own personal use as it were."

Dostoevsky told his friend Strakhov that the substance of *The Eternal Husband* was the same as that of *Notes from Underground.* ("My permanent substance," he called it.) This is to be understood primarily in a psychological, rather than philosophical, sense, because Dostoevsky's symbolic term "underground" stands not for any particular outlook or "deep" philosophy (existentialist or otherwise) but for psychic disorder and all the plotting and counterplotting in which the hurt and vengeful ego engages as it attempts to recover its self-esteem in a world that seems bent on depriving and humiliating it. Thus, when Velchaninov, the worldly Don Juan, berates the aggrieved husband Pavel Pavlovitch Trusotsky for his "underground vileness," it is himself as well that he incriminates, for it is in himself that Trusotsky's essential masochism encounters its sadistic counterpart. In another scene Velchaninov cries out to Pavel Pavlovitch: "We are both vicious, underground, loathsome people."

In psychological fiction there are few things as fine as the opening pages of this narrative, given over to the description of Velchaninov's nervous depression and the onset of memories and images that disorganizes his habitual equilibrium, estranging him from the world which he had always been disposed to take for granted and in which he had played his part not without some telling successes. It is a masterful account of neurotic decline toward the critical stage. But at this point there appears on the scene the incomparable figure of Trusotsky, the type of the eternal husband; and that is the *coup de force* which both arrests Velchaninov's descent into the depths of neurosis and provides the story with its dramatic complication.

But it is Trusotsky of course who is the undergroundling *par excellence*. He is unable to resolve the conflict that rends him between his vanity and craving for self-humiliation. He cannot make himself renounce his attachment to his deceased wife's lover even after he knows for certain that he had been cuckolded for many years and that his rival is the real father of the beloved daughter Liza. Even in this extreme situation, integrity and spontaneity of feeling fail him. It is never without ambivalence that he can hate the man who has wronged him. One might even go so far as to say that he hates him more out of a sense of duty and decorum, as it were, than because his nature unequivocally demands it. Hence he is driven to play the part of the buffoon, enjoying his jealousy at the same time that he is all the more humiliated by the sheer indecency of his enjoyment of it. Unresolved tormented feeling attaches him to Velchaninov, and only a few minutes after worshiping him, nursing him devotedly in his sudden illness, he sets upon him to cut his throat in the dark. At long last Velchaninov is convinced that "Pavel Pavlovitch certainly had meant to cut his throat, but that perhaps only a quarter of an hour before had not known that he would do it." And again: "Pavel Pavlovitch wanted to kill him, but didn't know he wanted to kill him. It's senseless, but that's the truth." The notion of the unconscious, as in the wake of Freud we now understand it, is altogether implicit in the psychic maneuvering that Dostoevsky portrays here. The dreams of Velchaninov — wonderfully psychodynamic dreams that enter so aptly into the pattern of action and serve as the eloquent medium of that knowledge that we at once possess and suppress — are a perfect instance of Dostoevsky's grasp of the processes of unconscious thinking.

Yet for all the pleasure of psychological revelation that this novella affords us, we cannot overlook the fact that it secures its imaginative effects and dramatic interest not through any descent into the clinical but through the formal mastery it displays — its unity of design and the just proportion of its parts. The psychogenic material it deploys with such marvelous assurance would in no way suffice to make it a work of art if it were not also for its perfection of structure. André Gide is surely right when he speaks of its uncommon narrative concentration, that responds, as he puts it, "to an ideal that we should nowadays call classical." It is somewhat strange to hear the word "classical" employed in connection with Dostoevsky, whom we usually think of as a spiritual profligate in whose fictional worlds tumult and excess reign. This impression of him is not false; it is merely one-sided. The term "classical" is not in the least far-fetched when applied to a work like *The Eternal Husband*, in which the content is thoroughly enveloped and shaped by the form. Dostoevsky demonstrates that in the matter of artistic method and economy he, too, could make the creative end issue strictly from the creative means.

1962

A NOTE ON BERNARD MALAMUD

THAT BERNARD MALAMUD is one of the very few writers of stature to emerge on our literary scene since the last war is now scarcely open to question. The author of four novels and two volumes of short stories, he has received several national prizes and his due measure of recognition from critics and reviewers. But he has also been frequently extolled for the wrong reasons, by critics who do not properly sort out or define with precision the imaginative qualities peculiar to him that make up his creative individuality; and sometimes he has been appraised as a special sort of genre-writer, dealing with the "laughter through tears," the habits of life, exotic to outsiders, of immigrant Jews, an ethnic group considered to stand in a marginal relation to American society at large.

Generally speaking, he has been assimilated all too readily to the crowd of American-Jewish writers who have lately made their way into print. The homogenization resulting from speaking of them as if they comprised some kind of literary faction or school is bad critical practice in that it is based on simplistic assumptions concerning the literary process as a whole as well as the nature of American

Jewry which, all appearances to the contrary, is very far from constituting a unitary group in its cultural manifestations. In point of fact, the American-Jewish writers do not in the least make up a literary faction or school. And in the case of Malamud, the ignorant and even malicious idea that such a school exists has served as a way of confusing him with other authors with whom (excepting his Jewish ancestry) he has virtually nothing in common.

The truth is that many writers are Jewish in descent without being in any appreciable way "Jewish" in feeling and sensibility; and I am noting this not in criticism of anyone in particular but simply by way of stating an obvious fact usually overlooked both by those who "celebrate" the arrival of American Jews on the literary scene and by those who deplore it. It is one thing to speak factually of a writer's Jewish extraction and it is something else again to speak of his "Jewishness," which is a very elusive quality and rather difficult to define. In this respect Norman Mailer may well serve as a conspicuous example. Mailer's consciousness of himself as a Jew is, I would say, quite unimportant to him as a writer, if not wholly negative. Among the protagonists of his fiction his favorite alter ego appears to be a character called Sergius O'Shaugnessy — a name not without significance. Other American-Jewish writers either back away from their Jewishness or adopt an attitude toward it which is empty of cultural value; it is only in their bent for comic turns that they call to mind some vestigial qualities of their ethnic background. In any case, what is mostly to be observed among these writers is ambivalence about Jewishness rather than pride or even simple acceptance. Malamud differs, however, from such literary types in that he fills his "Jewishness" with a positive content. I mean that "Jewishness," as he understands and above all feels it, is one of the principal sources of value in his work as it affects both his conception of experience in general and his conception of imaginative writing in particular. One can see this in the very few instances when his characters touch on literature in their extremely articulate but "broken" speech. Thus in the one-act play "Suppose a Wedding," the retired Yiddish actor Feuer tangles with a young man who can only speak of tragedy in terms of Aristotle's theory of catharsis. Feuer says:

Don't quote me your college books. A writer writes tragedy so
people don't forget they are human. He shows us the conditions that
exist. He organizes us for the meaning of our lives so it is clear to our
eyes. That's why he writes it, that's why we play it. My best roles were
tragic roles. I enjoyed them the most though I was also marvelous in
comedy. "Leid macht auch lachen."

The last sentence is a saying in Yiddish which means that suffering
also makes for laughter. If you are looking for Malamud's "poetics,"
it is in such speeches of his characters that you will locate it, not
in any explicit critical pronouncements. Another equally revealing
passage is to be found in his novel *The Assistant*, when Helen Bober,
the Jewish girl so pathetically aspiring in her dreams of a college
education, is on the verge of becoming involved with the unlettered
Italian clerk in her father's grocery. They meet in the branch library
of their neighborhood:

He asked her what she was reading.
"*The Idiot*. Do you know it?"
"No. What's it about?"
"It's a novel."
"I'd rather read the truth."
"It is the truth."

Malamud's conception of literature, as a mode of truth-saying, un-
dercuts all our old and new debates about the role of the aesthetic
motive in our lives. For in his context of profound commitments to
the creative word the very term "aesthetic," with the compartmental-
ization of the human faculties that it suggests, seems almost out of
place, if not frivolous; and it strongly reminds us of Kafka's moral
earnestness in his approach to the making of literature, of which he
conceived as a sacred expenditure of energy, an effort at communion
with his fellowmen, the reflected splendor of religious perception.

Malamud's "Jewishness" is also connected with a certain stylization of language we find in his fiction, a deliberate linguistic effort
at once trenchantly and humorously adapting the cool Wasp idiom
of English to the quicker heartbeats and greater openness to emotion of his Jewish characters; and it is particularly in the turns and
twists of their dialogue that this effort is most apparent and most
successful. These people are emotionally highly charged and des-

perate in their urgency to make themselves heard. Malamud insists on giving them their head, on letting them speak out of their genuine fervor — and to achieve this authenticity of speech he refuses to censor their bad, even laughable grammar, distorted syntax, and vivid yet comical locutions that sound like apt imitations of Yiddish. In this regard, any one of his narratives — such as "Take Pity," "The Mourners," "The Magic Barrel," "Idiots First," etc. — in which "Old World" Jewish types predominate can serve as a case in point.

Another "Jewish" trait in Malamud, as I read him, is his feeling for human suffering on the one hand and for a life of value, order, and dignity on the other. Thus he is one of the very few contemporary writers who seems to have escaped the clutch of historical circumstance that has turned nihilism into so powerful a temptation; nihilistic attitudes, whether of the hedonistic or absurdist variety, can never be squared with Malamud's essentially humanistic inspiration. The feeling for human suffering is of course far from being an exclusively "Jewish" quality. It figures even more prominently in Dostoevsky. The Russian novelist, however, understands suffering primarily as a means of purification and of eventual salvation, whereas in Malamud suffering is not idealized: suffering is not what you are looking for but what you are likely to get. Malamud is seldom concerned with the type of *allrightnik* Jews who lend themselves to satirical treatment (as in Philip Roth's *Goodbye, Columbus*); his chief concern is rather with the first-generation, poor hardworking immigrants, whose ethos is not that of prosperity but that of affliction and endurance. Hence he is at times inclined to speak of suffering as the mark of the Jew and as his very fate. Leo Finkle, who is among the major characters of that extraordinary story "The Magic Barrel," draws out of his very discomfiture the consolation "that he was a Jew and a Jew suffered." Frank Alpine in *The Assistant*, thinking of what it means to be a Jew, explains it to himself as follows: "That's what they live for . . . to suffer. And the one who has got the biggest pain in the gut and can hold onto it longest without running to the toilet is the best Jew. No wonder they got on his nerves." This is of course an outsider's point of view, and it remains for Morris Bober, the unlucky and impoverished owner of the grocery store, to correct his Italian clerk's assertion that Jews like to suffer:

"If you live, you suffer. Some people suffer more, but not because they want. But I think if a Jew don't suffer for the Law, he will suffer for nothing."

"What do you suffer for, Morris?" Frank said.

"I suffer for you," Morris said calmly.

Frank laid his knife down on the table. His mouth ached. "What do you mean?"

"I mean you suffer for me."

The clerk let it go at that.

Here Malamud transcends all sectarian understanding of suffering, seeing it as the fate of the whole of mankind, which can only be mitigated when all men assume responsibility for each other. The contrast between Jew and Gentile is thus resolved on the level of feeling and direct intuition, and what this resolution suggests is an affinity with the Dostoevskyean idea of universal brotherhood and mutual responsibility. Yet Dostoevsky's correlative idea that "we're all cruel, we're all monsters" (as Dmitri Karamazov phrases it) is quite alien to Malamud. Frank Alpine is the guilty one when he takes Helen Bober against her will just as she has begun learning to love him. After the violation she cried: "Dog — uncircumcised dog." What restitution can Alpine possibly make for abusing Helen's trust? After much brooding and many incidents Alpine enters a symbolic death and rebirth, and his decision is made without Helen's knowledge or prompting. "One day in April Frank went to the hospital and had himself circumcised. For a couple of days he dragged himself around with a pain between his legs. The pain enraged and inspired him. After Passover he became a Jew." So *The Assistant* ends, with the sentences I have quoted. Frank Alpine's act is not to be understood as a religious conversion. Within the context of the novel, what Frank's singular act stands for is the ultimate recognition by this former holdup man and thief of the humanity that he had so long suppressed within himself.

Along with the theme of suffering, one finds in Malamud the theme of the meaningful life, which is the antithesis of "the unlived life" against which his leading characters are always contending. The college teacher S. Levin, in *A New Life*, becomes involved in what threatens to become a sordid affair with Pauline, another man's wife. But when she probes him for what he thinks life offers at its best, his reply is: "Order, value, accomplishment, love." Levin, who is at times prone to consider himself "his own pathetic fallacy," struggles to discover an authentic self amidst the circumstances that surround him; nor is he likely either to overestimate or underestimate himself. "Why must Levin's unlived life put him always in peril? He had no wish to be Faust, or Gatsby; or St. Anthony of Somewhere who to conquer his torment nipped off his balls. Levin wanted to be himself, at peace in present time." And again: "He left to Casanova or Clark Gable the gourmandise, the blasts and quakes of passion." Levin comes to a state of the Far West looking for welcome and a chance of organizing his existence anew. He begins as S. Levin, a half-anonymous *schlemiel*, and in the last chapters he has turned into a *mensch* called Seymour Levin, who against all odds had become a husband to Pauline and the father of her children.

But the irony of the *schlemiel* turning *mensch* pervades the book, tempering the exaltation of the last pages. Levin's first lovemaking to Pauline takes place in a forest glade, and "he was throughout conscious of the marvel of it — in the open forest, nothing less, what triumph!" And when he first kisses her, "he was humbly grateful . . . They were standing under a tree and impulsively kissed . . . They kissed so hard his hat fell off." The displaced hat is an ironic counterpoint — the signature of reality inscribed in a romantic pastoral. An identical irony is to be encountered in many of Malamud's stories. In "The Last Mohican," Fidelman, "a self-conscious failure as a painter," gets off the train in Rome and soon discovers the remains of the Baths of Diocletian. "Imagine," he muttered. "Imagine all that history." He confronts history as Levin confronts nature in Marathon, Cascadia (Oregon?). Fidelman likes to wander in the old sections of Rome near the Tiber. "He had read that here, under his feet, were the ruins of Ancient Rome. It was an inspiring business, he, Arthur Fidelman, after all born a Bronx boy, walking around in all this history." But Fidelman, for all the thrills that history provides him, is a person lacking in genuineness — cautious, withdrawn, self-centered. It takes Susskind, the starving and demanding refugee, a nuisance to Fidelman, to supply him with the revelation he so badly needs. Susskind steals the briefcase containing the first chapter of Fidelman's scholarly work on Giotto — the only chapter he had managed to write. The last paragraphs of the story are wonderfully conceived and written: a model of economy in expression. After much importunity, Susskind returns the brief-case.

> Fidelman savagely opened it, searching frenziedly in each compart-ment, but the bag was empty. The refugee was already in flight.
> With a bellow the student started after him.
> "You bastard, you burned my chapter."
> "Have mercy," cried Susskind, "I did you a favor."
> "I'll do you one and cut your throat."
> "The words were there but the spirit was missing."
> In a towering rage Fidelman forced a burst of speed, but the refugee, light as the wind in his marvelous knickerbockers, his green coattails flying, rapidly gained ground.

It is only then that Fidelman, moved by all "he had lately learned, had a triumphant insight." Half sobbing, he shouts: "Susskind, come back . . . All is forgiven." So the spirit missing in his life and studies finally descends upon the hapless Fidelman.

Of the four novels that Malamud has written *The Fixer* has proven to be the most popular. But despite its impressive sales fig-ures, it seems to me to be the weakest of his longer narratives; and its success can be traced to fortuitous circumstances. Far too many chapters of the book are devoted to the account of the prolonged and unspeakable pain its protagonist, Yakov Bok, suffers while jailed on the false charge of the ritual murder of a Christian child. It so happens, however, that the long-spun evocation of sheer physical pain is poor novelistic policy. Bok is a victim pure and simple; he is deprived of the chance to exert his will and make significant moral choices by the very helplessness of his condition, and paradoxically enough, even by his complete innocence. A total victim, however, cannot attain the stature of a hero of a work of art, for, lacking even minimal freedom of choice, the only emotion he can arouse is com-passion; and Bok, save for the closing pages when he is transformed by a frenzied revolutionary imagination, remains inert as a charac-ter, a passive sufferer who stubbornly refuses to confess to the false charge leveled against him. Moreover, throughout the novel we stay within Bok's consciousness, perceiving all that occurs from his point of view alone. I think this procedure is mistaken. A superior narrative strategy would have required the picking of the Russian Bibikov as the novel's protagonist. This examining magistrate is torn by pangs of conscience as he becomes aware of Bok's innocence even as he is caught in the toils of the Czarist government's ruthless determination to convict the Jew. Bibikov is a humane person who is in a position to make a choice, to adopt one course or another. But we never see Bibikov from within, and Malamud kills him off much too early in the story. I suppose that insufficient familiarity with the Russian background frightened off Malamud, preventing him from adopting Bibikov as the center of consciousness or "point of view" in the technical sense of the term.

It appears to me that as a whole Malamud succeeds far more frequently in his short stories than in his novels; and of all his stories, surely the most masterful is "The Magic Barrel," perhaps the best story produced by an American writer in recent decades. It belongs among those rare works in which meaning and composition are one and the same. Who can ever forget the matchmaker Salzman, "a commercial Cupid," smelling "frankly of fish which he loved to eat," who looked as if he were about to expire but who somehow managed, by a trick of his facial muscles, "to display a broad smile"? The pictures of prospective brides that the matchmaker shows the rabbinical student Finkle, intent on matrimony, prove very discouraging — all these girls turn out to be either old maids or cripples. But Salzman contrives to leave one picture in Finkle's room by which his imagination is caught as in a trap. The description of the picture is full of mystery, yet admirably concrete; it is as good as, if not better than, the description of the picture of Nastasya Filippovna which makes so much for the vitality of the first part of *The Idiot*.

Caught, Finkle in turn must now pursue Salzman, who has suddenly become elusive. When tracked down, he swears that he had inadvertently left the fatal picture in Finkle's room. "She's not for you. She is a wild one, wild, without shame . . . Like an animal, like a dog. For her to be poor was a sin. This is why to me she is dead now . . . This is my baby, my Stella, she should burn in hell." But Finkle will not relent. It is Stella he must see, and Salzman arranges their meeting "on a certain street corner." The last sentences of this tale are like a painting by Chagall come to life.

He appeared, carrying a small bouquet of violets and rosebuds. Stella stood by the lamp, smoking. She wore white with red shoes, which fitted his expectations, although in a troubled moment he had imagined the dress red, and only the shoes white. She waited uneasily and shyly. From afar he saw that her eyes — clearly her father's — were filled with desperate innocence. He pictured, in her, his own redemption. Violins and lit candles revolved in the sky. Leo ran forward with flowers outthrust.

Around the corner, Salzman, leaning against a wall, chanted prayers for the dead.

Thus the rabbinical student who, as he confesses, had come to God not because he loved Him but precisely because he did not, attempts to find in the girl from whose picture "he had received, somehow, an impression of evil" the redemption his ambiguous nature demands.

It seems to me that "The Magic Barrel," a story rooted in a pathology that dares to seek its cure in a thrust toward life, sums up many of the remarkable gifts of insight and expressive power that Malamud brings to contemporary literature.

1967

ON F. R. LEAVIS AND D. H. LAWRENCE

THAT F. R. LEAVIS is a first-rate critical personality is certain, but that is by no means the same thing as saying that he is a first-rate literary critic. No doubt he has at times achieved that stature; at other times not at all. I am here primarily concerned with him as a critic, not with his reputation as a formidable teacher, nor with his educational theories, nor with his standing as the charismatic head of the sectarian *Scrutiny* group, consisting in the later years of that periodical mostly of epigones who have for some years now acquired positions of influence in the British schools. In the America of the late 1940s and early 1950s the "new critics" tried to annex him by gratuitously referring to him as one of their own, a comrade-in-arms. That was a mistaken assessment, if not something worse.

Actually, the peculiar combination of formalism and traditionalist ideology (*à la* Eliot), characteristic of the "new criticism," has always been foreign to Leavis. He has never committed himself to any kind of religiosity (covert or overt) and he has explicitly repudiated the formalist position. Typical of him is the following remark, repeated throughout his career in different critical contexts:

"Questions of technique — versification, convention, relation of diction to the spoken language, and so on — cannot be isolated from considerations of fundamental purpose, essential ethos, and quality of life." In his view, a "serious interest in literature" cannot be limited to the kind of local analysis, however intensive, associated with "practical criticism" — the effects of linguistic strategy, metaphor, symbol, etc. "A real literary interest is an interest in man, society and civilization, and its boundaries cannot be drawn." Clearly, this position is wholly at odds with the circumscriptions imposed upon the theory and function of literary criticism by the "new critics." Happily, their dominance of the American literary scene in the immediate postwar period is a thing of the past now and virtually forgotten; and my aim in recalling them in this discussion of Leavis is simply to set the record straight.

What I chiefly like about Leavis' work are its Johnsonian qualities: the robustness, the firmness, the downrightness. He is not one to beat around the bush, to play the diplomat, to cultivate ambiguity, or to shun controversy. A critic in the Arnoldian tradition, he aspires, in his own words, "to the highest critical standards and the observance of the most scrupulous critical discipline" — an admirable aspiration in the attainment of which, however, he has, to my mind, failed quite as often as he has succeeded. For he is plagued by all the defects of his virtues. What I have in mind is not his plain speaking, of course, but rather the *esprit de sérieux* animating many of his critical pronouncements. It expresses itself in a kind of provincial moralism (by no means to be equated with the "marked moral intensity" he so esteems in his literary preferences), a protestant narrowness of sensibility, basically puritan, resulting in what seems to me the thoroughly unjustified rejection of Flaubert, Joyce, and other important literary artists of the modern line, a tendency to elevate "English studies" to the status of a major force in the shaping of culture if not of society itself, and his endless and tiresome fulminations against Bloomsbury, the "London literary establishment," the system of "personal and institutional relations" that appears to him to dominate the British literary world and to obstruct the free play of the critical mind.

It is not my intention to defend the literary establishment, whether
of London or of New York, or to question Leavis' all-too-strenuous
distaste for such literary figures — of unequal stature, to be sure —
as Lytton Strachey, Clive Bell, Virginia Woolf, and Lord David
Cecil. The trouble is that his clamorous and prolonged campaign
against the establishment has all the marks of an obsession. It is
common knowledge that every major capital has one, and that it is
usually lacking in the seriousness and discrimination that Leavis
demands. It is quite possible to dissent from established opinion
without going on and on about it in a compulsive manner. After
all, Bloomsbury, which no longer exists, is at present merely a foot-
note in literary history. A class struggle in literature is one thing,
even if of doubtful value, as in the 1930s we saw in this country,
because the partisanship involved easily gets out of hand; but the
conversion of a petty social antagonism into a full-scale crusade
is something else again.

In truth, what Leavis is waging can in no sense be described as a
Kulturkampf, which invariably deals with basic values, the clash of
opposing world-views, not merely literary issues and personalities.
Leavis' obsession cannot be regarded otherwise than as a symptom.
Of what? I am afraid there is no other way to characterize it than
as a symptom of class *ressentiment*, and that very condition also sufficiently explains his uncritical identification with his supreme paragon among modern writers, D. H. Lawrence, upon whom he heaps
panegyrics in his regrettably influential book, *D. H. Lawrence: Novelist* (1955). But more about that book (and even earlier critical
studies) later. First one wants to take a close look at his new collection of essays and reviews.

In his new book, *Anna Karenina and Other Essays,* the lead essay
is excellent. Its interest lies not so much in any new insights it
offers — in that respect John Bayley's recent *Tolstoy and the Novel*
is certainly superior — but rather in the angle from which Leavis
approaches the novel. Given his age, critical background, and past
allegiances, he was bound to confront openly certain animadversions
on *Anna Karenina* expressed by Arnold, James, and, surprisingly
enough, D. H. Lawrence. Admiring as he is of all three of these
figures, especially Lawrence, he could not conceivably have arrived
at his major conclusion, that *Anna Karenina* is not only one of the

great European novels but "surely *the* European novel," without first challenging their negative views. A younger commentator on Tolstoy might well have ignored these views as being manifestly irrelevant. Leavis, however, immersed as he is in "English studies," is constrained to deal with them.

Arnold, though immensely struck by Tolstoy's novel, nevertheless characterized it as "not a work of art but a piece of life." Leavis demonstrates what hardly needs demonstrating today, that everything in the novel is fully rendered, fully "enacted," and that only of *a work of art* of such validity and force can one authoritatively say: "This is life." The antithesis of these formulas — "a piece of life" and "this is life" — is very apt, very neat. As for Henry James, his view was substantially the same as Arnold's. And given his peculiarly subjective conception of the art of the novel, what could he do, when faced with the Russian novel's centrality of experience and sheer comprehensiveness, but stress its alleged deficiency in "composition" and utter the phrase "fluid pudding"? One therefore welcomes Leavis' comment on James's "narrowly provident economy" in novel-writing, for it is about time that a critic of Leavis' stature should come right out with this sort of objection, thus implicitly calling into question the portentous, self-justifying, and self-loving mystifications that play no small part in his famous Prefaces. Leavis rightly insists that the creativity possessed by Tolstoy is of the highest kind — "a higher kind than James's." One might add that the Jamesian type of creativity, particularly as displayed in his later phase, is so idiosyncratic as to preclude his becoming a model for others. Moreover, it provides scarcely sufficient grounds for generalizing about the medium of narrative prose.

But in the case of Lawrence — whose opinion of *Anna Karenina* is thoughtless, to say the least — Leavis has a different problem on his hands. For, long before writing his book on him, he committed himself to the estimate of Lawrence as "the finest literary critic of our time — a great literary critic if ever there was one." So Leavis treats Lawrence's opinion of Tolstoy as a mere momentary aberration. But such an approach is evasive; it simply won't do. Just listen to Lawrence:

> Why, when you look at it, all the tragedy comes from Vronsky's and Anna's fear of society . . . They couldn't live in the pride of their sin-

cere passion, and spit in Mother Grundy's eye. And that, that cowardice, was the real "sin." The novel makes it obvious, and knocks all old
Leo's teeth out.

The novel makes obvious nothing of the sort. The impact of its
cumulative episodes convinces us that it was impossible for Anna
and Vronsky to live for long "in the pride of their sincere passion."
Leavis goes into great detail to show how adverse conditions (of
personality and environment) defeated them; thus the charge of
cowardice amounts to no less than "a refusal to take what, with all
the force of specificity and subtle truth to life, the novel actually
gives." The implied comparison with Frieda and himself (which
Lawrence alludes to in a letter) is fatuous. Being the kind of man
he was, Vronsky could not live just by devoting himself to being
Anna's lover — his attempts to become an artist and later a landed
magistrate are pathetic and come to nothing — while Lawrence had
his work cut out for him even before he met Frieda: he could wander from country to country and still do his writing with unpar-
alleled ease. As for Frieda, though the loss of her children made her
suffer, she was, as Leavis observes, "an amoral German aristocrat"
who finally attained "a floating indolence of well-being," remaining
"placidly undomesticated." Anna, however, could not be reconciled
to the loss of her son. And from all the evidence concerning Frieda
that we have, adds Leavis, "we can see that what Tolstoy makes
present to us in Anna is certainly something finer."

Still, in this very essay Leavis again praises Lawrence as a "marvelously perceptive critic." Is such high praise deserved? I think
not. Lawrence made some very percipient remarks about the relation of the truth of "art-speech" to the novel as a genre. But such
remarks are merely fine generalities; when it comes to specifics he
is nearly always wrong-headed, absurdly doctrinaire. Thus in a
letter he refers to Chekhov as "a second-rate writer and a willy wet-
leg." Dostoevsky enrages him: he is "foul," presumably for "mixing
sadism and God." About the characters in *The Possessed* he says:
"They bore me, these squirming sorts of people; they teem like in-
sects." So much for Verhovensky *père*, Stavrogin, Kirillov, Shatov,
Captain Lebyadkin, and his sister! And again about Dostoevsky:

He is . . . like the rat, slithering along in hate, in the shadows . . .
His will is fixed and gripped like a trap. He is not nice.

To be sure. Dostoevsky is far from "nice," but if niceness is to be
our criterion, then Lawrence's fiction, in which emotions of cruelty,
anger, and hatred so frequently dominate, is positively malignant.
Reviewing Thomas Mann's *Death in Venice*, Lawrence finds its
author "somewhat banal," suffering from the same complaint as
Flaubert, whose *Madame Bovary* seems to him "dead." Nor does he
in the least appreciate either Proust or Joyce.

The truth is that as a critic Lawrence is wholly lacking in disin-
terestedness and even a minimum of objectivity. Violently preju-
diced, he is a contemner of many works of great formal beauty, as
well as psychological and dialectical power, simply because their
contents fail to correspond to his own new Gospel of life, or "meta-
physic," as he sometimes called it. Even his *Studies in Classic
American Literature* is not the masterpiece it is reputed to be. It
contains one basic insight which has influenced some American
critics, and I too have been affected by it. He detects in "moral
duplicity" the "fatal flaw" of nineteenth-century American writers,
excepting Whitman, and in this insight he appears to me to be right.
Hawthorne, for instance, gives "tight mental allegiance to a morality
which the passional self repudiates." Yet in his essay "Hawthorne
and The Scarlet Letter," having made his point about that "blue-
eyed *Wunderkind* of a Nathaniel" he soon wanders off into sheer
rant about matters irrelevant to the text. Page after page of the
essay is given up to a furious denunciation of Hester Prynne as "a
demon, a devil when she was so meekly going around as a sick-nurse
. . . the great nemesis of woman." What Lawrence is doing is simply
exploiting his ostensible subject in order to indulge himself in a fit
of characteristic misogyny, damning a certain type of modern woman
whom he loathed. Whether such a type is more than a figment of
Lawrence's imagination is doubtful, but that she is not the Hester
of Hawthorne's novel, in either a latent or a manifest sense, is
certain.

The essay about Cooper opens well, only to turn into a romance.
Nor does Lawrence even begin to understand Poe, to see through his
neurotic rationality (his famous bent for ratiocination) and recog-

nize it for what it really is — a shield against the murderous fantasies that threaten to unhinge his mind. All that he notes in Poe is "the pride of human conceit in knowledge," with Ligeia, Berenice, and the rest as victims of his "obscene" will to know. Here Lawrence is again riding his favorite hobbyhorse, the execration of knowledge or "mental consciousness," his *bête noire* of which he cannot rid himself either in his discursive prose or in his fiction. Moreover, the Poe essay is entirely lacking in specific literary or critical interest, being a piece of amateur psychologism pure and simple, and offensively preachy at that. Yet even as psychology it is useless. One has only to compare it to Marie Bonaparte's psychoanalytic study of Poe — not to be classified as literary criticism either — to realize how wide of the mark it is.

But though the Lawrence question still haunts Leavis' new volume, there are essays in it deserving commendation, such as the two very satisfactory pieces on Conrad, the fine analysis of "Johnson as Critic," and the truly enlightening review of *The Letters of Ezra Pound,* in which he sums up with admirable economy and persuasiveness all that he previously said about him. Though paying generous tribute to Pound's beneficent influence on Yeats and Eliot (among others) at "crucial moments" of their creative careers, he nonetheless contends that his limitations are overwhelming. *Mauberley* is his only valid claim to significance as a poet, while "the spectacle of his degeneration is a terrible one." It is apparent in the "barren and monotonous" *Cantos,* as in his hapless politics, in which there is "something repellently brutal, a certain naive, tough and truculent insensitiveness turning into a positive vice."

In this fully supported judgment Leavis is at his best, and it should suffice to shatter the Pound cult, were it not for the fact that the cultists and their leading hierophant, Hugh Kenner, in their highly suspect, devious ideological bias and vain exegetical ardor had not already proven themselves immune to critical argument. I wonder how they will now react to the startling revelation by Daniel Cory (*Encounter,* May 1968), a reliable witness and a friend of Pound's of long standing, that the poet had but recently admitted to him in Italy that he had in fact "botched" the *Cantos.* ("I knew too little about so many things . . . I picked out this and that thing that interested me, and then jumbled them into a bag. But that's not the way to make a work of art.") There is much pathos in this belated confession, bringing a melancholy end to a long and remarkable career.

Pound's admission also makes fools of the cultists who have for a long time dominated the criticism of Pound. Even the late R. P. Blackmur, in an essay of the 1950s, in effect retracted his shrewd earlier reservations about Pound. And T. S. Eliot certainly lent a hand in promoting the cult in a variety of cordial and (perhaps) propitiatory remarks about Pound, finally announcing that his interest is not in what the latter had to say but only in the way he said it. Leavis comes down hard on this equivocal statement, in which form is so drastically isolated from substance as to convert it into a sheer abstraction.

In the last essay of this new collection, "The Orthodoxy of Enlightenment," we are again embroiled in the Lawrence question. Reviewing the Penguin documentary record of the trial of *Lady Chatterley's Lover,* he strains to show, though without any recognition of the irony involved, that his backing of Lawrence had been misconceived and misused in the trial by persons of a type that would have been inevitably hostile to Lawrence during his lifetime and who are now, to put it bluntly, kowtowing to him because of the new "enlightenment" of sex. It should be observed that even in his extravagant book about Lawrence (1955), Leavis excised *Lady Chatterley,* as well as *The Plumed Serpent,* from the canon. Now he speaks of it as "a bad novel," arguing that his distaste for it is something "that the normal Lawrence would have shared and justified," if the "abnormal state" he was in when writing the novel had not "violated his wholeness." What a way of putting it! This new evocation of a Lawrence split into normality and abnormality flagrantly contradicts the insistence in *D. H. Lawrence: Novelist* that there is "no profound emotional disturbance in Lawrence, no obdurate major disharmony; intelligence in him can be, as it is, the servant of the whole integrated psyche."

Plainly, there is something deeply wrong here, a tortuous, willed self-deception, on account of which this critic's reputation for integrity and independence of judgment incurs a damaging loss. No doubt there are stages to be noted in Lawrence's development as a thinker and artist, but the novels that Leavis disowns — including

Sons and Lovers which he manages to dismiss, without seeming to do so, as little more than a case history — embody the essential Lawrence just as much as those Leavis acclaims as supreme master-pieces. (To my mind, *Sons and Lovers* remains Lawrence's best novel, by far the most convincing, fully enveloping its Oedipal theme, which cannot be reduced to mere clinical material, and free of the patently compensatory overassertiveness and arbitrariness, that in no small degree mar his later work.)

Leavis' emphasis on "health" and "sanity" and his mandatory dis-tinction between what "makes for life" and what does not are singu-larly inappropriate to "placing" Lawrence. Terms like "health," "sanity," and even "life" are at once too vague and too inclusive, too invertebrate as it were, for use in any precise analysis, and, above all, too moralistic to make much sense in literary discourse. As cri-teria they are in constant peril of toppling over — though Leavis would hardly countenance such a fall — into the popular cure all of "the power of positive thinking." Evidently there is no getting away from the Lawrence question in examining Leavis' contribution to contemporary criticism.

The truth is that by radically separating his art from his doctrine without fully acknowledging what he is up to, Leavis has been able to create a Lawrence who never really existed. Hence the stress on the word *novelist* in his book on him. But this procedure is mislead-ing in Lawrence's case. For as E. M. Forster has observed, he was "both preacher and poet . . . though without the preaching the poetry could not exist. With some writers one can disentangle the two, with him they were inseparable." It is this very "inseparability," which cannot be said to affect in the same drastic manner Dostoev-sky and other novelists of intense ideological animus, which calls into question Lawrence's status as an artist. Furthermore, as Forster adds, as he grew older he became "more and more mannered and didactic." None of that is recognized by Leavis. Nor does the con-cept of neo-primitivism, of which Lawrence is the most extreme ex-ponent in modern literature, ever engage Leavis' attention, though that concept is far more cogently deployed in appraising Lawrence than the meager literary notions Leavis brings to bear in his apothe-osis of him as before all else an artist, "a creative writer of the greatest kind," as well as "an incomparable critic," and "one of the greatest masters of comedy." His determination to endow his *bel idéal* with every possible virtue is appalling.

I have already dealt to some extent with Lawrence's criticism. To attribute to him a mastery of the comic mode is equally spurious, for a kind of archness, even cuteness, was the only result of his occasional attempts to be amusing. Historically, Lawrence represents, as I see it, "the return of the repressed" (to use Freudian terminology) to English literary expression after the long Victorian epoch of inhibition and repression of the sensual life. Such a return, however, exalting the pleasure principle above the reality principle, cannot but take, under inauspicious social and historical conditions, a form at once anarchic and compulsive. Nor is this return, as embodied in Lawrence, in any sense complete, involving as it does frequent relapses and more than incidental backsliding. Thus even while protesting the repression of sexuality by civilization, he at the same time turns away from any real orgiastic freedom and actually *disincarnates* sexuality by preaching the continuance of traditional male domination, by envisaging marriage as "ultimate" and "final" (a lapse into the very idealism he otherwise repudiated), and by denying (emphatically in *The Plumed Serpent*) the orgasm to women.

Such obscurantist predications are not what I would call creative contradictions but rather a set of corrosive inconsistencies that add to his disabilities precisely in his role as novelist. He is not what Leavis says he is: he is not an up-to-date version of George Eliot, nor is he a realist, except superficially and only intermittently. Leavis maintains that modern civilization found in Lawrence "a student and analyst of incomparable range and insight." But he was not so much a student or analyst of civilization as its outright and rigorous opponent. He rejected culture, intellect, consciousness, knowledge — the values that Leavis is above all attached to. Lawrence wrote:

> My great religion is a belief in the blood, the flesh. We can go wrong in our minds. But what our blood feels . . . is always true. The intellect is only a bit and a bridle. What do I care about knowledge? All I want is to answer to my blood, direct, without the fribbling intervention of mind, or moral, or what not.

This is no abstraction but a solemn and programmatic avowal, the essential "message" informing most of his work, in the interest of which he was all too prone to disregard the modifications, reservations, and strategic reversals imposed by the discipline of novelistic art. Can Leavis honestly claim that he shares this "message" or faith? One can imagine a critic — though not much of one — who might find this faith acceptable, but my point is that Leavis' assertion of his own beliefs positively *disallows* his solidarity with Lawrence. The visionary neo-primitivism, the regression to an animistic and archaic mode of apprehending the world, which dissolves the distinction between the human and the inhuman and between nature and culture, are wholly alien to Leavis. The latter frequently affirms Lawrence's "intelligence"; and I for one have no doubt that he was very intelligent; at the same time I have no doubt that after *Sons and Lovers,* ever alert to the threatening inroads of the so abominated "mental consciousness," he more often than not refused to use his intelligence.

Psychic disorder is just as noticeable in Lawrence as it is in literary artists like Baudelaire or Dostoevsky or Kafka. But from a literary standpoint the significant difference is that, in Baudelaire, Dostoevsky, or Kafka, art is for the most part the consequence, even if neurosis is the occasion. This is only contingently and even at times fortuitously true in Lawrence. The conscientious critic, however, cannot adopt the psychiatrist's crude though useful distinctions between the normal and the abnormal without undercutting the fullness and complexity of his response to the manifold if contradictory "truths of art-speech." The many quarrels Leavis picks with T. S. Eliot seem to be chiefly motivated by the latter's disparagement of Lawrence. One of these concerns Eliot's "over-insistence" on Lawrence's "sexual morbidity," which Leavis finds very odd in a writer whose own attitudes "to sex have been, in prose and poetry, almost uniformly negative — attitudes of distaste, disgust, and rejection." This is as good an example as any of Leavis' tendency to circumscribe the literary medium by setting up preconceived and obligatory values for it.

For my part, I cannot see why an attitude of sexual disgust is not as valid a theme for poetic expression as an attitude of affirmation, of "health and sanity." The value of literary art cannot be judged

by the bias of its ideology or world-view, but rather by its rendering of felt experience, the intensity of its existential commitment,
and above all the incontrovertible force of its concrete enactment.
Eliot's awareness of this is shown by the unremitting attention he
gave to the problem of "belief" in poetry. There is something irksome
in Leavis' polemic against Eliot, to whom his best books, *New Bearings in English Poetry* and *Revaluations* are heavily indebted. Aside
from the discord relating to Lawrence, Eliot is accused of endorsing
Wyndham Lewis, not to mention Djuna Barnes' *Nightwood* and
Miller's *Tropic of Cancer*, of being too close to Bloomsbury, of
printing Auden and Spender in *The Criterion*, etc., etc. But all this
is trivial. What is really vulnerable in Eliot — his collapse into
Anglo-Catholicism in the late twenties and his embrace of the dogma
of original sin — Leavis leaves strictly alone. In other words, he
fails to perceive that given Eliot's militant new adherence to institutional Christianity, it was only logical for him to attack Lawrence
as a dangerous "heretic" in *After Strange Gods,* which is a primer
of heresy. There existed in Eliot an empirical critic of genius, usually
prevailing in his prose, as well as a fretful and conscience-ridden
Christian perceptor. The former produced his important literary
essays; the latter produced such nebulous tracts as *Notes toward the
Definition of Culture* and *The Idea of a Christian Society.* His
derogation of Lawrence as a writer "incapable of what is ordinarily
called thinking" is far from unjust, if we stress, that is, the word
"ordinarily." But Eliot in his moods of Christian fervor strikes me
as equally incapable of that kind of thinking, and so does Leavis,
who so plumes himself on his critical rigor, when he flaunts his identification with Lawrence.

I think that Lawrence was a unique and original writer, perhaps
the most "natural" writer in English literature by virtue of his innate
gift of fluidity and spontaneous free flow of expression. But this
is by no means the same thing as saying that he was a great novelist. In that respect his disabilities are irreducible. His most persistent fault is the unabashed eagerness with which he nearly always
subordinates art to prophecy and his ruthless manipulation of scene,
act, and character to justify his new Gospel of life at all costs.

While describing himself as "a fearfully religious man," he was unable, all the same, to believe in any religious tenet except in a purely symbolical manner; and his nostalgia for remote pre-Christian modes of relatedness to the world expresses nothing more than a desire to give his intuition free play, to escape the limiting and probing articulations of historical consciousness. As Philip Rieff has aptly observed, what he wanted to preserve was "the dynamic of religion" as form without any specific content. Thus he was a "literary Methodist," proposing attitudes of prayer "without mentioning anyone to whom to pray." And in the political sphere, into which he sometimes ventured, he was a fantast pure and simple. He understood neither socialism nor liberal democracy, invariably confusing political theory with individual psychology. However, the charges of proto-fascism, of having developed, as Bertrand Russell put it, "the whole philosophy of fascism before the politicians thought of it," seem to me almost grotesquely unfair. His preaching of "blood-consciousness" has nothing whatever to do with racial or national purity of blood, or the assertion of superiority of one race over another. (The notion of "blood-consciousness," if at all meaningful, can only be taken as the equivalent, and a very muddled one at that, of Freud's Unconscious or Id.) Moreover, Lawrence's fundamental rejection of industrialism places him in diametrical opposition to the fascists, who, glorifying the martial virtues, are the least ready to scrap the industrial machine.

The paradox is that, for all his denunciations of "the modern cult of personality," and his attack on the ego as "a vile entity," our interest in him as an artist is primarily called forth precisely by his personality. All the people who knew him, whether friend or enemy, invariably recalled "the strange and marvelous radiance" emanating from him, the "spritelike, electric, elemental" quality. That is what surely comes through in his writing, particularly in the passionate tenderness of his evocations of nature — "birds, beasts, and flowers." But the other side of his personality — the acrimony, the fits of jeering and hectoring — also comes through. His general ideas about the novel are unimpeachable, and very fine indeed. Let me cite some of my favorite dicta:

> Never trust the artist. Trust the tale. The proper function of a critic is to save the tale from the artist who created it.

302/Literature and the Sixth Sense

If you try to nail anything down in the novel, either it kills the novel, or the novel gets up and walks away with the nail.

The novel is the highest example of subtle inter-relatedness that man has discovered. Everything is true in its own time, place, circumstance, and untrue outside of its own place, time, circumstance . . . Morality in the novel is the trembling instability of the balance. When the novelist puts his thumb in the scale, to pull down the balance to his own predilection, that is immorality.

Unfortunately, his practice belies his theory. In the very novels and tales Leavis regards as masterpieces he seldom hesitates to put his thumb in the scales, "to pull down the balance to his own predilection." This is exactly what Dostoevsky never did, even in *The Possessed*, where a subtle balance is maintained in spite of its national and religious prepossessions. For he was able to identify not only with such children of light as Sonia Marmeladov and Prince Myshkin but also with the characters ostensibly set up for ideological rebuttal — Raskolnikov, Stavrogin, the elder Vorhovensky, Ivan Karamazov — all children of darkness whom he nonetheless absorbed creatively without depriving them of their essential humanity. And the secret of that is complicity, that is to say, the indispensable process of identification with the creatures of one's own imagination without regard to positiveness or negativeness of ultimate judgment. In this sense, Flaubert identified with Charles Bovary and M. Homais no less than with Emma. Not so Lawrence, who identified the people who speak for him, like Ursula in *The Rainbow* and Birkin in *Women in Love*, with himself, thus turning them into mere mouthpieces; while he treated his adversary characters, like Skrebensky and Gerald Crich, with punitive harshness, and he proceeded in the same manner against Clifford in *Lady Chatterley* and against Rico in *St. Mawr* — a novella rated very highly by Leavis but shown up, by both Eliseo Vivas and Graham Hough in their respective books on Lawrence, as the shabby performance it actually is. Even *The Fox*, a novella beautifully articulated and rendered in convincing detail, is spoiled in the last few pages when the young protagonist, having won the girl March after the willed death of her friend Jill, suddenly steps out of his role in order to assume as his own some of Lawrence's dogmatic notions. It is gratuitous as well as out of character for him to demand of March that she submerge herself in him. "He wanted to make her submit, yield, blindly pass away out of all her strenuous consciousness." This is no longer the simple farmer-boy we have been reading about but Lawrence conducting his continuous struggle with Frieda for dominance.*

What we are up against in Lawrence's fiction is a kind of "credibility gap" of his own making, the result of the excessive and willful intrusion of a personality inebriated with doctrinal salvationism.

In *The Rainbow*, as Graham Hough notes, Ursula loves Skrebensky physically while finding him inadequate spiritually, and that is "intelligible enough, but that she found him inadequate in both respects makes their love wholly unintelligible, merely makes one wonder what the basis of their affair can ever have been." This is even more true, I think, of the Gudrun-Gerald relationship in *Women in Love*, so bafflingly implausible in connecting motive and action. For much of the novel, despite occasional outbursts of hostility to Gerald, Gudrun is presented as standing apart and not as a mere mouthpiece for the author, as Birkin is. But in the last chapters, when she is with her lover in the Tyrolese Alps, she is suddenly bursting with Lawrentian ideas that make her want to destroy Gerald. What is wrong? Gerald is immersed in the "ethics of productivity," he is an industrial magnate concerned solely with efficiency and deriving his values from the established social order. Then, through some kind of typical Lawrentian legerdemain, she links these external traits, external, I mean, to his sexual being, with sexual defectiveness. Hence her fury and determination to do him in. It is as if a Marxist novelist were to deduce sexual characteristics of any given bourgeois protagonist from the propositions of *Das Kapital*. So Lawrence simplifies in the most ludicrous fashion the connection between quite different aspects of life. The trouble is,

* See his letter to Katherine Mansfield (December 1918): "In a way, Frieda is the devouring mother. It is awfully hard, once the sex relation has gone this way, to recover. If we don't recover, we die. But Frieda says I am ante-diluvian in my positive attitude. I do think a woman must yield some sort of precedence to a man, and he must take this precedence. I do think men must go ahead absolutely in front of their women, without turning around for permission or approval from their women. Consequently the women must follow as it were unquestioningly. I can't help it, I believe this. Frieda doesn't. Hence our fight."

as Hough observes, that Lawrence came to assume that "sexual compatibility and compatibility of mind and spirit are indissolubly linked." But existence is marked by startling incongruities, and human love is only very rarely so rounded and complete. Individuality is no more cut of the whole cloth than historical reality.

And for all of Lawrence's desire to adjust consciousness "to the basic physical realities" and his warm approval of "sex-stimulus" in art, he was quite unable to achieve in his favored female characters the sensual reality, the sense of desirability and carnal attraction that we find so affecting in Emma Bovary, Anna Karenina, or even in Kate Croy and Charlotte Stant — heroines of Henry James who is so frequently dismissed as a eunuch. Lawrence repeatedly tells us that Ursula and Gudrun are very alluring but he cannot make us feel it. Sometimes I think that Lawrence was much too overwrought, too morbidly sensitive to physical experience to cope with the sexual theme. William H. Gass was surely right, in a recent essay, in characterizing Lawrence's attempts to describe directly sexual feelings and sensations as "moments of disaster":

> . . . When Lawrence wishes to render these [sexual] feelings, he turns to an abstract, incantational shorthand, often full of biblical overtones and antique simplicities, phrases which are used like formulas, reiterated until they become meaningless: hearts grow bitter and black and cold, souls melt or swoon, bodies freeze or burn, people are rapt or blind, they utter strange blind cries, their feelings ebb and flow . . . they "go mad with voluptuous delight," they overmaster or submit, bowels move poignantly . . . and their eyes sing, laugh, dance, stab, harden, burn, flash, seize, subside, cool, dim and die. One lust could do for another, angers are peas, nothing is clearly envisaged, nothing is precise, and we pass through them soon in a daze.*

Lawrence is in essence very far removed from the "life-enhancing elements" that Leavis likes to celebrate in his favorite writers. The "obliteration of personality" that Mellors, for instance, demands from Connie, the radical ambition, that is, to "de-create" the self in its social aspects, is essentially hostile to the quite different form that Leavis' search for "life" has taken. The obsession with Lawrence is the incubus that weighs his criticism down, which, despite

* *New York Review,* August 1, 1968.

its protestant moralism, is nonetheless among the more heroic efforts in English of this century. He was at his best in his earlier work, but even in *The Common Pursuit* (1952), as in his latest volume, you find many excellent things. And in comparison with the sorry state of criticism today — when the older critics (Wilson, Tate, Trilling) are silent about contemporary writing, and the field has been preempted by younger men, swinging reviewers rather than critics in any proper sense of the term, who, in the name of a trivial-ized aestheticism and sophistication, welcome every whim of fad and fashion as a creative "breakthrough" and a "new" conquest of imaginative experience — Leavis looms large as a force and as a sur-passing example. He may be too moralistic and exclusive in his approach, but the currently modish idea that morality has nothing to do with literature is a sheer perversion, an accommodation to the indulgence of degeneracy that marks the arts in our age — an indulgence that on no account will deny artistic status even to ob-vious pornography.° Of course, there are exceptions among the younger critics; their influence, however, hardly counts against that of the promoters of a phony avant-gardism who draw no distinction between integral talent and the crude products of the celebrity-machine.

Ours is a consumers' society, in which culture has been trans-formed into another provider of goodies, to be processed, consumed, digested, and eliminated to make room for more. In a situation of

° The literary cheerleaders of the new porno-aesthetics are much inclined to embellish their lineage by including Lawrence among their precursors. To claim descent from De Sade is one thing, but to try appropriating Lawrence is something else again and is nothing less than falsification. For despite the spill of four-letter words in *Lady Chatterley*, Lawrence despised pornography and wanted it banned. Thus he wrote: "Then what is pornography? Not sex appeal or sex stimulus in art. But even I would censor genuine pornography, rigorously. It would not be very difficult . . . you recognize it by the insult it offers, invariably, to sex, and to the human spirit . . . The insult to the human body, the insult to a vital human relationship! Ugly and cheap they make the human nudity, ugly and degraded they make the sexual act, trivial and cheap and nasty."
And in a letter of 1929 about *Lady Chatterley*, he remarked: "You mustn't think I advocate perpetual sex. Far from it. Nothing nauseates me more than promiscuous sex in and out of season. But I want, with *Lady Chatterley*, to make an adjustment in consciousness to the basic physical realities." Surely this attitude has nothing in common with the kind of freaky excitement about sex fomented by our contemporary porno-aesthetes.

this kind, the appearance of another Leavis, or Eliot, or critics of like caliber, is no longer to be expected. No wonder that the more intelligent young people are turning away from literature to politics, where sensitivity of conscience and moral feeling can still find expression, even if only within a minority movement, and where cynical calculation masquerading as worldly sophistication can still be seen through for what it actually is.

1968

PART II
SKETCHES IN CRITICISM

A SEASON IN HEAVEN

IT IS ONLY NATURAL that T. S. Eliot, who has been sufficiently publicized as the fugleman of literary reaction, should have written *Murder in the Cathedral,* a verse drama asserting his belief in death and man's utter wretchedness. Eliot has long held the view that this is what any "really serious belief in life" must come to. Where the surprise came in — most unpleasantly for the Left critics — was the fact that Eliot spoke his message of darkness in the unmistakable accents of a major poem. The critics had decided that Eliot's godliness had done for him, and here he was flying in the face of their stigmas.

To say that great art has a way of making even the death rattle sound like the rattle of tambourines is all too easy, and withal quite useless. Caught short by the contradiction between their habitual simplicities and Eliot's performance, several of the Left critics declared the play to be fascist, and hence, by implication, beyond the pale of analysis and interpretation. By itself such procedure is ludicrous enough, but here it is doubly so. The conflict the play portrays is between Church and State, the spiritual and temporal orders, the spirit and the flesh; and this conflict is so pointed as to pillory all profane aspiration and power. If classic Christianity be fascism, then Christ becomes the prototype of Hitler and every priest a storm trooper. By the same token, in stressing another aspect of Christian doctrine, one can make out a case for Christ as the prototype of Marx. And, indeed, a horde of humanitarian gents are quite adept at this game.

It is true, of course, that of late Eliot has been steering close to fascism in his general attitude to the problems of our time. But that by no means signifies that his poetry, existing and potential, is automatically suffused with the fascist spirit. Every work of art no matter how sure we are of its origin, must be examined anew. There is always the possibility of creative contradictions, on which the dialectic feeds. The danger lies in the excess of confidence with which we tend to identify the *apparent* ideas of a work with the work as written, its intention with its actual meaning, and finally its individual quality with the quality of its creator's complete works.

In criticism, as in science, exactness of observation and statement is indispensable. Without it, even if our general principles are right, we somehow manage to be specifically wrong. Thus it is one thing to say that the religious denial of the world is purely theoretical, and that in the main religion accommodates itself to fascism as it has accommodated itself to capitalism. But to claim that Eliot's play is fascist is something else again. All we can say is that though its internal drive is really against all politics, in a sense its social use is nevertheless political. In essence the spiritual slavery promulgated by the Church is but the ideological reflex of real social slavery, in the flesh. But historic facts of this order cannot excuse the frivolity of some Marxist critics, who make a practice of skipping intrinsic stages and distinctions in order the more easily to blur the difference between the specific content of a work of art and its possible objective effects, which more often than not are rather vague and remote. Moreover, criticism that discards such basic distinctions must end in equating literature with life. And the failure to distinguish between literature and life is almost as bad as the failure to see their close and necessary relationship.

To my mind, in *Murder in the Cathedral* Eliot has written his best poetry since *The Waste Land*. Its magnificent lucidity, so much in contrast to the symbolic mazes of his previous devotional verse, mirrors itself in a trembling and dolorous music. The diction is lyrical, yet dry and firm, its slight biblical cast and rare ecclesiastical phrase tempered by the neutral words of current speech. The obligations of a definite historical theme as well as the clear pattern imposed by the dramatic medium seem to have prevented the poet from clawing his way through caverns of history and mythology, as is his wont. If *The Waste Land* was written in "water," this new poetry is cut into stone.

The structure, too, is simple. Thomas Becket returns to Canterbury after a long exile aboard. The first conflict represented is self-conflict, with Becket's soul as the arena, when he casts out the devils within himself — the four tempters, arguing earthly pleasure, ambition, treason, and pride. After the *entr'acte* of the Christmas morning sermon, in which Becket heeds the summons of martyrdom and resigns himself to die, the main conflict comes to a head. The four knights appear — messengers of the king, figures out of earth, cruel and lustful — who kill Becket as they blaspheme. At once a metaphorical curtain is dropped on the historic scene as the knights step out of their parts and address the audience in the corrupt and ingratiating speech of modern politics. This is the continuation of blasphemy, ironically transposed into the typical clichés of British respectability and parliamentary eyewash. After having heard the lofty incantation:

Destiny waits in the hand of God, shaping the still unshapen:
I have seen these things in a shaft of sunlight,

etc. or the lyric beat of a line like:

The New Year waits, breathes, waits, whispers in darkness,

we hear the honorific vocabulary of public meetings in sentences like: "In the answer to these questions lies the key to the problem," or, "I have nothing to add along their particular lines of argument." Here the poetry of exaltation takes the cure in the prose of private convenience and genial demagogy. The result is comic relief, a vertiginous reversal of tone and tempo. In an instant the reader or spectator, laughing cynically, turns hard-headed and a bit rowdy. The final chorus, intoning a beatific vision, sounds uninspired, as dull as a hymn or a patriotic ode. The spell has been broken. The poet wanted to show us the sameness of history, that nothing changes, but history threw him aside to repeat itself as farce. No doubt this interlude has its logic within the play's orthodox scheme, yet the effect is as if someone had pulled up a blind and instead of Dante's gloomy visage we had caught a glimpse of Sweeney's grinning mug. Or perhaps it is that small house agent's clerk we see, "the young man carbuncular" of the celebrated typist's episode, on his way for another bout of love? Can it be that Eliot's religion is really a form of willful aesthetics? If so he is man enough to be damned, and we shall not be prevented "from praying for his repose."

It has been said that every work of art is an act of collaboration between reader and creator. Let us measure, then, the truth of that statement against Eliot's play. Did our sensibility really respond to the desiccated pattern of theological salvation? It cannot be that we were pleased by the stale art of the old-time vamps! No, it is not Becket and the women of Canterbury, the knights and the tempters, but we ourselves who are here represented. The pattern has been rent asunder by a tragedy altogether temporal — and to the poet perhaps both absurd and terrifying — giving the play overtones and meanings in another sphere, one close to our interests and desires.

I believe that the chorus in this play, chanting the doom of man, develops a language and a meaning for that doom much in excess of its presupposition in the dogma of man's sinful nature and the need for expiation. Are we listening to the mournful cry of a doom "out of time," born in the jungle of prehistory, whence the religious ethos springs? or is this a doom posthumous to theology, very much in our time?

> Sweet and cloying through the dark air
> Falls the stifling scent of despair . . .

or:

> Here is no continuing city, here is no abiding stay.
> Ill the wind, ill the time, uncertain the profit, certain the danger.
> O late late late, late is the time, late too late, and rotten the year;
> Evil the wind, and bitter the sea, and grey the sky, grey, grey, grey.

The intensity mounts, the poet's thought is sensualized and trans-
muted into emotion. Eliot's civilization smells the death bringers, its
values disintegrate:

I have tasted
The savour of putrid flesh in the spoon. I have felt
The heaving of earth at nightfall, restless, absurd. I have heard
Laughter in the noises of beasts that make strange noises: jackal, jack-
    ass, jackdaw; the scurrying noise of mouse and jerboa; the laugh of
    the loon, the lunatic bird. I have seen
Grey necks twisting, rat tails twining, in the thick light of dawn. I have
    eaten
Smooth creatures still living, with the strong salt taste of living things
    under sea;

and further:

I have smelt
Corruption in the dish, incense in the latrine, the sewer in the incense,
    the smell of sweet soap in the woodpath, a hellish sweet scent in the
    woodpath, while the ground heaved. I have seen
Rings of light coiling downwards, leading
To the horror of the ape. Have I not known, not known
What was coming to be?

From the arteries of "God," cut open, streams the blood of secular
humanity. This is an apocalyptic vision of a death as much feared
as desired. With this the play hooks itself on to the positive elements
of our reality, that death's necessity, and the poet, though pining
for relief in the lap of the infinite, begets his bastard child — a
prophetic sense of our age.

Moreover, what has become of the Christian man, man in the
singular, that *identical* creature of dogma? Why does the chorus
harp upon the image of the "common man," the "small folk"?
Throughout the action Eliot-Becket, the clerical philosopher, answers the complaints of those "who acknowledge themselves the
type of the common man" in contrast to those who walk "secure and
assured" in their fate. Who hatched this heresy of a plural man,
veritably a class conception in disguise? Has Eliot heard of the role
of the masses in history, of their refusal to become the fodder of
eternity? Is the image of the small folk the poet's bad conscience?

> Archbishop, secure and assured of your fate, unaffrayed among the
> shades, do you realize what you ask, do you realize what it means
> To the small folk drawn into the pattern of fate, the small folk who live
> among small things . . .

The protest of the commoners, however, always meets the stopgap
reply: The sin of the world is upon your heads. Yet it is in the self-
portrayal of these plebeians that concrete life emerges. Sometimes
the corn fails them, one year is a year of dryness, another of rain,
there have been oppression and taxes, girls have unaccountably dis-
appeared, still they have gone on living, "living and partly living."
(This word *partly*, denatured, unpoetic, recurs throughout and
throughout turns into its opposite. Loaded with the burden of the
real, it violates its many "poetic" contexts, thus animating them
with a superior poetry, the genuine poetry of surprise and humility.)

The dislocation of the poet's intention continues. We do not feel
the "joyful consummation" heralded as the play ends. The formal
cause of the horror expressed by the chorus — the crime of murder
absolutized in "an instant eternity of evil and wrong" — remains an
abstraction. The horror is not realized as such, its language is nowise
equivalent to the peculiar logic of its indicated motivation. History,
ever determinate, will not be cheated of its offspring; though the
poem recoils from history, only history can give it life. And in his
essay on Baudelaire, Eliot has himself perceived why this is so.
Though Baudelaire, he says, was the first counter-romantic, he was
still inevitably the child of romanticism. If the poem is sincere, "he
must express with individual differences the general state of mind —
not as a *duty*, but simply because he cannot help participating in it."

I have suggested a creative contradiction in Eliot that makes him
our contemporary in more than a chronological sense. Yet there
are many whose distorted critical ideas allow them to see only explicit ideology in a work of art, and unable to share the poet's beliefs,
they find themselves unable to enjoy his poetry. This is the real
reason for the crude treatment the play received from some of the
Left critics. What these critics don't see is that their approach iso-
lates them from literature as a historical entity, particularly from

the literature of the past. We can understand the immediate pleasure a critic gets from an ideological correspondence between himself and the work he criticizes, but let him beware lest this immediate pleasure become a vice blinding him to other and related values.

1936

DR. WILLIAMS IN HIS SHORT STORIES

IN HIS PROSE as in his poetry William Carlos Williams is too hardy a frontiersman of the word to permit himself the idle luxuries of aestheticism. There are too many things to be seen and touched, too many cadences of living speech to be listened to and recorded. Kenneth Burke once said of Williams that he was engaged in "discovering the shortest route between subject and object." Perhaps that explains why in *Life on the Passaic River*, a collection of nineteen short stories, not one imitates in any way the conventional patterns of the genre. The directness of this writer's approach to his material excludes its subjection to the researches of plot and calculated form. What Williams tells us is much too close to him to lend itself to the alienation of design; none of his perceptions can be communicated through the agency of invented equivalents. The phenomena he observes and their means are so intimately involved with one another, the cohabitation of language and object is so harmonious, that formal means of expression would not only be superfluous but might actually nullify the incentive to creation.

These notations in a doctor's notebook, these fragments salvaged from grime and squalor, these insights gained during the routines of humble labor — such would only be given the lie by the professional mannerisms of authorship, its pomposities and braggadocio. Where a writer usually takes the attitude of an impresario toward his themes, calculating each entrance and exit, Williams will begin or end his story as the spirit moves him; pausing to face his reader, he will take him into his confidence and speak his mind without recourse to stratagems of ingratiation. Elliptical in some passages and naturalistic in others, Williams is perfectly conscious of writing but hostile to "literature." Out of "a straight impulse, without borrowing, without lie or complaint," he puts down on paper that which stirs him. His subjects are few and often minute, their scope is sharply circumscribed by his personal experience and by his voluntary seclusion within the local and immediate, he repeats himself frequently — yet these stories are exceptional for their authenticity and told not to provoke but to record. It is pain which is the source of values here. The dread of annihilation is ever present "Christ, Christ! . . . How can a man live in the face of this daily uncertainty? How can a man not go mad with grief, with apprehension?" No grand conceits, no gratuitous excitements, no melodrama. There is no doing away with the staples of existence; no gallivanting on the banks of the Passaic River.

For what could be more dismal than life in these small industrial towns of New Jersey? The mills are worked by immigrant laborers, and their youngsters are "all over the city as soon as they can walk and say, Paper!" The doctor visits these uprooted households, often angry at himself because of the tenderness in him that reaches out to these people, quite as often resigned to doing his job, to immersing himself in the finalities of human life. "To me," he writes, "it is a hard, barren life, where I am alone and unmolested (work as I do in the thick of it), though in constant danger lest some slip send me to perdition but which, being covetous not at all, I enjoy for the seclusion and primitive air of it."

The little girl, both of whose tonsils are covered with membrane, fights furiously to keep him from knowing her secret. Another one, a lank-haired girl of fifteen, is a powerful little animal upon whom you can stumble on the roof, behind the stairs "any time at all." A whole gang is on her trail. Cured of her pimples, how will this tenacious creature ever slash her way to the bliss recited on the radio?

"The pure products of America go crazy," Williams once wrote in a poem. And these stories are familiar images of the same, released by that active element of sympathy which is to be prized above all else in the equipment of an artist. But this writer has no hankering for consistent explanations, for the constancy of reason; he seldom permits himself to ask why. "What are you going to do with a guy like that. Or why want to do anything with him. Except not miss him," he says of one of his characters. This last is the point. He is content with grasping the fact, with creating a phenomenology; but the relations, social and historic, that might unify these facts and significate them on a plane beyond sensation or nostalgia or pathos he has no mind for. And this absence of what one might call, in his terms, ideological presumptuousness, while admirable in its modesty, also constitutes his defeat. However much of value there is in these facts of "hard history" and in the scrupulous gathering of their detail, the larger implications are systematically neglected. Thought is proscribed as anti-aesthetic. Yet, though habitually confined to the suggestive and purely descriptive, this prose nevertheless holds within itself some of the raw elements of a comprehensive consciousness.

But Williams does think about America, if only to sketch it in psychic outline. He is under the spell of its *mystique* and strains to encompass it in a vision. This need in him provides a contrast and relief to the phenomenological principle informing his work; and much of his charm flows from the interaction of his precise facts with his American mysticism. In his novel, *White Mule*, the fusion of these two qualities allowed a visible direction to emerge. "What then is it like, America?" asks Fraülein Von J. in "The Venus," which seems to me the best story in the collection. This German girl is a genuine Weimar-period object. She has a genius for formulating the most complex modern problems in the simplest terms. The daughter of a general, she comes to Italy to become a nun. But perhaps America — she questions the American, Evans, who carries a flint arrowhead in his pocket — could prove a satisfactory alternative to the Church? Evans speaks of the old pioneer houses of his ancestors, and of that "early phase" of America whose peculiar significance has been forgotten or misunderstood. The German girl holds the arrowhead in her hand, feeling its point and edge. "It must be even more lonesome and frightening in America than in Germany," she finally says. The story recalls us to the Williams of *In the American Grain,* a writer ravaged by this hemisphere's occult aboriginal past. In some ways Dr. Williams is really a medicine man.

1938

TWILIGHT OF THE THIRTIES:
PASSAGE FROM AN EDITORIAL

TO SPEAK OF MODERN LITERATURE is to speak of that peculiar social grouping, the intelligentsia, to whom it belongs. The intelligentsia, too, is a modern product, created by the drastic division of labor that prevails under capitalism. Restricted to the realm of technical and spiritual culture, which is their only real property, the intellectuals make their livelihood by preserving the old and by producing the new forms of consciousness. Now Marxist criticism, in discussing the social base of literature, has always laid too much stress on such terms as "bourgeois" and "proletarian." This is an error, I think, because literature is not linked directly to the polar classes, but associates itself with (or dissociates itself from) the life of society as a whole as well as the different classes within it by giving expression to the given bias, the given moods and ideas of the intellectuals. An examination of the special role and changing status of the intelligentsia is, therefore, essential to any social examination of modern literature.

Trotsky is, I believe, the only Marxist critic who develops his analysis of writers and literary trends largely around this concept. Thus he connects the symbolist schools that flourished in Russia before the October revolution with the growing self-determination, in that period, of the intelligentsia, which proclaimed that "it had its own value, regardless of its relation to the people." But Trotsky does not credit this factor with sufficient power. This self-determination occurred also in other countries and it was directed not only against the masses but against the ruling strata as well. Materially and politically it was an illusion, of course, since the intellectuals remained at bottom as dependent as ever; yet in other respects it encouraged the creation of moral and aesthetic values running counter to and often violently critical of the bourgeois spirit.

Regardless of their specific historical meanings, most of the typically modern literary tendencies, such as romanticism, naturalism, symbolism, expressionism, surrealism, etc., could not have become articulate save through the support, through the necessary social framework, provided by this relative detachment of the intellectuals from a society intrinsically hostile, and at best indifferent, to the rights of the human personality and to everything imaginative, gratuitous, natural, and commercially devoid of advantages. In American literature, for instance, the typically modern did not appear until late, until the years before the First World War in fact; and the reason seems to be that in America, because of the concentration on the physical mastery of the continent, it was not until the twentieth century that a separate intellectual class emerged conscious of itself as standing apart from society and as possessing special and superior interests and ideals.

The modern artist has been rebuked time and again by social-minded critics both of the Right and of the Left for his obsessive introversion, his jealously maintained privacy, his aesthetic mysticism, his bent toward the obscure and the morbid. Yet without such qualities, given the boundaries of the bourgeois world, he could not have survived. These qualities are not derived from a limitless confidence that this artist has in himself (the opposite is often the case) but from the group-ethos, from the proud self-imposed isolation of a cultivated minority. It is this isolation which was translated ideologically into various doctrines — the theory of art for art's sake is a striking example — that could simultaneously be put to aristocratic and bohemian uses. For a long time it enabled the art-object to re-

21

sist being drawn into the web of commodity relations. Being an impersonal exchange value, a commodity is a product that dominates its producer; and whereas in almost every other sphere the conversion of products into commodities robbed the producers of their individuality, in the sphere of art many producers still found it possible — through a valiant effort, certainly, and at the cost of much suffering — to remain the masters instead of the victims of their products.

But the contradiction in this is that it is precisely its integrity which is to a large extent synonymous with the "antisocial" character of so much of modern art. Inevitably so, for during the greater part of the bourgeois epoch not to conform meant to repel the social, and rather than pay the price of being at one with society, the artist chose to be alone with his art: he preferred alienation from the community to alienation from himself. "Anywhere out of the world," said Baudelaire: and Flaubert formulated the belief of a whole race of artists in claiming that "now that the bourgeoisie is all humanity" art had become particularly valuable, since in art, at least, "all is liberty in a world of fictions." "When there is no encouragement to be derived from one's fellows," he wrote, "when the exterior world is disgusting, enervating, corruptive, and brutalizing, honest and sensitive people are forced to seek within themselves a more suitable place to live . . . The soul, made to overflow, will be concentrated in itself."

Flaubert and the other protestants of art and thought did not so much retire into themselves, however, as into their group lives and group cultures. They immersed themselves in the "destructive element," which has been defined as the awareness of "a void in the present." Moreover, in their desire to recover the lost unity of consciousness, they created a whole range of what might be called idealized negations of the society they scorned: some made a religion of art, some denied the reality of ideas in order to gain freedom in a life of sensations, some embarked on expeditions into the past in search of ancient mythologies and the old religions. From *René* to *The Waste Land*, what is modern literature if not a vindictive, neurotic, and continually renewed dispute with the modern world?

But the effect of the crisis of our time has been to undermine this tradition, so that at present it is fast breaking up. In the first place its social equilibrium was destroyed as soon as the weakened capitalist system withdrew the privilege of limited self-determination hitherto granted to its intellectuals. Once the very existence of this system was threatened, it could no longer afford to "keep" its intelligentsia in a state of even semi-independence; nor could the latter, now that it was compelled to think seriously of its future, afford any longer to belittle and neglect political creeds and political action. Despite all their postures of objectivity, it is the law of social gravitation toward the ruling class which, in the last analysis, determines the behavior of the intellectuals. Still, their problem was not simple, for the actual location of the ruling class was not at all obvious anymore. The question was: Who is the real ruler? Is he the benighted and visibly decaying bourgeois or is he that enlightened and mighty proletarian who, as they were assured, was successfully building socialism in Russia as well as preparing the revolution the world over? And many decided to throw in their lot with the youthful contender for power.

The modern literature of individualism was then belabored on all sides by the new converts to the socialist cause. Those of its critics who remained friendly admired its past splendors while insisting that it put political teeth into its abstract-spiritual dissent from bourgeois values. On the other hand the whole-hog Leftists, led by the impassioned party-liners, attacked it outright for projecting its ideals back into history instead of forward into the classless society, for being self-centered, pessimistic, obscurantist, and so on and so forth.

But now that this movement has abandoned its social goal, it can be seen that in reality it was not to the revolution that so many writers were converted but simply to politics. Yet politics — ordinary reformist and parliamentary politics — has nothing to offer to the literary artist. It was one thing to criticize the individualist tradition from a revolutionary standpoint, but it is something else again to criticize it from the standpoint of Stalinist social-mindedness. In view of what has happened, is it not clear that the older tradition was a thousand times more "progressive" — if that is to be our criterion — was infinitely more disinterested, infinitely more sensitive to the actual conditions of human existence, than the shallow political writing of our latter days?

Is a new tendency in literature possible today? Is there a basis for a new vanguard group whose members, not frightened by isolation, know how to swim against the current? After all, not all writers have reverted to some safe-and-sane way of thinking, and among those who consider themselves liberals and even Marxists not all are held on a leash by some pseudo-radical organization. The revolution may have sunk out of sight and the intelligentsia may be sticking close to its paymaster-mentors, but the impulse to represent experience truthfully persists. The impulse persists, even though the job of judgment and representation has seldom been so arduous, so perplexing, so enmeshed in ambiguous claims and counterclaims. Yet part of the job is to evaluate these claims. If one is to be equal to the contemporary subject matter, one cannot shut one's eyes to the unruly presences that beset it.

I do not believe that a new avant-garde movement, in the proper historical sense of the term, can be formed in this prewar situation. For obituaries, however, the time is not yet; despite multiple pressures a literary minority can still maintain its identity. And even if it cannot look forward to an expansive career, still what it can do is to warn. We should remember the fateful words of Wilfrid Owen, spoken during the last war: "All a poet can do today is to warn. That is why the true poets must be truthful."

For this minority, which has learned how to resist the reactionary *Zeitgeist,* there is surely no turning back to prepolitical modes of expression; but neither should it bind itself to some closed and definitive political doctrine. For it is in becoming a mouthpiece that the writer defeats himself. His work is vitiated not so much by the errors he commits in his own right, not so much by the errors he has actually *lived,* as by the seemingly impersonal errors which are for that very reason all the more abjectly mindless, by the errors that he imitates out of cowardice and the servile desire to ingratiate himself.

Moreover, even the best of doctrines is thick with prohibitions. It is much too remote and narrow a base for literature, which relates itself to life through experience and only secondarily through ideas. If a sufficiently organic, active, and broad revolutionary movement existed, it might assimilate the artist by opening to him its own avenue to experience; but in the absence of such a movement all he can do is to utilize the possibilities of individual and group secession from, and protest against, the dominant values of our time. Needless to say, this does not imply a return to a philosophy of individualism. It means that all we have left to go on now is individual integrity — the probing conscience, the will to repulse and to assail the forces released by a disintegrated society.

The dissident artist, if he understands the extremity of the age and voices what it tries to stifle, will thus be saved from its sterility and delivered from its corruption. Instead of deceiving himself and others — either by playing with bureaucratized visions of the shining cities of the future or by turning his art into a shrine for things that are dead and gone — he would be faithful to the metamorphosis of the present. And every metamorphosis, as Marx wrote, "is partly a swan song and partly a prelude to a great new poem."

1939

MRS. WOOLF AND MRS. BROWN

IN HER WONDERFULLY high-spirited essay "Mr. Bennett and Mrs. Brown," written in 1924, Virginia Woolf came out for scrapping the conventional realism of the Edwardian generation, the generation of Wells, Galsworthy, and Bennett. The new course for English fiction, she declared, is being set by novelists like Joyce and Forster and Lawrence and herself, who were discarding the old outworn methods. Confident that they could be relied on to make good the promise of the age, she boldly predicted that it would prove to be "one of the great ages of English literature." But in conclusion she warned that it could be reached only "if we are determined never, never to desert Mrs. Brown."

Mrs. Brown, the old lady in the railway carriage, served Mrs. Woolf as the symbol of reality — of reality as we think we know it and of the human character as we live it daily and hourly. It was Mrs. Woolf's idea, in other words, that no adequate substitute for Mrs. Brown can be found but that it is possible to devise new ways of coping with the rather stodgy yet ever so obstinate old lady. Now, however, in evaluating the actual literary practice that followed and by some years even preceded the theoretical flights of her manifesto against the Edwardians, the questions that need to be asked are these: What really happened between Mrs. Woolf and Mrs. Brown? Did Mrs. Woolf succeed in holding on to Mrs. Brown or was she finally forced to desert her? And if she deserted her, as I think she did, what were the consequences of this act? Did it reduce or increase her powers as a novelist who was also one of the leading innovators in modern writing? Our judgment not only of Mrs. Woolf's fiction but of contemporary fiction in general is affected by whatever answers can be given to such questions.

E. M. Forster is among the critics who have applauded Mrs. Woolf's creative efforts; and he appears to snub Mrs. Brown when speaking of *The Waves*, surely the most abstract of Mrs. Woolf's novels, as her best work. But in another passage of the same essay he implicitly modifies his estimate of her achievement. There are two kinds of life in fiction, he observes, "life on the page and life eternal," and it is only the first kind of life that Mrs. Woolf was able to master. "Her characters never seem unreal, however slight or fantastic their lineaments, and they can be trusted to behave appropriately. Life eternal she could seldom give; she could seldom so portray a character that it was remembered afterwards on its own account." Mrs. Woolf no doubt made a very brave attempt to break through conventional realism and to create new forms for the novel. *Mrs. Dalloway* and *To the Lighthouse* are minor successes and unique in their way, but on the whole she failed. Some years ago William Troy outlined the full extent of this failure in a brilliant essay, in which he demonstrated that Mrs. Woolf's style is the product of a "facile traditionalism," that the unity of her novels is "merely superficial or decorative, corresponding to no fundamental organization of the experience," and that her characters are "unable to function anywhere but on the plane of the sensibility."

Mr. Troy's definitive analysis may be supplemented by several observations. There is the fact, for example, that at one time Mrs. Woolf thought of herself as an associate of Joyce, whereas actually there is little kinship between them. Consider to what totally different uses they put such a device as the interior monologue. While in Joyce the interior monologue is a means of bringing us closer to the characters, of telling us *more* about them than we could learn from a purely objective account of their behavior, in Mrs. Woolf it becomes a means of telling us *less* about them, of disengaging their ego from concrete situations in life and converting it into a vehicle of poetic memory. Her tendency is to drain the interior monologue of its modern content and turn it back to the habitual forms of lyrical expression — and reverie. Where Joyce performs a radically new act of aesthetic selection, Mrs. Woolf performs what is in the main an act of exclusion; for she retains no more fictional material than will suffice to identify the scene and its human inhabitants; beyond that all is sensation and impression of a volatile kind. And it is so volatile because only on the surface does it flow from the actual experience of the characters — its real source is the general tradition of English poetry and of the poetic sensibility. However, there is a crucial fault in Mrs. Woolf's grasp even of this tradition, for she comprehends it one-sidedly, and perhaps in much too feminine a fashion, not as a complete order but first and foremost as an order of sentiments.

In *Between the Acts,* Mrs. Woolf's last and most unhappy book, the following complaint is sounded time and again: "None speaks with a single voice. None with a voice free from the old vibrations. Always I hear corrupt murmurs; the chink of gold and metal. Mad music . . ." One feels that this is the author's requiem for a lost art, that here she is pronouncing judgment against herself. But it is by no means the final judgment. Something remains that is deeply moving, an expiatory tenderness, the soul's searching of its own roots. To read her closely is to catch the strains of that "mad music" that sometimes possessed her, a music which breaks through the "old vibrations," the used-up words and disembodied imagery of such "poetic" abstractions as Time and Change, Life and Death. It is the deranged song of Septimus Smith, who is Mrs. Dalloway's double and who dies that she may live. Septimus is the mysterious stranger, the marked man, the poet upon whom an outrage had been committed; he is at once the sacrificial goat and a veritable "lord of creation." This apparition haunted Mrs. Woolf, but always she strove to escape from it. She felt more at home with Mrs. Dalloway.

The ultimate failure of Virginia Woolf's experiments might perhaps be explained by going back to her initial conception of reality as an old lady in a railway carriage called Mrs. Brown. For what is Mrs. Brown if not the product of the traditional realism of the English novel? What is she if not the dominant figure of that world so scorned by Mrs. Woolf — the world of Messrs. Wells, Galsworthy, and Bennett? The truth is that she tacitly accepted, even as she revolted against her elders, their innermost vision of reality. Hence all she could do is turn their vices inside out — since they had materialized the novel she was to devote herself to spiritualizing it. Forgotten was the pledge "never, never to desert Mrs. Brown." But Mrs. Woolf was profoundly mistaken in her belief that she had seen through Mrs. Brown and was now free to dismiss her. If literature can be said to have a permanent theme, that theme is precisely The Mystery of Mrs. Brown, who is a creature of many paradoxes and truly unfathomable. She is not to be encompassed either by the materialist or by the idealist approach and she lets the novelists make what they can of her. To some she appears as a commonplace old lady; to others as a tiger in the night.

Mrs. Woolf's idea of Mrs. Brown is expressive of all the assumptions she was born to, of the safety and domestication of that upper class British culture to which she was so perfectly adjusted. Now the breach between poetry and prose, conceived as opposed to each other in the same absolute way (but is it absolute?) that pleasure is opposed to pain, is one of the most secure assumptions of that culture; and Mrs. Woolf carried its traditional dualism to its furthest extreme. Therefore she was forced to invent a definition of what is real, of what life is, quite as artificial as the one she repudiated. "Life," she declaimed in her essay "Modern Fiction," "is not a series of gig lamps symmetrically arranged; life is a luminous halo, a semi-transparent envelope surrounding us from the beginning of consciousness to the end." That is the essence of idealism, of that other, that sacrosanct reality in which Mrs. Woolf luxuriates but from which Mrs. Brown is excluded.

Yet if Mrs. Woolf was not a great literary artist, she was surely a great woman of letters. "She liked writing," as Mr. Forster says, "with an intensity that few writers have attained, or even desired." *The Death of the Moth,* her last collection of essays and reviews, while not quite so impressive as the two volumes of *The Common Reader,* contains at least a half dozen pieces that are first rate. Never a systematic critic, she was a master of such neglected forms as the literary portrait and the familiar essay. And it is her enthusiasm and the purity and passion of her devotion to writing, rather than the poetic code which she endeavored to impose on the fictional medium, that will in the end secure a place for her, even though of the secondary order, in the history of English letters.

1942

THE UNFUTURE OF UTOPIA

GEORGE ORWELL has been able to maintain an exceptional position among the writers of our time seriously concerned with political problems. His work has grown in importance and relevance through the years, evincing a steadiness of purpose and uncommon qualities of character and integrity that set it quite apart from the typical products of the radical consciousness in this period of rout and retreat. A genuine humanist in his commitments, a friend, that is, not merely of mankind but of man (man as he is, not denatured by ideological abstractions), Orwell has gone through the school of the revolutionary movement without taking over its snappishly doctrinaire attitudes. His attachment to the primary traditions of the British empirical mind has apparently rendered him immune to dogmatism. Nor has the release from certitude lately experienced by the more alert radical intellectuals left him in the disoriented state in which many of his contemporaries now find themselves. Above all endowed with a strong sense of reality, he has neither played the prophet in or out of season nor indulged in that willful and irresponsible theorizing at present so much in vogue in certain radical quarters where it is mistaken for independent thought. It can be said of

Orwell that he is the best kind of witness, the most reliable and scrupulous. All the more appalling, then, is the vision not of the remote but of the very close future evoked in his new novel, *1984* — a vision entirely composed of images of loss, disaster, and unspeakable degradation.

This is far and away the best of Orwell's books. As a narrative it has tension and actuality to a terrifying degree; still it will not do to judge it primarily as a literary work of art. Like all utopian literature, from Sir Thomas More and Campanella to William Morris, Bellamy, and Huxley, its inspiration is scarcely such as to be aesthetically productive of ultimate or positive significance; this seems to be true of utopian writings regardless of the viewpoint from which the author approaches his theme. *1984* chiefly appeals to us as a work of the political imagination, and the appeal is exercised with gravity and power. It documents the crisis of socialism with greater finality than Koestler's *Darkness at Noon*, to which it will be inevitably compared, since it belongs, on one side of it, to the same genre, the melancholy mid-century genre of lost illusions and Utopia betrayed.

While in Koestler's novel there are still lingering traces of nostalgia for the Soviet Utopia, at least in its early heroic phase, and fleeting tenderness for its protagonists, betrayers and betrayed — some are depicted as Promethean types wholly possessed by the revolutionary dogma and annihilated by the consequences of their own excess, the *hubris* of Bolshevism — in Orwell's narrative the further stage of terror that has been reached no longer permits even the slightest sympathy for the revolutionaries turned totalitarian. Here Utopia is presented, with the fearful simplicity of a trauma, as the abyss into which the future falls. The traditional notion of Utopia as the future good is thus turned inside out, inverted — nullified. It is now sheer mockery to speak of its future. Far more accurate it is to speak of its *unfuture*. (The addition of the negative affix "un" is a favorite usage of Newspeak, the official language of Ingsoc — English socialism — a language in which persons purged by the Ministry of Love, i.e., the secret police, are invariably described as *unpersons*. The principles of Newspeak are masterfully analyzed by Orwell in the appendix to his book. Newspeak is nothing less than a plot against human consciousness, for its sole aim is so to reduce the range of thought through the destruction of words as to make "*thoughtcrime* literally impossible because there will be no words in which to express it.")

The prospect of the future drawn in this novel can on no account be taken as a fantasy. If it inspires dread above all, that is precisely because its materials are taken from the real world as we know it, from conditions now prevailing in the totalitarian nations, in particular the Stalinist nations, and potentially among us too. Ingsoc, the system established in Oceania, the totalitarian super-State that unites the English-speaking peoples, is substantially little more than an extension into the near future of the present structure and policy of Stalinism, an extension as ingenious as it is logical, predicated upon conditions of permanent war and the development of the technical means of espionage and surveillance to the point of the complex extinction of private life. Big Brother, the supreme dictator of Oceania, is obviously modeled on Stalin, both in his physical features and in his literary style ("a style at once military and pedantic, and, because of a trick of asking questions and then promptly answering them . . . easy to imitate"). And who is Goldstein, the dissident leader of Ingsoc against whom Two Minute Hate Periods are conducted in all Party offices, if not Trotsky, the grand heresiarch and useful scapegoat, who is even now as indispensable to Stalin as Goldstein is shown to be to Big Brother? The inserted chapters from Goldstein's imaginary book on "The Theory and Practice of Oligarchical Collectivism" are a wonderfully realized imitation not only of Trotsky's characteristic rhetoric but also of his mode and manner as a Marxist theoretician. Moreover, the established pieties of Communism are at once recognizable in the approved spiritual regimen of the Ingsoc Party faithful: "A Party member is expected to have no private emotions and no respites from enthusiasm. He is supposed to live in a continuous frenzy of hatred of foreign enemies and internal traitors, triumph over victories, and self-abasement before the power and wisdom of the Party." One of Orwell's best strokes is his analysis of the technique of "doublethink," drilled into the Party members, which consists of the willingness to assert that black is white when the Party demands it, and even to believe that black is white, while at the same time knowing very well that nothing of the sort can be true. Now what is "doublethink," actually, if not the technique continually practiced by the Communists and their liberal collaborators, dupes, and apologists. Nor is it a technique available exclusively to Soviet citizens. Right here in New York any issue of *The Daily Worker* or of *The Daily Compass* will provide you with illustrations of it as vicious and ludicrous as any you will come upon in Orwell's story. As for "the control of the past," of which so much is made in Oceania through the revision of all records and the manipulation of memory through force and fraud, that too is by no means unknown in Russia, where periodically not only political history but also the history of art and literature are revamped in accordance with the latest edicts of the regime. The one feature of Oceanic society that appears to be really new is the proscription of sexual pleasure. The fact is, however, that a tendency in that direction has long been evident in Russia, where a new kind of prudery, disgusting in its unctuousness and hypocrisy, is officially promoted. In Oceania "the only recognized purpose of marriage was to beget children for the service of the Party." The new Russian laws regulating sexual relations are manifestly designed with the same purpose in mind. It is plain that any society which imposes a ban on personal experience must sooner or later distort and inhibit the sexual instinct. The totalitarian State cannot tolerate attachments between men and women that fall outside the political sphere and that are in their very nature difficult to control from above.

The diagnosis of the totalitarian perversion of socialism that Orwell makes in this book is far more remarkable than the prognosis it contains. This is not to deny that the book is prophetic; but its importance is mainly in its powerful engagement with the present. Through the invention of a society of which he can be imaginatively in full command, Orwell is enabled all the more effectively to probe the consequences for the human soul of the system of oligarchic collectivism — the system already prevailing in a good part of the world, which millions of people even this side of the Iron Curtain believe to be true-blue socialism and which at this time constitutes a formidable threat to free institutions. Hence to read this novel simply as a flat prediction of what is to come is to misread it. It is not a writ of fatalism to bind our wills. Orwell makes no attempt to persuade us, for instance, that the English-speaking nations will inevitably lose their freedom in spite of their vigorous democratic temper and libertarian traditions. "Wave of the future" notions are alien to Orwell. His intention, rather, is to prod the Western world into a more conscious and militant resistance to the totalitarian virus to which it is now exposed.

As in *Darkness at Noon,* so in *1984* one of the major themes is the psychology of capitulation. Winston Smith, the hero of the novel, is shown arming himself with ideas against the Party and defying it by forming a sexual relationship with Julia; but from the first we know that he will not escape the secret police, and after he is caught we see him undergoing a dreadful metamorphosis which burns out his human essence, leaving him a wreck who can go on living only by becoming one of "them." The closing sentences of the story are the most pitiful of all: "He had won a victory over himself. He loved Big Brother." The meaning of the horror of the last section of the novel, with its unbearable description of the torture of Smith by O'Brien, the Ingsoc Commissar, lies in its disclosure of a truth that the West still refuses to absorb. Hence the widespread mystifications produced by the Moscow Trials ("Why did they confess?") and, more recently, by the equally spectacular displays of confessional ardor in Russia's satellite states (Cardinal Mindszenty and others). The truth is that the modern totalitarians have devised a methodology of terror that enables them to break human beings by getting inside them. They explode the human character from within, exhibiting the pieces as the irrefutable proof of their own might and virtue. Thus Winston Smith begins with the notion that even if nothing else in the world was his own, still there were a few cubic centimeters inside his skull that belonged to him alone. But O'Brien, with his torture instruments and ruthless dialectic of power, soon teaches him that even these few cubic centimeters can never belong to him, only to the Party. What is so implacable about the despotisms of the twentieth century is that they have abolished martyrdom. If all through history the capacity and willingness to suffer for one's convictions served at once as the test and demonstration of sincerity, valor, and heroic resistance to evil, now even that capacity and willingness have been rendered meaningless. In the prisons of the M.V.D. or the Ministry of Love suffering has been converted into its opposite — into the ineluctable means of surrender. The victim crawls before his torturer, he identifies himself with him and grows to love him. That is the ultimate horror.

The dialectic of power is embodied in the figure of O'Brien, who simultaneously recalls and refutes the ideas of Dostoevsky's Grand Inquisitor. For a long time we thought that the legend of the Grand Inquisitor contained the innermost secrets of the power-mongering human mind. But no, modern experience has taught us that the last word is by no means to be found in Dostoevsky. For even the author of *The Brothers Karamazov*, who wrote that "man is a despot by nature and loves to be a torturer," was for all his crucial insights into evil nevertheless incapable of seeing the Grand Inquisitor as he really is. There are elements of the idealistic rationalization of power in the ideology of the Grand Inquisitor that we must overcome if we are to become fully aware of what the politics of totalitarianism come to in the end.

Clearly, that is what Orwell has in mind in the scene when Smith, while yielding more and more to O'Brien, voices the thoughts of the Grand Inquisitor only to suffer further pangs of pain for his persistence in error. Smith thinks that he will please O'Brien by explaining the Party's limitless desire for power along Dostoevskyean lines: "That the Party did not seek power for its own ends, but only for the good of the majority. That it sought power because men in the mass were frail, cowardly creatures who could not endure liberty or face the truth, and must be ruled over and systematically deceived by others stronger than themselves. That the choice for mankind lay between freedom and happiness, and that, for the great bulk of mankind, happiness was better. That the Party was the eternal guardian of the weak, a dedicated sect doing evil that good might come, sacrificing its own happiness to that of others." This is a fair summary of the Grand Inquisitor's ideology. O'Brien, however, has gone beyond even this last and most insidious rationalization of power. He forcibly instructs Smith in the plain truth that "the Party seeks power for its own sake. We are not interested in the good of others; we are interested solely in power . . . Power is not a means; it is an end. One does not establish a dictatorship in order to safeguard a revolution; one makes a revolution in order to establish the dictatorship. The object of persecution is persecution. The object of torture is torture. The object of power is power. Now do you begin to understand me?" And how does one human being assert his power over another human being? By making him suffer, of course. For "obedience is not enough. Unless he is suffering, how can you be sure that he is obeying your will and not his own? Power is in inflicting pain and humiliation. Power is in tearing human minds to pieces and putting them together again in new shapes of your own choosing." That, precisely, is the lesson the West must learn if it is to comprehend the meaning of Stalinist Communism. Otherwise we shall go on playing Winston Smith, falling sooner or later into the hands of the O'Briens of the East, who will break our bones until we scream with love for Big Brother.

But there is one aspect of the psychology of power in which Dostoevsky's insight strikes me as being more viable than Orwell's strict realism. It seems to me that Orwell fails to distinguish, in the behavior of O'Brien, between psychological and objective truth. Undoubtedly it is O'Brien, rather than Dostoevsky's Grand Inquisitor, who reveals the real nature of total power; yet that does not settle the question of O'Brien's personal psychology, the question, that is, of his ability to live with this naked truth as his sole support; nor is it conceivable that the party-elite to which he belongs could live with this truth for very long. Evil, far more than good, is in need of the pseudo-religious justifications so readily provided by the ideologies of world-salvation and compulsory happiness, ideologies generated both by the Left and the Right. Power is its own end, to be sure, but even the Grand Inquisitors are compelled, now as always, to believe in the fiction that their power is a means to some other end, gratifyingly noble and supernal. Though O'Brien's realism is wholly convincing in social and political terms, its motivation in the psychological economy of the novel remains obscure.

Another aspect of Orwell's dreadful Utopia that might be called into question is the role he attributes to the proletariat, a role that puts it outside politics. In Oceania the workers, known as the Proles, are assigned to the task of production, deprived of all political rights, but unlike the Party members, are otherwise left alone and even permitted to lead private lives in accordance with their own choice. That is an idea that appears to me to run contrary to the basic tendencies of totalitarianism. All societies of our epoch, whether authoritarian or democratic in structure, are mass-societies; and an authoritarian state built on the foundations of a mass-society could scarcely afford the luxury of allowing any class or group to evade

22

its demand for complete control. A totalitarian-collectivist state is rigidly organized along hierarchical lines, but that very fact, so damaging to its socialist claims, necessitates the domination of all citizens, of whatever class, in the attempt to "abolish" the contradiction between its theory and practice by means of boundless demagogy and violence.

These are minor faults, however. This novel is the best antidote to the totalitarian disease that any writer has so far produced. Everyone should read it; and I recommend it particularly to those liberals who still cannot get over the political superstition that while absolute power is bad when exercised by the Right, it is in its very nature good and a boon to humanity once the Left, that is to say "our own people," takes hold of it.

1949

Postscript 1969 — Orwell's novel and my review were published twenty years ago, precisely at a time when the totalitarian perversion of socialism established by the Stalinist bureaucracy in the Soviet Union appeared to us to be very secure, durable, and its horrors immitigable. None of us foresaw the disarray into which that system fell soon after Stalin's death. Still, I was able to say that *1984* should be judged primarily as a diagnosis rather than as a prognosis of things to come. I praised the book for "its powerful engagement with the present," slighting its prophetic element, and I saw clearly enough that this work, like all utopian as well as anti-utopian literature, is not "aesthetically productive of ultimate or positive significance." Thus somewhat gently, to be sure, I denied it the status of a literary work of art claimed for it in certain quarters, even as in a political sense I shared its vision composed entirely, as I put it, of "images of loss, disaster and unspeakable degradation." Also, I disagreed on psychological grounds with Orwell's notion of totalitarian power as expounded by O'Brien, the Ingsoc Commissar. Fortunately for humanity, historical events since 1949 have shown our extreme pessimism of that period, though plausible enough under the circumstances, to have been in the long run unjustified. The human mind has proven itself to be finally resistant to the methodology of terror devised by totalitarian regimes. In the last analysis, as more recent historical experience has disclosed, "Big Brother" can only earn the hatred and contempt of the Winston Smiths of this world. Happily for us, in this important matter Orwell has turned out to be quite wrong. To say that, however, is not at all to detract from the value of his novel as a timely momentous warning.

MELVILLE AND HIS CRITICS

NEWTON ARVIN's *Herman Melville* is, to my mind, the finest critical biography of an American author that we have had for a long time. It is also the best book Arvin has written; he transcends in it the limitations of tone and method manifest in his works on Hawthorne and Whitman. Here he is in complete possession of his subject and uninhibited by ideological preconceptions. He treats text and context with equal authority, combining in a masterly way the traditional resources of literary criticism with a flexible and entirely apposite use of the insights provided by the newer psychological disciplines. The result is a critical interpretation so just and clear that it may well become the classic study of Melville in our literature.

Melville has of late nearly eclipsed Henry James as the much-favored object of critical inquiry. A few of the new studies devoted to him are welcome contributions to scholarship; but some of the others, in which a critical approach is attempted, are of dubious value, since what is displayed in them is less insight into Melville than an addiction to the more aberrant tendencies of the contemporary literary mind. There is the new pedantry of myth, for instance, which is well on its way to converting a valid though by no means inexhaustible cultural interest into a pretentious and up-to-date version of the kind of source-and-parallel hunting now rapidly going out of fashion in the more alert academic circles. That there is a genuine mythic element in Melville is hardly open to doubt. But the myth-happy critics blow it up to vast proportions, laboring gratuitously, and in a mode of erudition peculiarly arid, to interpose between us and the reality of Melville a talmudic elaboration of mythology portentous to the point of stupefaction.

Not quite so one-sided yet unsatisfactory on the whole is the traditionalist approach to Melville. The literary traditionalists (whose point of view is scarcely distinguishable these days from that of the "new critics") make what they can of him with their means, and their means are well adapted to eliminate the contradictions in him. But these contradictions are really of an immitigable nature. At once creative and frustrating, agonizingly personal yet deeply expressive of national and universal culture, they are at the very core of Melville's modernity and the symbolic fate of his genius. Now a Melville relieved of his contradictions is, of course, a Melville removed from the shifting and perilous terrain of history and safely committed to a transcendent realm where, ceasing to be fallible and alive, no longer desperately striving for illumination in a siege of darkness, he is canonized as an exalted witness to metaphysical faith and aesthetic order.

The traditionalist aesthetic, with its profound revulsion from historicism and psychology and its inner drive toward standards of the normative-classicist type, cannot accept the real Melville or sustain him without doing violence to itself. Hence it constructs an ideal figure who is but a ghost of the man of whom Hawthorne wrote that he could neither believe nor be comfortable in his unbelief, reasoning endlessly about "everything that lies beyond human ken" even as he despaired of immortality and "pretty much made up his mind to be annihilated." Hawthorne, who was so frequently made inaccessible by the cold clarity of his nature, was moved by Melville's passion and believed in his integrity. None would now deny that integrity, but what is it, actually, if not the integrity of his riven and dissonant consciousness? This consciousness is inseparable from his art — an art which, in transforming the business of whaling into a fiery hunt ("wonder ye at the fiery hunt?"), makes us see the artist in the image of those sea captains of whom he said in *Moby Dick* that though they sailed anonymously out of Nantucket they yet became "as great and greater than your Cooke and your Krusenstern, for in their succorless emptyhandedness, they, in the heathenish sharked waters, and by the beaches of unrecorded, javelin islands, battled with virgin wonders and terrors." Conrad's dictum, "In the destructive element immerse," comes to much the same thing. These "heathenish sharked waters" compose an element situated on the other side of the planet from the inland lakes of traditionalism.

Arvin, who in his present phase is perhaps freer of confining allegiances than most critics, is able to lay hold of the contradictions in Melville and to disclose their psychodynamic meaning without any squeamishness or failure in sympathy. There is no separation of man and artist in this critical portrait but an integration of the two which enforces the understanding of both in their organic unity. Eschewing all stress on biographical and historical facts for their own sake, and so controlling his account of the man Melville, of his background and character, as to enable the reader to see more clearly into his art, Arvin demonstrates anew the relevance of the biographical mode to the job of criticism when it is properly utilized and not made an end in itself. Equally credible is Arvin's use of the Freudian psychology. It is brought to bear upon Melville's experience with a maturity of judgment and power of modulation rarely found in literary contexts, where the amateurish shuffling of the formulas of neurosis is still the rule rather than the exception. In spite of long and intensive discussion, the issue of psychoanalysis in its application to literature remains unsettled, arousing hostile distrust in some quarters and excessive confidence in others. From this standpoint Arvin's book might be taken as a practical experiment, offering concrete evidence which neither the friends nor the enemies of the psychoanalytic method can afford to overlook.

All of Melville's work, including the poems, is minutely examined in this study, resulting in a valuation that differs considerably from accepted judgments. Thus "Benito Cereno" is pulled down from its high place in the canon and shown to be basically lacking in the imaginative quality conventionally attributed to it. "An artistic miscarriage, with moments of undeniable power," Arvin calls it in a passage of exhaustive analysis, which lays bare the story's defective moral structure as well as the relative poverty of its technical devices and verbal texture. In his judgment of *The Confidence Man*, however, Arvin restores the negative estimate of it commonly accepted until it was recently challenged by an ambitious ideological approach which put a load of interpretation upon the book which it cannot carry.

The Confidence Man is a narrative which Arvin finds even more disappointing than *Israel Potter*, and that precisely because its "ideal" intention is such that had it been realized it might have become a "vaster, more animated, and of course more modern *Ship of Fools*, or even an American *Gulliver*." There is a wonderful felicity in the western river-scene that Melville conceived for it and the richest meaning in its theme, the exposure of "contemporary shams, and particularly the quackeries of a false humanitarianism, an insensate optimism." This, in fact, was the most pertinent of all subjects in Melville's age. But *The Confidence Man* was never really written. It is a worse book than *Pierre*, I think. Though *Pierre* is a failure, and even a failure of a peculiarly monstrous kind, it still exercises a certain appeal, a certain power of evocation, because it is full of passion and swarms with unconscious life. Not so *The Confidence Man*, which, except for its opening pages, strictly enforces the lesson that in art nothing speaks to our mind which does not simultaneously engage our senses: that is the supreme lesson, and one which criticism fails to heed only at the risk of utter irrelevance. And the reason, obviously, that this disputed work of Melville's remains, as Arvin says, "a tantalizing scenario for a book that never came into being," is that it is scarcely at all a living narrative. "One is alleged to be on a steamboat descending the greatest of American rivers, but sensuously, pictorially, kinesthetically . . . the river does not flow and the boat does not move ahead." As a fiction the book is "meager and monotonous . . . all but motionless . . . a series of conversations rather than an action . . . which keep recurring to the same theme too compulsively, with too few variations, to be anything but unendurably repetitious." Arvin pursues his analysis to the ultimate conclusion that this work is "one of the most completely nihilistic, morally and metaphysically," of American books, suffering from a "fatal want of moral chiaroscuro," Melville's *Timon of Athens* without a Flavius. Its actual effect is more of tameness than of terror, since what "it expresses, except at rare moments, is not a passion of bitterness but a dull despondency of mistrust and disbelief." Melville wrote it in a state of morbid suspiciousness when he had lost the vision of tragic grandeur that makes *Moby Dick* the chief masterpiece of American letters.

The most richly assimilative of his critical tasks Arvin undertakes in his comprehensive scrutiny of that masterpiece. Varied resources of literary and philosophical investigation are pressed into service in an unflagging effort to grasp, to understand, to bring to light. The analysis is conducted on the four levels of the literal, the psychological, the moral, and the mythic; and it is so comprehensive an analysis that it would be impossible to do it justice in a brief résumé. Suffice it to say that it yields a reading of *Moby Dick* summing up the best that we have learned about it at the same time that it establishes some wholly new relations of meaning and a sharper perception of the coherence of its parts in the unity of imaginative possession.

The Shakespearean influence on Melville has been sufficiently charted by scholars like Olson and Matthiessen, and on that score Arvin has little to add that is newly suggestive. Of more original value is his examination of Melville's problem in seeking to discover the proper form for his narratives. Melville was working in isolation from the central currents of European writings, an isolation from which he both lost and gained. As *Pierre* shows, he foundered in attempting to adopt as his own the typical novelistic forms developed by his contemporaries in Europe. This problem and the fashion in which Melville proceeded to solve it are of far more than technical importance. We are confronted here with an aspect of the national literary experience that indirectly but significantly connects certain elementary considerations of manner and technique with the higher considerations of form and value.

1950

T. S. ELIOT: THE POET AS PLAYWRIGHT

THE SUBJECT of poetic drama has been for some thirty odd years now among T. S. Eliot's most enduring interests. It has preoccupied him in his capacity both as practitioner and critic, and in his latest essay, "Poetry and Drama," comprising the text of the first Theodore Spencer Memorial Lecture delivered at Harvard, he proceeds to sum up, with his usual precision and with a fine candor so surprising as to be anything but usual, what the experience of his self-education as a poet "trying to write for the theater" has come to so far.

It is a lively summing-up, engrossing in its general formulations and even more so in its author's extended comment on his own experiments in verse drama, their "intentions, failures and practical successes." This comment, admirably concrete and sensible, and all in all an unequaled feat of self-criticism, ought to confound the swarming idolizers and cultists of Eliot among the younger academic *literati* of reactionary allegiance, the *nouveaux* "new critics" as someone has aptly called them, whose habit it is to extol every new opus of their master regardless of its specific value in relation to his work as a whole. The ponderous exegeses of *The Cocktail*

Party that have appeared during the past year in some of the literary quarterlies — exegeses marked by a maximum of unreliable assumption and a minimum of relevant evaluation — are the latest and more egregious products of this sterile and fatuous cultism. Now when Eliot informs us that it is "an open question" whether there is any poetry in that play at all, and when he puts his finger on the chief structural defect of the play in remarking that its third act is more in the nature of an epilogue than a true dramatic resolution of the action, one wonders how it is that the eager-beaver exegetes failed to notice anything of the sort. The faults Eliot notes are hardly of an esoteric nature, and they relate solely to the form of the play. I think that it has other faults, too, bearing upon its basic meaning and conception, that are perhaps undiscerned by the author and that are equally lost on the cult-ridden commentators.

I doubt that these people are in a position to learn anything really essential from their master. They have by now converted Eliot into a vested interest, fastening upon the worst side of him, his bent toward scholasticism in matters of belief and partly in matters of art too, thus erecting a traditionalist aesthetic which has of late grown into a barrier to the renewal of the creative impulse in American letters; and this they have done mostly on the strength of Eliot's eminence as an example. What is objectionable is the stupefying one-sidedness of their citations of this example. If one thing is certain, it is that Eliot could with justice disclaim the image of himself presented by his disciples. Marx once declared that he was no Marxist, and Eliot may soon be forced to resign from the school of Eliot. For the truth is that his contribution to the practice of modern poetry and criticism is by no means exhausted by his traditionalist bias. In the future it will be seen, I believe, that the link between him and his disciples was forged by the *Zeitgeist* rather than by what is most real in his achievement. The disciples dote on his dogmatic ideology, turning it into a proof of impeccable literary virtue, at the same time that with singular regularity they shy away from recognizing the empirical genius displayed in his best insights into the creative process.

It is instructive to compare what Eliot now says about poetic drama with his remarks in the "Dialogue on Dramatic Poetry," which dates back to 1928. It is the change of tone which is above all noticeable. The "Dialogue" is full of arrogant pronouncements and the tone is combative throughout, reflecting the exasperation of a poet straining to repel the apparently irresistible encroachments of the prose medium on the drama, which he is opinionated enough to regard as belonging peculiarly to the domain of poetry. In this latest stocktaking, however, there is no longer any question of cavalierly dismissing the play in prose as a mere "by-product" of the play in verse; nor is there any trace left of such grotesque opinions as that ranking Tourneur above Ibsen as a dramatist. The current word as to Ibsen is "a great prose dramatist." Thus many years of trying to adapt versification and idiom to the needs of a modern dramatic poetry, a poetry so flexible as to be able to deal with the most matter-of-fact things no less than with the most exalted, have taught Eliot that poetic drama can be restored only if it is willing to enter into "overt competition" with prose. The easy victory scored over prose in the "Dialogue" is now implicitly seen as the illusion typical of the poet venturing into the theater with insufficient appreciation of dramatic technique.

The conclusions Eliot comes to are, firstly, that no play should be written in verse for which prose is dramatically adequate; and, secondly, that the play, whether in prose or verse, should be so absorbing to the audience that the effect of style and rhythm would prove to be nearly "unconscious." In other words, what Eliot now calls for is a more complete fusion of action and speech — a fusion helping to overcome the resistance both of those listeners who dislike poetry altogether and those who like it so much they are prepared to abstract the poetry from the play in order to enjoy it in splendid isolation as it were. Hence it will not do to employ poetry in a play merely as a means of formalizing or decorating speech. Poetry in dramatic form is unjustified if "it merely gives people of literary tastes the pleasure of listening to poetry at the same time that they are witnessing a play." For then the poetry becomes superfluous, and perhaps even harmful, in that it tends to reinforce the habit of taking poetry as the speech of an unreal world.

Eliot is nothing if not intent on coping with what Henry James once called "the beautiful difficulties of art"; and, in the case of poetic drama, the difficulty which now appears to him to be most patently and stubbornly there is that of retaining the poetry while so subordinating its immediate effect as to make its integration into a dramatic whole possible. I have heard poets express suspicion of this notion, which they somehow associate with a "reductive" attitude toward their medium. Yet what Eliot is saying here is actually no more than what Keats said in his statement that "poetry should be great and unobtrusive, a thing which enters into one's soul, and does not startle or amaze with itself but with its subject." And it is because of this new conviction of the necessity of unobtrusiveness that Eliot now renounces the use of choral verse in drama. The chorus is seen as anachronistic in essence, leading nowhere so far as a general solution of the problem of poetic drama is concerned. After all, it is much easier for a poet to write choral verse than to master dramatic dialogue. The chorus was no doubt appropriately placed in a ritual play like *Murder in the Cathedral,* but in a normal dramatic context it inevitably tends to interrupt rather than to intensify the action.

In the main, the lesson that Eliot draws from his continual experimentation is that the writing of verse for a play must be approached in an entirely different frame of mind from the writing of other verse. Ordinarily a poem is written "in terms of one's own voice," and it is addressed, initially at least, to a narrow circle of readers disposed not only to receive the poet's communication favorably but to study and meditate upon it. In the verse play, on the other hand, every line "must be judged by a new law, that of dramatic relevance." One might have thought that this elementary law, with which every middling Broadway craftsman is thoroughly familiar, would have been apparent to Eliot at the very start of his experiments. But no, as is shown by his present declaration and by the evidence of *The Family Reunion,* which contains not a few passages that are dramatically irrelevant and dispersive in effect, it has taken him years of constant application to acquire a working knowledge of that law. It is true, of course, that at least for two centuries now English poets, attempting to reinstate verse as a language of the theater, have been confronted with enormous difficulties in adjusting metric and idiom to a living and natural speech-tone; it is for that reason perhaps that they have tended to make far too little of the problems of characterization and plot — and plot, in the Aristotelian sense of it as an action that is "serious and complete," is the very soul of drama.

I must confess that Eliot's latest audit of his experience in writing for the theater has made me more skeptical than ever of the ability of poets to master dramatic form while maintaining a high level of poetic expression incorporating the movements of modern speech. *The Cocktail Party* is a case in point. Here Eliot, following the "ascetic rule" of avoiding lines of verse without dramatic utility, has produced a poetry so "unobtrusive" as to be virtually nonexistent. Thus what he gains in theatrical technique he loses in poetic power. The plain conclusion is that the play might as well have been written in prose.

Also, it seems to me that *The Cocktail Party* is so deficient in plot and characterization as to merit not at all the encomiums that greeted its production on Broadway. There is a discord between the convention of drawing-room comedy it employs and its deeper aim, which is nothing less than of getting at the essence of the human situation. What the audience warms up to is the familiar trappings of comedy; but the deeper meaning, since it remains dramatically unrealized, is impressed upon it, if at all, with the shallowness of a pious lesson or message — the price paid for the evening's diversion. For in its aspiration to get at the human essence, the play falls short as lamentably in its way as did the plays of the German Expressionists, upon whose failure the philosopher Georg Simmel once commented with great astuteness that they "attempt to seize life in its essence but without its content." And in its dramatic structure *The Cocktail Party* is indeed the epitome of essence without content.

The two ways of life — that of resigned mediocrity on the one hand and saintliness on the other — are expatiated upon by the playwright through his mouthpiece Harcourt-Reilly, but are so inadequately embodied in a living action that what comes through to us is no more than another theory of human existence rather than a lively representation of it. The Chamberlaynes are a couple without any life of their own; they have no motive-power except that of illustrating as neatly as possible the *Weltanschauung* which the author imposes upon them by main force. And what is one to make of Celia Coplestone, the exemplar of the second, that is, the saintly way? What can be more hollow than this attempt to enforce the claims of transcendent goodness by releasing the claimant from her dramatic obligations, so to speak, and packing her off to Africa to perform missionary work and die the death of a Christian martyr? It is too easy, too pat. The portrayal of goodness is among the most difficult tasks that any writer can undertake. Dostoevsky said many incisive things about the problem of portraying "a positively good man" in literature, and surely he would have failed utterly if in *The Idiot* he had removed Myshkin from the net of human relationships in which he becomes involved in order to transport him to some other realm, conveniently free from the pressure of such demonic beings as Rogozhin and Nastasya Filipovna, where he could perform the deeds traditionally associated in devotional writings with the Christian character assigned to him by the author. To substantiate Celia's choice of the "second way" by immersing her in the experience of modern London is one thing; to send her off to Africa to be crucified is something else again. It is religious melodrama of an appallingly conventional sort. For in the context of Eliot's play, Africa is not a real place but the domain of abstraction pure and simple. And there are other things in the play, such as the psychiatric masquerade of the clerical Sir Harcourt-Reilly, which are equally bad. Nor does it help us to appreciate the play any better when Eliot now tells us that its point of departure is the *Alcestis* of Euripedes. Only the cult-ridden exegetes will take seriously the intellectual "conceit" of treating "one-eyed" Reilly as the mythic offspring of Heracles and identifying Lavinia, the woman whom no one can love, with the lost and recovered wife of Admetus. Neither by way of contrast nor similarity is this mythic correlation very interesting or revealing.

We are fortunate to have Eliot's account of his self-education as a playwright. It is a scrupulous account, convincing us of the positive nature of his effort to restore poetic drama. The effort is its own justification even if at times the result strikes one as wide of the mark.

1951

HEMINGWAY IN THE EARLY 1950s

T HE FIRST THING to be remarked about *Across the River and into the Trees* is that it is so egregiously bad as to render all comment on it positively embarrassing to anyone who esteems Hemingway as one of the more considerable prose-artists of our time and as the author of some of the finest short stories in the language. Hence the disappointment induced by this latest work of his, a work manifestly composed in a state of distemper, if not actual demoralization.

This novel reads like a parody by the author of his own manner — a parody so biting that it virtually destroys the mixed social and literary legend of Hemingway that has now endured for nearly three decades. For it can be said that not since the days of Dickens and later of Mark Twain has a writer of fiction in English succeeded in beguiling and captivating his readers to the extent that Hemingway did; and his success had a quality of ease and naturalness that was essentially exhilarating. In this latest book, however, the legend suffers irremediable damage. Here he really goes too far in the exploitation of it, indulging himself in blatant self-pity and equally blatant conceit, with the result that certain faults of personality, and the moral and intellectual immaturity which he was never able to overcome but which heretofore, in the greater part of his creative work, he managed to sublimate with genuine artistry, now come through as ruling elements, forcing the reader to react to Hemingway the man rather than to Hemingway the artist. And the man in Hemingway — in his literary appearances at any rate — has nearly always struck one as the parasitical double of the artist in him.

This cleavage between man and artist was long ago perceived by his more acute critics. Thus Edmund Wilson observed that "something frightful seems to happen to Hemingway as soon as he begins to write in his own person. In his fiction, the conflicting elements of his personality, the emotional situations that obsess him, are externalized and objectified; and the result is an art which is severe, intense, and deeply serious. But as soon as he talks in his own person he seems to lose all his capacity for self-criticism and is likely to become fatuous or maudlin." Now though this new narrative is written not in the first person but in the fictional third person, still it is precisely the element of the fatuous and the maudlin that predominates in it. The explanation for that lies, I think, in the insecure division between man and artist in Hemingway. The strain of sustaining it has been obviously getting him down and the artist has been gradually giving way to the man.

That this was the case was already becoming apparent in sections of *To Have and Have Not,* a poor novel on the whole, whose protagonist, Harry Morgan, was presented, in a manner unmistakably and disagreeably subjective, as a kind of totem of sexual virility. The infantile nature of the fantasy was plain and so was the sub-literary effect. Then one came upon the same sort of thing in parts of *For Whom the Bell Tolls,* particularly in the parts celebrating the love-making of Robert Jordan and Maria; and in *Across the River and into the Trees* the personal brag and splutter is even more jarring, for here the artist appears to have been entirely displaced by the man. In fact there is hardly any aesthetic distance between the author and Colonel Richard Cantwell, the hero of the novel. They have so much in common, in their private history and war experience no less than in their opinions, tastes, attitudes, and prejudices, that there is no telling them apart. Thus the author intrudes everywhere, violating the most elementary specifications making for verisimilitude in a work of fiction. For example, why is this colonel of the regular U.S. Army, who on the face of it is no great shakes as a worldly character, treated in the luxurious Venice hotels and bars with the minute deference usually reserved for the celebrities of international café society? As for the obsessive consumption of food and liquor, especially liquor, and the pride taken in the knowledge and selection of them, that certainly belongs to the more recent versions of the Hemingway legend; but it is wholly unconvincing as an integral part of the characterization of an army officer of the type of Colonel Cantwell. Though these may be small details they point to an identification of author and hero disruptive of the primary and indispensable aesthetic illusion.

The time span of the story is three days, the scene is Venice and the Adriatic countryside, and the action consists of a duck shoot, which is far and away the best bit in the book, and, for the rest, of prolonged love passages between the Colonel and his girl, the nineteen-year-old Countess Renata, who is not a recognizable human being at all but a narcissistically constructed love-object. She is even less credible than Maria of the Spanish novel. Both belong to the tradition of adoring and submissive Hemingway girls, a type that has been getting more and more adoring and submissive as the years pass. Renata, the latest incarnation, is surely the most unreal of the lot, wholly the product of an adolescent reverie of irresistible mastery and perfection of experience in love. The ritualistic love-talk between the Colonel and this girl is of an indescribable tediousness, and the way in which he introduces his war memories into the talk is structurally so artificial as to deprive the recalled experience of the authority it implicitly lays claim to. The war scenes evoked in this book come off very badly in comparison with the actual representation of war in *A Farewell to Arms* and *For Whom the Bell Tolls*. What is missing here is "the real thing, the sequence of motion and fact which made the emotion," as Hemingway once put it with the precision of a conscientious artist speaking of his craft.

The stated themes of love and death are unrealized in this novel. The Colonel dies of heart disease as the action ends, but we are prepared for his death only factually, not imaginatively. It is an occurrence, nothing more, devoid of expressive implications, since the story turns on no significant principle of honor or valor or compassion such as invested some of Hemingway's earlier narratives

with value and meaning. This could not but happen once the author
became involved with his hero in exactly the wrong way, shifting
from the role of creator to that of devotee pure and simple. He is
unaware, or only dimly aware, of his hero's vanity and brutality and
of the ugly competitiveness exhibited in his relations to other human
beings. There can be no evaluation of character or behavior in such
a context, and no intelligible meaning to the action.

It is true, of course, that Hemingway has always been more closely
involved with his hero than most novelists. The relation in which
he stood to him, however, was not that of literal and helpless identification but that of the ego to the ego-ideal. Seeking to "find himself" in this leading character, he endowed him with all the qualities
he considered admirable; and the world into which he turned him
loose to do or die, though real enough, was nonetheless specially
selected and ordered so as to provide him with the conditions he
needed for self-fulfillment. These were conditions of relative freedom from normal circumstances and routine compulsions, for it is
only within the special ambience of combat and virile sports that he
performed his part, discovering the fate that awaited him. It seems
to me that a good many qualities of Hemingway's prose are accounted for by this disengagement of his hero and his typical situation from the thick coils of environment, from its confusion of objects and facts. It certainly helped Hemingway to form a style of
unusual lightness and freshness, but it did not make him a novelist
of the first rank.

There is a certain kind of freedom which the greater novelists can
neither afford nor care to solicit. Still, the fact that the binding
agent of Hemingway's work was the personality of the hero, who
alone held sway and in whom all the compositional elements were
merged, made for a unity and concreteness of effect matched by
very few of his contemporaries. But within this creative process
there always lurked the danger of a possible merger between ego
and ego-ideal that would disrupt the delicate balance allowing the
author to live through his leading character imaginatively while
standing apart from him as a man. That this balance has been lost
is now evident. Colonel Cantwell is not Hemingway's ego-ideal,
like Jake Barnes and Lieutenant Henry: he is the ego-ideal taken
as achieved and absorbed into the ego of Hemingway, who is thus

turned into his own complete ego-ideal. It is greatly to be hoped
that in his future work the man recedes as the artist regains control.

1950

Hemingway's new story happily demonstrates his recovery from
the distemper that so plainly marked his last novel, *Across the River
and into the Trees*. In *The Old Man and the Sea* the artist in him
appears to have recouped some of his losses, curbing the over-
assertive ego so easily disposed to fall into a kind of morbid irritabil-
ity of self-love mixed with self-pity. It is to be hoped that the
recovery is more than temporary.

But free as this latest work is of the faults of the preceding one,
it is still by no means the masterpiece which the nationwide publicity set off by its publication in *Life* magazine has made it out
to be. Publicity is the reward as well as the nemesis of celebrities,
but it has nothing in common with judgment. Though the merit of
this new story is incontestable, so are its limitations. I do not believe
that it will eventually be placed among Hemingway's major writings.

Moreover, it is in no sense a novel, as the publishers would have
us believe. At its core it is actually little more than a fishing anec-
dote, though one invested with a heroic appeal by the writer's art,
which here again confirms its natural affinity with the theme of combat and virile sports. This art is at its best in the supple and exact
rendering of the sensory detail called for by its chosen theme; and
in telling of the old fisherman's ordeal on the open sea — of his
strenuous encounter with a giant marlin, the capture of him after a
two-day struggle, and the loss of the carcass to the sharks in the end
— Hemingway makes the most of his gifts, turning to good account
the values of courage and endurance and discipline in action on
which his ethic as an artist depends.

The premise of the story — its moral premise at any rate — is the
purity and goodness and bravery of Santiago, the Cuban fisherman.
And given Hemingway's habitual attitude of toughness coupled
with sentimentality, one can easily make out the chief threat to the
integrity of the writing; and it is in fact to the circumvention of
sentimentality that the story owes its success. The two scenes (in
which the boy displays his adoration of Santiago) that are not quite

exempt from the charge of sentimentality are but indirectly related to the action. They form a lyrical prelude and postlude to the action, which is presented in fictional terms that are hard and clear. And it is saved from false sentiment by Hemingway's wonderful feeling for the sea and its creatures — a feeling that he is able to objectify with as much care and devotion as he lavishes on the old man. This creates the rare effect of our perceiving the old man and the fish he catches as if they existed, like a savage and his totem, within the same psychic continuum. No wonder that at the height of his battle with the fish Santiago exclaims: "You are killing me, fish . . . But you have a right to. Never have I seen a greater, or more beautiful, or a calmer or more noble thing than you, brother. Come on and kill me. I do not care who kills who."

When all this has been said, however, one is still left with the impression that the creative appeal of this narrative is forceful yet restricted, its quality of emotion genuine but so elemental in its totality as to exact nothing from us beyond instant assent. It exhibits the credentials of the authentic, but in itself it promises very little by way of an advance beyond the positions already won in the earlier phases of Hemingway's career. To be sure, if one is to judge by what some of the reviewers have been saying and by the talk heard among literary people, the meaning of *The Old Man and the Sea* is to be sought in its deep symbolism. It may be that the symbolism is really there, though I for one have been unable to locate it. I suspect that here again the characteristic attempt of the present literary period is being made to overcome the reality of the felt experience of art by converting it to some moral or spiritual platitude. It goes without saying that the platitude is invariably sublimated through the newly modish terms of myth and symbolism. As Lionel Trilling reported in a recent essay, students have now acquired "a trick of speaking of money in Dostoevsky's novels as 'symbolic,' as if no one ever needed, or spent, or gambled, or squandered the stuff — and as if to think of it as an actuality were subliterary." Perhaps this latter-day tendency accounts for the inflationary readings that Hemingway's story has received, readings that typically stress some kind of schematism of spirit at the expense of the action so lucidly represented in its pages. Hemingway's big marlin is no Moby Dick, and his fisherman is not Captain Ahab nor was meant to be. It is enough praise to say that their existence is real, and that their encounter is described in a language at once relaxed and disciplined which is a source of pleasure. In art, as Wallace Stevens once put it, "Description is revelation. It is not / The thing described, nor false facsimile." And I would suggest to the ingenious interpreters that they look to the denotations of a work of literature before taking off into the empyrean of pure connotation.

1952

ART AND THE HISTORICAL
IMAGINATION

ARNOLD HAUSER's *Social History of Art* is concerned with literary as much as with pictorial art. Its insights into the creative process are provocative and its ideas of a more general nature are brilliantly developed. It is a work remarkable above all for its intellectual energy.

Remarkable, too, is the fact that the method deployed in it is basically that of Marxism, though not of the type we have become accustomed to and against which we have so strongly reacted in the recent past. Purged of crudities and stultifying obligations to a party line, what Mr. Hauser's Marxist bias really comes to is a kind of radical historicism which has nothing in common with the shifty and specious ideology manipulated by the culture-commissars. Yet even so Mr. Hauser's merit as critic and historian will doubtless be excessively resisted among us. The current dogma has it that radicalism, in all the diversity of its possible revisions, combinations, and permutations, is played out for good and nothing more can be said for it. This dogma I take to be a falsification committed by the *Zeitgeist*, essentially as groundless as the dogma prevailing in the thirties that assigned to radicalism a monopoly of critical thought. The abrupt swings of consciousness from one demoralizing extreme to the other that we have experienced of late are typically of our time and belong to its intellectual pathology.

As for Mr. Hauser's political attitude, to judge by the skittishness of his references to the censorship of the arts in the Soviet empire, he is far from prepared to believe the worst. Still, it would ill become us to emulate the party-line strategy of examining books strictly in terms of their authors' political opinions of the moment rather than in the light of their stated intention and inherent value. What counts for us, chiefly, is the writer's handling of his subject and the return it yields for our mental loss or gain — and Mr. Hauser's subject is not the present world situation but the social and historical background of the arts beginning with the magical drawings of the Old Stone Age (pp. 23ff) and ending with the emergence of the film as a powerful new medium and the impact of the democratization of culture in the twentieth century (p. 958).

Since the vastness of Mr. Hauser's undertaking has imposed a rigorous selectivity, our consideration of it must of necessity also be highly selective. One can hope to discuss only some aspects of the work he has produced. The particulars of his approach to painting I shall leave to the critics in the field, making what I can of his interpretation of literary figures and movements, his general method and a few of the leading ideas he has put to use in integrating his material.

For Mr. Hauser the key word is "history" not because he is literally engaged in writing a history of art but rather because in his view the modern conception of history is the heuristic principle *par excellence*. This puts him into the camp of the historicists, to be sure, but scarcely into the camp of the academic practitioners of the "historical method." Our "new critics" have by now nearly succeeded in discrediting that method, and one should go along with them insofar as their motive is to devise a more adequate mode of teaching literature and writing about it. At the same time, however, one is appalled by the intellectual naiveté manifest in their failure to distinguish between creative historical insight (as you find it in such diverse thinkers as Herder, Goethe, Marx, Nietzsche, and Toynbee, or, for that matter, in T. S. Eliot at his empirical best or in a fine scholar-critic like Erich Auerbach) and the "historical method" of the old-time professors, whose laborious tracing of sources and mechanical accumulation of historical facts for their own sake is at its best merely a form of documentation, no matter how useful, and at its worst a form of antiquarianism. If the "purpose of historical research is to understand the present," as Mr. Hauser maintains, then the academic researchers in literature evade that task by retreating into the sheer facticity of the past. The "new critics" on the other hand, converge on the literary text, which, after all, regardless of the age it was composed in, is in a sense a piece of irreducible presentness. Their attachment to the text is what is appealing about the "new critics"; what is unappealing is their neglect of context. Only in the medium of historical time is that context to be apprehended; and there is a dialectical relation between text and context, which, if ignored in principle, must eventually lead to the impoverishment of the critical faculty and a devitalized sense of literary art. Thus in the long run the neglect of context is paid for by the increasing misuse and misreading of the text itself. For the historicity of a text is inextricably involved in its nature and function, just as it is involved in the nature and function of language, law, religion, political institutions, etc. Nor is the historicity of a text to be equated with any given series of historical facts. The historical fact is as such no more than a neutral datum, whereas historicity is a value created by the power of the historical imagination.

The historical sense is at once an analytic instrument and a tonic resource of the modern sensibility. To confuse it with conventional historical studies is an elementary blunder. It has led the "new critics," particularly the men of the younger academic generation, who appear to be bitten by the spirit of faction and the conceit of up-to-dateness in method, to reject the historical appeciation of literary art, replacing it with a narrow textual-formalistic approach which cannot account for change and movement on literature and which systematically eliminates ideas from criticism; and without ideas it is impossible to connect the literary interest with other interests. Nor is an inflated and abstruse terminology a substitute for ideas. It is mainly for the lack of such connective ideas — which alone enable us to assimilate literature to the historical world at large whence it comes and whither it longs to return — that the "new criticism" has lately exposed itself to the charge of sectarianism and downright tediousness. The complaint is justified, I think, though it scarcely applies to such older critics as Tate, Ransom, and Blackmur, whose virtues and faults are primarily their own; they are intractably their own men, so marked in their individual character and high critical intelligence as not to fit neatly into any school. It is the epigone-like disciples, coming upon the scene too late to have absorbed the exhilarating literary spirit of the twenties, who really make up the school of the "new criticism." And what, at bottom, is that criticism, considered not in the sense of Ransom's book of that title but in the sense of its actual practice during the past decade? It is essentially an amalgam of diluted formalism and diluted traditionalism (Eliot's version of it). I call it an amalgam because its two elements are artificially combined, in a forced congruity. The diluting results from the domestication habitually enforced by the academy.

Where Mr. Hauser comes in after this digression is that his book, like Erich Auerbach's *Mimesis,* so patently offers us at least one instructive alternative to critical sectarianism. The stimulative effect can be gauged by comparing Mr. Hauser's passages on such writers as Balzac and Flaubert with the treatment of them in *The Novel in France,* a recent work by Mr. Martin Turnell, who might be said to belong to the British wing of the "new criticism." Mr. Turnell, attempting to run down both Balzac and Flaubert, judges the former to be a writer of sloppy prose with an immature outlook on life and the latter as perhaps even more immature, a cynic in fact, whose fiction represents "an attack on human nature." To my mind, this attempted revision of the canon of the French novel falls wide of the mark. It draws no support from the historical sensibility. This is not to say that Mr. Turnell is unaware of the factual-historical background of the novelists he has set out to depose. It is rather that the historical dimension of their art escapes him. Hence he is forced back into a tight moralism of judgment; also to disregard the variability of the novelistic gift, which is not an abstract potential but is actualized on the historical plane and is to be perceived on no other plane. Balzac is by now so far removed from us that a response to the historicity of his work is essential to our enjoyment of it. This is less true of Flaubert, who is in a sense still our contemporary; but the contemporaneous too is badly understood when the historical sense is weakly operative.

Mr. Turnell, for example, attributes the faults he discerns in Flaubert to his personal manias. For my part, I find unacceptable this approach to a writer of Flaubert's stature and immensely symbolic significance in modern letters. Mr. Hauser sees quite as clearly as Mr. Turnell the inhumanity of Flaubert's aesthetic fanaticism and his lack of a direct relationship to life. But he also sees something else, something more ambiguous and touching and inevitable: the torment of an artist in whom romanticism had turned so self-conscious and problematical that it compelled him to outrage his own instincts and inclinations, thus enacting a sacrificial role. Certain things had become historically inescapable in Flaubert's time and it is exactly because he chose to take the burden of them upon himself that he is so authentic, so formidable even in his failures. Is his struggle for the *mot juste* merely a personal aberration? It is a sign, Mr. Hauser notes, of the gulf that had opened up in the artistic career between "the 'possession' of life and the 'expression' of it." One thinks of Henry James, whose stylistic distillations of the later period are likewise implicated in this division. James, of course, was not forced to struggle for the *mot juste*. It came to him with an ease as astonishing as it is suspect. For James, unlike the disconsolate Frenchman, finally succeeded only too well in repressing within himself the human hunger for immediacy and spontaneity. His rules of art, i.e., his vaunted aesthetic of the novel, is intrinsically an effort to vindicate the consequent estrangement and to derive from it a discipline of creative work. His triumph was that he achieved the discipline and that even in his state of estrangement he continued to pay homage to the "possession" of life.

Mr. Hauser's long passage on Flaubert is built along the lines of synoptic characterization, the classic resource of criticism. It is a masterful critical-historical *récit*, as are the passages of Rousseau, Richardson, Stendhal, Balzac, Dostoevsky, and Tolstoy. Of *Madame Bovary* he writes:

Flaubert's statement, "*Madame Bovary, c'est moi*," is true in a double sense. He must often have had the feeling that not merely the roman-

ticism of his youth but also his criticism of romanticism . . . was a life-
fantasy. *Madame Bovary* owes its artistic veracity and opportuneness
to the intensity with which he experienced the problem of this life-
fantasy, the crises of self-deception and the falsification of his own personality. When the meaning of romanticism became problematical, the
whole questionableness of modern man was revealed — his escape
from the present, his constant desire to be somewhere different from
where he has to be . . . because he is afraid of the proximity and responsibility for the present. The analysis of romanticism led to the
diagnosis of the disease of the whole century, to the recognition of the
neurosis, the victims of which are incapable of giving an account of
themselves, and would always prefer to be inside other people's skins,
not seeing themselves as they really are, but as they would like to be.
In this self-deception and falsification of life . . . Flaubert seizes hold
of the essence of the modern subjectivism that distorts everything with
which it comes in contact. The feeling that we possess only a deformed
version of reality and that we are imprisoned in the subjective forms
of our thinking is first given full artistic expression in *Madame Bovary*
. . . The transformation of reality by the human consciousness, already
pointed out by Kant, acquired in the course of the nineteenth century
the character of an alternately more or less conscious and unconscious
illusion, and called forth attempts to explain and unmask it, such as historical materialism and psychoanalysis. With his interpretation of romanticism, Flaubert is one of the great revealers and unmaskers of the
century, and, therefore, one of the founders of the modern, reflexive
outlook on life.

L'Éducation sentimentale Mr. Hauser analyzes as a novel of
which the true hero is time. Time serves in it in a double role, both
as "the element which conditions and gives life to the characters"
and as the principle by which "they are worn out, destroyed and
devoured." It was romanticism which discovered creative, seminal
time, while in the reaction against romanticism time was discovered
to be a corrupting element, undermining and draining man's life.
Thus "this gradual, imperceptible, irresistible pining away, the silent
undermining of life, which does not even produce the startling bang
of the great, imposing catastrophe, is the experience around which
the *Éducation sentimentale* and practically the whole modern novel
revolves" — an experience nontragic and undramatic and therefore
appropriately cast in the narrative mode. Here we have a key to the

dominant position of the novel in the modern age. It is the medium which lends itself more easily than the play or the poem to the representation of life in its mechanized, commonplace, and frustrating aspects, and of time as a destructive force. The novel develops its formal principle from this idea of the corrosive effects of time, just as tragedy derives "the basis of its form from the idea of the timeless fate which destroys man with one fell blow. And as fate possesses a superhuman greatness and a metaphysical power in tragedy, so time attains an inordinate, almost mythical dimension in the novel."

This analysis of the time-experience of the present age is developed in the last chapter with greater complexity and absorption in detail. Time has for contemporary man a quality of immediateness such as it could never have had in the past. Modern technics have made him conscious of "the contiguity, the interconnections and dovetailing of things and processses," with the result that he has become fascinated by "simultaneity" which is a kind of universalism of the temporal dimension. Not only the cinema, the medium most naturally adapted to produce effects of "simultaneity," but modern art as a whole reaches out for this same magical illusionism of time, borrowing from the cinema whatever it can. Mr. Hauser sees this Bergsonian *simultanéité des états d'âmes* as the basic experience of painting, for instance, connecting its multiform tendencies, the futurism of the Italians with the expressionism of Chagall, the cubism of Picasso with the surrealism of Chirico, Ernst, and Dali. The film Mr. Hauser evaluates as a form that accommodates itself above all to the analysis of time, capable of representing visually those processes which previously only music could express. But the film is still an empty form, whose "real life has not yet arrived." In the meantime the novel has appropriated some of its techniques. Thus "the discontinuity of the plot and the scenic development, the sudden emersion of the thoughts and moods, the relativity and the inconsistency of the time-standards, are what remind us in the works of Proust and Joyce, Dos Passos and Virginia Woolf of the cutting, dissolves and interpolations of the film, and it is simply film-magic when Proust brings two incidents, which may lie thirty years before, as closely together as if there were only two hours between them." Joyce is even more radical in his effort to free time of its chronological articulation; and one may add the poetry of Pound and Eliot as further examples. But what is the meaning of this intermingling of past and present across the boundaries of space and time? "Simultaneity" is hardly an end in itself. In heightening our sense of time it also induces in us the feeling that all our experiences occur at one and the same time. Thus the ultimate effect is that of the negation of time — a negation implying an effort for the recovery of that inwardness for which we long in the midst of our chaotic modernity.

Mr. Hauser evaluates writers and painters almost entirely by indirection, through a phenomenological description and analysis of the worlds they wrested from chaos. He does not share the predilection of contemporary Anglo-American criticism for the outright "ranking" of artists in a strictly graded hierarchy of achievement. I have sometimes wondered whether this passion for "ranking," for establishing with an almost obsessive conscientiousness the exact degree of one writer's alleged superiority to another and his precise place in the hierarchy, does not actually mask an inner uncertainty and even skepticism as to the value of art altogether? A skepticism so threatening would naturally seek compensation in ideas and procedures of a diametrically opposite order, such as the fetishism of art and the urge to control the imaginative process by setting up fixed and conclusive standards that are good for all time and thus serve as a barrier to the nihilism of the age, which affects everything and everybody, including the hierophants of art and culture. Mr. Hauser's historicism enables him to resist the temptation to idolize the art-object and to overestimate its saving power. But his approach is not immune to the relativization of value inherent in historicism. The peril is real, and his endeavor is to save himself by plunging into the reality of history as into a restorative medium. While not going so far as Ortega y Gasset, who has put forth the claim that man has no nature but only a history, nevertheless his practice throughout is to grasp all ideas and ideals by disclosing their historical import, which thus becomes the main guaranty of their actuality.

The expository mode he adopts is that of the polyphonic organization of historical themes, enormously varied in their bearing and significance, dealt with not summarily but with extraordinary informedness and wide-ranging scholarship, taking in all major art-movements and coming to rest in the extended consideration of single figures who might be said to sum up their time or to initiate the transition to a new epoch. And at all points he is concerned with determining the public status of the artist in any given period, the social value attached to the phenomenon of art, the meaning of the idea of artistic freedom and autonomy, and the evolution of the concept of genius.

This latter concept is so familiar to us that we tend to project it backward into past ages, ascribing a permanence to it which it wholly lacks, since it is thoroughly imbued with historical motives. It was foreign to the Middle Ages, whose superpersonal, objective, and authoritarian culture allowed for no strong sense of intellectual property and individual originality. The basic change occurs in the Renaissance, when famous masters like Michelangelo, Raphael, and Titian begin to outshine their patrons, becoming great lords themselves. Mr. Hauser perceives in Michelangelo "the first example of the modern, lonely, demoniacally impelled artist . . . who feels a deep sense of responsibility toward his gifts and sees a higher and super-human power in his own artistic genius." Genius, both as cult and idea, is a fundamentally new element in the valuation of art; implicit in it is the notion that "the work of art is the creation of an autocratic personality, that this personality transcends tradition, theory and rules, even the work itself, being richer and deeper than the work and impossible to express adequately within any objective form." From this notion it is but a step — though the Renaissance never made this step — to the notion of the misunderstood genius and the appeal to posterity against the verdict of the contemporary world. The idea of the autonomy of art parallels the idea of genius, for it gives expression in an objective manner, that is from the standpoint of the work, to what is expressed subjectively, from the standpoint of the artist, in his claim to be a uniquely creative person. But there is far more content than that in the idea of the autonomy of art. Indeed, I am conscious of simplifying Mr. Hauser's exploration of this and other themes, which take him into shifts and modulations of meaning that depend on elaborate excursions into social and economic history. His method enforces the constant recourse to the means of analysis furnished by sociology and psychology, and the use of such means are indispensable to the fulfillment of his purpose. There are certain problems and attitudes in art, not open to the direct "intrinsic" approach, which become accessible through the detour of the approach from without. An instance of this sort of problem is aestheticism, more specifically the attitude of *l'art pour l'art*, which Mr. Hauser interprets as being "partly the expression of the division of labor which advances hand in hand with industrialization, and partly the bulwark of art against the danger of being swallowed up by industrialized and mechanized life. It signifies, on the one hand, the rationalization, disenchantment and contraction of art, but simultaneously the attempt to preserve its individual quality and spontaneity, in spite of the universal mechanization of life."

Mr. Hauser is quite aware of the limitations of his method. He knows very well that artistic quality cannot be explained sociologically, nor does he offer such explanations. And time and again he asserts that artistic progress — in the sense of movement, change, and innovation — is frequently compatible with political conservatism, that not only is there no direct relation between progressiveness in art and conservatism in politics but that they are indeed "incommensurable in the two spheres." What is important is the artist's sincerity and fidelity to his vision of life, which sufficiently account for his enlightening influence on his age. There is, however, a complication in the idea of "compatibility," as exemplified in the case of novelists like Balzac and Dostoevsky. Not a few works of art display an internal antagonism between their material and spiritual qualities or an antithesis between their latent and manifest content: hence the contradiction which is sometimes to be observed between a writer's proclaimed ideology and the inner meaning of his imaginative creations. For instance, the first generation of French romantic writers were to begin with legitimists and clericalists while at the same time assaulting with might and main the conservative classical tradition in literature, which was then defended mainly by the liberals; a more modern instance are certain poets of traditionalist bias in whom a genuine aesthetic liberalism and openness toward the future go hand in hand with historical reaction. Neither in art nor in life is there a preestablished harmony guaranteeing the even and unified development of all the elements that combine to form objects of value. Advance in one sphere is often paid for by regression in another.

The literature of the modern period is particularly exposed, I would say, to inner antagonisms and contradictions. Critics who are perturbed by these contradictions, preferring the writers they deal with to be of one mind, are prone to expend much ingenious cerebration in inventing unified creative personalities where none perhaps exists. They would do better to try getting at a writer's truth by fathoming the depth and intensity of the contradiction of which he is the carrier and which more often than not proves to be the wayward secret of his power over us. Fortunately, literature is not a function of criticism, no matter how methodologically refined or overbearingly intent on moral suasion. It makes its own arrangements with life, and its victories and defeats are also its own.

1952

THOMAS MANN AT EIGHTY

M ANN'S LATEST NOVELLA, *The Black Swan*, will scarcely add
anything substantial to his fame. Its theme of the fatal attraction of age to youth reminds us, though far from irresistibly, of
Death in Venice. Actually it reads like a feeble parody of that early
work of genius, with Frau Rosalie von Tümmler, a middle-aged
Düsseldorf widow, put in as a ringer for the truly formidable
Aschenbach, and with Ken Keaton, the young American, who has
nothing in common with Tadzio but sheer youthfulness, somewhat
casually enacting the role of that splendid and richly meaningful
figure. Missing are the ardors and rigors of the Venetian tale: the
closed form and classical discipline of style and craft triumphantly
containing a thoroughly modern fiction of ambiguous desire, dissolution of personality, and death conceived of both as the secretly
longed for consummation and inevitable issue of the collapse into
guilty love — the *Liebestod*, in other words, fully brought up to
date.

Moreover, in *The Black Swan* the dazzling dialectic of life and
art, providing *Death in Venice* with its ruling idea, is replaced by
the more restricted polarization of psyche and soma. These the

author, in his typically dualistic fashion, assimilates to the traditional idea of a struggle between "Nature" and the soul. So conceived, these antagonists turn out to be metaphysical essences, all the more ferocious because of their abstract dynamism, and between them they make short shrift of Rosalie's love for young Keaton. In the end the antagonist that goes by the name of Nature wins the battle by playing a peculiarly malignant trick on the poor deluded cheated woman (*Die Betrogene* in the German title) even as she proclaims her victory over her aging flesh in speeches at once passionate and magisterial. Fulsome are her praises of "great beneficent Nature" for the miracle it had wrought in her in arresting the dreaded menopause and restoring her to the status of a "functioning female." But it is exactly this dubious physiological "miracle" that marks her doom. At the point, virtually, of surrendering to her lover she has a hemorrhage and a few weeks later dies of cancer of the womb.

Thus Rosalie, like so many of Mann's protagonists, suffers a kind of *Liebestod;* and where her version of it differs from the others is that it is rendered almost entirely in psychosomatic terms. Now what must be kept in mind is that for Mann, with his penchant for irony at all costs, the psychosomatic is merely another correlate of the ambiguous, that is to say, it is emptied of all definable empirical content and invested with those sinister qualities which his dialectic of disease and disorder calls for. No wonder, then, that one cannot really say whether the rejuvenescence and sexual revitalization that Rosalie finds so gratifying as she is swamped by erotic feeling is in some mysterious way induced by the cancerous growth in her body, or whether, on the contrary, it is this revitalization which lays her open to illness, inciting the cancerous cells to do their worst. It is not Mann's intention that we learn the answer to this question. It is true, of course, that in her deathbed speech Rosalie, pious to the end, absolves Nature of all blame for her fate. These last words, however, may well be taken as spoken "in character"; it is unlikely that her understanding of what has happened coincides with that of the author. For one must allow here for his all-pervasive irony and unending delight in the problematic and equivocal.

Mann has always been a very deliberate artist. Temperamentally incapable of spontaneity, if not actually hostile to it, he succeeded in turning this very deliberateness into an imaginative resource of a high order. But in some of his recent works, and particularly in such shorter ones as this latest novella, he seems to overreach himself in deliberateness, taxing our patience with effects not so much subtle as cunning, effects ultimately discountable as the products of a contriving will. Thus one comes, in this grisly tale, upon a species of symbolism so obviously and neatly predesigned for its purpose that it generates resistance rather than assent on the part of the conscious order. What is one to make, for instance, of a piece of symbolism such as that of the dank and moldy passageway in the castle where Rosalie, confessing her love, embraces Keaton for the first time? "Ugh, it smells of death . . . I will be yours, but not in this mould . . . In your room . . . tonight." In the context it becomes altogether plain that this scene of passionate avowal has been rigged up with a décor of decay simply as a convenient means of prefiguring symbolically the disaster to come. Similarly, in an earlier chapter there is a great to-do made about Rosalie's "sensual fervor" in absorbing "whatever Nature offers to gratify our sense of smell — sweetness, aromatic bitterness, even heady and oppressive scents"; and in the very next page we are brought up short by a repellent scene, that of Rosalie and her daughter walking in the woods and coming upon a teeming little mound of putrid stuff the smell of which makes the women run. This again strikes me as artificial and arbitrary. The symbolic detail of the teeming little mound is much too starkly antithetical to the exposition of Rosalie's "sensual fervor" preceding it; it has been maneuvered rather than integrated into the narrative.

More impressive is the long interior monologue in which Rosalie discloses her state of complete abandon; and equally good are some of the dialogues she conducts with her daughter Anna. It is especially the mother's speeches that at times achieve a very fine effect, suggesting those "tirades" of classic tragedy in which analytic finesse is unaccountably though brilliantly combined with the unrestrained expression of feeling. To secure this effect Mann disregards the modern conventions of realistic dialogue. Rosalie's language has nothing in common with the breaks, pauses, falterings, and ellipses of "real" speech. It is an utterance formal yet impassioned, oratorical yet at the same time emotionally fluent. One might characterize it as a kind of "'educated" rant of a smitten middle-aged woman of culture who, with true Germanic earnestness, cannot help enlisting higher ideas in the service of her libidinal strivings.

But virtuosity of this sort cannot undo the general impression that the story is at bottom lacking in significance. It means too little for the frightfulness it contains. One would be hard put to it to say what the author had in mind in constructing his insidious plot. Are we to take it as a satire on the nature-worship to which his country-men are known to yield so readily? If so, the means are peculiarly ill adjusted to the end. Then there is the fact of Keaton's American-ism, which appears to be gratuitous in the sense of being essentially unrelated to the scene and the action. Keaton is an expatriate who runs down his own country in favor of Europe's historical opulence, but what he says and thinks is entirely unconnected with Rosalie's situation. In the last analysis what catches one's interest is not the story in its own right but the fact that it was produced by a writer close to eighty years of age; and at this point the literary concern gives way to an interest in the writer's personal psychology. I have heard Mann praised for his audacity in composing at his age the plot of this book. I prefer to describe the plot as insidious. It suggests not so much the boldness of a poet like Yeats who in late life found in "lust and rage" the spur to song but rather a sensibility seeking to discover in meaningless enormities a cure for ennui.

1954

PULLING DOWN THE SHRINE

M AXWELL GEISMAR's *Henry James and the Jacobites* is an all-
out assault on Henry James, his person and his work. For
Mr. Geismar it is not a matter simply of cutting the James cult down
to size — an operation for which there is surely some felt need
for some time now. No, Mr. Geismar is out for blood. Nothing else
will do but the total annihilation of James, the dignity of the man no
less than the integrity of his art.

James is charged here with every sin in the calendar: from being
a practitioner of "literary deceit" and a self deluded expatriate snob
for whom America was "death," to rabid racist prejudice and "social
shame" even so far as his own family is concerned. His work, consisting of an "endless series of puzzles to fill up the empty box of
his art and his life," shows the growth of "a frustrated, devouring
and sealed-off egotism." Despising poor people and valuing "wealth
as the highest human good," he was primarily "the novelist of our
primitive finance-capitalism in its first flowering of titans and robber
barons." Moreover, he invariably linked sexuality with "sin and
crime," and in his later years he was no less than obsessed by sex —
"rather like a prurient old maid when he was not playing the role

of the infantile voyeur. . . ." A chapter entitled *The Psychology of the Keyhole* ends with what its author must have thought of as a killing sentence, a real clincher: "But let us note in passing that Henry James had a dirty mind." Such is the manner in which Mr. Geismar interprets anew the Lesson of the Master. Nor does he do so "in passing." Far from it; the impeachment of indecency, sexual as well as social, is what he positively luxuriates in throughout the book.

As for the major novels of the Jamesian canon, Mr. Geismar characterizes *The Ambassadors* as "perhaps the silliest novel to be taken seriously in world literature"; he is harsh on *The Golden Bowl* — from the standpoint of social morality he finds it absolutely vicious; and *The Wings of the Dove* "concerns itself with human daydreams of a very special order." And so it goes. Hardly any Jamesian fiction, short or long, of the early, middle, or late period, is spared Mr. Geismar's invective. In sum, his thesis is quite simply that James is, if not some kind of literary malefactor, then surely an impostor. Never in the history of American criticism (or even in what passes for it) has an American writer of stature been subjected, so far as I know, to such ruthless abuse.

It seems to me that nearly all that Mr. Geismar has to say about James is politically motivated. There is scarcely a literary valuation he commits himself to that will stand the test of serious analysis. He appears to have learned nothing from the debacle of the Leftist literary movement of the thirties, for like so many of his predecessors in that ill-fated movement, he shows no capacity to draw distinctions in principle between political and literary judgments of works of art. (The two types of judgment are by no means unrelated, but they are certainly not identical; the connection between is often indirect and quite elusive.) The truth is that for Mr. Geismar Henry James is not a literary artist worth examining in his own right but a socio-political symbol, pure and simple — a symbol of everything he detests in the American literary situation as it has developed in the past two decades — an epoch, as he describes it, of "conformity and sterility . . . of the 'peace' which went under the name of the Cold War." In this perspective James is thus seen as a cultural agent "for changing and distorting, or for eliminating the realities of world history which a large sector of the American intellectuals no longer wished to understand and deal with." This, I think, is the real source of Mr. Geismar's rage. It is like the "sacred rage" of Waymarsh that James has so much fun with in *The Ambassadors,* and it is just as ludicrous.

Ideological and political allegiances, whether of the Left or Right, have little relevance to the critical question of James's achievement as a man of letters. As long ago as 1918 the late Joseph Warren Beach observed in an early appreciative study of James that he is basically "a gentleman of cultivated and conservative, not to say, reactionary instinct." No perceptive critic of James has ever denied this obvious fact, without taking it as anything but a descriptive statement rather than as an evaluation of his work. The fuss that Mr. Geismar kicks up precisely about this obvious fact is so much waste motion. For James was not interested in "ideas" in the usual sense of the term; only some very minor aspects of his fiction relate in any significant sense to ideological issues. He is not all of a piece, but the creative contradictions in him differ radically from those you find in the greater European novelists. Of course, besides intrinsic literary causes, there are certain sociological factors involved in the rise of James to supreme eminence in our contemporary literary culture, just as there are other sociological factors involved in the long neglect he suffered previously. (In his *Main Currents of American Thought* V. I. Parrington dismissed James in three pages while devoting eleven pages, in the main laudatory, to James Branch Cabell. According to Mr. Geismar, James has been "used to mislead at least two generations of college and university students." In my opinion, the widespread influence of a text as popular as that of Parrington on earlier generations of students was far more deplorable.) But such sociological factors, while worth taking into account whether favorable or unfavorable to James, are in the long run quite external to the substance of his narrative art. From this point of view Mr. Geismar strikes me as not at all functioning in this book as a literary critic properly speaking, but as a left-wing sociologist *manqué.* And his is the kind of sociology applied to literature that in the thirties we used to call "vulgar Marxism."

But even worse than the sociologism is the irresponsible, amateur and punitive Freudianism which Mr. Geismar employs so copiously in his attempt to discredit James. It is quite incomprehensible to me how a literary critic can permit himself the use of the Freudian approach to creative writers not as a means of understanding them but chiefly in order to expose and punish them. But this is exactly what Mr. Geismar does when he consistently reduces James's fiction to real or imaginary psychoneurotic strains in him. You would not know, reading Mr. Geismar on James's Oedipal feelings, that the Oedipus complex is conceived of by Freud as a universal human condition, not as a personal fault. To apply the Freudian method with punitive intent is a sheer corruption of it; there is hardly a major novelist, Dickens, Dostoevsky, Proust, or whoever, who could not be beat down in this way, precisely as Mr. Geismar tries to beat down James. Thus in his analysis of "The Turn of the Screw" he declares that "James was not only 'identified' with the nameless governess; he *was* the governess, in the sense that her snooping, prurient, obsessive sexual curiosity was his own." And "The Aspern Papers," that perfectly realized, shapely *nouvelle*, is not what it purports to be about: no, the "primary human basis of the story is, of course, a barely infantile-sexual 'curiosity' and guilt." Such statements are, to my mind, no more than pure willful assertion, unvalidated by evidence that any sound Freudian investigator would accept.

James "identifies" with the governess in "The Turn of the Screw" no more and no less than most novelists identify with their characters. Nor has it been textually proven, by Mr. Geismar or others, that her relationship to the haunted children in her charge is necessarily that of "prurient" sexual curiosity. To be sure, there is a strong morbid sexual element in the story, but imaginatively that is entirely to its advantage rather than the opposite. If Mr. Geismar wants sexuality in fiction without morbidity, then he would be well advised to turn his back on modern literature altogether. As for his "Freudian" interpretation of "The Aspern Papers," I find it strictly without meaning. He may be writing in some dim speculative way about James the man, but he is certainly not saying anything pertinent about "The Aspern Papers." In James, as in many writers, there are no doubt neurotic derivations and patterns to be discovered. For the intelligent reader, however, their presence in literature can never be a pretext for depreciating it. The creative act is to be judged by its outcome as art, not by the private occasions, embarrassing or not, that might have given rise to it.

Naturally, Mr. Geismar does all he can to impugn the judgment of the "Jacobite critics," as he calls them — that "bewitched, bemused and Circe-ish circle"; and in their case, too, his penchant for gratuitous psychologizing gets the better of him. Among those attacked are Edmund Wilson (accused of "swallowing whole the Jamesian confectionery"), Lionel Trilling, F. O. Matthiessen, R. P. Blackmur, F. W. Dupee, Leon Edel, W. H. Auden, Stephen Spender, Morton Zabel, and the present writer. His quotations from the "Jacobites" are for the most part abbreviated in a tendentious manner, if not downright inaccurate and misleading. Nor, if I may speak of myself for a moment, does he bother, in his determination to convict me of cultism at all costs, to quote an observation I made as far back as 1948 (in the foreword to my book *Image and Idea*) that "the apotheosis of James is not quite what is wanted. For it appears that the long-standing prejudice against him is now giving way to an uncritical adulation equally retarding to a sound appraisal of his achievement." So is Edmund Wilson presented as a cultist, when the fact is that in his 1948 appendix to his famous essay "The Ambiguity of Henry James," he spoke up with extreme sarcasm about the cultists, even while reaffirming his conviction that we do well to be proud of James. "Alone among our novelists of the past," he wrote, "Henry James managed to master his art and to practice it on an impressive scale, to stand up to popular pressures so as not to break down or peter out, and to build up what the French call an *oeuvre*."

Though not a figure of the first magnitude in the literature of the world, James is a great writer nevertheless — if not on an international scale, then purely on a national one.

1963

TWO SUBVERSIVE RUSSIANS

One Day in the Life of Ivan Denisovich (translated by Max Hayward and Ronald Hingley) is a significant book, perhaps the most significant that has come out of Russia in many years. A completely authentic account of life in the forced-labor camps under Stalin, it is cast in a fictional form superbly adapted to its subject. Its narrative tone and method, relying on the selective accumulation of minute factual particulars, finely controls the powerful emotional content, never getting out of hand, never descending to rhetorical presentation or to any sort of preaching and moralizing.

The author, Alexander Solzhenitsyn, who is at present teaching physics and mathematics in a secondary school, served with distinction in the Red Army during the war but was arrested in 1945 on what is now officially admitted to be a "baseless political charge," and was sentenced to eight years' imprisonment. The experience recorded in *One Day* no doubt parallels his own, but he is not the novel's protagonist. That role, from first page to last, is reserved for the simple village workman, Ivan Denisovich Shukhov, who has no head for politics or any kind of "learned conversation." He is a wonderful creation, exhibiting certain traits that are new as well as traits deeply rooted in the Russian literary tradition. The figure in that tradition he most reminds me of is Tolstoy's Platon Karatayev. But there is also a significant difference between them. For Karatayev, standing somewhat apart from the other characters in *War and Peace*, who are portrayed with surpassing realism, is in the main a mythic figure, an abstraction of Christian goodness, while Shukhov, in no way dependent on religious doctrine or precept, is invested with a goodness that is altogether credible, altogether imbedded in the actual. He fills in every crevice of his own nature, without appeal to higher powers or utopian and ambiguous dreams of saintliness.

As all ideologies are alien to Shukhov, so none can ruin him. Neither hero nor saint, existing in an environment where the only time the prisoners are not marched out to work in the early mornings is when the thermometer goes down to forty-two degrees below zero, he yields neither to hope nor despair but depends for survival on his own largely unconscious and invulnerable humanity. Though in no way exceptional, he is the unbeatable human being whom the regime can at any time destroy but never convert nor make over in its own image, thus giving the lie to Orwell's nightmare of total demoralization in *1984*. Humble yet extremely resourceful in small ways, a man whose self-respect demands that he do his work properly and even joyfully, Shukhov has been "walking this earth for forty years. He'd lost half his teeth and was getting bald. He'd never given or taken a bribe from anybody, and he hadn't learned that trick in the camp either." He knows that the authorities twisted the law any way they wanted. "You finished a ten-year stretch and they gave you another one. Or if not, they still wouldn't let you go home . . . So you just went on living like this, with your eyes on the ground, and you had no time to think about how you got in and when you'd get out." And why was Shukhov put in a concentration camp? He had escaped from a German prisoners-of-war cage and upon returning to his own lines found himself accused of treason. Though guiltless, he was forced to give evidence against himself: "The way he figured, it was very simple. If he didn't sign, he was as good as buried. But if he did, he'd still go on living for a while. So he signed." Shukhov's fate is the essence of the Stalinist terror-system.

However, the way in which the author chiefly succeeds in his characterization of Shukhov is not by harping on his innocence or putting any kind of political gloss on his ordeal but by depicting him throughout as a person in his own right — not merely a victim and least of all a symptom but always a person, even when ill, starving, and freezing. The secondary characters, such as Alyoshka the Baptist and Tuyrin the boss of the work-squad, are portrayed with equal responsiveness to their personal qualities. Now it is precisely this newly won and truly existential personalization of vision, so long outlawed in the Communist theory and practice of literature, which surprises and impresses us most in *One Day*. As a novel it is not, in my view, the "great work of art" that some people say it is; its scale is too small for that. But it is a very fine book in which not a false note is struck. Its theme, the nature of man under extreme conditions of inhumanity, is treated unpretentiously, without despair or overt bitterness, and, above all, without the distempers and consolations of ideology. It is the same theme that Dostoevsky developed, though in a manner quite different, in his *House of the Dead*, another account of life in a Siberian prison, published almost exactly a hundred years ago. Dostoevsky, too, was a political criminal, sentenced by the Czar to penal servitude. How greatly the Russian people have suffered that their writers thus tragically echo each other across a century!

One Day first appeared in the Moscow literary monthly *Novy Mir* for November in 1962 in an edition of 95,000 copies that was at once sold out. Its publication in Russia thus clearly marks some kind of breakthrough toward freedom in Soviet writing. Thank God, the world is still unpredictable after all. No one, not even the most astute Kremlinologist among us, could possibly have foreseen that the party-hierarchs would be prevailed upon to permit the publication of a work so devastating in its implications. It's all very well to say that its subject fits in with Khrushchev's renewed campaign against Stalin. That is true only in an immediate and narrowly political sense.

The novel's meaning, in its broader aspects, is scarcely open to political manipulation. It is senseless to see its meaning serving the partisan interests of any faction in the Soviet power structure. No, the integrity of this story of an ordinary winter day, from reveille to lights out, in the life of Prisoner No. S-854 is inviolable. In the long run it cannot conceivably benefit any authoritarian elite, whether Communist or anti-Communist. The lessons it enforces — such as "How can you expect a man who's warm to understand a man who's cold?" — are of a down-to-earth simplicity that should make any ideologue of power quail. And in the one "learned conversation" in the book, overheard on the run by the protagonist, we come upon the following words in a very brief discussion of Eisenstein's famous film *Ivan The Terrible*: "The politics of it is *utterly* vile — vindication of a one-man tyranny. An insult to the memory of three generations of Russian intellectuals . . . Don't call Eisenstein a genius! Call him a toady, say he carried out orders like a dog. A genius doesn't adapt his treatment to the taste of tyrants!" If Khrushchev can turn such sentiments to his own use, he is by all means welcome to them.

1964

II

The paperback edition of this book, containing *The Trial Begins* (translated by Max Hayward) and *On Socialist Realism* (translated by George Dennis), appears at an opportune moment. We know now, of course, that Abram Tertz, a name the mysterious anonymity of which has long intrigued us, is the pseudonym of the Russian author Andrei D. Sinyavsky, recently tried in a Soviet court, along with Yuli M. Daniel, and sentenced to seven years of hard labor on charges of smuggling anti-Soviet writings to be published abroad. This trial has had international repercussions and was protested even by some foreign Communist newspapers and leading personalities, such as Louis Aragon.

Smuggled out of the Soviet Union in the late 1950s, *The Trial Begins*, a short novel, was originally printed in *Encounter*, and the long, exceedingly brilliant as well as highly informative essay on socialist realism originally appeared in *Dissent*. What these two works demonstrate, above all, is a very considerable talent that functions with ease both in the creative and critical spheres. There is uncommon wit, irony, and immense cleverness in Mr. Sinyavsky's fiction, while his criticism is distinguished by the same qualities as well as an astonishingly agile historical imagination.

The Trial Begins is a satirical account of Soviet society in the last years of Stalin's life, when ever-newer and more monstrous purges were in the works and the atmosphere in Moscow was very gloomy indeed. But the tone of the story, written some years after Stalin's death, clearly reflects the new mood prevailing among Soviet intellectuals — a mood, if not necessarily of hope, then certainly of relief and some measure of relaxation. It is a tone essentially light-hearted, mocking, even laughter-provoking, and is oriented, in my opinion, toward Western models in matters of style and technique. There are no "lacerations" here à la Dostoevsky or that impression of "depth" that we usually associate with the Russian novel.

Nor is this work simply a satire on conditions in the Soviet Union, which it surely is, and very successfully at that. Its satirical thrust goes beyond its political specifics toward the actualities of the human state everywhere, as in the enticing portrait of Marina, the married woman intent on making a career out of being irresistibly beautiful. To be beautiful is to her in itself "a worthy and sufficient end, and all the rest — men, money, clothes, apartments, cars — were only a means to serve it." Perhaps the funniest thing in the story is a dialogue concerning the sexual act in which a character named Karlinsky attempts to seduce Marina by means of a display of verbal fireworks. Almost intolerably brilliant, Karlinsky goes so far as to describe the brain as "only a cognitive adjunct of the sexual organs," but when Marina finally succumbs, the occasion turns into a fiasco — in his case an all-too-active brain evidently nullifies the sexual impulse. The spoofing dialogue about sex is among the wittiest in fiction and should prove an eye-opener to the increasing number of writers in America who approach the same subject with pious solemnity and are even disposed to regard pornography as no less than a literary genre on a par with tragedy and comedy.

There is very little plot in this story, and what there is of it has a look of improvisation. But plot is not its point, for its appeal is mainly in the dialogue and in the narrator's droll comment. As for the Communist bureaucrats that appear in it, they are surely more grotesque than menacing. They are characters out of Gogol brought up to date. Even when Seryozha, a charming boy, is accused of being "an unconscious Trotskyite" and packed off to a concentration camp, the effect is more gently sardonic than sorrowful. And in terms of political interest, the passage I found most impressive is that describing Stalin's funeral: "The Master was dead. The town seemed empty as a desert. You felt like sitting on your haunches, lifting up your head, and howling like a homeless dog." I suspect that this passage, from which I have quoted only the first two sentences, is historically more authentic than most accounts of that event which have reached us. Yet the principal impression one gathers from this short novel is that ideology plays a very small part in the author's scheme of values. I suppose that from his point of view both the petrified ideology of official Communism and our own rabid variety of crusading anti-Communism are equally obsessive forms of mental enslavement. He writes with the kind of inspired frivolity (or appearance of it) that reminds one of the early Evelyn Waugh, and with the energy of a fine literary intelligence at long last released from the confinement of officially "permitted" publication. No wonder he took his chances in transmitting his manuscripts abroad.

On Socialist Realism is in its analytic way as witty and ironic as *The Trial Begins*. What is socialist realism? It is the literary and artistic wing of a culture that is "teleological" through and through, that is to say, subject "to a higher destiny, from which it gains its title of nobility. In the final reckoning we live only to speed the coming of Communism." It is art with a Purpose. Works produced by socialist realists vary, of course, in style and content, but "in all of them the Purpose is present, whether directly or indirectly, open or veiled. They are panegyrics on Communism, satires on some of its many enemies, or descriptions of life in its revolutionary development, i.e., life moving towards Communism." Hence the inevitable appearance in this literature of a cast of "universally respected" and "privileged" characters called "positive heroes." "This is the Holy of Holies of socialist realism, its cornerstone and main achievement." But the trouble is that these "positive heroes" are cardboard figures, mere dummies of ideology, in whom no one but the very stupid can believe.

Now, as Mr. Sinyavsky sees it, what kills socialist realism as a form of art is not that it presents what should be as what actually is but rather that it is not consistent enough or bold enough to erect its own classical canons in the manner of the religious cultures of the past. For no matter what we hear to the contrary in the West, art is not really "afraid of dictatorship, severity, repressions, or even conservatism and clichés. When necessary, art can be narrowly religious, dumbly governmental, devoid of individuality — and yet good. We go into aesthetic raptures over the stereotypes of Egyptian art, Russian icons and folklore. Art is elastic enough to fit into any Procrustes bed that history presents to it. But there is one thing it cannot stand — eclecticism." And the misfortune of Soviet writers is that they are socialist realists with insufficient conviction. They went to school, are well-read in all sorts of literature, and know only too well that there were great writers before them — "Balzac, Maupassant, Tolstoy, and yes, what's his name? — Chekhov. This is what has undone us. We wanted to become famous and write like Chekhov. This unnatural liaison has produced . . . a loathsome literary salad." Who was the most orthodox of socialist realists, even before the term was invented? According to Mr. Sinyavsky, the most orthodox as well as the most successful artistically was none other than Mayakovsky; and the reason is that he was thoroughly consistent, setting out to glorify the Revolution without looking back to the Russian nineteenth century — a century of "searchings, of ardent or calm aspirations . . . torn by uncertainties and doubts."

Mr. Sinyavsky holds out little hope for socialist realism, though not for the reasons usually given in the West. For my part, I believe that its vogue in Russia will prove to be short-lived and that the State will gradually if reluctantly withdraw its support of it. In a society dominated by rapid technological change and with a political system devoid of stability, there is no room for a new kind of classicism — "that most stable of styles." Communist society is real but its ideology is ossified. Under such conditions a new kind of dynamic realism can be expected to emerge.

1966

ARTHUR MILLER AND THE
FALLACY OF PROFUNDITY

IN HIS SECOND PLAY, *Incident at Vichy*, at the Repertory Theater of Lincoln Center, Arthur Miller recovers somewhat, even if only to a limited extent, from the disaster of *After the Fall*, a piece so pretentious and defensive that virtually nothing good can be said about it. In an openly subjective or confessional mood, bringing his own life behavior into question, Miller is more pitiable than ingratiating. In this new play, however, what is perceptible is not callow subjectivity but an overstrain of intellectual capacity. Still, its director, Harold Clurman, has very ably succeeded, insofar as it was at all within his power, in staving off some of the hazards of the author's ideological ambition and the frequent sententiousness of his language.

The play is basically a discussion piece. The scene is a detention room at Vichy in the fall of 1942, where a number of "suspects" rounded up by the Nazis with the help of the French police are awaiting an interrogation presided over by a German "professor" of racial science — an interrogation from which the Jews among the "suspects," who are in the majority, are never to return. For the

386/*Literature and the Sixth Sense*

hour and a half that it lasts (there are no intermissions) it does generate an unquestionable dramatic tension not to be explained away
by reference to the appalling historical experience it invokes. Recalling the gruesome suffering inflicted by the Nazis does not in
itself create dramatic order and consequence — only the dramatist's
integrative hand can accomplish that. The part that is best conceived and that does provide a certain meager element of plot is
that of the non-Nazi German major who enacts his revulsion at
what his superiors are making him do at the same time that he
accepts it as a decree of our modern historical fate; and the per-
formances, the parts of the Jewish psychoanalyst, of the sensitive
and humane Austrian prince caught in the dragnet, of the German
major, and of the actor still full of consoling illusions of what the
future holds for him, are not only credible but sometimes even
better than that.

What *au fond* I find objectionable, in a dramaturgical as well as
in a plain logical sense, is the surprise ending of the play (welcomed
by not a few reviewers as giving it "a jolt it badly needs," as one of
them put it), in which at the very last moment the Austrian prince,
a liberal of refined sensibilities, is released by the interrogators only
to hand over his exit-permit to the doomed Jewish psychoanalyst.
This Myshkin-like act of self-sacrifice seems to me to belie the entire
portentous dialectic of guilt, responsibility, the horror of Nazism as
the horror of human nature, etc., which Miller develops throughout
the production. It is an ending dramatically unearned, so to speak,
because on the symbolical plane at least it contradicts the entire
emphasis of the ideas that preceded it. It is a melodramatic contrivance pure and simple, a sheer *coup de théâtre*. It may give the
audience a lift, but it drops the play's intellectual baggage with a
heavy thud. After all, liberalism, especially the aestheticized type
of liberalism represented by the prince, has been belabored throughout, and here all of a sudden he gives his own life to save another
man's, who is a stranger at that; nothing whatever in the play has
prepared us for this exhibition of saintliness. Thus the author has it
both ways: he condemns human nature ("We're all scum") at the
same time that he appears to exonerate it in the way he brings his
action to a close. Everything is indeed possible in life, but in dramatic art what is required is the seeming inevitability of an end, how-

ever tragic, which is truly a conclusion vindicating the organizing principle of the work as a whole.

I prefer to think that it is not theatrical opportunism but sheer intellectual confusion which brought Miller, who is one of our few authentic playwrights, to close his piece with such a patently arbitrary ending. The confusion is in his ideas, which have that stylish "profundity," masking a retreat from socio-political realities, that has been for many years now so much in vogue among our intellectuals. The collapse of Marxism has left them high and dry in an ideological sense, and they have long been looking for "profundities," from whatever source, to cover their nakedness; and the "profundities" they have gone in for, ostensibly explaining totalitarianism in all its varieties, have led in the long run to little more than idle theorizing and moralistic attitudinizing. The aim is somehow to replace at all costs the concrete analysis of historical forces in their specific social and political manifestations, for such analysis seems to many people nowadays to be so very stale and boring compared to the *divertissement* of "deep" thoughts, which commit them to nothing but more thoughts. Hence the attempt to understand Nazism — as for instance by resorting to individual psychology (e.g., Hannah Arendt trying to understand Eichmann's character) or to notions of human nature in general or Evil capitalized — has resulted in nothing so far but outright mystification.

What the Nazis did is in fact no mystery. It is implicitly or explicitly contained in their program, which they openly proclaimed long before coming to power; nor did they do anything which had not been done before throughout history; think of the Turks slaughtering the Armenians or of the Church-inspired Western crusaders slaughtering not only the Moslems but the Greek Orthodox Christians as well, to cite but two examples out of an innumerable array. The difference is that the Hitlerites commanded technological means permitting them to commit atrocities on a scale hitherto unknown. There is nothing "new" in terror; what is new is the means at the disposal of the terrorists. In the Nazi experience the point for us does not lie so much in what the Nazis did — what they did cannot be undone — but in the question of how they managed to take power in the first place without being forced to fight for it; only by examining the latter question can some useful lessons for the future be drawn. Hitler's greatest success was in sparing himself civil war while nevertheless grabbing the state power. And the blame for that is to be laid at the door of German big business no less than that of German small business, also of the German military, also of the Communists, ruinously manipulated by Stalin, also of the Social Democrats, in part immobilized by their Communist rivals and in part by their inherent lack of militancy. Nor can one absolve from blame the German intellectuals who, for the most part, instead of thinking and acting politically, were engaged as usual in misinterpreting life and history with their seductive abstractions and profundities. (There is an extremely revealing picture of that type of intellectuality, which is by no means a German monopoly, in Thomas Mann's *Dr. Faustus,* a picture far more interesting and historically instructive than his so much more talked about invocation in that novel of its hero's Satan-inspired aesthetics.)

Now Arthur Miller appears to have absorbed quite a few of the mystifications with which some of our intellectuals have been at once perplexing and diverting themselves. Thus in his play the Austrian prince, who in this instance is clearly speaking for the author, says: "Many times I used to ask my friends: To be a good German why must you despise everything that is not German? Until I realized the answer. They do these things not because they are Germans but because they are nothing. It is the hallmark of the age — the less you exist the more important it is to make a clear impression." On the surface this may sound profound and, to be sure, it has the modish "existentialist" ring; but does it actually explain the German contempt for other nations? No human beings are "nothing," and to equate "good German" with "nothing" is a pointless piece of cleverness. The German contempt that Miller refers to is at bottom far from mysterious. It was a willed contempt functionally serving as the rationalization, politically and culturally, of their urge to exterminate other peoples in order to make *Lebensraum* for themselves. They thought it was a practical urge, but it turned out to be wholly impractical. German imperialism, in its first nationalistic as in its second totalitarian edition, was a historical phenomenon much too belated to realize its aims; and its worked-up claims of superiority, like its frightful ruthlessness, was an essential

part of what one might call its character-armor. Why mystify ourselves with the metaphysics of "nothingness" when the explanation
is really so much simpler?

Nor am I impressed by Miller's notion of anti-Semitism as his
psychoanalyst voices it: "And Jews is only the name we give to that
stranger, that agony we cannot feel, that death we look at like a
cold abstraction. Each man has his Jew; it is the other. And the
Jews have their Jews." But gentiles are drawn to anti-Semitism not
because otherness as such repels them but for simpler reasons, such
as the tempting contradiction in their image of the Jews. On the
one hand they seem to them to be "pushy" and all too prosperous
while on the other hand they seem so very helpless. It is this particular combination which invites the blows. And if Miller merely
means to say that everyone wants to find someone he can look down
upon or who might serve him as a scapegoat, that is the sheerest
cliché. Again, the psychoanalyst says to the prince: "It's not your
guilt I want, it's your responsibility." This too sounds deep, but
what does it mean? Guilt feelings are essential if our conscience is
to be stirred, and without pangs of conscience there can be no taking of responsibility. The thesis of the play, insofar as it has any
coherent thesis at all, is that each of us is responsible for all, that
whatever evil we do, however small, contributes to the greater evil
that destroys humanity. Actually, this is one of Dostoevsky's ideas,
which is scarcely convincing even in this context. It is a Christian
thought put to false uses. He used it as apologetics for the absolutist
Czarist regime, its state-dominated Church and other malign forces
holding down the Russian people in ignorance and misery. Responsibility cannot be other than specific: if all are responsible none are
responsible. It is simply not true that we are all responsible for the
Nazi horrors, and to universalize in this fashion the German guilt
is to transfer it to human nature in general and thus vaporize it. The
argument from human nature in general is insubstantial because it is
so exceedingly vague, explaining everything and nothing at the
same time.

Miller is no ideologue, no thinker, but he has written some good
things. Apart from *Death of a Salesman*, about which I have mixed
feelings, I think his best play is *A View from the Bridge*, a simple

but trenchant dramatic poem. *The Crucible,* too, is a fine work, once we disregard the analogies with McCarthyism, an entirely different phenomenon from the Salem witch trials, analogies that are not really in the text which I have recently read, but in the mind of the audience that first saw it produced. Now *Incident at Vichy* has been criticized by reviewers, though for reasons that seem to me somewhat external. Its actual ideas have not been examined in detail but mostly sneered at for not being deep enough. The trouble with these ideas, however, is precisely their apparent depth — depth without content.

The reviewer in *Newsweek,* for instance, after lambasting Miller, has written his prescription for the theater, which, in his opinion, needs "to become again the forum for the boldest confrontations with the truths of history and the moral life of man in society." Why "again"? I for one cannot remember the time when our theater fulfilled this exalted role. Yet some very good plays have been written by Americans — on the basis, however, not of "the boldest confrontations" of history and morality but of emotional commonplaces.

I am not, of course, recommending emotional commonplaces, but why overlook the fact that some very good drama has been written on that basis and so has some great poetry, in English as in other languages (Pushkin is an excellent example).

Moreover, the present cultural situation in the United States is hardly conducive to the "boldest confrontations," either in drama or in literature generally. We are living at a time when anything goes, when much of our theater is given over to a debased kind of Freudianism, when in the name of literature and art, no less, the right to pornographic writing is affirmed, strategically omitting to mention the cold cash which is its huge reward, as if it were almost a new kind of civil liberty; when people who should know better are proclaiming a moral idiot like Jean Genet to be a great novelist, a worthy successor to Joyce and Proust and Mann and Kafka and Lawrence and Faulkner, while other people are so frightened of being called square that they are willing to accept this unlikely estimate.

And, unlike the reviewer in *Newsweek,* I do not think that highbrowism as such is the answer. It is not an end in itself. Intelligence is one thing, and programmatic highbrowism is something else. That reviewer strikes me either as a confirmed optimist or as one of the many who are blind to what is actually transpiring among us. It is not more high-sounding and utopian demands that we need but a strict and perhaps harsh examination of what we are in fact faced with.

1964

SAUL BELLOW'S PROGRESS

WITH THIS NEW WORK, *Herzog,* his sixth novel, Saul Bellow emerges not only as the most intelligent novelist of his generation but also as the most consistently interesting in point of growth and development. To my mind, too, he is the finest stylist at present writing fiction in America.

For some time now the critical consensus has been, expressed not so much formally in writing as in the talk of literary circles, that *Seize the Day,* published some nine years ago, was his best single performance. However, I think *Herzog* is superior to it, even if not so tightly organized and in fact a bit loose on the structural side. For one thing, it is a much longer and fuller narrative than *Seize the Day,* which is hardly more than a novella. For another, it is richer in content, in the effective disposition of tone and language, as well as in intellectual resonance and insight of a high order in the makeup of modern life — insight into what is really new and perhaps all too hazardous about its strange, almost inconceivable mixture of greater freedom and maddening constriction.

Above all, this novel positively radiates intelligence — not mere brightness or shrewdness or that kind of sensitiveness which all too

often passes for mind among us. This intelligence is a real endowment, coherent, securely founded and of a genuine intellectual quality which, marvelously escaping the perils of abstractions, is neither
recondite nor esoteric. It is directed toward imaginative ends by
virtue of a true and sharp sense of the pain that rends the human
world, of its ills both curable and incurable, and equally by a bracing, unfailing sense of humor and irony serving to counteract such
chronic vulnerabilities and intelligence as oversolemnity of mind on
the one hand and perversity of sensibility on the other.

It is important to stress this element of intellectual mastery in
Bellow, for in the milieu of our creative writers intellect has by no
means played a conspicuous part. Hence the immaturity of even
the best, like Hemingway for instance, and the aborted careers of
not a few other gifted writers, aborted among other things by the
repetition compulsion that results not so much from neurotic disturbance, though that may be present too, as from thematic poverty and
narrowness of the mental horizon. To be sure, intellect is not art;
in some ways it might even be said to be corrosive in its effect on
artistic production. But without intellect it becomes impossible for
the artist, the verbal artist particularly, to transform into consciousness what is offered by experience and the manifold and at times
infinitely varied and subtle emotions it gives rise to. After all, thinking too is an experience. Without thought the writer may be able
to relate the particulars of experience well enough, though usually
at inordinate length, but he is at a loss when it comes to extracting
values from experience that will make it meaningful to the reader
(and perhaps to himself also).

Herzog is far and away the most personal novel Bellow has writ
ten, and the most immediate in self-reference. But the personal
element in this case in no way strikes us as an intrusion, as it makes
for a clear gain in impact and reality-mindedness. By comparison,
The Adventures of Augie March seems like a wonderfully inventive
exercise in mere narrative fantastication, projecting an affirmative
message that falls short of conviction. *Herzog*, moreover, despite its
deeply personal provenance, betrays none of that orgastic self-glori-
fication that you may find in our hipster writers who make do with
the self (the ravenous, raging self of erotic fantasy and adolescent
daydreams of power) when talent and moral intelligence fail them.

As a maker of prose fiction, Bellow is far too scrupulous and his personality too complicated to engage in such capers. He has put a great deal of himself into his protagonist Herzog, but always with a twist of irony and a minimum of self-display.

Herzog is a Chicago professor, author of a work entitled *Romanticism and Christianity* (a good stroke, that, for the novel is in its own way a kind of exploration of latter-day versions of romanticism), who is suffering a near breakdown when his second wife, Mady, leaves him. She appropriates house and child to take up with his best friend, Gersbach, a purveyor of the latest cultural goodies, like Buber's "I and Thou" relationship, the more portentous varieties of existentialism, and Yiddishisms of phrase and stance. At the very start of the story we are told that some people thought Herzog was cracked, and he himself is uncertain whether this is so. The truth is, however, that he "had fallen under a spell and was writing letters to everyone under the sun," feeling an irresistible need "to explain, to have it out, to justify, to put in perspective, to clarify, to make amends." The letters teem with ideas, thus converting Herzog's personal crisis into the more impersonal crisis of modern thinking. Herzog moves from place to place carrying a valise full of papers, which he takes with him from New York to Martha's Vineyard and back again almost at once. Two days later he flies to Chicago, keyed up to the highest pitch, to have it out with his wife and her lover (at this stage the latent violence almost erupts), and then back again to a village in western Massachusetts where, hidden in the country, he again "writes endlessly, fantastically, to the newspapers, to people in public life, to friends and relatives, and at last to the dead, his own obscure dead and finally the famous dead." The story ends in this village, where Herzog evades his brother's efforts to get him to a psychiatrist even as he makes ready for a visit from his New York mistress, a superbly rendered figure of "sex and swagger."

There is nothing in any novel I have read quite like these letters Herzog writes. In no sense formal in tone, they represent at once a fictional device and a prodigiously productive aggression of the mind. The writer is richly ironic, at his own expense too, and intolerant of the typical platitudes of modern thought, letting go in a strange intermixture of "clairvoyance and spleen, *esprit de l'escalier*, noble inspiration, poetry and nonsense, ideas, hyperaesthesia . . ."

To the philosopher Heidegger he addresses himself, "I should like to know what you mean by the expression, 'The Fall into the Quotidian.' When did this fall occur? Where were we standing when it happened?" Another letter, to Nietzsche, opens with the sentence, "Dear Herr Nietzsche — my dear sir, may I ask a question from the floor?," followed by an outburst against the German thinker's celebration of the Dionysian spirit's pride in allowing itself the luxury of pain and evil. In still another letter, to a fellow scholar named Shapiro, he writes that "we must not forget how quickly the visions of genius become the canned goods of the intellectuals. The canned sauerkraut of Spengler's Prussian socialism, the commonplaces of the Wasteland outlook, the cheap mental stimulants of Alienation, the cant and rant of the pipsqueaks about Inauthenticity and Forlornness. I can't accept this foolish dreariness. We are talking about the whole life of mankind. The subject is too great, too deep, for such weakness, cowardice ... A merely aesthetic critique of modern history! After the wars and mass killings! You are too intelligent for this. You inherited rich blood. Your father peddled apples."

Herzog, with his talent for polemics, bears down with particular force on those German existentialists who tell you that guilt and dread are good for you; their story is that "God is no more but Death is." Human life, writes Herzog, "is far subtler than any of its models. Do we need *theories* of pain and anguish?" Now such ideas will scarcely please our academic popularizers of existentialism who imagine that with delusions of concreteness borrowed from Germany and France, they are actually escaping the basic and very comfortable abstraction of their professorial stance. Herzog protests vehemently against the seeming profundities of the modern cult of pain and suffering. Himself in a state of extreme anguish, he needs no theories to rub it in.

Among the characters of the novel other than Herzog (of whom there is a richly varied cast, some beautifully drawn), Ramona, his mistress, is an outstanding creation. Mady, the treacherous wife, does not really come through except as an object of hostility, though a weirdly interesting one, whereas Ramona is the best portrait I have encountered in contemporary fiction of the modern woman *par excellence* who has made good on the sexual revolution. That kind of woman is the chief beneficiary of the revolution, made mostly by men. How is it possible, muses Herzog, to run out "on fragrant, sexual, high-minded Ramona? Never in a million years. She has passed through the hell of profligacy and attained the seriousness of pleasure." She believes in no sin but "the sin against the body, for her the true and only temple of the spirit." If you are under stress and Ramona likes you, then the only thing to do, the perfect restorative indeed, is to fly to her at once; she will "feed you, give you wine, remove your shoes, flatter you, put down your hackles, pinch your lips with her teeth. Then uncover the bed, turn down the lights, disclose the essentials."

In his state of feeling betrayed, Herzog voices a certain animus against women, and this animus is not without heuristic value. He notes: "Will I never understand what women want? What do they want? They eat green salad and drink human blood." This short last sentence, with its startling juxtaposition of the tame and the fierce, is good vivid writing and by no means purely rhetorical. For nowadays women do expect all the privileges of the sex-inhibited past plus all the freedoms of the swinging present. In other words, the modern female is hugely avid and expects nearly everything, and from her husband most of all. She expects him to provide nightly erotic "gratification, safety, money, furs, jewelry, cleaning women, drapes, dresses, hats, night clubs, automobiles, theater!"

As the story progresses it becomes clear that poor Ramona will receive none of those valuable things from Herzog, who is much too ironically observant of her modern ways to fall in love with her, even though, far from young, she is touching enough as a woman who more than once has taken matters into her own hands. It is scarcely easy to live on an ideological diet of permanent sex, and Ramona is "fairly fanatical about that." On the theme of the erotic, Herzog has his mordant say: "The erotic must be admitted to its rightful place, at last, in an emancipated society," but why put such a great value on the sexual act as "actually socially constructive and useful, an act of citizenship" no less? Salvation through sex is among the more fatuous illusions of our age. In this novel there are sexual scenes galore, but none of them clinical, none of them fired with the vulgar *ne plus ultra* fervor of our contemporary sexologists in fiction.

Bellow's style in this narrative, as in most of his fiction, provides a

very meaningful pleasure in its masterful combination of the demo-
tic and literary languages. At once astringent and poetic, it neither
muffles nor distends his themes. Among the elements back of it is,
no doubt, a deep sense of humor derived from his Jewish background and thoroughly assimilated to his sensibility. This style is
sensibility in action.

1964

THE CRITIC AS *LITTÉRATEUR:*
LESLIE FIEDLER AND JOHN ALDRIDGE

I

TWO NEW WORKS of criticism, George P. Elliott's *A Piece of Let-tuce: Personal Essays on Books, Beliefs, American Places, and Growing Up in a Strange Country* and Leslie A. Fiedler's *Waiting for the End,* dealing mainly with the American literary experience, make a startling contrast. Elliott, who has published fiction and poetry, is not a professional critic, but insofar as he ventures into criticism (mixing it, in some parts of his book, with personal remi-niscences and asides that are much to the point), his writing is sensible, modest, pertinent, and for the most part reliable in judg-ment. He does have something definite to say on every subject he tackles — whether it be Raymond Chandler or Ezra Pound, George Orwell, or Henry Miller — and he says it as plainly as he knows how; and where one cannot agree with him the grounds of disagree-ment are clear, as in the essay on Dante in which the critical argu-ment is weakened by pledges of faith too tenuous to be redeemed and gratuitous besides. He is remarkable, however, among latter-day literary men, for affecting few mannerisms and refraining altogether from straining for that facile and fashionable brilliance of phrase and reference to which we have recently become, if not accustomed exactly, then surely indurated. Elliott is still old-fashioned enough to be concerned with the sensibility of the common reader and with the virtues of plain prose. Quite alien to him is the ambition to dazzle with an impresssion of virtuosity, an impression more often than not deceptive because so largely derived from the kind of manic verbalization nowadays widely confused with excelence of style.

Fiedler, on the other hand, is nothing if not brilliant, even at the cost of adopting postures that betray and attitudes that pall. His enormous knowingness about literature and patent intelligence are laid waste, it seems to me, by the stance to which he has of late given himself. His prose, in which the phrase now invariably goes beyond the content, is more vehement than virulent, needlessly vehement at times because excessive to the subject, and better adapted to the sheer display of superficially "daring" notions than to any true commitment to ideas or rigorous concern with them. Again, in this latest book, he is long on generalizations, most of them dubious in the extreme, and short on evidence. Once more we are belabored with the race-sex thesis ("the dream of a great love between white and colored men"), which is tied in with the contention that repressed and/or sublimated homosexuality is the inner secret of the American novel. Such notions are too prankishly childish to be worth serious examination. Fiedler has merely added a literary gloss and a homosexual twist to what are in essence the stereotypes of the popular folklore of the menace of miscegenation. No wonder his pages teem with terms like "stereotype" and "counter-stereotype," not to mention "myth" and "archetype," of which he never tires. (When his essay "Come Back to the Raft Ag'in, Huck Honey," since become notorious, was printed in *Partisan Review* some fifteen years ago, the editors of that magazine thought of it as a talented young man's *jeu d'esprit*, a spoof on academic solemnity, not at all as the weighty contribution to the understanding of American letters that Fiedler, who is still pushing its proposition as hard as he can, apparently takes it to be.) Moreover, in this new book Fiedler's tone is irritatingly jeering, even in discussing such superior literary artists as Faulkner and Hemingway; it is not exactly that he is tactless as that he is virtually allergic to tact. And in *Waiting for the End* he above all gives free rein to his worst impulse — that of shocking or scandalizing the reader and playing the *enfant terrible* at any price.

Yet in our present social and cultural stalemate he who plays the *enfant terrible* among us typically turns out to be no genuine rebel or heretic or prophet, even if he has the look of one; on the contrary, he is someone who characteristically expects to pay no penalty for his escapades but rather to be hugely rewarded for them. And with good reason too, for there is more diversion in him than dissidence, more impudence than courage. After all, if he violates or mocks national pieties, like sexual prohibitions and inhibitions, they are on the point of breakup anyhow. To be explicit about sex nowadays, even about its most scabrously technical detail, is like walking through an open door. When it comes, however, to orthodoxies still firmly held, as in the political sphere for instance, our *enfant terrible* either keeps mum or indulges in idle utopian fancies more amusing than threatening. Clearly, the stance of the bad boy has proved to be quite profitable of late, making for an easy climb to celebrity status — that American sort of celebrity whom Daniel Boorstin has so aptly defined as a person known, not for any actual or lasting achievement, but primarily for his well-knownness. To judge by the welcoming and pleased reviews that *Waiting for the End* has received in some of our mass-circulation periodicals, Fiedler, if he fails to curb his appetite for histrionic blatancy of statement, will soon be officially certified by the publicity-media as the perennial bad boy of literary criticism.

The definition of avant-garde literature to which Fiedler has committed himself in a recent article is all too characteristic of him. "Highbrow or truly experimental art," he tells us, "aims at *insult*; and the intent of its typical language is therefore exclusion. It recruits neither defenders of virtue nor opponents of sin; only shouts in the face of the world the simple slogan, *épater les bourgeois*, or 'mock the middle classes,' which is to say, mock most, if not quite all, its readers." Now it is patently impossible to recognize such "highbrow or truly experimental" writers as, say, Proust, Gide, Sartre, Mann, Kafka, Joyce, Yeats, Eliot, and Stevens in this singular definition. Its emphasis is wholly on the writer's putative attitude toward his prospective readers rather than toward himself. If the work of such literary artists is difficult and complex, it is surely because it reflects a highly intellectual consciousness, the artist's resolve not to simplify his imaginative experience and psychic obsessions, to remain true to the vision that compels him even in the teeth of convention and tradition. The specific Flaubertian hatred of the bourgeois is scarcely present in their books. Least of all are they willfully motivated by any such intent as excluding, or even merely provoking, the middle-class reader by means of the stategy of "insult." Nothing can be more shallow than this bohemian theory of *épatisme* as the essence of avant-garde expression. *Épatisme* may well be Fiedler's own stock-in-trade but it is largely foreign to the ethos of serious modern artists.

Moreover, the bourgeois of our time is no longer the solid citizen and respectable householder of Flaubert's day. Having thrown over the moral code by which he was traditionally bound, he is now a nihilist like everyone else. Fiedler's dream of the bourgeois as the ideal enemy is quite out of date, a mere memory of past literary wars; the bourgeois is not so easily frightened as in the past. A snob as well as a nihilist, he has ceased to be baffled or intimidated by culture, even culture of the more advanced sort that remains incomprehensible to him, for he has learned to deal in its prestige value as he deals in more material commodities. No longer deterred by considerations of piety or gentility, he wants his good time and enjoys even the new sexology that our "liberated" novels provide; the only thing that scares him is the possible loss of his economic and social privileges. On this score alone he is still quite adamant — adamant and dangerous. But it is precisely on this score that Fiedler makes not the least effort to challenge him.

In his essay, "Who Is We?" Elliott voices, not without humor and with a good deal of justice, a provincial's protest against the presumption of some of the New York literati, and among other things he has his mordant say about the role that Fiedler plays: "He has developed to perfection an ingroup tone which appeals very potently to outsiders who like the illusion of being let in. He is especially fond of telling his betters what their *real* (i.e., nastiest) motives are, and his attitude of superiority, often of indulgence, applies to everyone he discusses, even to those he is trying to praise . . . He constantly finds archetypes and symbols where you least expect them: 'the bum as American culture hero'; 'the young Jew as writer and thinker is the very symbol of our urbanization (as also our ambivalent relationship to Europe, the atomization of culture, and our joyful desperation).'" Elliott is equally perceptive in nailing down Henry Miller and Norman Mailer as writers who have developed a kind of craft of self-promotion and have succeeded in converting themselves into their own scandal. This is a phenomenon symtomatic of our contemporary literature which Fiedler, unlike Elliott, is apparently more than willing to put up with.

For instance, he repeatedly makes his obeisances to the beats and hipsters, announcing the "triumphs of Ginsberg and Ferlinghetti" and assuring us that "willy-nilly the beats have triumphed in the academy too, and Whitman with them." I have heard of the publicity triumphs of these two beat poets, of the former in particular, but that they have already, with so little effort and smaller accomplishment, triumphed in the academy is news to me. Fiedler is exceedingly literal-minded about the supposed Whitmanesque connection of the beats; in his view Ginsberg is no less than Whitman's latest metamorphosis. But what does this connection finally consist of? There is of course Ginsberg's long, loose, and unmetered line, but apart from that the connection is flimsy indeed. As for his apostrophes cursing out America, so many American writers have gone in for such flights that it scarcely requires the enlistment of Whitman as the great exemplar. Nor is Fiedler more accurate in his notion of the influence William Burroughs, in whom he sees veritably the king of the beasts (or beats). "Any American abroad," he writes without irony, "has come to expect to see hordes of the new young descending on Athens or Paris or Florence or wherever, bearded and sandled and carrying under their arms the holy books, *Naked Lunch* and *The Soft Machine;* and if they do not sing, 'Burroughs is our leader, we will not be moved,' they might just as well."

Such is the fantasy elaborated by our gullible critic. No report that has ever reached me or any friend of mine has ever so much as alluded to these "hordes of the new young," one and all devotees or *hasidim* of Burroughs. I would guess that Fiedler's students have not in the slightest degree appreciated *Naked Lunch* (assuming, that is, that some of them have read it), which is not the portentous antinovel "exploding" the novel form from within that Fiedler makes it out to be but truly a nonnovel full of sadistic homosexual extravagance, a dream sequence of gruesome and impossible pleasure, larded with plain, flat talk about narcotics. Nor have I heard any of my students, even the most self-consciously bearded and literary among them, express the enthusiastic rapport with Burroughs of which Fiedler brings us the glad tidings. The trouble with this critic, in my opinion, is that he has an excessively, even stiflingly literary imagination. It is a morbid state of mind leading him to conceive of literature as always overpowering life. The actual is seldom real to him; its sole appeal is in its literary reflection. Hence it is no wonder that in his aberrant condition he is so obviously fascinated by the politics of literary careers and the public legends they give rise to. One has only to read him on the Hemingway legend to see that he can't leave well enough alone.

It is primarily in connection with literature that ideas of race and ethnic origin seem to intrigue him, for he writes extensively about Negro and American-Jewish writers. In some few passages about the latter I seem to detect the tone of an informer to the *goyim*, and the less said about that the better. As for the Negro writers, his comment on Baldwin's *Another Country* is that it "demonstrates that the hatred between black and white, only exacerbated by attempted interracial unions between men and women, can in fact be resolved in homosexual love." Of course, "demonstrates" is about the worst possible word in this context, as no novel can ever be said really to demonstrate anything, least of all the kind of proposition (What a boost for civil rights!) that Fiedler professes to discover in Baldwin. I, for one, do not find this proposition either in *The Fire Next Time* or in Baldwin's other utterances on the race issue. To be sure, there is a strong personal homosexual bias in *Another Country*, but it is no kindness to its author to interpret this bias in any sense as a programmatic statement. The attribution of it to Baldwin is rather to be explained by Fiedler's persistent and futile effort to justify and confirm his early essay, "Come Back to the Raft Ag'in, Huck Honey!," which is more like a burlesque account of Mark Twain's novel than a serious examination of it. It is in Elliott's book that I came upon an essay, "Wonder for Huckleberry Finn," which I admire. It is the best piece in the collection, I think, synthesizing with rare critical insight and revitalized interest the not inconsiderable studies of that novel which American scholarship and criticism have accumulated.

1964

II

This collection of critical articles and reviews, *Time to Murder and Create: The Contemporary Novel in Crisis,* sports a wildly inappropriate title taken from Eliot's "Prufrock." However resonant Eliot's line may be in its context, it stands in no literal or symbolic relation whatever to what Mr. Aldridge has to say, and in thus appropriating (or expropriating) it, he displays a sense of self-importance which is excessive, to say the least, and a taste for histrionics not at all suitable to the critical medium. Nor is his subtitle — *The Contemporary Novel in Crisis* — any more apt or accurate. For one thing, he is not actually examining the contemporary novel in any representative sense but only American examples of it, and, for another, even within this restricted framework Mr. Aldridge is inadequate, for he fails to discuss quite a few writers of consequence in American fiction, such as Flannery O'Connor, John Barth, John Hawkes, Thomas Pynchon, and Philip Roth, among others. It appears to me that novels like Barth's *The Sot-Weed Factor* and O'Connor's *Wise Blood* cannot rightly be left out of account in any book which advances, as this one does, such overtly large claims of concern with the performance of American novelists since the end of the Second World War.

The truth is that this somewhat miscellaneous collection offers no comprehensive appraisal of present-day American fiction. My impression is that what Mr. Aldridge is mainly after is to check up, as it were, on the authors he dealt with in his earlier book, *After the Lost Generation,* published nearly fifteen years ago; and he lets us know in emphatic terms that he feels let down by them, badly let down. The trouble is, however, that he writes about them in a tone somehow suggesting that they are personally responsible to him, and this peculiar tone, so alien to critical discourse, induces an uneasy feeling in the, reader, who finds himself at a loss to discover when and where Mr. Aldridge was officially appointed to serve as the Inspector-General of contemporary fiction in America. In this unlikely role he is quite unimpressive, almost fatally so, reminding one more of Khlestakov, the hero of Gogol's great comedy, than of any real authority.

The one novel recently produced that wins this critic's unstinted praise is Norman Mailer's *An American Dream*, a work whose merits are still very much in question and in defense of which he offers what seems to me to be an utterly inane piece of apologetics, scrambling together all sorts of notions, mostly irrelevant to his text, in support of his extravagant and improbable opinion of it. Yet in articles, written a year or longer before *An American Dream* appeared, he is just as rough on Mailer ("peddling his megalomania in *Esquire* . . . the antics of a man sick for publicity at any price," etc., etc.) as he is on his coevals. Thus, William Styron is taken to task with what strikes me as incredible rudeness and rancor; Updike is dismissed out of hand, Mary McCarthy is psychologized and "motivated" to pieces; and Bellow's *Herzog* is so willfully interpreted that it emerges as a book "wholesome and nutritious as a dish of corn flakes, a clearly 'major' Establishment work," whose epitome is "the platitude of Accommodation and Togetherness."

Now it should be obvious that no ordinary critical terms can possibly cope with a judgment so nonsensical: this is in no way a critical reading of *Herzog* but sheer fabulation, and the only question is whom Mr. Aldridge is trying to please by thus setting out to degrade Bellow at all costs. And yet in another article Mr. Aldridge decries the anti-intellectualism of many of our writers, contending that "the novel is not nearly intellectual enough . . . contemporary writers generally think too little to be able to feel . . ." But if intellectual capacity is your prize, then certainly Bellow is your man, for, whatever his other qualities, he is surely the most genuinely intellectual of contemporary American novelists, whose ideas, moreover, never take the form of modish apocalyptic preachments but are inextricably a part of his narrative structures. Mr. Aldridge, let it be said, is aware of this objection and tries to counter it by the glib assertion that Bellow's "thematic and stylistic interests" happen also to coincide with those most in favor with his audience. This is an argument as foolish as it is false. Interests and ideas that are in favor with a given audience are not necessarily worthless on that account. But that is neither here nor there, as what Mr. Aldridge really wants to insinuate is that Bellow is not a true intellectual but some kind of fashionmonger in the realm of ideas. Now as to that, taking *Herzog* as a test case, I would say that the greater part of the public that made the book a best seller, far from being in tune with its author's ideas, simply did not know what he was talking about. In my view, the sales figures of *Herzog* are a more or less accidental symptom of the current culture-explosion and in no sense a proof of Bellow's popularity as a thinker or, least of all, as a leader of fashion in the literary world. For he is not a thinker or ideologue but a novelist who is also able to think — that is to say, one of our very few imaginative writers who has managed to transcend the cult of experience in American literature.

Also included in this collection are some comments on writers of an older generation, such as Katherine Anne Porter, John O'Hara, Fitzgerald in *The Great Gatsby*, the very last works of Hemingway, and, of all people, P. G. Wodehouse. About some of these older writers Mr. Aldridge does at times contribute plausible judgments, as in the piece on Miss Porter, whom he sees as not nearly deserving, in spite of the famed lucidity of her English, the high artistic reputation she has acquired and as being in the last analysis a regionalist writer most truly at home "in only one place, the American Southwest of her childhood." Mr. Aldridge is even more severe on John O'Hara, whom he dismisses with some cogency as "a pious pornographer" for the middlebrows. O'Hara is easy pickings for any critic, and even at that Mr. Aldridge ignores the obvious fact that he is just as vulnerable on the ground of his cheap snobbery as he is on the ground of his cheap sexology. And some things that Mr. Aldridge says about O'Hara are quite uncalled for. I have in mind a sentence like the following: "O'Hara is an example of a once talented novelist who has sold out his original talent to write well for middlebrow success." Here Mr. Aldridge indulges himself again in his bad habit of "motivating" writers he dislikes. In a context of literary criticism — which is very far from gossip — the imputation of low motives is entirely gratuitous; since personal motives are something one can only vaguely speculate about, undocumented assertions with reference to them are useless as well as offensive. About Hemingway in decline Mr. Aldridge makes statements with which, having heard them so often before, one can hardly disagree.

And why did this critic include in his collection yet another essay on *The Great Gatsby?* Though managed dexterously enough, it contains nothing particularly new, merely adding another tribute to the hundreds, if not thousands, already published. Wonderful in its way as *The Great Gatsby* is, it has been worked to death in the past fifteen years or so both by Fitzgerald's critics and biographers. It should be left alone for at least several decades. One should know a case of critical superfetation when one sees it.

If Mr. Aldridge has any thesis to offer at all, it is that on the whole the contemporary American novel is disappointing. Admittedly this is so and most of us have long known it. But what might have caused this falling off? It appears that our novelists are unable "to imagine with an intensity and complexity equal to their sophistication"; what is wrong is that "the imagination of the contemporary novel . . . has remained locked in certain stereotypes and modes of perceiving and recording reality that it has inherited from the modern classic literary past." It soon turns out, however, that what Mr. Aldridge means by referring to "the modern classic literary past" is hardly anything more than the novels of the American twenties and thirties, mainly those of Fitzgerald, Hemingway, and Faulkner. "We have too often and eagerly accepted the version of reality supplied by these novels, and that has prevented us from arriving at our own version."

At bottom what is Mr. Aldridge really saying? Merely that if our novelists were able to forget their predecessors and applied their imagination more intensely and in a more complex fashion they would produce superior work. This is finally the extent of this critic's tautological wisdom. Such factors as the climate of ideas or the cultural situation, which has changed so enormously since the last war, and in general the present state of American society, so greatly affluent and almost perversely narcissistic in spirit, are not brought to bear on the question. Mr. Aldridge is singularly unaware of the larger environment in which literature functions. Nor does he have any plausible ideas about the intricate relationship between literary conventions and traditions on the one hand, and new talent on the other. He wants writers to break away from "the literary formulations" of the past, and we have already seen how restricted is his view of it. What he has in mind is the immediate past only. Yet the history of literature shows that writers make use of "the literary formulations" of the immediate past even in the process of changing them. Dostoevsky never abandoned but rather built on the foundations of the novelistic methods and conceptions of such predecessors as Gogol, Dickens, Balzac, and Hoffmann; nor did Henry James forget the lessons of Hawthorne, Balzac, and Turgenev. Mr. Aldridge's notion that in each decade or so writers must start from scratch in devising their "version of reality" is preposterous on the face of it. As T. S. Eliot once put it, all one can do in art is the next thing possible and the effort to be totally original can only result in the totally unintelligible.

Mr. Aldridge is concerned with American novels and with making provocative statements. But that is not enough to establish his authority as a critic. Innocent in matters of literary theory and indifferent to ideas of any sort, political, philosophical, religious or whatever, he is manifestly a narrowly unideological type of critic, who brings to bear very little to the novels he examines besides his interest in novels. Is that sufficient? I think F. R. Leavis was essentially right in remarking some years ago that "one cannot be seriously interested in literature and remain purely literary in interests."

1966

CRIME WITHOUT PUNISHMENT

An American Dream is, to my mind, the most eccentric of the four novels Norman Mailer has written. It is far more eccentric, I think, than *Barbary Shore* — his second novel and a better one than literary opinion has generally taken it to be — which alienated readers not so much by personal singularity as by the extreme sectarianism of its political theme. In the case of that work it might well be said that the reader, wholly unprepared for that kind of statement, was in a certain sense quite as much at fault for its failure as the author. This latest book, however, has very few if any of the qualities that redeemed *Barbary Shore* as well as Mailer's other fiction.

There is nothing here like the brilliantly observed comic episodes in *The Deer Park* (involving the Hollywood producers Teppis and Munshin), or the powerfully sustained narrative-sequence comprising the second part of *The Naked and the Dead* (the Sergeant Croft section). And the title, *An American Dream*, strikes me as a misnomer. It implies a generalization about the national life palpably unsupported either by the weird and sometimes ludicrous details of the story or by the low-level private mysticism informing its imaginative scheme. That mysticism is more or less pseudonymously presented in Mailer's articles under the flashy and ostensibly impersonal heading of Hip. Now whatever the origin of the term in the underworld of jazz and narcotics, the explication of it that he has been engaged in for some years is at bottom scarcely a report on something that exists outside himself but is basically a programmatic statement of his own desires, power-drives and daydreams. It amounts to a kind of personal mythology projected unto something he chooses to call Hip. I venture to say that real-life hipsters, not romantic youths reading Mailer with relish, would hardly recognize themselves in his free-wheeling description of their motivation and behavior.

The time-span of this new novel is thirty-two hours, and its frantic action consists of a great deal of sexual exertion and is centered on a murder — the protagonist's killing of his wife, a bitchy wealthy heiress, during a violent tussle in which hard words and harder blows are exchanged. It is true enough that the murder is unpremeditated, but neither can it be said that this act of ultimate violence commited by Stephen Rojack, the protagonist, is merely an accident; and he commits it with enormous exhilaration. Already on page 8, before the episode of the killing is introduced, Rojack acknowledges that he had long known there was murder within him, and he speculates that the exhilaration accompanying it must come "from possessing such strength." "Besides," he adds, "murder offers the promise of vast relief. It is never unsexual." (How would he know that, since these thoughts occur to him prior to the experience itself?) Moreover, the long paragraph describing Rojack's choking of Deborah to death is full of positive imagery, and it closes with the following sentences: "I was weary with a most honorable fatigue, and my flesh seemed new. I had not felt so nice since I was twelve. It seemed inconceivable at this instant that anything in life could fail to please. But there was Deborah dead beside me . . ." And immediately after absorbing this to him so ecstatic an experience, a true renewal, Rojack rushes to the maid's room to engage her in sex-acts both plain and fancy. It is not that he had been having an affair with her; killing excites him sexually. Then he returns to the scene of the killing and dumps the corpse out of the tenth-floor window to the East River Drive. So much for hipster heroics!

The curious thing about it is not only that this murder goes un-punished (Crime without Punishment) but that it is also without any kind of consequence, either public or private. Clearly the plot is all too intentionally manipulated by the author so as to free Rojack from paying any sort of price, even if only psychologically, for what he had done. At the last moment and even as the detectives are clos-ing in on him, they are held back by a call from Washington. We are astonished to learn — just as the husband is — that Deborah had all along been engaged in "amateur espionage." As the maid, Ruta, ex-plains to him: "Last night they must have had electricity burning in government offices all over the world . . . Yes, they had to let you go . . . Since nobody can know if you know a little or a lot, a real investi-gation would be ending *der Teufel* knows where." But this novel is not designed as a spy-thriller nor as a wacky tale the absurd hap-penings of which are not meant to produce consequences; it is writ-ten in the realistic convention and without a trace of irony. The business about espionage, arbitrarily introduced at the last moment, is simply the author's *deus ex machina* — a device confirming Rojack in his lordly "existentialist" freedom at the same time as it confirms him in his ecstasy of violence. Only in a hipster's fantasy is society so easily cheated of its prey and only in his fantasy can the self become so absolutized, so unchecked by reality, as to convert itself with impunity into the sole arbiter of good and evil.

It is evident that Mailer has repressed in this novel his common sense as well as the moral side of his nature. He has of late been arguing in his neo-primitivistic fashion, that civilization threatens to "extinguish the animal in us." This yea-saying to instinct is a common error of neo-primitivism. It is well known that patterns of instinct are rigid and conservative; the original and spontaneous are virtually a monopoly of human consciousness. Moreover, neo-primi-tivists seem unaware that not only "the animal in us" but also our Superego, as Freud and other analysts have repeatedly shown, is subject to repression. If Freud's motto was: "Where the Id once was there shall Ego be," Mailer's should read: "Where the Ego once was there shall Id be." Nor is the objection to the imaginative scheme of this novel a matter of morality pure and simple. It is also a matter of the novelist's primary responsibility to his craft. A writer like Mailer, who aspires to be something more than an intellectual version of Mickey Spillane, who takes himself seriously and in turn expects us to take him seriously, cannot without self-stultification center a story on so portentous a theme as murder (think of what novelists like Dostoevsky and Stendhal and Faulkner, among others equally preeminent, have made of this theme!) and then proceed to evade its multiple consequences in the dimensions of character and fate by means of sheer plot-manipulation. But I suppose this kind of thing was more or less in the cards ever since a number of our literary people have gone in in a big way for what is known as swinging. The swingers want to make the scene, to be "in," to be "with it." Their great pretension is that they are protesting against a genteel, conventional, and conformist society, but the fact is that they are not truly protestants or rebels at all. What they are doing is expressing the fickle moods of a certain sector of American society, by no means the least affluent, which in every sphere but the political has collapsed into total permissiveness. There is money in it and fun too, though in the long run the fun runs out as the law of diminishing returns takes over. And as the shock of riotous explicitness in the handling of sexual subject matter by writers wears off, murder and other forms of brutal sadism beckon from the wings. Engaged in raising the ante all the time, the swingers must come to that.

Who is this protagonist of Mailer's? He is not at all the anti-hero of modern fiction but one of the most lamentably old-fashioned heroes, in the dictionary meaning of a man of distinguished valor and performance, I have come across in years. Hence as a novelistic character he never quite comes to life: he remains a vacuity. He is "the one intellectual in America with a Distinguished Service Cross," an ex-Congressman, a television celebrity, a professor of "existentialist psychology with the not inconsiderable thesis that magic, dread and the perception of death were the roots of motivation," author of a work entitled *The Psychology of the Hangman,* and, needless to say, a prepotent lover and expert in fisticuffs. Though as conformist as anyone else in his bedazzlement by power and success ("there's nothing but magic at the top"), he is so full, however, of obsessions almost clinical in nature, and outright superstitions to boot, that the last thing one can say about him is that he stands generically for

Americans at large. On all levels but that of literal biography he is a facsimile of the author, down to the most absurd details of his personal mythology; and some of the secondary characters, like his girl friend Cherry and his millionaire wheeler-dealer father-in-law, are also mere mouthpieces on occasion. The national experience, whether conceived in the broadly typical manner of Dreiser and Dos Passos or in a latent imaginative form, is not to be found in this novel. Its true *raison d'être* is a dream of romantic omnipotence, in which what is projected is a mana-figure, a being of occult and enchanting powers. Mailer is testing here (or acting out, to be more precise) a whole cluster of notions to which he has committed himself. But unfortunately for him the fictional medium is far more exacting in its demands than the discursive form of the article, in which charm and personal vehemence take you a long way.

To make sense of *An American Dream* one must use as a gloss the articles he has collected in *Advertisements for Myself* and *The Presidential Papers*. There he declares that "the existentialist moment, by demanding the most extreme response in the protagonist, tends to destroy psychotic autonomies . . . and then one is returned to the realities of one's personal strength or weakness." Also, "whether the life is criminal or not, the decision is to encourage the psychopath in oneself." Also: "Postulate a modern soul marooned in constipation, emptiness, boredom and a flat, dull terror of death. It is a deadened existence, afraid precisely of violence, cannibalism, loneliness, insanity, libidinousness, perversion and mess, because these are states which in some way must be passed through, digested, transcended, if one is to make one's way back to life." The language here is a bit circumlocutory, a bit on the "tactical" side, but its meaning is clear enough. It appears that the way to "transcend" violence is to commit it, the way to overcome perversion is to indulge in it: get it out of your system once and for all. The "extreme response" (presumably not excluding murder) is regarded as therapeutic and heuristic. The psychopath in oneself is to be encouraged, and if that is indeed Mailer's program he has certainly succeeded only too well so far as this latest novel at least is concerned. And the most curious thing about it all is the way in which in all his invocations of violence he nearly always identifies with its perpetrators, almost never with its victims. And violence, however extreme, is plainly for him a testing ground of courage which he is inclined to understand, with excessive reiteration and emphasis, in a strictly physical sense. Yet because of such ideas Mailer has been saluted by some people as a "moralist" no less, an expositor of sacred mysteries, a religious type in fact.

The one religious notion of the novel is expressed by the girl friend Cherry in this wise: "There is no decent explanation for evil. I believe God is just doing His best to learn from what happens to us. Sometimes I think He knows less than the Devil because we're not good enough to teach Him. So the Devil gets most of the best messages we think we are sending up." This same belief is elaborated by Rojack's father-in-law, who holds that God is engaged in a war with the Devil and God may lose. — "God might be having a very bad war, with troops defecting everywhere." Thus when the God-Devil relationship is not conceived of as a kind of celestial prize fight it is conceived of as a scene from a war novel. This echo of an old Christian heresy, a sort of flattened out Manichaeism, is solemnly offered as a contribution to theology. It also seems to contain a vague, distorted, late American military-style reminiscence of *Paradise Lost*. More than ever, then, we should now cry out with Wordsworth: "Milton! thou shouldst be living at this hour . . ."

Then there is Mailer's obsession with explaining cancer in his own inimitable manner, here repeated by Rojack: "In some madness must come with breath . . . In some it goes up to the mind. Some take the madness and stop it with discipline. Madness is locked beneath. It goes into the tissues, is swallowed by the cells. The cells go mad. Cancer is their flag." With what ease Mailer thus outmaneuvers the biochemists! And there are other far less "original" beliefs of a magical nature in the book, such as Rojack's compulsive involvement with "the phases of the moon," which now and then invites him to commit suicide; but these thoughts of suicide, induced by the guileful moon, appear to have nothing to do with guilt-feelings or remorse; in fact they occur to him before the murder. Rojack also hears voices and messages from some unspecified beyond, which at one point order him to walk three times around a parapet twelve inches wide at the Waldorf Towers thirty stories above the street, and this feat he virtually manages to accomplish too. Then there is a whose series of extravaganzas of the olfactory sense, a kind of olfactory mysticism, permitting Rojack to smell what are really states of mind rather than states of the body.

On the technical side what the novel obviously lacks is verisimilitude, even in the most literal sense. In his thirty-two hours in New York Rojack, a man no longer young, engages in feats of strength — consuming vast quantities of alcohol, fighting, making strenuous love to two different girls, not to mention murder — that would lay low not one but several younger men. The characters don't emerge into reality, especially Rojack and his girl Cherry; Deborah is drawn rather better than the rest. In Chapter 7 the Negro singer Shago Martin engages in a near-monologue of hipster talk which is worldly-wise, heady and strangely effective. It is a pity that he does not stay around long enough, for he is soon beaten up by Rojack and thrown downstairs. Eventually, in the very last paragraph, the words "I was something like sane again" occur, but here Rojack is referring not to the main action in New York but to his last and least credible experience in Las Vegas, where the story ends. It is important to stress that Rojack is not considered by his author to be insane — inspired, if you please, but not mad.

But Mailer is no ordinary swinger. For one thing, he cannot be accused of pornographic intent, as the sex-writing in his more recent work, however rank and dense, is so mixed up with concepts of the self's salvation that it cannot be mistaken for exploitative commercialized sexology. For another, he is a prose-writer of considerable gifts; and this novel is likewise written with a certain sharpness, though to my taste there are too many purple passages in it. The trouble with Mailer, to my mind, is that he has let himself become a victim of ideas productive of "false consciousness"; and these ideas are willful, recklessly simple, and too histrionic. He has too many ambition-fed notions and he does not sufficiently value the artistic function. His habitual stance of toughness and the "advertisements" of his own special brand of excruciated sexology have not been helpful in resolving the discords of his creative personality. Salvation is not to be seized by force of heroics or diabolics. Life's cruel and inexorable processes can be arrested neither by the brain nor by the phallus, least of all by the phallus. But if Mailer ever extricates himself from his entanglement with the hocus-pocus of power and the glamor-dream of the romantic domination, physical and psychic, of existence, he might yet emerge as one of our greater talents.

1965

Postscript 1969 — There is surely something to be said about Mailer's development since the publication of *An American Dream*. His next novel, *Why Are We in Vietnam?*, struck me as an even worse performance. The author's frenetic language, the failure to discover in the youthful hero-narrator anything but one more souped-up version of himself and, above all, the extravagant and (to my mind) wholly unfounded claim of having gained deep insights into the American psyche — what does all that come to but more play-acting, more gimmickry? The fact is that though Mailer is overly fascinated by the actuality of America, he has no real ideas about it. All you find in him on this subject are outlandish notions, mostly psychosexual projections of his own confused inner life; nor has the personality cult which the media have by now secured for him proven to be anything but damaging to that inner life. And in the literary world he has become the hero of a claque whose outrageous puffery cannot but abort his creative career in the long run. If he takes it seriously, that is. And I am afraid he does. He is not very discerning in distinguishing his talent for self-promotion from his genuine talents as an imaginative writer.

However, Mailer appears to have recovered somewhat his élan in his more recent journalistic works, *Armies of the Night* and *Miami and the Siege of Chicago*. For Mailer is really far more effective as an observer and reporter of immediate situations than as an ideologue. In the latter role he seldom conveys an impression of authenticity; what you mostly get is mere idea-mongering in a dashing manner. In this respect he reminds me of what T. S. Eliot once said about Chesterton: that his "brain swarms with ideas; I see no evidence that it thinks." At bottom Mailer is a man of divided consciousness, ambivalent in the extreme. Instinctively an extremist of the Left, if not a complete anarchist, he nevertheless prefers to speak of himslf as a "left conservative," whatever that may mean. So he strives with might and main to seem more "original" in his political and intellectual attitudes than it is within his power to be. Even in *Armies of the Night* he by no means overcomes his besetting vice of playing ego-games and flaunting his personality. Yet the famous Mailer personality is not actually very interesting. It affects animal vitality and pride of life, but what comes through mainly, apart from all-too-obvious charm, is unbounded egocentrism and flamboyance of phrase and posture. It is only in *Miami and the Siege of Chicago* that he manages to stick to the job at hand and thus succeeds in checking his bent for self-exploitation. For this reason I think it is a far better book than *Armies of the Night*.

ON PORNOGRAPHY, BLACK HUMOR,
NORMAN MAILER, ETC.

Interviewer: Is there any particular way in which contemporary literature can be characterized?

Rahv: The present situation in American literature is one of perplexity and confusion, of marking time, actually, while most of the attention goes to the hipsters, militant homosexuals, and pornographers, who claim the title of avant-garde even while trying to "make it" in a big way in the wordly world. They are tremendously concerned with publicity and success at the same time as they come on as moral and literary rebels. But what exactly would you like to talk about?

Interviewer: How about the pornographers?

Rahv: The pornography written today, as well as the old pornography, like *Fanny Hill*, reissued in new editions and widely distributed, is being played up as a form of literature, but it still remains pornography no matter what the label.

This interview appeared in the undergraduate Brandeis literary magazine, *Folio*.

Terry Southern's book, *Candy,* consists of a series of dirty jokes. It uses one of the standard gimmicks of pornography. The main character is not in any sense a person. She is supposed to be a liberal type, all too open to experience, anxious to help the deprived, and the novel is ostensibly a satire on liberal credulity. This is simply a gimmick making it easy for Southern to take her through a whole series of scabrous incidents. None of the other people in the book are real characters either. The humor of the story, real enough on a low level, has nothing to do with literature. Yet *Candy* was built up by the reviewers as a spoof on pornography, some kind of sophisticated product no less. In my judgment its impulse is basically commercial, and we know, in fact, that it was originally written for a few hundred dollars to feed the Olympia Press in Paris.

Actually, it is not possible for pornography to be a literary form because its aim is too "practical," so to speak. Its aim is to appeal to prurient interests and to satisfy the public's inexhaustible interest in sexual details; nor does the public care whether the information given is in any sense accurate or not. Now literature can never have such a limited and "practical" goal.

Interviewer: Do you think that pornography is bad on moral grounds?

Rahv: As a critic, I am not concerned with the question whether pornography is good or bad for young people, or old people for that matter. This is something for the courts or other governmental bodies to worry about. Nor am I a sociologist. I have opinions on the subject but they are no better qualified than yours. As a literary critic I am qualified — or at least I think I am — to judge whether it is a form of literature, as it now claims to be, or not.

The publishers have succeeded in putting something over on reviewers and critics who are confused by the cultural atmosphere of the 1960s and who live in mortal fear of being called squares or philistines. Now the reviewers have nothing to gain when a pornographic work becomes a best seller. The publishers, however, stand to make a lot of money, yet reviewers, and even some academic types, have apparently chosen to play their game.

There is a large distinction to be made between a novel like *Candy* and one like *Lolita.* The latter work has a literary framework within which the sexual events take place. The characters are interesting and credible, the author's sensibility is superb, and the erotic scenes are validated by the context. But *Candy* is a novel with sex but no people, no psychology; it is mere organ-grinding in words, as pornography inevitably tends to be; even the book's sexology is not real, because you can't have sexuality without relationships, without people. You can't create a character by limiting yourself to purely physical sexual acts. People are not reducible to their private parts.

It is in the nature of novelists — American novelists especially — to be very competitive with one another. And now that the clinical sex-scene has virtually become obligatory, most novelists feel that they must bring in this scene into their work, whether it belongs there or not, or risk losing out in the competitive game. I think this situation is causing a good deal of damage to the literary effort, for what you have here in consequence is a new and terribly tyrannical literary convention imposed by commercial considerations.

Pure physical sensation is very difficult to render in literature anyhow. The sensation tends to be pretty much the same no matter who is involved, and this leads to monotony or else to totally irrelevant rhapsody. On the other hand, desire and erotic states in general can be rendered with far more interest and variety, as for instance in *Madame Bovary,* where actual intercourse is not described though an air of sensuality pervades the novel.

Pornography is essentially a sub-literary form. All it has in common with literature is the written word.

Interviewer: What about the black humorists?

Rahv: Black humor seems to me — as a phrase — to have become a mere fashionable label for elevating all kinds of shoddy work to artistic status. The best piece of black humor in American literature that I know of is *Miss Lonelyhearts* — a very good book published in the early 1930s. But why use the expression anyway? Most of the writers called black humorists today are mere buffoons of one sort or another. To call them black humorists is to flatter them. The expression suggests a desperate state of negation, but our writers are far too worldly-wise and ambitious for that sort of thing. They are still immersed in the cult of experience.

Interviewer: Do you have any thoughts as to why Mailer's novel, *An American Dream*, did not become a best seller?

Rahv: Not because it was too shocking but rather because it was so childish. There is a small literary clique which is furious because it did not make the best-seller list, and the members of that clique, mostly hangers-on of Mailer, are very angry at Bellow for the success of his novel, *Herzog*.

In his novel Mailer is out to show that he can outsex all the sexologists. But the sex-scenes are not sexy; they are mostly repulsive. But that is not important as such. Rojack (the novel's hero who is so closely identified with his author in his ideas and general demeanor) appears to consider bed an arena in which to show off his prowess as a male. What he is after is domination, not pleasure; he wants to subdue women, to bring them to subjection by exercising some kind of magic. The feeling of competition with other men is very prominent throughout the work, and one of the women tells Rojack that he is a sexual genius.

On the question of murder, the main event of the book, Mailer indulges himself in pure uninhibited fantasy. He pretends that the act of murder has no moral relevance. But whatever may be true of life, where people both literally and figuratively sometimes "get away with murder," this cannot be true of the novel, a literary form that cannot ignore moral experience. This is not just moralizing. The prohibition of murder is not a mere convention of society, a pious prejudice or some kind of bourgeois leftover: it has existed in every society, however primitive. The serious novelist must see it as a significant act with consequences. Now Mailer does not attempt to reevaluate murder morally. He presents it as a self-justified. Why does his hero kill his wife? Because she makes some sarcastic remarks about his virility. No wonder Prof. Coser has called the novel "an apologia for murder." Actually, Rojack is the comic-strip fantasy of an adolescent. The neo-primitivism, which has played a considerable role in modern literature, is reduced in this work to mere gratuitous violence and sexual braggadocio.

1966

HAWTHORNE IN ANALYSIS

O NE CANNOT SPEAK of Hawthorne these days without observing that of all the classic American writers he is perhaps the one least understood by the academic scholarship and criticism of our time. It is to be hoped, therefore, that Frederick C. Crews's book, *The Sins of the Fathers: Hawthorne's Psychological Themes*, with its unabashedly and relentlessly Freudian analysis of what really goes on beneath the didactic surface of his fiction, will induce serious misgivings in the circle of Hawthorne specialists and lead to a significant revision of the genteel orthodoxies they now find so serviceable. But somehow I doubt it.

The academic mind, particularly when it comes into possession of some small specialty, has its own way of absorbing insights it finds disagreeable and in the long run rendering them harmless; and the psychoanalytic method, having been so frequently and grossly abused by popularizers and sensation-mongers among both laymen and analysts, is peculiarly open to the charge of being academically disreputable. Hence I expect that for some years to come Hawthorne will continue to be presented in the classrooms as a kind of "religious tutor to posterity," a Christ-like figure no less, or else, in a more secular version, as a diligent and accurate student of American history. This second approach is almost as bad as the first: It depersonalizes Hawthorne's tales and romances, turning them into documentary source-material readily annexed by that proliferously ambitious, empire-building new academic "discipline" called American Studies.

Mr. Crews — an academic himself, though of an uncommon kind — applies Freudian techniques to his literary subject matter in an acute and highly sophisticated fashion; and in the process he easily controverts both approaches, with the religious-didactic one, which is the most influential in Hawthorne studies, receiving most of his polemical thrusts. Unfortunately, but not at all unexpectedly, it is exactly these approaches that are copiously exemplified in the collection of essays designed as collateral reading for students that A. N. Kaul has edited for the critical series advertised as "Twentieth Century Views." I don't believe that students will get much out of it. Only a few entries in it deserve our esteem, such as, notably, Yvor Winters' chapter on Hawthorne taken from his book, *Maule's Curse*. Even if Mr. Winters never gets anywhere near considering Hawthorne as an individual writer with a temperament and personal background specifically his own, and not just as the focus of New England's theological bias and allegoric bent, still his essay traces with precision the impact of the dogmas and habits of mind of the Puritans and their successors on the literary imagination of New England; and his critical estimate of Hawthorne is far from inflationary.

Not so Q. D. Leavis, who, I am bound to say, prodigiously inflates his achievement in her essay, "Hawthorne as Poet." She sees him as "the critic and interpreter of American cultural history" (why the definite article?), compares him, entirely to his advantage, with Milton, and commits herself to the view, wholly unacceptable in my opinion, that "the just comparison with *The Scarlet Letter* is not *The Pilgrim's Progress* but *Anna Karenina*, which in theme and technique it seems to me astonishingly to resemble." It is hard to conceive of a more inapt comparison. What, after all, do these two books have in common? The subject of adultery (and in the language of criticism *subject* is by no means the equivalent of *theme*), which they share with any number of novels. Moreover, as is well known, in matters of art the subject is a more or less neutral element; what counts primarily is treatment, and in this respect the two novels are obviously poles apart. So what are we left with? The idea of sin presumably. Yet *The Scarlet Letter* is not in fact the novelistic representation of a sin (if we can call it that, for its author's ambivalence, as the text shows, forced him repeatedly to voice his doubts even about that) but only of its aftermath. It goes without saying, of course, that nothing whatever in Tolstoy's novel reminds us in any sense of the two strains that mingle in Hawthorne's literary nature: the spectral strain of the Gothic tale and the pietistic strain of Christian allegory, both of which contribute to his estrangement from the actual. But it is of the actual above all that Tolstoy is in secure possession. No doubt *The Scarlet Letter* is in its way a masterpiece, though only if measured on a strictly national if not provincial scale, whereas *Anna Karenina* is one of the four or five great novels of the world, incomparably superior, in its total vision as in its creative resources, to anything that Hawthorne, with his fear of life induced by bare and crabbed circumstances and his obsessive memories of the past, could possibly have produced. How Mrs. Leavis, richly endowed as she is with a sense of literary history, could insist on a "just comparison" here, is beyond me.

So much for twentieth-century views! What the essays in Mr. Kaul's collection mainly attest to is that "process of canonization" which Mr. Crews rightly deplores as having contributed to the fact that Hawthorne, like all saints, "has ascended to dullness." But Hawthorne is in essence far from being a dull writer; it is only necessary to learn how to read him, how not to confuse the manifest with the latent content of his work. And it is in this regard, precisely, that the theologically-minded critics are at fault, having failed to apply the resources of modern intelligence to his fiction. They have refused to see that Hawthorne's religiosity was of the surface only, not a matter of the deepest personal feeling but a traditional rhetoric he adopted as a protective screen for his fantasies. The most that can be said is that though the faith of his forefathers had lost its rational appeal to him, it still, in part, ruled and imprisoned him psychologically. Hence the inherited beliefs appear in his work as phantoms rather than convictions. "How plausible is it," writes Mr. Crews, to make a saintly allegorist of a man who almost never went to church, who described his masterpiece as a "hell-fired story," and who confessed to his journal, "We certainly do need a new revelation — a new system — for there seems to be no life in the old one." And indeed, once we have ceased trying to make him into a source of oracular wisdom, "we perceive that Hawthorne's keynote was neither piety nor impiety, but ambivalence . . . In short, Hawthorne was emotionally engaged in his fiction, and the emotions he displays are those of a self-divided, self-tormented man."

In the not so remote past, however, some very good things were written about him, though hardly at all from a rigorously psychological point of view — by Henry James, for instance, by Paul Elmer More in his penetrating essay, "Hawthorne, Looking Before and After," by Van Wyck Brooks in a few pages of his book, *America's Coming-of-Age,* and of course by D. H. Lawrence. The James volume of 1879 in the "English Men of Letters" series exerts a perennial charm and is of lasting interest to students of the native culture; but James was scarcely in a position to expand his analysis of his chief predecessor beyond calling attention to his care "for the deeper psychology," and to the glimpses his work offers "of the whole deep mystery of man's soul and conscience." He also carefully explained why he thought Hawthorne's allegorizing a weakness, even if an inevitable one under the circumstances, for allegory "was apt to spoil two good things — a story and a moral, a meaning and a form." In 1915 Van Wyck Brooks wrote some pages on Hawthorne that set the tone for the moderately candid biographies of him that appeared during the twenties. According to Brooks,

> this being who passed twelve years of his youth in a solitary, close-curtained room, walking abroad only in the twilight . . . was himself a phantom in a phantom-world.

Not long afterwards, D. H. Lawrence remarked on "the duplicity of that blue-eyed *Wunderkind* of a Nathaniel," accurately noting the split in him between outward conformity and "the impeccable truth of his art-speech." This was a valuable hint, ignored, to be sure, by the Hawthorne specialists, who in the past two decades or so have transmogrified the "haunted" Hawthorne, a phantom-like being, into a figure of nearly Goethean repose, a wide-awake American culture-hero, at once a didactic writer and a symbolist in the version of symbolism cooked up by the New Critics. What happened to the allegorizing that James took exception to? It was somehow metabolized into myth and symbol. By 1950 this distorted evaluation of Hawthorne had gained so much ground in the academy that Professor Hyatt H. Waggoner, one of the principal specialists, was able to claim in his Introduction to the Rinehart edition of his *Selected Tales and Sketches*, a text widely used in the schools, that "Hawthorne's views were those of democratic Christian humanism, and the key word here is Christian . . . Hawthorne's sensibility was primarily Christian, and his instinct was for the central catholic tradition of Christian humanism." Now this is nothing more than a bland fiction, designed to adapt Hawthorne to the demands of the *Zeitgeist*, a compound, at that time, of the triple alliance of the New Conservatism, the Revival of Religion, and the New Criticism. It is literally impossible to understand what our scholars and critics were then saying about Hawthorne (and numerous other writers) without accounting for it by the prevailing *Zeitgeist*.

Given the backwardness of Hawthorne studies, that is, the determined refusal of the specialists to examine his work realistically, one cannot but welcome Mr. Crews's psychoanalytical investigation, which succeeds, to my mind, in uncovering what is beneath "the layers of euphemism and rationalization" we find in this classic American writer. There is nothing new, of course, in the psychoanalytic approach; it is a modern platitude, but in the case of Hawthorne, so protected by genteel academic prejudice and sheer timorousness, the approach Mr. Crews has chosen is something of a daring novelty. He concentrates not so much on his subject's biography as on his psychological themes and patterns; nor is he primarily writing literary criticism, though his study contains a good deal of it. If criticism is, among other things, the evaluation of literature, then it is plain that psychoanalytic statements about literature are not in themselves criticism. What they are is a form of research, precisely in the same sense that historical or formal analysis is a mode of research. But research, all types of it, constitutes the indispensable material on the basis of which the critic forms his judgment, his evaluation of a work of literature. And in Hawthorne's case we have long missed the kind of research that Mr. Crews has undertaken: therein lies its value.

He clearly establishes that the emphasis in Hawthorne is "on buried motives which are absolutely binding" because of their unavailability to consciousness. With his "sense of guilt rooted in the twin themes of incest and patricide," he exhibits "a definable, indeed classic, conflict of wishes at the heart of his ambivalence that provides the innermost configuration of his plots"; and in his writings he nonetheless succeeds in "simultaneously *analyzing* and *indulging*" his psychological excess. It should be stressed that Mr. Crews nowhere contends that Hawthorne is ingeniously concealing his meanings or playing any games. The point is, rather, that though as anxious as anyone to view his protagonists superficially, he could not help but "*represent* their motives" in fictional terms. The inescapable conclusion is that "sexual obsession is the governing force" of his work.

Mr. Crews's thorough reading of Hawthorne takes us through all his writings, from the early "Alice Doane's Appeal," in which the ostensible interest in the historical past is "nothing other than the sense of family conflict writ large," the four novels, his better short stories, and finally the four aborted romances with which he wrestled toward the end of his life but could never finish. They remain mere fragments, inconsistent as imaginative works, for what is clearly apparent in them is "the return of the repressed" in a form so powerful that it could no longer be controlled; we find in them "an unceasing flow of repressed fantasy which is counteracted by unceasing denial and distortion." It is characteristic of the Hawthorne specialists that they usually make very little of the unfinished romances, dismissing them for the most part as the products of weariness or the senility of old age. But Hawthorne was only sixty years old when he died. So what is ordinarily said to explain the incoherence of these late works is mere evasion; it is only in Mr. Crews's analysis of them that they become relevant, showing that his "creative breakdown" occurred when "he surrendered to a neurotic despair whose origins he did not quite dare to understand."

Limitations of space do not permit me to reproduce Mr. Crews's closely reasoned argument or the wealth of evidence he cites from Hawthorne's texts. I have indicated only his conclusions, which to our present psychological sense cannot appear startling. For given the time and place in which Hawthorne lived, and taking into account the fact that he was a writer not of vaporous "transcendental" essays or apotheoses of "nature" but of imaginative prose, his neurosis was indeed exemplary — exemplary as private penalty and as expiation of "the sins of the fathers," his brutal and bigoted ancestors who hanged witches and persecuted Quakers. Therefore it comes as no great surprise to learn that the classic Hawthorne of the schoolbooks was indeed a classic "Freudian" case. The social environment and culture in which he grew up was intensely repressive of the more intimate emotions: no wonder he was as irresistibly drawn to sexuality as he was repelled by it. In his work he depicted a persistent character-image (Hester, Zenobia, Miriam, and Beatrice — "the dark lady of Salem," as I once named her) who is as beautiful and voluptuous as she is "inexpressibly terrible," a temptress offering the ascetic sons of the Puritans "the treasure-trove of a great sin." The very juxtaposition in one phrase of two such words as "treasure-trove" and "sin" is deeply expressive of the conflict that at once fired his imagination and depressed his life. His constant plaint was: "I have not lived but only dreamed of living."

As Mr. Crews sees it, his outward conformity, his conspicuous respectability as a father and public official, do not erase the sense of "melancholy isolation" he gives us,

> any more than his professed love of Dutch painting, of Trollope, of factual journalism can erase the fact that his own art was based on fantasy. Only an indifference to mental suffering can make us grateful for the emotional starvation that perversely nourished Hawthorne's art; we must admire the art and separately regret the life. And yet it is a fact that the two are inextricable. As Freud remarked in a moment of self-dramatization . . . "No one who, like me, conjures up the most evil of those half-tamed demons that inhabit the human breast, can

expect to come through the struggle unscathed." Let that be our epitaph for a writer whose anguished brooding has given us an urgent, a subtle, and an emotionally profound fiction.

The author of this fiction is, needless to say, quite unknown to the Hawthorne specialists. So much the worse for them.

1966

T. S. ELIOT IN HIS
POSTHUMOUS ESSAYS

THERE IS MUCH to interest and even fascinate students of T. S. Eliot in his posthumously published collection, *To Criticize the Critic and Other Writings,* consisting for the most part of public lectures and addresses delivered between 1942 and 1961. Of the earlier articles not heretofore reprinted only two, both dating back to 1917 — one on *vers libre* and the other on the metrics of Ezra Pound — are included in this volume. The analysis of *vers libre* is as lively as it is discriminating, keyed to the highest pitch of poetic intelligence; but the essay on Pound's metrics is less satisfactory. It is full of technical argumentation that somehow steers clear of any truly evaluative judgment. It has generally been my impression that, in his various statements on Pound, Eliot seems to be laboring under an intolerable burden of personal indebtedness that inhibits candor. As a result, what we get is a kind of embarrassed formalism that makes more for the appearance than the substance of criticism. He is always ready to praise Pound; yet the grounds of his praise, apart from the purely technical points involved, remain obscure.

The title essay of the volume is indispensable for the understanding of Eliot's development. He reviews in it the entire corpus of his critical writing with great tact and a good deal of humor. The self-deprecatory manner characteristic of his later years is also much in evidence in his remarks on errors of judgment and errors of tone: "the occasional note of arrogance, of cocksureness and rudeness, the braggadocio of the mild-mannered man safely entrenched behind his typewriter." As he grew older Eliot was never fanatical about his literary ideas and opinions, and he mixed grace with courage in retracting quite a few of them, as on the subject of Milton, for instance; nor did he ever lose sight of the literary object in expounding his religious convictions. The one interlude of fanaticism in his career that I recall occurred in the early 1930s, and its upshot was *After Strange Gods*. This book, harsh and even supercilious in tone, has not been reprinted for a long time, probably because its author regretted its publication in the first place. The fanaticism has been voiced mainly by his disciples, who did their master little good by converting his insights, perhaps inseparable from their specific contexts, into dogmas; and Eliot does in fact express here his irritation at having his words, uttered decades ago, quoted as if he had written them yesterday. Even the famous statement (in the Preface to *For Lancelot Andrewes*) that proclaimed him to be "a classicist in literature, a royalist in politics, and an Anglo-Catholic in religion," is considerably hedged in 1961 — the Anglo-Catholicism is still firmly retained, while the royalism is reduced to an empty gesture, and the classicism is brushed aside altogether. It is clear that Eliot is no system-builder, has no great flair for logical consistency, and is scarcely if ever concerned with the more abstract concepts of aesthetic theorizing. If a number of influential commentators have insisted on deriving a system from his work, it is largely due, it seems to me, to their willfully confusing his religious ideas, which belong to an entirely different order of discourse and are even at best quite unoriginal, with his literary and critical ones. There is no real interdependence, either logical or substantive, between the two orders of ideas. For it can be shown, I think, that his more valuable literary ideas are mostly empirical in nature and can easily be disengaged from his religious commitments. That this disengagement is stubbornly resisted by some people points to the vested interest in Eliot that the religious ideologists have acquired. The religious experience that he records in his poetry is validated by the poetry, not the other way around; the ideology, insofar as it enters his criticism, is something else again, and should be separated out if we are to make the best use of it. Deliberately or not, it is exactly in this fashion that we proceed with Dr. Johnson, with Coleridge, and with Arnold. Why not with Eliot, who, to my mind, is as good a critic as any of them?

Eliot distinguishes three periods in his criticism, and attributes the "enduring popularity" of his earlier essays, in which, as he says, he was implicitly defending the sort of poetry he was then writing, to a kind of "urgency, the warmth of appeal of the advocate," which his later, "more detached and judicious essays cannot claim." (Of course, there is more to it than that: The authority and enormous influence of that earlier criticism, though it must always be considered in close relation to the poetry, are by no means fully accounted for by his successful poetic practice.) In the first period the influences he was chiefly aware of were those of Irving Babbitt and Ezra Pound, "with a later infusion of T. E. Hulme and of the more literary essays of Charles Maurras" — influences apparent in the recurrent theme of Classicism vs. Romanticism, an opposition he later abandoned when he realized that its literary implications were meager indeed, and that its origins lay mainly in political conservatism. As for the emphasis on "tradition" — transmogrified by the disciples, of whom there were far too many until very recently, into a reactionary status-symbol — it came about, he states, as a result of his reaction against the poetry, in English, of the nineteenth and early twentieth centuries, and his "passion" for the poetry, both dramatic and lyric, of the late sixteenth and early seventeenth centuries. But this much we have known for a long time. He is "certain of one thing," however, that he wrote best about the poets who influenced his own poetry.

The essay "To Criticize the Critic" is full of very informative asides and excellent formulations. Thus he comments on his varying attitudes toward D. H. Lawrence through the years, confessing that, in spite of Mr. Leavis' repeated animadversions, his antipathy to Lawrence remains, "on the grounds of what seems to be egotism, a strain of cruelty, and a failing in common with that of Thomas

Hardy — the lack of a sense of humor." This may not be the last word on Lawrence, but it surely adumbrates a more realistic approach, and a more sensible one, than can be inferred from the overwrought opinions of Dr. Leavis, whose addiction to a limited, social-moralistic, edifying interpretation of Lawrence has now for the most part prevailed in academic circles. Eliot persists in his view that it is impossible "to fence off literary criticism from criticism on other grounds," that standards other than those of "literary merit" cannot be excluded in the long run. I think that he made this point with greater precision in an earlier essay, "Religion and Literature": "The greatness of literature cannot be determined solely on literary grounds; though we must remember that whether it is literature or not can be determined only by literary standards." Certainly the practice of most literary critics, past and present, bears out this simple but very important truth.

It is disturbing to observe that this simple truth, substantiated by the whole history of literature, is hardly understood any longer by our younger, articulate critics of art and letters, whose twaddle about something they call "aesthetic bliss," setting immediate sensation above thought and feeling, has lately acquired a fashionable ring. What this represents, finally, is a falling back to *fin-de-siècle* aestheticism, only in a souped-up, modish version. Now in the van of fashion — and fashion invariably goes in for change for its own sake and novelty at all costs — those people are not critics at all but the tastemakers of the newly affluent whose vulgar yearning it is to consume culture, as it consumes any product that makes for "excitement." Since these tastemakers have learned that "culture" goes down all the more easily if diluted with *kitsch*, they exhibit no reluctance whatever to issuing certificates of aesthetic chastity to *kitsch* of all sorts. The true function of criticism, however, is more frequently to resist the *Zeitgeist* rather than acquiesce in its now rampant aberrations. As Eliot notes in his book, criticism at its best acts "as a kind of cog regulating the change of literary taste," since it is well aware of "the antiquarianism of the old and the eccentricity and even charlatanism of the new . . ."

It is necessary to add that the parts of this volume dealing with nonliterary subjects are not very impressive, reminding us, unhappily, of such laborious compositions as *Notes toward a Definition of Culture* and *The Idea of a Christian Society*. In such works the author's superior intelligence and ironic bent recede before his sense of duty as a responsible Anglican churchman. An example is the long piece, "The Aims of Education," which, though bristling with carefully staged definitions, does not really get us very far beyond Arnold's "the best that has been said and thought in the world." But the literary essays are as superb as ever. Even if more "detached and judicial" than Eliot's earlier work, certainly they display no falling off in the assured grasp of issues relevant to a literary discussion, no loss of vigor in the tactful but firm avoidance of concerns that are basically academic. For instance, in the short essay on "American Literature and Language," he dissects a number of questions which most of our critics are not properly equipped even to identify. Thus Eliot persuades us once again that he is the finest literary critic of this century in the English language. His only possible rival is Edmund Wilson. But the comparison is not quite to the point, because Wilson's merits and demerits are of a different order. In the future the comparison will no doubt be made often enough, but only after essential distinctions between *kinds* of criticism have been drawn.

To my mind the most admirable piece of criticism in the book is the essay "From Poe to Valéry" — a marvel of precision and insight. Eliot begins by giving us his impression of Poe's status among English and American readers and critics, an impression accurate enough, and then proceeds to develop his own estimate of him. I take it to be the definitive estimate; I certainly find it far more convincing than either the wholly negative, virtually demolishing, view that Yvor Winters adopted in *Maule's Curse*, or the somewhat implausibly positive opinion of Poe to which Wilson has committed himself. In some of Poe's poems Eliot detects "an irresponsibility towards the meaning of words," and he has no trouble refuting in detail the theory of the impossibility of writing a long poem. According to Eliot, that Poe had a powerful intellect is undeniable, but it was also a fatally immature intellect. Though the variety and ardor of his curiosity delight and dazzle, yet in the end the eccentricity and lack of coherence of his interests tire. There is just that lacking which gives dignity to the mature man: a consistent point of view. An attitude can be mature and consistent, and yet be highly skeptical: but Poe was no skeptic. He appears to yield himself to the idea of the moment: the effect is that all his ideas seem to be *entertained* rather than believed.

But the heart of the essay is in Eliot's consideration of the manner in which three French poets, Baudelaire, Mallarmé, and Valéry, representing three different generations, responded in different ways to Poe. Their response is, of course, the truly significant factor in his reputation. As Eliot sees it, Baudelaire primarily appreciated Poe as a prototype of *le poète maudit*, and in this sense he was first of all interested in Poe the man. With Mallarmé the interest shifts to Poe the poetic technician, while with Valéry "it is neither the man nor the poetry but the theory which engages the attention." Thus Eliot arrives at the strategic point where he can undertake a thorough analysis of *la poésie pure* and all the possible relations between subject matter and poetic language grown increasingly self-concious. Eliot does not come down on the side of purity. On the contrary, he thinks that "poetry is only poetry so long as it preserves some 'impurity' in this sense: that is to say, so long as the subject matter is valued for its own sake." Valéry represents above all a change of attitude toward the subject matter. It is not so much that it has become less important but rather that its importance is that of a means only — the end is the poem. Furthermore, in Valéry, the interest in the compositional process, and in observing himself in the act of composition, finally displaces even the belief in ends. This represents the culmination of ideas that can be traced back to Poe. And what about the future? Eliot holds it as "a tenable hypothesis that this advance of self-consciousness, the extreme awareness of and concern for language which we can find in Valéry, is something which must ultimately break down, owing to an increasing strain against which the human mind and nerves will rebel . . ." That in this respect Eliot is essentially right is shown by the work of the latest generation of poets, post-Eliot and post-Auden, who are in full retreat from the more complicated verbal and structural modes of the recent past.

Eliot is dead, and we will not soon see his like again. He was one of the principal educators of the imaginative life of his age, a uniquely great shaping influence both as poet and critic. In the latter capacity he was never deceived by the stratagems and artifices of "methodology," and taught us to understand that the only method is to be very, very intelligent, that, in the words of Henry James, "the deepest quality of a work of art will always be the quality of the mind of the producer." His commitment to orthodox beliefs must have answered an irresistible inner demand of his nature for a discipline to shore him up against chaos, against his fears of "shape without form, shade without color/Paralysed force, gesture without motion." In this sense it was no more than an anodyne, yet we who have not suffered his pains are seldom in a position to reproach him. No, it was not in the titanic ambition to steal fire from heaven that he sought his inspiration but rather in a kind of patience of suffering and wonderment of scruples forbidding him ever to try purloining the things that rightly belong to the gods.

1966

AN OPEN SECRET

JOHN R. HARRISON's *The Reactionaries: Yeats, Lewis, Pound, Eliot, Lawrence: A Study of the Anti-Democratic Intelligentsia,* is an important book, which is scarcely likely to win favor in the Literary Establishment. It rattles too many skeletons in the closet. The importance of the book does not lie in the incidental literary criticism it contains but in its undertaking a necessary job of systematic research into the "beliefs" present in the work of some of the major writers of our age. Why, then, do I anticipate this negative reaction of defensive maneuvers and clever alibis? Because four of the five writers (Wyndham Lewis is the least famous among them) examined by Mr. Harrison — and he finds the ideas about history and society of all five to be lamentably reactionary — belong to the exalted company of the "sacred untouchables," as they have rightly been called, of the modern creative line. Read and praised everywhere, they have been speedily converted to classics of the college classroom, where they are almost invariably presented in a heroic light. Thus they have come to represent a vested interest not so readily affronted.

I suppose there is a natural propensity among critics, scholars, and teachers of literature to equate superior works of the imagination with creedal wisdom and beneficence. Few can resist the temptation to swallow a doctrine implicit in a body of poetry that gratifies the aesthetic sense; most cannot bear to admit to themselves that the relation between literature and truth or moral insight is sometimes very erratic, if not altogether deceptive. This is a weakness that fits very nicely with the megalomaniacal disposition of modern art, a disposition easily diverted in our latter days from the close appreciation of the work to the apotheosis of the artist's person. People in the aging twentieth century, prostrate amid their material affluence and spiritual bankruptcy, surveying the wreckage of all the earlier schemes of salvation, whether secular or religious, are impelled to seek in art the highly consolatory, if not absolute, values they crave. As a consequence we have the culture explosion so called, the promoters of which, all too ubiquitous at present, are sometimes touching in their naiveté but more often frenetic and offensive in the impostures and dissimulations they subject us to. How much closer to the truth is Jean Dutourd, who observes in his latest novel that "loving beautiful things doesn't mean that one has a beautiful soul but that one has a taste for luxury. The supreme luxury, which is the prerogative of artists of genius, doesn't presuppose that one possesses the supreme virtue, which is charity." Though this is by no means the whole story, Dutourd's way of putting it is certainly worth keeping in mind, if only as a corrective to the cultism of art nowadays rampant among us. The tacit assumption of this cult is that art by itself is capable of conferring ultimate value and meaning upon life. In the long run such vain expectations are bound to lead to total disillusionment with culture.

The virtue of charity is the last one can look for in the "sacred untouchables" whose programmatic ideas Mr. Harrison (somewhat ingenuously, to be sure) has undertaken to investigate. But he is on to an open secret, which is simply, as he puts it in an early chapter, that

> what Yeats, Pound, Lewis and Eliot wanted in literature . . . was a hard intellectual approach ruled by the authority of strict literary principles. They rejected the humanist tradition in literature, and in society the democratic humanitarian tradition. The same principles governed their

social criticism as their literary criticism, and led them to support the fascist cause, either directly as Pound and Lewis did, or indirectly, as Yeats and Eliot did.

As for Lawrence, though emphatically not a believer in any kind of intellectual approach, he was quite a reactionary, as in his preaching a return to primitive life forms and his idealizing of blood sacrifice, his hostility to the democratic process and rant against the "mob-spirit" and "democratic mongrelism," his acclaim of power, of mastery and lordship, as a marvelous life-giving "mystery," and his urging us to surrender to "the natural power of the superior individual, the hero." Mr. Harrison hastens to note that "Lawrence's views on social leadership are inherently close to the fascist conception of society." I see no real gain in such a formulation. Admittedly Lawrence's views and attitudes are as false as they are dangerous, but what they represent is a private dream rather than a political plan or design; it is far more profitable to approach them through individual psychology and the precise analysis of the moment in Western culture that encouraged their emergence. Bald political terms, with their inevitable crudity of labeling, cannot provide illumination in this particular context. For all the coincidence of certain moods and preconceptions, neither Mussolini's Italy nor Hitler's Germany could find any real use for Lawrence in their cultural propaganda.

Hence I am inclined to object to Mr. Harrison's rather gummy use of the label "fascist" in his indictment of all five writers under consideration, just as I object to Empson speaking, in his Introduction to the book, of "the political scandal of their weakness for Fascism." Not that I deny that for a time Pound and Lewis supported the fascist cause — though Lewis reversed himself in later years, perhaps for the wrong reasons. Surely the "scandal" invoked by Empson can easily be made out to be real, but only if the entire theme of reaction in modern literature is transposed into strictly political terms. This transposition does not get us very far because it tends to stop discussion. In their social and political thinking all these writers were sheer amateurs, wonderfully alert in their own verbal medium but unable to grasp that politics is a specific medium — of action in history and society — and that it is preposterous to introduce into this medium notions of "personal supremacy" (Yeats) or of "the natural power of superior individuals" (Lawrence) as serious recommendations for the organization of society. They were drawn ideologically to authoritarian positions but were not in any definite way committed (not even Pound, who is by far the most vulnerable) to the shifting demands and intolerable dogmas of any given political party. Not one of them was in any meaningful sense a political man or even capable of consistent political thought. I doubt whether they understood how capitalism actually functions or exactly what socialists have in mind in proposing a different system. Their social-political unworldliness shows through all their denunciations of liberal ideas. There is in all five of them a radical want of modesty, and I am using the word as Chekhov used it in deploring Dostoevsky's "spiritual immodesty." What they can be truly accused of is presumption in undertaking to speak portentously about matters they knew little about. This presumption by quite a few men of letters is a cultural phenomenon — a symptom of certain antinomian qualities intrinsic to the literature of the modern age — which deserves more attention than Mr. Harrison, bemused by the political terminology he has adopted, has given it.

Yeats, for example, looked forward to a new aristocratic society, the rise of which he deduced from his theory of "cycles," with concentration of power in a small ruling class, "every detail of life hierarchical, every great door crowded at dawn by petitioners, great wealth in a few men's hands . . . an inequality made law." Despising democracy as a standardizing process, he idealized previous modes of social life. But these earlier periods, the model of which he saw in the custom of patronage supposedly beneficial to artists and in the "great houses" (Coole Park) of the eighteenth-century patricians, actually knew no such equality of aristocrat and artist as he had in mind. (Even in his own lifetime he imagined the "great houses" to be centers of civilized discourse and behavior, but according to the testimony of Louis MacNeice, a far less subjective observer than Yeats, those old houses contained no culture worth speaking of — "nothing but obsolete bravado, insidious bonhomie and a way with horses.") In Yeats a strain of social snobbery and resentment of certain features of the modern art era (such as the prestige of science) combined to produce a kind of historical snobbery scarcely at all concerned with historical truth. Vision was all; the facts didn't matter. An exacerbated imagination, over-stimulated by certain poems and graceful phrases he found in old books, conjoined with a coldness and aloofness of temper, "a lack of sympathy with ordinary humanity," as Mr. Harrison notes, generated in him a dream of the unity of art and life established in an order powerfully conducive to the creation of works of art.

This type of historical snobbery, though not necessarily always mixed with social snobbery, is also found in Eliot, Pound, Lewis, and Lawrence. Thus Pound, in the *Cantos*, locates his ideal society in the China of the eighteenth century and the time of Malatesta in the Italian Renaissance; he casts Jefferson and John Adams in the role of precursors of Mussolini, whose execution he laments in sincere poetic words: hung dead by the heels before his thought in proposito/came into action efficiently." It is not difficult to recognize in all five the vagaries of those who at once abuse the present and undercut the Utopias of the future by placing theirs in the past.

In discussing the variety of reactionary prejudice to be found in these writers Mr. Harrison's tone is on the whole judicious. His book is free of moral tantrums or outbursts of liberal rhetoric. It is more in sorrow than in anger that he painstakingly presents the evidence from their writings. These men of the 1880s (only Yeats was considerably older) came of age in a cultural atmosphere shot through with yearnings for the mystical and occult, and marked by "the growth of a powerful neo-romanticism which revived the theories of the older romanticists of the early nineteenth century and refashioned them for an attack on rationalist and liberal humanitarian democracy." The supreme irony is that this modernist version of romanticism was presented in a magisterial manner as a restoration of classical norms. A whole generation of poets and critics was taken in by this self-deception.

In the sections dealing with the cultural and historical background of these archaistic Utopias Mr. Harrison is both perceptive and thorough: he is one of the very few critics who do not skirt the question of the enormous influence exerted on Eliot by Charles Maurras and the *Action Française* movement. The anti-Semitic feelings divulged in the early poems, as well as the emphasis on *the* tradition (with the obligatory definite article enforcing exclusion), by means of which he set out to instruct his recusant British hosts — so prone to fall away from allegiance to "Outside Authority" and ecclesiastical monarchical domination — are derived not from native sources but primarily from Maurras. In his Introduction Empson remarks that Joyce was one of the few men of the 1880s to escape this pervasive archaism and reaction: he quotes a letter of 1934 in which Joyce says he is "afraid the poor Mr. Hitler will soon have few friends in Europe apart from my nephews, Masters W. Lewis and E. Pound." Perhaps Joyce resisted the lure because "he had actually escaped from a theocracy such as many of the authors examined in this book recommend."

There is one exaggerated claim, which Mr. Harrison advances on his own behalf, that one would want to challenge. He defines his aim as that of showing "the relationship between the 'tendency' of these five writers and their literary style, also their literary principles." As for establishing any kind of direct relationship, particularly in style, Mr. Harrison has not, in my opinion, succeeded. Between their "tendency" and their literary principles the connections drawn are much clearer. Principles, however, are one thing and practice another. Some of the best qualities of these writers crystallize around the contradiction between stated principle and actual practice. Eliot, for instance, boosted for a long time the virtues of classicism, whereas as a practitioner he developed in his poetry what is unmistakably a new version of romanticism. In his nostalgia for the past he is openly romantic, and in his patrician-puritan scrupulosity and feelings of sexual disgust he is the romantic turned inside out. (He was writing before the onset of the present period of "positive" sex, so grossly romantic in its hankering to discover in pornography yet another and quite acceptable literary form.) No wonder that the late Paul Elmer More was gratified by Eliot's principles, finding them impeccable, and at the same time appalled by his creative practice.

Mr. Harrison would have been well advised, I think, to be persuaded by George Orwell's judgment, quoted in the book, that "no one has succeeded in tracing the connection between 'tendency' and literary style. Texture cannot seemingly be explained sociologically." Texture or style is the product of the workings, at once extremely minute and extremely complex, of individual sensibility; and though the entire process is no doubt in some way affected by the writer's "belief," it cannot be altered fundamentally. This question of "belief" in poetry caused Eliot no end of worry (cf. especially his 1929 essay on Dante) and he wrestled with it vigorously and with exemplary truthfulness in essay after essay. He never came to any definite conclusion and finally let the matter rest. The case of Bertolt Brecht will serve as a good example in this respect. However orthodox he may have been in his communist principles, his unquenchable and highly original sensibility got him into trouble with the Soviet commissars of culture. What goes for radical writers goes equally for the reactionary ones.

Let me approach this question from another angle. One can show, I believe, that virtually all of Lawrence's novels after *Sons and Lovers* are considerably damaged as works of art by his undue insistence on his own "belief"; but what shall we say about the numerous works which despite the salient element of "belief" in them easily transcend the level of idea-mongering and doctrinal bluster? *The Possessed* is admittedly a counterrevolutionary novel politically and in the writer's explicit intention but that does not deter those of us who spurn its propagandistic "message" from fully enjoying it. Nor do the antipathetic social-political views of W. B. Yeats deter me from appreciating his poetry. Perhaps V. S. Pritchett is right in claiming that "propaganda does not become art until it has the grace and courage to welcome the apparent defeat of its purpose." The occasion of Pritchett's apt comment is to be found in his analysis of *Oblomov*, of which it can be presumed that its author set out initially to chastise the sloth and torpor of the landlord class in Russia, only to produce in his protagonist, that prodigious and ineffable "absentee" from life, one of the most extraordinary characters in fiction. This is equally true of the portrait of elder Verhovensky in *The Possessed*, by which Dostoevsky meant to scourge the liberal idealists of the 1830s and 1840s only to find himself, as he gave free rein to his creative impulses, with a human being on his hands so genuine and appealing as to surpass wholly our awkward categories of "belief." I think that posterity will no doubt forgive the ideological aberrations of at least three of the writers discussed in this book — certainly Yeats and Eliot and in part Lawrence — as it has already forgiven Dostoevsky and many other great artists of word and image.

But I agree with Mr. Harrison when he takes to task such critics as L. C. Knights and F. R. Leavis for glossing over the real meaning of some of the ideas of these writers. "It is one thing to see and accept his [Yeats's] prejudices, and another to conjure them away, to pretend that they were something different." This false stance is one of which most literary critics who have dealt with Yeats and the others are notoriously guilty. Thus Mr. Harrison justly attacks Dr. Leavis' position on Lawrence as a social critic. The conclusions of this criticism, writes Dr. Leavis, "were Lawrence's and Lawrence was an artist of genius: that is why they are to be considered." Mr. Harrison has no trouble demonstrating that such an approach is irresponsible even from a literary point of view. "One has not only to understand Lawrence's ideas but to make some attempt to sympathize with them before one can begin to appreciate a novel such as *The Rainbow*." After all, Lawrence did not primarily conceive of himself as an artist but as a leader and prophet. And he himself, I have no doubt, would have protested against such cavalier treatment of his ideas as he gets from Dr. Leavis; for he went so far as to assert that "even art is utterly dependent on philosophy: or, if you prefer, on a metaphysics." It is precisely this metaphysics, so important to Lawrence, that Dr. Leavis, in his book *D. H. Lawrence: Novelist,* willfully ignores in his anxiety to promote Lawrence as an artist of narrative prose in the "great tradition" (of whose existence I am not at all persuaded). Lawrence is admirable, to be sure, in the immediacy and spontaneity of his language, but there is more to the fictional medium than language and he is not nearly so good a novelist as Dr. Leavis makes him out to be.

To my mind, what these five writers have in common is a conviction, not always conscious, of the sovereignty of the word, not only in literature but also in life. This is their real "heresy," to use an expression much favored by Eliot and his disciples. In their school of modernity the view prevails that words somehow command reality. What this view represents, of course, as Leon Trotsky once said while polemicizing against the Russian formalists, is a kind of obdurate philosophical idealism. Such literary idealists, he then noted, are proselytes of St. John in that they believed, as is written, that "In the beginning was the Word." And Trotsky added that he on the other hand believed that in the beginning was the deed, with the word following as its "phonetic shadow."

1967